THE CONTROLLED ECONOMY

He thought it unsuitable to a
reasonable being to act without a
plan, and to be sad or cheerful only
by chance.

SAMUEL JOHNSON : *Rasselas*

Volumes One and Two of a
Principles of Political Economy
are

THE STATIONARY ECONOMY

and

THE GROWING ECONOMY

'This is a splendid and bold idea. Professor
Meade is a master of lucid and rigorous
theoretical exposition' *The Economist*

'It is outstandingly lucid' *New Society*

other books by J. E. Meade

EFFICIENCY, EQUALITY AND THE OWNERSHIP OF PROPERTY

PLANNING AND THE PRICE MECHANISM

THE GEOMETRY OF INTERNATIONAL TRADE

PROBLEMS OF ECONOMIC UNION

A NEO-CLASSICAL THEORY OF ECONOMIC GROWTH

(Allen & Unwin)

CONTROL OF INFLATION

(Cambridge University Press)

INTRODUCTION TO ECONOMIC ANALYSIS AND POLICY

THEORY OF INTERNATIONAL ECONOMIC POLICY

(Oxford University Press)

THE CONTROLLED
ECONOMY

BY

J. E. MEADE

C.B., F.B.A.

Being Volume Three of A
PRINCIPLES OF POLITICAL ECONOMY

STATE UNIVERSITY OF NEW YORK PRESS
ALBANY
1972

Published by State University of New York.
Thurlow Terrace, Albany, New York 12201

Library of Congress Cataloging in Publication Data

Meade, James Edward, 1907–
The controlled economy.

(His Principles of political economy, v. 3)
1. Economic policy.   I. Title.

HB171.M478 vol. 3 [HD82]   330   79-37998
ISBN 0-87395-204-9

Printed in Great Britain

CONTENTS

PREFACE

This volume continues the series of volumes, of which *The Stationary Economy* and *The Growing Economy* have already appeared, and which are designed to put into a general conspectus the major advances of economic analysis which in recent years have been numerous, important, and often highly sophisticated. *The Growing Economy* brought the story up to the point at which a closed economy without indivisibilities or externalities was moving with perfect foresight on an equilibrium growth path through time. The present volume was basically designed to consider the progress of a similar economy in conditions of uncertainty without perfect foresight on a disequilibrium path through time. I thought at first that this would involve primarily, if not solely, the old familiar problem of 'the trade cycle' or, perhaps more accurately, the problems of economic fluctuations and of their stabilization. Accordingly, I announced boldly in the Preface to *The Growing Economy* that I would call the present volume *The Fluctuating Economy*; and I thought that I was faced with the boring task of putting down on paper what little I knew about ideas with which I was in general already familiar.

But how wrong I was. The first thing that happened to me was that some of my younger colleagues, better educated than I, would not allow me to ignore the fact that the controls used by the government for short-run stabilization policies (interest rates, tax rates, etc.) were the same as the instruments which would have to be used to implement any long-term structural plan. What, I was asked, should be done, if the long-term structural planning of the economy demanded a level for some control which was incompatible with the level required for short-term stabilization purposes? I was told that if only I would study my Pontryagin and my Bellman I would soon see how outmoded was the idea of controlling an economic system by an automatic built-in feedback mechanism (a servo-mechanism) based on three-point proportional, derivative, and integral control. The implication was that short-term stabilization and long-term structural planning should be a single exercise in optimal control, designed to find that plan for present and future controls which would maximize the expected value of some social welfare function over the whole span of planned time, taking all the effects of the controls—long-term and short-term, micro and macro, productive and distributive, and so on—into account. But, thought I, the Chancellor of the Exchequer, on going into his office one morning and being presented with the question whether an unexpected overnight change in the economic situation does not call for a rise in Bank Rate to offset an imminent inflation, would not feel impelled to demand a revision of the whole of the nation's five-year structural economic plan before giving an answer. My colleagues' argument was logically compelling and yet I stubbornly felt in my bones that something was amiss. It took me a long time to find some rationalization of my instinctive conviction that there is almost a distinction in kind to be made between a short-term stabilization programme and a long-term structural plan.

I will not spoil for the reader the plot of my book by revealing here the nature of my dénouement, except to say that it has got something to do with the nature of uncertainty. And it was in this connection that I learned my second great lesson by being made aware of the famous Arrow-Debreu way of considering uncertainty. As a consequence, a very large part of the present volume is devoted to the question how best to use present policy controls in view of the uncertain nature of their future effects. In a review of *The Growing Economy,* Professor Solow suggested that it would have been better not to have included any reference to uncertainty in that volume. I heartily agree now with that view. *The Growing Economy* should have dealt exclusively with conditions in which 'environmental uncertainties' (as they are called in the present volume) were wholly absent and in which, therefore, perfect foresight and so equilibrium growth could have been attained by means of comprehensive forward markets or indicative planning. But unfortunately I went off at half-cock and the result is an overlap—and sometimes a somewhat unhappy overlap—in the treatment of uncertainty in the two volumes.

I must repeat what I said in the Preface to *The Growing Economy,* namely that it is impossible for me to acknowledge the sources of all the ideas in the present volume. My debt is to a vast army of economists. But I cannot refrain from explaining how I owe my basic education in the design of stabilization policies to Professor A. W. H. Phillips to whom, above all, I would express my gratitude. I shall never forget the hours which I spent with him at the London School of Economics discussing these matters. More recently, I have continued my education in a small seminar in Cambridge; and I would like to thank many members of that seminar, but very specially David Livesey, Tony Atkinson, Geoff Heal, and David Newbery for giving me ideas and for criticizing much of what I have written in the present volume. David Livesey, like Bill Phillips a control engineer turned economist, has been simultaneously building an econometric model of the United Kingdom economy to which to apply his control techniques. It was he who suggested to me that I should call this volume *The Controlled Economy* and I am struggling with my conscience as to whether, in view of what I said in the Preface to *The Growing Economy*, I am morally bound to pay him $1 or its equivalent in sterling. A close reading of that Preface will, I think, absolve me from any binding obligation to do so.

It will be clear to the initiated how much I owe in this volume to the ideas of Professors Arrow and Debreu on the treatment of uncertainty. The term and the idea of 'residual uncertainty' I owe to Professor Lombardini. I have been particularly fortunate in having been able to discuss many of these ideas with four visitors to Cambridge from the United States—Professors Radner, Scarf, and Stiglitz as well as Professor Arrow. Professor D. G. Champernowne and Dr C. J. Bliss have read, and greatly improved by their comments, the Note to Chapter XX of this volume. Chapter XVI owes much to comments made by Professor Inada.

Much of Part 3 of this volume is reproduced from lectures which I gave at the University of Manchester in March 1970, subsequently published by the Manchester University Press under the title *The Theory of Indicative Planning*. Chapter XVI of the present volume is based upon a paper which I presented at Tokyo in June 1970 to the Fifth Far Eastern Meeting of the Econometric Society, subsequently published in *The Economic Studies Quarterly*, Vol XXI, No 3 (December 1970). Some passages in Chapter XXIV are reproduced from the Inaugural Lecture which I gave at Cambridge in 1958, subsequently published by the Cambridge University Press under the title *The Control of Inflation*. I am grateful to all those concerned for permission to make use of these materials in the present volume.

Finally I would like to express my deep gratitude to the Nuffield Foundation and to the Master and Fellows of Christ's College, Cambridge for the opportunity which has been given to me, as Nuffield Senior Research Fellow at Christ's College, to devote my time wholly to this enterprise.

J. E. MEADE

Christ's College
Cambridge
December 1970

PART 1

Some Basic Concepts

The present state of things is the
consequence of the former; and it is
natural to inquire what were the sources
of the good that we enjoy, or the evil
that we suffer.

SAMUEL JOHNSON : *Rasselas*

CHAPTER I

UNCERTAINTY, FRICTION AND DISEQUILIBRIUM GROWTH

Both in *The Stationary Economy* and in *The Growing Economy* we have been dealing with an economy in which conditions were such that perfect competition or perfect potential competition was possible. That is to say, we assumed that, if decisions were left to the whim of uncontrolled individuals, no individual decision-maker would be able by his own individual action significantly to affect the prices at which he could buy or sell the goods and services with which he was concerned. We showed that, in the unchanging conditions assumed in *The Stationary Economy*, any equilibrium reached in such conditions would represent an efficient situation in the sense that it would be impossible to make one citizen better off without making any other citizen worse off. (See Chapter XII of *The Stationary Economy*.)

In *The Growing Economy* we introduced three major factors of change into this type of economy, namely population growth, capital accumulation, and technical progress. It was a major theme of that volume that once again, provided that competition was perfect, any equilibrium reached in such conditions would represent an efficient outcome provided that one basic condition could be fulfilled. The efficient outcome would in this case take the form of an efficient time-path of the economy, in the sense that things would so develop through time that it would be impossible to make any one citizen better off at any one point of time without making someone worse off either at that point of time or at some other point of time; and the basic conditions for this result to be achieved was that each individual decision-maker should not only know the current levels, but should also correctly foresee the future course, of all the prices with which he was concerned. (See Chapter XXIII of *The Growing Economy*.)

Of course, this basic condition can never be exactly, or even perhaps approximately, fulfilled. Uncertainty about future basic conditions (for example, about the future course of technical knowledge) makes it impossible. This was recognized in *The Growing Economy*, where there was some discussion of the way in

3

which unavoidable risk and uncertainty might affect decisions (Chapter XXI) and of some ways in which inefficiencies due to uncertainty about the future might be reduced (Chapter XXII). But the central theme and purpose of *The Growing Economy* was to consider equilibrium growth and efficient time-paths of the economy. The great bulk of the problems which arise when false expectations about future market conditions are formed and when, as a result, disequilibrium growth occurs and the economy threatens to move along an inefficient time-path was severely neglected. It is the purpose of the present volume to consider these issues.

We shall continue in this volume for the most part to assume that basic conditions are such that perfect competition or perfect potential competition is possible. At a few very important points in our argument we shall modify this assumption but whenever we do so we shall do so with an explicit discussion of the point. The basic subject matter of the present volume is: to watch a competitive economy moving through time when, because of uncertainties about the future, false expectations are formed; to observe how in such conditions it may diverge from an equilibrium time-path; and to consider by what means and in what ways the government might attempt to control the course of such an economy in order to make its development through time approximate more closely to the most desirable or optimum time-path.

In *The Growing Economy* (p. 344) we defined equilibrium growth as the state of affairs in which the economy so moved through time that no decision-maker ever came to regret at any future time the decision which he took today. We argued that in a perfectly competitive economy this would be the case if every decision-maker did in fact correctly foresee the future course of all the prices with which he was concerned. We argued further that in these conditions the economy would move on an efficient path through time. But what happens when people form false expectations? Clearly, by definition, the economy will no longer move on an equilibrium path. But can it nevertheless be so controlled as to make it move on an efficient path?

That this is conceptually possible is shown by the following example. Mr A is considering the installation now of some additional machinery to produce a product X. Conditions are such that if there were a perfect forward market for all products (see pp. 467–9 of *The Growing Economy*) the future 'equilibrium' price of X would be known to be \$2 and in these conditions A would now decide to instal the 'equilibrium' and 'efficient' amount of 100 new machines. Suppose, however, that A expects that the future selling price of X will be \$4 and, in view of this, intends to instal not 100, but 150 new machines. This is a decision which he would come to regret if and when the selling price of X in fact turned out to be only $2.

The government becomes aware of this excessive optimism on the part of A and of other similar investors in this machinery. As a result, in order to control the excess investment in this line of activity which threatens to take place, it imposes a special tax on the installation at this time of this type of machinery. As a result of this, A in fact decides to instal only the 'efficient' number of machines, namely 100. His excessive optimism about future prices is offset by the present special control on investment imposed, in the form of a special tax, by the government.

As a result of this and of other well-devised governmental controls, the price of X, we will assume, does in fact turn out to be only $2. The efficient number of machines (100) has been installed and the efficient level of the future price of X (namely $2) has been achieved by means of government controls which have offset the false price expectations of private decision-makers such as A.

In these conditions (of a high rate of tax on the installation of the machines plus the low future equilibrium level of the selling price of the product) A may well regret that he installed 100 machines. He may wish that he had installed only 50. The controlled time-path is an efficient, but not an equilibrium, path.

Government controls are needed for many other purposes besides the offsetting of false dynamic expectations. Already, in the perfectly competitive conditions assumed in *The Stationary Economy* and *The Growing Economy*, we have pointed out that a competitive *laissez faire* efficient solution does not necessarily lead to the most desirable distribution of income and wealth so that, even in conditions of perfect competition and perfect foresight, governmental controls may be needed to offset distributional evils. When, in later volumes, we come to allow for indivisibilities (which imply monopolistic conditions) and externalities (which imply all sorts of conflicts between private and social advantages) we shall find many other reasons for governmental controls.[1]

We must imagine, therefore, a state of affairs in which the government has at its disposal a certain limited number of feasible controls (such as the supply of money, certain rates of taxation and of subsidy, and so on) and in which it has a number of objectives (such as the distribution of income, the control of monopolies, and so on). One, but only one, of these objectives is to offset the undesirable effects of dynamic disequilibrium due to the formation of false expectations. The optimum or best possible policy is to use these various controls in the way which obtains the optimum time-path

---

[1] These are enumerated in Chapter XV of the present volume.

for the economy. This optimum time-path is not necessarily an efficient time-path in the narrow sense in which we have used that term. It is the time-path which, given the feasible use of the limited number of available controls, obtains the best possible balance between the various social objectives. This may involve a state of affairs in which, as far as the conditions of production are concerned, it would be technically possible (if more suitable controls were feasible and available) to make someone better off without making anyone else worse off.[2]

In the present volume, we shall be concerned primarily with the use of governmental controls to offset the inefficiencies due to dynamic disequilibrium. But we cannot do this without some references to the other objectives of control policy, although we shall restrict these references to the inevitable minimum.

There is, however, one very important phenomenon connected with economic change in conditions of uncertainty, which we will call 'market friction' and which can play a central role in the control problems with which we are primarily interested in this volume. This phenomenon can perhaps be best explained by considering the particular case of the determination of the level of wage rates and of employment in the labour market. In *The Growing Economy* (p. 33) it was assumed: that at 8 a.m. each day a given number of workers came forward seeking work; that a given number of employers came forward seeking workers, each with a fixed schedule in his mind as to the number of workers he would want to employ at any given wage rate; and that the forces of competition between workers and employers then *instantaneously* determined a market wage rate at which the total demand for labour equalled the total supply on the market. Thus full employment was always achieved at a competitive wage rate.

But even the most flexible and well lubricated market mechanism cannot, of course, work like that. Quite apart from any other imperfections, in conditions of uncertainty on the part both of the workers and employers at the opening of the labour market at 8 a.m. on any day as to what the day's wage rate would turn out to be there would be some process of higgle-haggle by means of which the wage rate was determined. There are many forms which this higgle-haggle may take and all of them take some time. Since 'a day' stood in our analysis for a very small atom of time, there is no reason to believe that the higgle-haggle relevant to the conditions of day 1 would, as it were, be finished before the beginning of day 2.

---

[2] We have already, in Chapter XXIII of *The Growing Economy*, considered one particular reason why the optimum time-path may not be an efficient time-path, namely the need to compromise between efficiency and the best distribution of wealth.

One particular form of the higgle-haggle might be on the following lines. The labour market is open for half an hour each day, from 8 to 8.30 a.m. Each worker comes into the market stating the wage at which he will do a day's work. Each employer comes into the market knowing how many men he would like to employ at any given wage rate. Workers and employers meet each other in a random way and each employer decides, when he meets a worker, whether or not he will hire that worker for that day at the wage demanded by that worker. At 8.30, each employer goes off with the workers whom he has by then hired.

This process could well mean that, at the end of the bargaining half hour, (i) there were still some workers who had not been hired and who would remain unemployed for that day, (ii) there were some employers who went to their factories with less labour than they would have liked and who regretted having refused to hire some of the workers whom they met but refused to hire because they hoped to find other workers at a lower wage, and (iii) there were some employed workers who found that they were working at a lower wage than most of their colleagues and who regretted not having gone into the market demanding a higher wage. If everyone learned from experience, those in group (i), which would contain a more than average proportion of workers who had demanded an exceptionally high wage, might well ask for a lower wage on the following day, and those in group (iii) might well ask for a higher wage, while the employers in group (ii) might well accept workers more readily at a higher wage on the next day. Thus there would be a process, but not an instantaneous process, tending to cause (a) a single wage for labour to rule in the market, since those who had asked a high wage would tend to lower their demands and those who had asked a low wage to raise their demands, and (b) a level of the wage which gave full, but not over-full employment, since the unemployed would tend to lower their wage demand and the employers who were short of labour to improve their wage offers. But new and unforeseen conditions in the labour market might well cause the equilibrium wage rate to change before this process of adjustment had brought the labour market into full equilibrium. There would be a tendency all the time for wages to move towards an equilibrium level but, with the equilibrium level itself moving, the actual wage rates might never be actually at the equilibrium level. 'Market friction' would cause a less than instantaneous response of the wage rate to changes in the underlying conditions of demand and supply for labour.

In *The Growing Economy* we were concerned above all with equilibrium growth. In that context it was perhaps legitimate to make the assumption that, by some admittedly all-defined process, the price of labour (and indeed the prices of all other factors and products) was instantaneously fixed each day at a level which cleared the market, i.e. which equated the total predetermined supplies available on that day to the total which purchasers would take off the market given their demand schedules on that day. But this mysterious instantaneous market-clearing mechanism cannot be permitted in an analysis which is expressly designed to discuss disequilibrium possibilities. We shall, accordingly, assume that markets behave in the following sort of way. Sellers announce, at the latest by the beginning of day 1, the price list at which they will sell their goods on day 1; purchasers receive these price lists and then decide how much they will purchase on day 1. At 8 a.m. on day 1 the purchasers set out to acquire those quantities at those prices. The sellers may be disappointed at the amount sold, finding as a result that they have unexpectedly large unsold supplies which may result in an undesired piling-up of stocks or a simple waste of perishable goods or unemployment among workers. Alternatively, the amounts which purchasers seek to acquire may be larger than the sellers had expected at the prices which they had quoted and the result may be an unexpected depletion of stocks or 'shop shortages' of one kind or another such as unfilled vacancies for labour, a lengthening unfilled order book for durable goods, or simply unfilled wants on the part of consumers of perishable goods and services. As a result of such experiences on day 1, sellers may revise their price lists for future days. Thus the search for a short-run equilibrium between supply and demand (which in *The Growing Economy* we assumed to take place instantaneously at 8 a.m. each day by some undefined mysterious process) is in the present volume itself assumed to proceed by a market friction process of the general kind indicated above.

This phenomenon of market friction as described above is, of course, only one aspect of the general problem of the formation of expectations in conditions of uncertainty. If, to return to the labour market example, there had been a perfect forward market for labour as well as for everything else, it would have been possible to have carried out in the far distant past all the higgle-haggle that was relevant for today's labour market condition, and workers and employers could have come into today's labour market already, all of them, expecting just that one single wage rate which would in fact just clear today's labour market. They would yesterday (when they were considering what offers they should make today) have had no uncertainty about today's outcome. In the absence of such certainty, some degree of market friction is inevitable even in the most perfectly competitive atomistic market.

But in fact, in many markets in the real world, and in particular in the labour market, there is an element of market friction which is due to the absence of perfectly competitive conditions. The existence of a trade union, which is a monopolistic organization of a body of workers, may mean that all the workers in a particular group come, as it were, into the labour market at 8 a.m. on any given day all demanding the same agreed wage rate. Each employer then hires a certain number of workers at that predetermined wage rate. If the wage rate is set high (given the expectations of employers about future market conditions for the sale of their products) some workers in that group may remain unemployed. If the wage is set low, some employers may be unable to find as many men for their employment as they would wish and there will be unfilled vacancies in their factories.

If the resulting unemployment is high and the unfilled vacancies low, it is possible that the workers in their trade union will, after some delay, agree to ask for a lower wage rate than would otherwise have been the case. After a considerable period of low unemployment and high unfilled vacancies, they may be moved to ask for a higher wage rate than would otherwise have been the case. The monopolistic organization of the workers in their trade union may thus well have a double effect. First, it may cause the equilibrium wage rate to be permanently higher than it would otherwise be, this being the well-known phenomenon of some degree of monopoly power. But, second, it may increase the degree of market friction. For the speed with which a large monopolistic organization will adjust its agreed offer to changing conditions may well be slower than the speed with which private individuals would so react.

In this volume, we wish to neglect as far as possible the problems of monopolistic power (which will be an important subject matter in a later volume). But, in a volume on the control of the economy, it would be pedantic to overlook the implications of a market organized in the way in which the trade unions may cause the labour market to be organized. We shall, therefore, allow for the fact that some markets may be so organized that the sellers all offer the good or service at a single predetermined price and that this price responds more or less sluggishly to an excess supply or demand in the market. But we shall treat this simply as a case of market friction and we shall give as little attention as we reasonably can in this volume to any implications which it may in fact carry with it about the exercise of monopolistic power.

In brief, we are concerned in this volume essentially with a competitive growing economy. But it is an economy in which there are a number of government interventions (typified by taxes and subsidies of various kinds) which are undertaken for such structural objectives as a better distribution of wealth, the offsetting of external economies and diseconomies, and the control of monopolistic powers. An outstanding feature of the economy is uncertainty about the future which means that private decision-makers are bound to form false expectations and which inevitably introduces friction into the markets for goods and services. An economy of this kind is most unlikely to move through time on an equilibrium path. It will be liable to fluctuations, hesitations, and lurches. It is the purpose of this volume to examine the special considerations which affect the design of governmental controls in a basically competitive economy for the purpose of offsetting the dynamic disequilibrating effects of false expectations and market frictions.

CHAPTER II

ENVIRONMENT, EXPECTATIONS, DECISIONS, CONTROLS AND THE STATE OF THE ECONOMY

When we consider the movement of the economy through time, we are considering the state of the economy at successive points of time. By the state of the economy at any point of time we mean simply a catalogue of all the economic variables at that point of time: the size of the capital stock of various machines, etc; the levels of the outputs of the various sectors of the economy; the levels of the various kinds of income (wages, profits, rents, etc.) received by various classes of citizen; the prices of the various inputs and outputs; the level of different rates of interest; and so on. Yesterday, each of these variables was at one level; today, they are at another level. We call all these variables the 'state of the economy' and watch the way in which it changes with time.

Today's state of the economy is determined by three main classes of factor.

(A) In the first place, the present state of the economy will, in many respects, be directly and materially affected by the past state of the economy. The most obvious example of this relationship is to be found in the influences affecting the present stock of capital equipment. The number of houses that exist today is clearly affected by the number which existed yesterday. It is not necessarily, of course, exactly the same, since some houses may have been demolished and others may have been built; but the stock of houses in the recent past will in fact be a major determinant of the present stock.

(B) Second, there are a number of factors which we will call 'the environment' which will greatly affect the state of the economy but which are not themselves affected by the state of the economy and cannot themselves be influenced by the economic decisions of any human agents. In the case of our housing example, an earthquake or the explosion of a nuclear bomb would be an obvious example. We assume, that is to say, that the earthquake or nuclear explosion would have occurred whatever were the past history of the state of the economy and whatever economic decisions were made.

(C) But the process of economic development is not one in which

11

the present state of the economy is exactly predetermined by the past state of the economy together with the environment. If this were so, our search for optimum policies or optimum decisions would be futile. The course of the economy can ᒫ affected by the 'decisions' reached by the decision-makers in the economy. To continue with our example of the stock of houses, the number of new dwellings under construction today is not inexorably predetermined by the past state of the economy and the environment. It will depend also upon decisions recently taken by human agents to devote more or less resources to the building of new houses. The stock of houses may not be affected until a later date when the houses have been completed. But recent decisions will have affected the present state of the economy which includes not only the number of houses in existence but also the number of houses under construction, and this will in turn affect the number of houses in existence at a future date. Past decisions have affected the present state of the economy which will in turn affect the future state of the economy.

Decision-makers can be divided into two categories in our economy, namely private citizens and governmental authorities. In our housing example, the number of new houses which it is decided to build may have been left to the decision of private individuals operating in a free competitive market or it may have been determined as part of a governmental house-building operation. In some respects the problems facing both of them can be regarded as very similar. The private entrepreneur, for example, controls some variable (e.g. the level of the output of his product) and he fixes this variable in such a way as to achieve the best possible outcome from his own point of view (e.g. to maximize his profit). The public authority controls some variable (e.g. the rate of income tax) and fixes this variable at a level which will achieve the best possible result from its own point of view (e.g. maximize 'social welfare' in some sense.) But, in spite of this, we shall treat the two types of decision-making in essentially different ways in this volume.

We may best explain the reason for this difference of treatment by considering the distinction between two types of influence, namely 'exogenous' and 'endogenous' factors. Exogenous factors are factors whose occurrence would not have been affected by a different past history of the economy. Thus, whether there is an earthquake today or not will not be affected by the past economic history of the community concerned. The endogeneous factors are factors whose occurrence is itself affected by the past history of the economy. Thus yesterday's stock of houses (which affects today's stock of houses) was itself in turn affected by the stock of houses of the day before yesterday, which in its turn was in part determined by the stock of houses of the day before that and so on. It should be noticed in passing that, while the distinction between exogenous and endogenous factors is of the first importance, it is not a distinctly clear-cut or absolute one. Where the line should be drawn depends upon the set of problems under consideration and the degree of simplification of the model of reality which one is prepared to accept.

One may, for example, be considering the situation only in one sector of a total economy. Suppose that one is considering the economic development of one small country in a large total world economy. The country's exports will depend among other things upon the total level of demand throughout the world for the sort of things which the country exports. This level of demand will in its turn depend upon many things including, theoretically, the amount of income which the rest of the world can earn by selling its produce to the small country in question. In so far as this is so, the world demand for the country's exports should properly be treated as an endogenous variable in considering the country's economic development, since the present events inside the small economy will affect its demand for imports which will in turn affect the world's demand for its exports, so that the world's demand for its exports is indirectly influenced by previous events inside the economy. But in the case of a very small country in a very large world the small country's demand for the products of the rest of the world will have a negligible effect upon the degree of prosperity or depression in the rest of the world and thus a negligible effect upon the outside world's demand for the country's own exports. In considering the economic development of the small country only a negligible error will be introduced by treating the world level of demand for its exports as an environmental or exogeneous variable.[1]

But let us return to our consideration of the nature of decisions. Are the economic decisions of human agencies to be treated as exogenous or as endogenous factors? Decisions by human agents, in fact, constitute a separate category of factor. In some respects they must be treated as exogenous factors, i.e. as similar to environmental factors, but in other respects they must be treated as endogenous variables. How they should be treated depends in the first

[1] Of course, the level of total demand in the rest of the world would have to be treated as an endogeneous variable in any investigation of what determined the economic development of the rest of the world. The point is that, once having been determined, it could be treated as an exogenous variable in considering separately the problems of the single small country. As we shall see later, the fact that what is an endogenous variable for one investigation may be an exogenous variable for another and *vice versa* is an essential feature of the task of fitting together different plans and policies of control which are devised for different purposes. (See Chapter XIII.)

instance upon the type of question to which one is seeking an answer and there are in fact three and not only two types of question to be considered. Let us illustrate this by considering a basic governmental decision.

(i) Suppose that one is seeking an answer to the question: 'What will happen to the development of the economy if tax rates are set at such-and-such levels and are held at those levels whatever may be their effect upon economic events?' Such a question may be a perfectly legitimate question to ask, even if it is asked only in order to decide whether or not to set tax rates at the specified levels. But clearly if such a question is asked, then tax rates must be treated as exogenous factors; they are already assumed to be like a given environmental factor in the formulation of the question.

(ii) Suppose, however, that the question asked is a different one, namely: 'What will happen to the development of the economy if tax rates are always raised (or lowered) each year by an amount which, on some rule of thumb calculation based on past experience, is reckoned to lead to a balance between budgetary expenditure and tax revenue?' Then equally clearly the rate of tax must itself be regarded as an endogenous variable; it has simply become a factor which is itself determined by past economic events.

(iii) But there is a third type of question which might be asked—a type of question which, in fact, it is the ultimate object of the analysis of this volume to help to answer. We may ask: 'What is the principle upon which the rates of tax should be set in order to make the economy move as nearly as possible upon the optimum path through time?' In coping with this problem, the rate of tax must be treated in the first place as an exogenous variable, but as an exogenous variable which is itself capable of being controlled and thus turned, as it were, into an endogenous variable. That this is so can be clearly seen as soon as it is realized that, in principle, one can seek the answer to the present question by examining the answers to a very large number of questions of the type asked under (i) above. Thus one could ask: "What will be the course of the economy (a) if the rate of tax is set at 50% this year, 50% the next year, 50% the year after; or (b) if it is set at 50% this year, 60% next hear, 70% the year after; or (c) if it is set at 40% this year, 30% next year, 70% the year after?" and so on through a very large number of combinations of tax rates. The different time-paths of the state of the economy which would result from policies (a), (b), (c), and so on could then be compared and that time pattern which was nearest to the optimum could then be selected. This would then indicate which pattern of tax rates should be chosen.

In asking each of the questions (a), (b), (c) and so on above, it is to be noted, the pattern of tax rates must be treated as an exogenous variable whose level does not depend upon the actual development of the economy. But when the best pattern of tax rates has been selected, the tax rates will have become, as it were, endogenous variables, since they will have been determined as a result of governmental decisions which can only be based upon knowledge and expectations formed in the light of past experience. They will no longer (like an earthquake) be set at levels which are independent of the past state of the economy. Decisions thus constitute a quite distinct category of factor.

The fact that decisions must first be treated as exogenous factors (while one is considering the effect of different patterns of decisions on the development of the economy) and then later as endogenous factors (when one has selected that strategy for the decisions which is expected to lead to the optimum development of the economy) explains the difference between our treatment of decisions by private citizens and decisions taken by public authorities.

Consider a private competitive producer who is trying to decide on the output policy which will maximize his profit. He can decide the level of his output. At first, he must treat this as an exogenous variable, in order to consider what his profit would be if he set his output at various levels when the selling price was $1, what his profit would be if he set his output at various levels when the selling price was $1.1, and so on. From these schedules he could select for each selling price that output which would maximize his profit. He would now have an optimal policy schedule which would tell him at what level to set his output as soon as he knows the day's selling price. His output is now no longer exogenously given; it is now determined according to the level of the ruling selling price. By choosing the optimal strategy his decision about his output has passed from an exogenously-given, to an endogenously-determined factor.

We may regard the analysis of *The Stationary Economy* and *The Growing Economy* as having dealt essentially with the problems of private citizens making their decisions (e.g. the competitive consumers deciding how much of each product to consume and the competitive producers deciding how much to produce) so as to maximize their utilities in the competitive *milieu* in which no one citizen can affect the prices at which he can buy and sell the various goods and services. For this reason, in this volume we are assuming that private decision-makers are already adopting their optimal policies so that their decisions must be treated as being determined by the course of events, i.e. as endogenously-determined factors. We are concerned, however, with the process by which the public authorities' decisions actually pass from the category of exogenously-set, to endogenously-determined, factors; that is to say, we are concerned with the choice by the public authorities of the optimal policy for the making of their decisions in the light of past events.

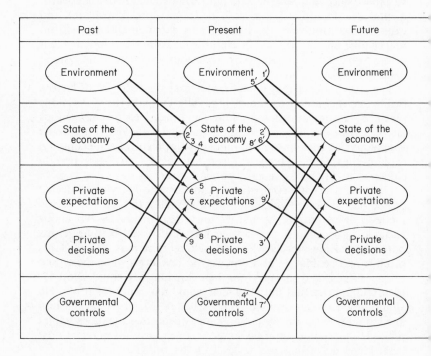

Figure 1

Thus, we shall treat private decisions as factors which are themselves determined by past events. But it is essential for much of the analysis of this volume to realize that a large part of the influence of past events on private decisions is exercised not directly but indirectly through the effect of past events upon 'expectations' and the effect of expectations on decisions.

Consider, for example, the factors which will influence a citizen in deciding whether or not to purchase a motor-car today. Clearly his decision will be much affected by past events such as his existing wealth (i.e. the amount of savings he has already managed to accumulate or the amount of capital he has received by way of gift or inheritance in the past), his existing stock of means of transport (e.g.

whether he already possesses a car, a motor-cycle, and so on), and the habits he has formed (e.g. whether he is accustomed to go to his work by public transport). But his decision will also be much affected by his expectations about future events. For example by his expectation of future income (will he be able to afford to run the car?) or of future needs (will he want his present accumulated savings to educate his children?). We can thus conclude that private decisions are themselves determined by the past state of the economy and by expectations of the future state of the economy.

But the decision-maker's expectations will in turn have been formed on the basis of past experience. Thus, our citizen's expectations of his future income and needs will be affected by his past income and needs (for example, his income has been rising regularly for some time at about $x\%$ per annum and he sees no reason why this trend should not be continued) and also by environmental events (a particular war has just come to an end which, he expects, will cause a change in the demand for his type of labour and so in his income).

The interrelations between the environment, the state of the economy, expectations, and private and governmental decisions are summarized in Figure 1. The arrows leading into the middle column of that figure show how the present is influenced by the past. The present state of the economy depends upon past environmental factors[2] (arrow 1), upon the past state of the economy (arrow 2), upon private decisions (arrow 3), and upon past governmental decisions (arrow 4); the expectations in the process of formation in the present depend upon past environmental factors (arrow 5), the past state of the economy (arrow 6), and past governmental decisions (arrow 7); present private decisions depend upon the past state of the economy (arrow 8) and upon expectations of the future formed in the immediate past (arrow 9). The arrows leading out of the middle section show how present events will affect future events. Present environmental events will affect the future state of the economy (arrow 1') and the future formation of expectations (arrow 5'); the present state of the economy will affect the future state of the economy (arrow 2'), future expectations (arrow 6'), and future private decisions (arrow 8'); the expectations formed at present will affect future decisions (arrow 9'); present private decisions will

[2] In the figure we have shown the present state of the economy as being affected not at all by present, but only by past, events. We have done this to indicate that, conceptually at least, there is always some delay between cause and effect. In some cases this may be minimal (as in the case of the effect of an earthquake upon the stock of houses) but in others it may be prolonged (as in the case of the effect of a change in a rate of tax in influencing consumers' habits.)

affect the future state of the economy (arrow 3′), and present governmental decisions will affect the future state of the economy (arrow
4′) and the future formation of expectations (arrow 7′).

Diagrams of the type shown in Figure 1 draw one's attention
to the fact that the process is one which occurs through time and
which links past with present and present with future. But it obscures
another most important feature of these relationships, namely the
element of feedback in these interconnections. As we have described
the process and as it is depicted in Figure 1, we can deduce that

      (a) the state of the economy affects private decisions which
      in turn affect the state of the economy, and

      (b) the state of the economy affects expectations which affect
      private decisions which in turn affect the state of the economy.

Both these interconnections are instances of feedback. If, to start
the ball rolling, some environmental event or a change in some
governmental decision affects the state of the economy, this will
set in motion a series of repercussions through expectations and
private decisions which will eventually react back on the state of
the economy. This secondary effect on the state of the economy will
itself set in motion secondary repercussions through its effects on
expectations and private decisions which will in turn exercise a
tertiary effect on the state of the economy; and so on through an
infinite series of repercussions, the nature of which we will examine
later (see Chapter V).

These feedback repercussions are not immediately observed in
Figure 1. But the same relationships can be depicted in an alternative fashion which, while it brings out less forcibly than Figure 1 the
working of the process through time, displays the feedback relationship much more clearly than does Figure 1. This alternative method
of depiction is shown in Figure 2, and in order to make the comparison between the two figures easier, the lines of causal interconnections in Figure 2 are given the same numbers as in Figure 1.
Thus, environmental events and governmental decisions after some
time-lag affect the state of the economy (lines 1 and 4) and expectations (lines 5 and 7). The present state of the economy affects the
future state of the economy (line 2), expectations (line 6), and the
decisions of private decision-makers (line 8). Expectations then
affect future private decisions (line 9) and private decisions, after
some delay, in turn affect the state of the economy (line 3).

The method of representation in Figure 2 enables one to see
more clearly the feedback relationships. For example, the state of
the economy affects expectations (line 6) which affect private decisions (line 9) which affect the state of the economy (line 3) and so
once more round this closed loop of causation. Also, the state of

the economy directly influences private decisions (line 8) which affect the state of the economy (line 3), which represents another closed loop of causation.

There is one important way in which, in the rest of this volume, we will simplify the representation of the forces at work in the economy as depicted in Figures 1 and 2. In terms of the relationships represented by the numbered lines shown in Figure 2, it can be seen that the *present state of the economy* depends upon

    (1) *previous states of the economy* (line 2),

    (2) *previous environmental events* (line 1),

    (3) *previous governmental decisions* (line 4), and

    (4) previous private decisions (line 3) which in turn depend upon

        (4a) *previous states of the economy* (line 8), and

        (4b) expectations (line 9) which in turn depend upon

            (4bi)   *previous states of the economy* (line 6),

            (4bii) *previous environmental events* (line 5), and

            (4biii) *previous governmental decisions* (line 7).

Thus, the causes affecting the state of the economy can be ultimately traced back to previous states of the economy, environmental events, and governmental decisions. Some of these causes will have operated directly, but some will have operated indirectly, through their effects upon expectations and private decisions. In every case, if these direct and indirect influences are known, each state of the

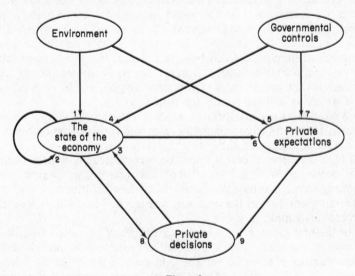

Figure 2

economy can be represented as the outcome of earlier states of the economy and of earlier governmental decisions and environmental events.

To take one example, the number of private cars successfully sold today by the manufacturers of cars will be determined by the decisions just made by their customers, these decisions being formed (a) in the knowledge which these purchasers have already acquired about certain relevant features of the state of the economy (e.g. the price at which cars are offered for sale, the price at which competing goods are available, the amount of cars of different kinds and age which they already have at their disposal, the spendable income which they have just earned, the amount of money and of other realizable capital assets which they possess, etc.), (2) in the knowledge of various environmental events and governmental decisions (e.g. the current rates of tax recently announced by the government), and (3) in the light of expectations which have themselves been determined by past events (e.g. in the light of expectations about future changes in the purchasers' incomes or in the price of cars, these expectations in turn having been determined by past experience of changes in incomes, prices, and other variables).

We may now divide all the events which are relevant to the study of the economy into three groups: (i) ENVIRONMENTAL EVENTS consisting of all those events which are not affected in any way directly or indirectly by the past, present, or future economic decisions by the private or governmental decision-makers in the economy (for example, earthquakes or the world demand for the exports of a small country); (ii) GOVERNMENTAL CONTROLS, which comprise all those variables (for example, the rate of income tax) which are determined simply and solely by governmental decisions; and (iii) all those other variables (such as market prices) which are affected by environmental events, by governmental controls, and by each other and which we will call simply the INSIDE EVENTS.

We can thus say that present inside events depend simply upon past inside events, environmental events, and controls, remembering always that many of these causal relationships will work only through the effect of events upon the private citizens' expectations and decisions. With this most important proviso, we can redraw Figures 1 and 2 in the greatly simplified form of Figures 3 and 4. The representation of the economy in Figures 3 and 4 is, however, deceptively simple.

In the first place, in each of the categories of variable—environmental events, inside events, and controls—there is included a very large number of separate variables. In each of these figures, therefore, a single line will represent a very large number of separate

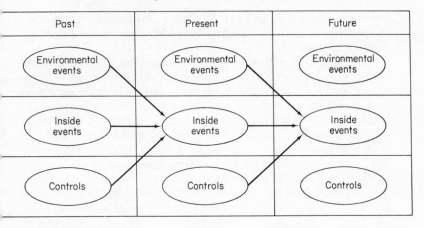

Figure 3

causal relationships. Theoretically, each variable in the category of present inside events might be affected by each of the past environmental events, each of the past inside events, and each of the past controls. Thus, if there were n variables in the category of inside events, m in the category of environmental events, and q in the category of controls, there would be no less than $n (n + m + q)$ possible separate lines of causality in Figures 3 and 4.

Secondly, as we have already seen, a number of these separate causal relationships would operate through their effect upon the citizens' expectations and decisions and this makes it especially difficult in many cases to assess their importance.

Thirdly, as we shall be at pains to show in the following two chapters, these causal relationships between the variables may take

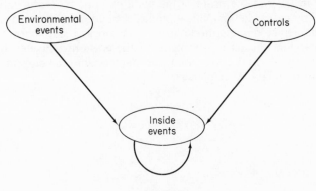

Figure 4

C

B

many different forms and this fact will in turn greatly complicate the problem of analysing the movements through time of the whole economic system.

One thing is clear from the outset, namely that in the real world the number of variables is so vast (comprising every price, every output, every income, every employment and so on in the economy) and the interconnections between them so numerous and complicated that it is totally impossible to construct anything but a much simplified model of reality. The questions immediately arise: In what way and to what extent should the model of reality be simplified? How far should one go in breaking down the economy into its components? For example, how detailed should be one's classification of goods? Into the two divisions of capital goods and consumption goods? Or into 1,000 groups of different types of product? For the purpose of examining the general control of the economy, does one want to break down into great detail one part of the economy (e.g. distinguish precisely between all the different groups of financial institutions in the economy) or another part of the economy (e.g. leave the financial institutions in one big composite but break down the productive apparatus of the economy into a very large number of separate industries and occupations)? How far, for the purposes of controlling the economy, must one build a model of the economy with a very large number of separate variables and interconnections? Or how far can one understand the main problems in which one is interested by considering a much simplified model of the economy with a relatively small number of variables and interconnections?

We must return to these questions in due course. Our present purpose in raising them is merely to underline the fact that there is no single *a priori* correct way of simplifying one's representation of interrelationships within the economy. Simplification there must be but in the end the proof of the pudding must be in the eating. When any particular simplification has been adopted, one can only ask whether or not the model has in fact worked satisfactorily in the sense that the past movements of the economy through time which it would imply correspond reasonably well to the movements which have in fact taken place.

CHAPTER III

IDENTITY, TECHNOLOGICAL AND BEHAVIOURAL RELATIONS

The formal problem of the dynamic control of the economy can now be expressed as follows: (i) given the interrelationships between the variables represented in Figures 3 and 4, (ii) given a forecast of the possible future courses of the environmental events, and (iii) given some principles upon which to base a judgment as to whether one particular development of the economy is to be held better or worse than another, we have to choose that pattern for the controls which will result in the socially most-preferred development of the economy.

The first step in this procedure is to determine what are the interrelationships between the variables represented in Figures 3 and 4—that is to say, to decide the structure of the simplified model of the economy which is to be constructed and what are the form and the importance of the various causal links connecting the variables in the model. This is the basic problem of the construction of the economic model to which Part 2 of this volume will be devoted.

This model, as we shall see in more detail later, can be expressed as a system of equations, the number of the equations being equal to the number of variables included in the category of inside events and each particular equation explaining how one particular variable in the category of inside events is to be explained as a result of previous environmental events, controls, and inside events. Given this set of relationships, given the state of the economy with which we start, and given the future course of the environmental events and controls, the future development of the economy will be determined. For (see Figures 3 and 4) present inside events will then be determined by past environmental events, controls, and inside events; and thus, in turn, the approaching future inside events will be determined in terms of past and present environmental events, controls and inside events, and so on into the future.

The economic model of the economy is thus made up of a set of equations, each of which explains the causal relation which determines the current value of one inside event in terms of past environmental events, controls, and inside events. These relations can fall into three types which we may call 'identity', technological', and 'behavioural' relations respectively.

The nature of identity relations can best be explained by means of an example. Let P be the money price of some good, X the amount of that good brought in any period (say, in the course of today), and M the amount of money spent on that good in the course of the same period of time. We can then (i) define M by the equation

$$PX = M$$

or (ii) define P by the equation

$$\frac{M}{X} = P$$

or (iii) define X by the equation

$$\frac{M}{P} = X.$$

All these three expressions are, of course, different ways of expressing the same identity relation between P, M and X.

Although each of these three expressions states the same identity relation, yet it will be useful in what follows to use each of the three forms to express a different causal sequence.

(i) Suppose that the market for this product is formed in the following way. Events on day 0 cause producers to decide to offer the good for sale at a price P on day 1; other events on day 0 cause consumers to decide to purchase an amount X on day 1. Then, separate sets of events on day 0 determine day 1's values of P and X and there results from these decisions the expenditure PX on day 1. We might depict this as in case (i) of Figure 5.

(ii) But the market might operate differently. Suppose, as before, that certain events on day 0 cause producers to decide to charge a price P on day 1. But suppose now that consumers behave differently. They decide on day 0 not how many units of the good they will purchase, but how much money—namely M—they will spend on the product on day 1. The result of these two decisions, through our identity relation, is the amount of X which consumers find they can purchase for M and the amount of X which producers find they can sell at P. We then have case (ii) of Figure 5.

(iii) Yet another possibility would be that consumers, as in case (ii), decide how much they will spend on the product on day 1 (M) while producers decide how much they will put in the market for sale on day 1 (X). The result will now be the price (P) which the

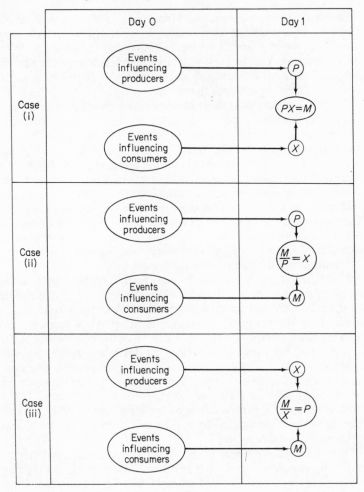

Figure 5

producers can get for each unit they sell.[1] We then have case (iii) of Figure 5.

[1] The reader may at this point well ask what happens if on day 0 the producers decide how much they will sell—as in case (iii)—while the consumers decide how much they will purchase—as in case (ii). The answer is, of course, that if the two quantities are unequal, both these decisions cannot be carried out. There will be either an unplanned change in producers' stocks (more or less being sold than was produced for sale) or else the consumers or the producers will be frustrated in their plans as to the amounts to be produced or consumed. We deal later in this chapter with the case of unplanned changes in stocks.

In other words an identity relation is not itself a causal relation. There is, for example, in case (i) above, not even conceptually, any time-lag between P and X on the one hand and the outcome M on the other hand. Yet the form in which the relationship is expressed can itself, in the way indicated above, show the direction in which causality is flowing through the system.

There is one special class of identity relations which we may call 'balancing relations' and which, as we shall see, are of particular importance in a dynamic model of the economy. Some variables are necessary equal to the sum of other variables or to the difference between some other variables. Thus, the increase in the stocks of a commodity in the course of any one day is necessarily equal to the excess of the production of that commodity in the course of the day over the consumption of that commodity in the course of the day. The stock of the commodity in existence at the beginning of day 2 is thus necessarily equal to the stock existing at the beginning of day 1 plus the production of the commodity during day 1 minus the consumption of the commodity during day 1.

This relationship is necessarily true; the list of the origins of the supply of a commodity and the list of the destinations of that supply must necessarily add up to the same total. And yet a relationship of this kind does imply a causal relationship. Thus suppose that certain people (the producers) hold a stock of the commodity at the beginning of day 1 and have decided on day 0 how much they will produce on day 1 and suppose that some other persons (the consumers) have decided on day 0 how much they will consume on day 1. Then the stock left over for the beginning of day 2 is the residual item which is determined by the three 'causes': (a) the stock existing at the beginning of day 1, (b) production during day 1, and (c) consumption during day 1.

Of course, the producers in the above example are very likely to be greatly concerned with what happens to their stocks during day 1. They may well have decided on day 0 to produce an amount on day 1 which they expect to be equal to what consumers will buy on day 1, i.e. they may have planned to keep their stocks constant during day 1. But their forecast of day 1's sales may turn out to be over-optimistic, in which case their stocks—which are, in our example, the residual or balancing item which keeps total supplies equal to total uses of the product—will in fact have gone up. And, in its turn, this rise in stocks during day 1 may cause them to decide on day 2 to produce less than they would otherwise on day 3, so as to reduce again their now excessive stocks.

In an economic system there are many relationships of this kind. One more example must suffice at this point. The amount which a man saves today may be defined as the amount of income which he receives today less the amount which he spends on consumption goods and services today and less the amount which he pays in taxes today. Savings (like stocks in our previous example) may well be the balancing or residual item. Thus, it may well be that on day 0 the citizen decides how much he will spend on day 1 (expecting a certain income and a certain tax liability on day 1 and thus planning for a certain level of savings on day 1), but that his actual income and tax liabilities are decided by others (by his employer and by the government). His actual savings on day 1 (which together with the property which he owned at the beginning of day 1 and any gifts or bequests which he received during day 1 will constitute the amount of property which he owns at the beginning of day 2) are thus caused by his expenditure on consumption on day 1 and by the amounts which in fact he receives in income or has to pay in taxes during day 1.

A second set of relationships in the economy may be called technological relations. These are straighforwardly causal relationships. These comprise all the productive possibilities. Thus (cf. *The Growing Economy*, Chapter XV), with any given state of technical knowledge on day 1 the outputs of various products that will be produced as a result of that day's operations will depend upon the inputs of labour, of land, and of intermediate products of various kinds and qualities that have been put into the various processes in the productive apparatus at the beginning of the day. If we treat all improvements in technical knowledge as a process of 'learning by inspiration' (see p. 111 of *The Growing Economy*) we can treat technical progress as an environmental event.[2] The outputs available for sale at the beginning of day 2 are thus determined by the inputs of day 1 and by the exogenously-given state of technical knowledge of day 1. These relationships describe the technological constraints on the production of goods and services available for use each day.

These technological relations are typically those in which past inside events affect present inside events (line 2 on Figure 1 above); the actual inputs of one day determine the actual outputs available for use on the next day.

The third group of relationships, the behavioural relations, are also straightforwardly causal. They are typically those through

---

[2] If we treated technical progress as a process of learning by one's own or other's research or doing (cf. Chapter IX of *The Growing Economy*) it would cease to be an environmental variable and would itself be an inside event dependent on previous inside events (i.e. on the amounts of past resources invested in research and development or the past amounts of the particular activities from the doing of which the new technical knowledge was acquired.)

which inside events are determined by the decisions of the private decision-makers (line 3 of Figure 1). How do past environmental and inside events working either directly or through their effect upon expectations, cause decision-makers to decide to do this rather than that? What past events (e.g. levels of income, prices, existing stocks of goods, value of property owned, and so on) cause consumers to decide on day 1 to purchase this amount of one particular product and that amount of another? What past events (profitability of different enterprises, rates of interest at which loans can be financed, changes in prices of inputs and outputs, and so on) cause business managers to invest in this amount of this instrument of production and that amount of that instrument? What past events (e.g. costs of various inputs, levels of demand for various products, changes in consumers' incomes, and so on) cause sellers to quote this price for the sale of this product and that price for the sale of that product?

A complete dynamic model of the economy will consist of a complete set of identity, technological, and behavioural relations which together will provide for each variable in the category of inside events an explanation of how its present level is determined by past inside events, environmental events, and controls.

CHAPTER IV

FORMS OF RESPONSE AND OF TIME-LAG

In depicting the process by which these identity, technological and behavioural relations cause the economy to move through time we shall adopt the convention, which we adopted throughout *The Growing Economy*, of splitting time up into small discrete units which we call days. We then consider the change in the state of the economy between one day and the next.

Since all causes precede their effects in time, this means that in the great majority of instances the relationships which explain the level of one variable in terms of other variables will be such that the effect (i.e. the explained variable) occurs on a day later in time than the day or days on which the causes (i.e. the explanatory variables) have occurred. But this is not invariably so for two reasons.

In the first place we have the identity relations of the kind already depicted in Figure 5. Here the relationship is one of simultaneous identity. The expenditure of money on a product on day t—$M(t)$— is equal to the price of the product on that same day—$P(t)$—multiplied by the quantity bought on that same day—$X(t)$—, so that we have

$$M(t) = P(t) X(t).$$

This is clear from the way in which the relations are depicted in Figure 5, though it is still true that the way in which it is depicted will show the channels through which causality is operating in the system.

Secondly, even in the case of straightforward causal relationships, the cause and the effect may occur on the same day because the day itself has some duration. An example will serve to make the point. Suppose some market were of the following kind. At the beginning of the day the sellers of a product set the price at which they offer to sell the product during the day and the buyers are then free to buy as much or as little as they like at this price during the day. $P(t)$ thus represents the price set AT THE BEGINNING OF day t and $X(t)$ represents the quantity subsequently bought DURING THE COURSE OF day t. $P(t)$ may thus causally affect $X(t)$. We could depict

29

this situation as in case (i) of Figure 6, where both the arrowed lines marked 1 are causal relationships.

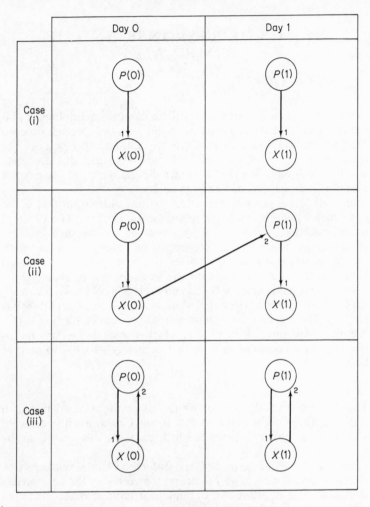

Figure 6

In the above example $P(t)$—the price set by the suppliers—affects $X(t)$—the amount bought by the demanders. Now it may also be true that the amount bought by the demanders will in turn affect the price set by the suppliers: when the demand is high, the suppliers may decide to ask a high price for the product. But the amount bought IN THE COURSE OF day t must then in our present model affect the price set AT THE BEGINNING OF day $t + 1$; we cannot have the amount bought DURING day t affecting the price set earlier, i.e. AT THE BEGINNING of day t. This would be to make the cause follow its effect. Thus we can have the situation depicted in case (ii) of Figure 6, where $P(0)$ and $P(1)$ are the prices set at the beginning of day 1 respectively, where $X(0)$ and $X(1)$ are the amounts bought during day 0 and day 1 respectively, where the lines marked 1 represent the causal affects of price on demand, and the line marked 2 the causal effect of demand upon supply price. What we cannot have is the situation depicted in case (iii) of Figure 6.

In other words, in the systems which we shall be examining we shall never have a feedback relationship (e.g. P affecting X and X in turn directly or indirectly affected P) which occurs within the course of a single day. All causal relationships flow in a single direction, as it were, from one day to the next day and without any simultaneous feedback occurring within the course of any one day.[1]

Having, then, adopted the convention of carving time up into very small discrete intervals called days, let us now consider the way in which the various identity, technological and behavioural relations may show themselves in such a system. We shall consider three basic forms for the way in which one variable may respond to (i.e. be affected by) another variable. These three basic forms of response may be called (1) a 'proportional' response, (2) a 'derivative' response, and (3) an 'integral' response; and each of these responses may in turn be a 'positive' response or a 'negative' response.

(1) *Proportional Effects.* Let us first consider a positive proportional response. As an example we may take the dependence of the level of consumption expenditure upon the level of spendable income. Suppose, to take the simplest possible example, that citizens always spent three-quarters of their disposable incomes and

---

[1] This is what is known technically as a recursive system. It should be emphasized that we are making this assumption purely for the sake of elucidating the logic of the relationships between the variables in our system. If the 'day' is a short enough period of time, then our assumption would also correspond closely enough to reality for it to be justified in actual statistical and empirical work. But, in fact, in constructing an actual econometric model of an economy, it may be necessary to carve time up into periods much longer than a day—i.e. into monthly, quarterly or even annual periods—simply because the statistical information is not available for shorter periods. In this case the periods may be so long that feedback influences which take place during the period cannot be neglected; and this can greatly complicate the problem of statistical and econometric estimation of the actual values of the influences at work in the economy.

always saved a quarter of their incomes. Then the effect of disposable income upon consumption could be called a positive proportional effect, since consumption would vary in a positive way proportionally to variations in disposable income. The level of disposable income would determine the level of consumption expenditures. We shall depict a relationship of this kind in the following way:

Y represents the level of disposable income and C the level of expenditure on consumption. The line leading from Y to C indicates that Y in some way or another affects C. The fact that the line is a continuous line and not a broken line indicates that Y exercises a positive effect on C, an upward movement in Y causing an upward movement in C. The arrowhead (⟶) indicates that the response of C to Y is a proportional effect. In short the diagram expresses the fact that a high level of Y leads to a high level of C.

Now we are assuming that every cause is followed in time by its effect. The level of C at one time must, therefore, in this case depend upon the level of Y at some previous time. The length and form of these time-lags between cause and effect can be very varied and can very greatly affect the way in which the economy will behave. We will return later in this chapter to a consideration of the various kinds of time-lag which may be operative in the economy. For the moment, let us assume the very simplest time-lag possible, namely that the level of consumption expenditure on day 1 is proportional to (for example, three-quarters of) the level of spendable income received on day 0.

In this case we could express this positive proportional relationship in the following way:

$$C(t) = aY(t - 1) \dots\dots\dots\dots\dots (4.1)$$

where $a = 0.75$. The level of consumption on any day (t) is three quarters of the level of disposable income received on the previous day $(t - 1)$.

Let us next give an example of a negative proportional response. Suppose that the amount of some commodity (X) which is bought is high when the price (P_x) is low and is low when the price is high. The level of X thus depends upon the level of P_x; but the relationship is now a negative one. A high level of P_x leads to a low level of X, and vice versa.

We can depict this as:

Once again the variables (the price and the amount bought) are enclosed in circles; the line shows the direction of causality (the price affects the amount bought); the broken line indicates that the effect is a negative one; and the arrowhead (———►) indicates once more that the relationship is a proportional one. Thus a high level of P_x leads to a low level of X.

Let us for the moment assume that this is a strictly proportional effect, i.e. that for every rise in P_x by \$1 there is a given constant reduction in X, by, say, five units; and let us also assume that there is the simplest possible delay between cause and effect, namely that the amount bought in the course of any one day depends upon the price fixed at the beginning of that day (see above). Then we could express this relationship as:

$$X(t) = A - bP_x(t) \quad \dots \dots \dots \dots \dots (4.2)$$

where $b = 5$. A is now a constant which expresses the amount of X which would be consumed if P_x were zero and X were a free good. Then for each unit increase in P_x there would be a reduction of b units in the consumption of X.

(2) *Derivative Effects.* The negative proportional effect of price upon the amount bought which we have just discussed is, however, not the only possible form of response of purchases to price changes. There may, for example, be a speculative influence of price changes upon purchases. In the case of a durable product, the amount bought today may be much affected by what purchasers expect will happen to the price in the near future. If they expect the price to go up in the near future they may increase their purchases now in order to acquire the product at today's uninflated price.

But what determines their expectations of future price movements? Let us suppose, for the purpose of illustration, that purchasers make the very simple assumption that prices will rise (or fall) in the near future at the same rates as they have been rising (or falling) in the immediate past. In this case a rise of price in the immediate past will indirectly, through its direct effect in causing an expectation of a continued rise in price in the near future, cause a speculative rise in today's purchases of the product in question. This we will call a positive derivative effect, which we can depict as follows:

Once again the line indicates the fact that the behaviour of the price is influencing the amount bought. The fact that the line connecting P_x to X is a continuous and not a broken line indicates that P_x exerts a positive effect on X. But in this case it is the rate of increase in the price (and not the level of the price) which raises the level of the amount bought, and this form of response of X to P_x is called a derivative effect. The double arrowhead (⟶) is used to show that in this case a derivative and not a proportional influence is at work. When the level of one variable (X) is raised by a rise in the rate of increase of another variable (P_x), then the latter is said to exercise a positive derivative effect upon the former.[2]

Let us once more assume the simplest form of time lag between cause and effect, namely that today's speculative demand for X is affected solely by yesterday's rise in price, i.e. by the difference between the price set at the beginning of today's transactions and that set at the beginning of yesterday's transactions; and let us further assume that for every \$1 increase in the price there is a speculative demand for, say, four units of the product. Then we could represent this relationship as:

$$X(t) = B + c\{P_x(t) - P_x(t-1)\} \dots\dots\dots\dots\dots (4.3)$$

where B is the amount of X which would be bought in the absence of any speculative demand and $c = 4$. The demand on day t is $X(t)$; and yesterday's rise in price is the excess of this morning's price ($P_x(t)$) over yesterday morning's price ($P_x(t-1)$).

Just as one may purchase more of a durable product now if one expects its price to rise in the near future, so one may decide to hold less money now if one expects a rapid inflation of money prices in the future. Money is held for the convenience of market transactions; if money prices in general are rising rapidly, any stock of money which one holds will be losing its real value quickly, a loss which could be avoided by holding some other asset (such as an ordinary share) whose money price may be expected also to rise during a period of general price inflation; and thus the more rapid is the price inflation which is expected, the less money will people be willing to hold, since they will sacrifice the convenience of a large cash holding in order to avoid the loss of real value of their assets.

If the degree of price inflation which is expected in the near future is itself determined by the degree of price inflation which has been experienced in the recent past, we have an example of negative derivative response. The HIGHER is the RATE OF INCREASE of the general level of prices, the LOWER will be the LEVEL of the money stocks

[2] The derivative of P_x, namely dP_x/dt, exerts a positive influence on the level of X, namely X.

people wish to hold, which we can depict as follows:

where *P* stands for the general level of prices and *M* for the amount of money people wish to hold. The higher is the rate of increase of *P*, the lower will be the level of *M*.

Suppose once more that we have the simplest form of time delay (the desired level of *M* on day *t* being affected by the rate of inflation of prices between the mornings of day *t* and of day *t* − 1) and that for each point by which the price level is rising there is a reduction of $500 in the amount of money, then we could express this relationship as:

$$M(t) = C - d\{P(t) - P(t - 1)\} \quad\dots\dots\dots\dots\dots\dots\dots (4.4)$$

where *C* is the amount of money which people would want to hold in the absence of general price inflation or deflation and *d* = 500.

(3) *Integral Effects.* The derivative effects which we have been considering are those in which the LEVEL of one variable depends upon the RATE OF INCREASE of another variable. But one can have instances of the reverse relationship where the RATE OF INCREASE of one variable depends upon the LEVEL of another variable. Such a relationship is called an integral effect.[3] Such integral effects can be either positive or negative.

As an example of a positive integral effect, consider the relationship between the amount spent on new machines and the number of machines available for use. Suppose, solely for purposes of simplification, that machines last for ever. Then the rate of increase in the stock of machines will depend simply upon the amount spent on new machines, which we can depict as:

where *I* represents the amount spent per day on machines and *K* the stock of machines in use. We will use a spearhead (——————◇) to represent an integral effect. Thus the diagram represents a positive integral effect of *I* on *K*, so that the higher is the level of expenditure on machines, the greater will be the rate of increase in the stock of machines.

[3] Suppose that dX/dt depends upon *Y*, in the sense that $dX/dt = \alpha Y$. Then $X = \alpha \int Y dt$. *X* depends upon the integral of *Y*. Thus, in the example, given in the text, we say that the RATE OF INCREASE in the size of the capital stock depends upon the annual OUTPUT of machines; and this is equivalent to saying that the present SIZE of the capital stock depends upon the SUM of past annual outputs of machines, i.e. upon the integral of outputs of machines over past years.

Suppose that we have the simplest form of time-lag, namely that machines bought yesterday become available for use today, and suppose that a machine costs \$100. Then we could express the above relationship in the following way:

$$K(t) - K(t - 1) = eI(t - 1) \qquad \dots\dots\dots\dots\dots\dots\dots (4.5)$$

where $K(t) - K(t - 1)$ is the increase in the stock of machines available for use as between the mornings of day $t - 1$ and day t, $I(t - 1)$ is the number of dollars spent on new machines in the course of day $t - 1$, and $e = 1/100$.

A straightforward form of negative integral effect is the relationship between the budgetary surplus and the national debt. If the excess of revenue over expenditure is used to redeem the national debt, then one can say that the HIGHER is LEVEL of the budgetary surplus, the LOWER will be the RATE OF INCREASE of the national debt, or

where B_s is the budgetary surplus and R is the national debt.

If the whole of yesterday's budgetary surplus is used to reduce the debt that would otherwise be outstanding today, we can express this as:

$$R(t) - R(t - 1) = - B_s(t - 1) \qquad \dots\dots\dots\dots\dots\dots (4.6)$$

where $R(t)$ is the amount of debt outstanding at the beginning of day t, and $B_s(t - 1)$ is the budgetary surplus realised in the course of day $t - 1$.

We have expressed an integral effect of variable X on variable Y as being the case in which the RATE OF CHANGE in Y depends upon the LEVEL of X. We can express this (see footnote 3 above) equally well by saying that the LEVEL of Y depends upon the SUM OF THE LEVELS of X over past periods of time. We can illustrate this very easily from the example of positive integral effect given above. Thus we can equally well express the same relationship (i) by saying that the rate of increase of the stock of machinery available for use depends upon the current level of expenditure upon new machines, or (ii) by saying that the level of the stock of machinery now available for use depends upon the sum of expenditures upon new machinery over the last years.

It is worthwhile considering this point at greater length. Suppose that the amount of new shoes bought by consumers depends, among other things, upon the number of shoes which they already have in their wardrobes. The greater the stock of shoes which they have, the lower will be their demand for new shoes. This again can be expressed as a negative integral effect of X (the number of shoes bought) upon itself. The level of the current demand for shoes will by the lower, the higher is the sum of purchases of shoes over the past periods.

Suppose that shoes lasted only three days and then were fully worn out. We could then express this influence on the demand for shoes by:

$$X(t) - X(t - 3) = E - d\{X(t - 1) + X(t - 2)$$
$$+ X(t - 3)\} \dots\dots\dots\dots\dots\dots\dots\dots\dots\dots\dots\dots (4.7)$$

where E stands for the number of shoes which the consumer is buying for other reasons (e.g. because his income is high, because the price of shoes is low, because he is speculating on the price of shoes being higher in the future, and so on); $X(t - 1) + X(t - 2) + X(t - 3)$ is his existing stock of shoes, since shoes last only three days; and $-d$ times this stock represents the fact that the higher is his stock, the lower will be his desire to add to it. However, since shoes last only three days he must purchase $X(t - 3)$ shoes on day t in order to replace the shoes that will be worn out on that day, so that his net demand for shoes to add to his stock of shoes is only $X(t) - X(t - 3)$. $X(t) - X(t - 3)$ represents the consumer's net demand on day t. But his net demand on day $t - 1$ was determined by exactly the same influences, all the variables being simply dated one day earlier, so that:

$$X(t - 1) - X(t - 4) = E - d\{X(t - 2) + X(t - 3)$$
$$+ X(t - 4)\} \dots\dots\dots\dots\dots\dots\dots\dots\dots\dots\dots\dots (4.8)$$

Subtracting 4.8 from 4.7, we have

$$\{X(t) - X(t - 3)\} - \{X(t - 1) - X(t - 4)\}$$
$$= -d\{X(t - 1) - X(t - 4)\} \dots\dots\dots\dots\dots\dots\dots\dots (4.9)$$

Equation 4.7 expressed the negative integral effect of the stock of shoes on the demand for new shoes by stating that the level of the net demand for shoes was lower, the higher the past accumulated stock of shoes. Equation 4.9 expresses the same relationship by saying that the rate of increase in the net demand for shoes is the lower, the higher the current level of the net purchase of new shoes.

Up to this point, in discussing all the positive and negative, proportional, derivative, and integral effects we have made the simplest possible assumptions about the time-lags between cause and effect, namely that each cause exerts its full effect as quickly as is consistent with the logic of our day-by-day type of analysis. But in fact the form and length of time-lags may be very different from this; and, as we shall see, the exact form and length of the time-lags can be of the greatest importance in determining the way in which the economic system moves through time.

Let us then consider some of the main forms which a time-lag may take. Let us illustrate these by considering the example which we took earlier of a positive proportional effect. We assumed simply that the amount spent on consumption on any one day was three-quarters of the disposable income received on the previous day or

$$C(t) = 0.75 \ Y(t - 1) \ \ldots \ldots \ldots \ldots \ldots \ldots (4.10)$$

We will proceed to consider different sorts of time-lag which may modify the simple basic equilibrium relationship that consumers wish to spend always three-quarters of their disposable income.

The first obvious possibility is that there is a simple time delay but of a greater length than one day. Suppose that citizens take not one, but four days, to do their personal accounts. It is only on day t that they know how great their disposable income was on day $t - 4$. Being very uncertain about their future prospects, they simply adopt the rule of thumb behaviour that they will spend on day t three-quarters of their disposable income of day $t - 4$, which is the most up-to-date accurate information about their actual earnings. Then we would have:

$$C(t) = 0.75 \ Y(t - 4) \ \ldots \ldots \ldots \ldots \ldots \ldots (4.11)$$

This time delay is illustrated in section (i) of Figure 7. We assume there that disposable income (Y) has been running steadily at $100 a day for a long period in the past but that on day 0 it suddenly rises to $150 a day and then stays steady at this new and higher level. The broken line shows the consequential equilibrium value of consumers' expenditure (C) which would have to rise on day 0 from $75 to $112.5 a day in order to remain at three-quarters of disposable income which rose that day from $100 to $150 a day. But consumers did not realize until day 4 that their incomes had risen and in consequence did not make the corresponding 50% rise in their consumption until four days after the rise in their incomes.

But this is by no means the only possible form of time-lag. Let us tell another story which is illustrated in section (ii) of Figure 7. Let us suppose that citizens are aware on day 1 as to what has happened to their incomes on day 0. But they are uncertain about the future and are cautious. On day 1 they realize that on day 0 their income was $150 and not $100 and that their equilibrium level of consumption was therefore \$112·5 and not the \$75 which they actually spent on consumption. On day 1, that is to say, they realize that on day 0 their actual consumption was \$112·5 − \$75 = \$37·5 below its equilibrium level. Being cautious they decide on

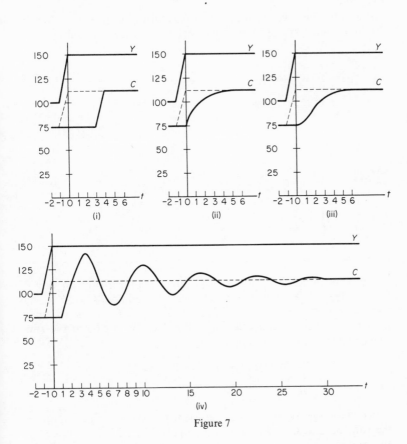

Figure 7

day 1 to raise their consumption not by the full amount of its shortfall on day 0 but by a certain fraction of that shortfall—for example, by half of the shortfall or \$18·75. Suppose, in brief, that consumers raise their consumption expenditure on day t not by the full amount of the shortfall on day $t − 1$ of their actual consumption below its equilibrium level but by some fraction λ of this shortfall.

Then consumption expenditure would be given by the formula:

$$C(t) - C(t - 1) = \lambda \{0.75Y(t - 1) - C(t - 1)\}$$

$$\ldots\ldots\ldots (4.12)$$

or $C(t) = 0.375Y(t - 1) + 0.5C(t - 1),$

if $\lambda = 0.5$.[4]

If $\lambda = 0.5$ then the movement in C resulting from a once-for-all rise in Y from 100 to 150 on day 0 is given in case (ii) of Table I.

Table I

t	-3	-2	-1	0	1	2	3	4	5
Y	100	100	100	150	150	150	150	150	150
Case (ii)									
$0.375Y$	37.5	37.5	37.5	56.25	56.25	56.25	56.25	56.25	56.2
$0.5C$	37.5	37.5	37.5	37.5	46.9	51.6	53.9	55.1	55.7
C	75	75	75	75	93.75	103.1	107.8	110.2	111.3
Case (iii)									
$0.125Y$	12.5	12.5	12.5	18.75	18.75	18.75	18.75	18.75	18.7
$0.5C$	37.5	37.5	37.5	37.5	40.6	45.3	50.8	53.3	54.9
C	75	75	75	75	81.25	90.6	101.6	107.1	109.9
Case (iv)									
$0.6Y$	60	60	60	90	90	90	90	90	90
$-0.8C$	-60	-60	-60	-60	-60	-84	-108	-114	-94
C	75	75	75	75	75	105	135	141	117

The row marked Y shows disposable income rising on day 0 from a steady 100 to a steady 150. The row marked $0.375Y$ is the row marked Y multiplied by 0.375. On day -2, C was at its equilibrium value of 75 and thus for day -2 we have 37.5 in the row marked $0.5C$. Now equation 4.12 states:

$$C(-1) = 0.375\,Y(-2) + 0.5C(-2)$$
$$= 37.5 + 37.5$$
$$= 75$$

which is the figure shown in the last row for day -1. Each figure in the row marked C is the sum of the figures for $0.375Y$ and $0.5C$ of the previous day. In the table, there is no change in any figure until $0.375Y$ goes up to 56.25 on day 0. This causes C to go up to 93.75 and $0.5C$ to go up to 46.9 on day 1, which causes C to go up to 103.1 and $0.5C$ to 51.6 on day 2, and so on. The way in which C

---

[4] It is to be observed that, if $\lambda = 1$, the formula becomes $C(t) = 0.75\,Y(t - 1)$, i.e. equation 4.10 with which we started the analysis. This is simply the case in which consumers adjust their expenditure completely to their disposable income of the previous day.

Forms of Response and Time-Lag   **41**

rises towards its new equilibrium level of 112·5 is shown in the last row of case (ii) of Table I; and this is illustrated in section (ii) of Figure 7.

The nature of this adjustment is clear. On any day C is raised by 0·5 of the extent to which C fell short of its equilibrium level on the previous day. Thus C goes up quickly when it is far below its equilibrium level and very slowly when it is very near its equilibrium level. C rises towards its equilibrium level at a speed which is proportional to the shortfall of actual C below equilibrium C. Citizens

6	7	8	9	10	11	12	13	14	15	16	17	18	19
150	150	150	150	150	150	150	150	150	150	150	150	150	150
119·9													
18·75													
55·6													
111·2	111·9												
90	90	90	90	90	90	90	90	90	90	90	90	90	90
−74	−71	−84	−99	−104	−97	−86	−80	−83	−91	−96	−96	−91	−86
93	89	105	124	130	121	107	100	104	114	121	120	114	108

raise consumption expenditure at a rate which depends upon the extent to which their actual expenditure is below the desired level.

But the reaction of our citizens in adjusting their consumption expenditure to a change in their spendable incomes might well depend not only upon the size of the shortfall of their actual expenditure below the equilibrium level, but also upon the length of time for which this shortfall had continued. Thus suppose as before that spendable income rises on day 0 from a steady 100 to a steady 150 and that in consequence the equilibrium level of consumption expenditure rises from $0·75 \times 100 = 75$ to $0·75 \times 150 = 112·5$. Because of uncertainty as to whether the rise in income was a permanent one or not, citizens might react in two ways: first, as we have already assumed, they might raise their consumption on any day by only a fraction—in our illustration, half—of the shortfall of their actual expenditure below the equilibrium level; but, second, they might also calculate that equilibrium level of consumption not merely in terms of the level of disposable income of the previous day but in terms of the average level of disposable income of a number of previous days. In other words, when their spendable income rises they might calculate their continuing disposable income not in terms simply of yesterday's income but in terms of the income of yesterday, the day before that, and the day before that. What they regard as their 'target' level of consumption will now depend not only on yesterday's income, but on an average of their income over a series of previous days; and as before they will on any day raise their expenditure by an amount which is greater, the greater is the shortfall of their actual expenditure below this newly calculated target level of expenditure. In the result, the rate at which they will adjust their expenditure will be the higher (1) the longer the discrepancy between the actual and the new equilibrium level has continued and (2) the larger this discrepancy is.

We can express this form of time-lag in the following way:

$$C(t) - C(t-1) = \lambda \left\{ 0.75 \, \frac{Y(t-1) + Y(t-2) + Y(t-3)}{3} \right.$$
$$\left. - C(t-1) \right\} \quad \dots \dots \dots \dots \dots \dots \dots \dots \quad (4.13)$$

if we assume that the target level of consumption is now not three-quarters of the previous day's income but three-quarters of the average of the previous three days' income. If we take $\lambda = 0.5$ as before, then the formula becomes

$$C(t) = 0.5 \, C(t-1) + 0.125 \left\{ Y(t-1) + Y(t-2) \right.$$
$$\left. + Y(t-3) \right\} \quad \dots \dots \dots \dots \dots \dots \dots \quad (4.14)$$

In case (iii) of Table I, we can see how the level of C would adjust itself to a once-for-all rise of Y on day 0 from 100 to 150. Up to day 0, Y has been steady at 100 and C at 75. On day 0, Y rises once for all from 100 to 150 (and $0.125 \, Y$ therefore from 12.5 to 18.75). The value of C is then calculated day by day as the sum of $0.125 \, Y$ for the three previous days and of $0.5 \, C$ for the previous day.

The resulting figures for the change in C are shown in the last row of section (iii) of Table I and in section (iii) of Figure 7, where, as in sections (i) and (ii) of the figure, the broken line shows the change in the equilibrium value of C and the solid line marked C shows the actual movement of C towards this equilibrium level. If one compares section (iii) with section (ii) of the figure, one can see that the rise of C is now slow at first (since citizens do not make big adjustments until the rise in income has lasted some time), then becomes rapid (as the rise in income has now lasted some time and the shortfall of actual below equilibrium expenditure is also large), and then becomes slow again (as there is very little remaining discrepancy to make good).

But there is yet another kind of time-lag which may lead to a quite different type of result. Let us suppose that Mr Smith keeps the family accounts and that Mrs Smith does the family shopping. The Smith family aim at spending three-quarters of their income. On Wednesday, Mr Smith does the family accounts for Tuesday and reckons that, on Tuesday, Mrs Smith underspent by an amount equal to $0.75 \, Y$ (Tuesday) $- \, C$ (Tuesday). He tells Mrs Smith that she can spend more on the coming day (Thursday) than she is spending today (Wednesday). He is fairly optimistic in view of Tuesday's balance, but in order not to be too rash tells Mrs Smith to increase her expenditure on Thursday by $0.8 \, \{0.75 \, Y$ (Tuesday) $-$ C (Tuesday)$\}$, i.e. by only a fraction, namely four-fifths, of the shortfall of expenditure on the last day on which he did the family accounts. As a result C (Thursday) $- \, C$ (Wednesday) $=$ $0.8 \, \{0.75 \, Y$ (Tuesday) $- \, C$ (Tuesday)$\}$ or

$$C(t) - C(t - 1) = 0.8 \, \{0.75 \, Y(t - 2) - C(t - 2)\}$$

or

$$C(t) = C(t - 1) - 0.8 \, C(t - 2) + 0.6 \, Y(t - 2) \ldots \ldots (4.15)$$

We have, as before, the idea of raising actual consumption by a fraction of its shortfall below an equilibrium level, but in this case there are two days' lag between the measurement of the shortfall and the actual increase in expenditure.

In this case, the way in which C will respond to a once-for-all rise of Y on day 0 from 100 to 150 is shown in case (iv) of Table I. In this case, Y rises, as in previous cases, on day 0 from a steady 100 to a steady 150. Up to this point, C has been steady also at its equilibrium level of $0.75 \times 100 = 75$. From this point on, the level of C for any day is calculated as the value of $0.6 \, Y$ two days before less the value of $0.8 \, C$ two days before plus the value of C one day before. The resulting figures are shown in the last row of case (iv) of Table I and are illustrated in section (iv) of Figure 7.

The outstanding feature of this case is that the actual level of C overshoots the equilibrium mark, turns down and undershoots the equilibrium mark, turns up again, and so approaches the equilibrium mark in a series of diminishing fluctuations. Why does this happen? Let us return to the housekeeping arrangements of the Smith family. On Wednesday, Mr Smith in essence tells Mrs Smith how much to raise the housekeeping expenditure on Thursday above its level on Wednesday, but he does this on the basis of a shortfall of expenditure that occurred on Tuesday. But Wednesday's expenditure may already have been raised considerably as a result of a big shortfall on Monday calculated by Mr Smith on Tuesday and leading already to a big increase in expenditure between Tuesday and Wednesday. To give another big boost to expenditure on Thursday on the basis of Tuesday's large shortfall when the shortfall on Wednesday was already much reduced may cause expenditure to rise above the equilibrium level on Thursday; in our particular example this is what in fact happens.

On Friday, when Mr Smith comes to do Thursday's accounts, he will realize that the equilibrium level has been much exceeded and will decide on a drastic cut for Saturday. In this way there may come to be an excessive economy in expenditure. When this becomes apparent, the process will again be reversed. And so the swing may continue. In our example these swings will gradually become less and less marked; this will always in fact be the case provided that Mr Smith tells Mrs Smith to add to her expenditure on day *t* only a fraction of the shortfall of expenditure on day *t*-2.[5]

In the earlier sections of this chapter we gave examples of a number of different particular relationships between one variable and the other variables upon which it may depend. We enumerated examples of cases of positive and negative proportional, derivative and integral effects. In those earlier sections, however, we confined our attention to cases in which only one of these relationships was at work in any one case. But in the real world, of course, these relationships may be combined in many different combinations. Let us illustrate this from one particular possibility.

Suppose that the gross number of pairs of shoes which will be purchased on any one day t, namely $X(t)$, will be the greater (i) the higher are the consumer's incomes; (ii) the lower is the market price of shoes; (iii) the more quickly prices are expected to rise in the future; and (iv) the smaller the number of still wearable shoes which the consumers own in their wardrobes.

Influence (i) is a positive proportional effect which we may represent by $aY(t - 1)$ if we assume that it is yesterday's income which influences today's purchase (cf. equation 4.1).

Influence (ii) is a negative proportional effect which we may represent by $A - bP_x(t)$ (cf. equation 4.2).

Influence (iii) is a positive derivative effect which we may represent by $B + c\{P_x(t) - P_x(t - 1)\}$ (cf. equation 4.3).

Influence (iv) is a negative integral effect which we may represent by

$$E - d\{X(t - 1) + X(t - 2) + X(t - 3)\} + X(t - 3),$$

[5] The equation for the system which we are examining is $C(t) - C(t - 1) + \lambda C(t - 2) = \lambda\alpha Y(t - 2)$, where α is the proportion of income which will be spent in equilibrium (in our example 0.75) and λ is the proportion of any shortfall of expenditure on day $t - 2$, which is added to the expenditure of day $t - 1$ to determine the expenditure of day t (in our example 0.8). The roots of the characteristic equation are $\frac{1}{2}\{1 \pm \sqrt{1 - 4\lambda}\}$. These roots will be conjugate complex and there will be fluctuations if $\lambda > 0.25$. But so long as $\lambda < 1$ these fluctuations will be damped.

if we assume that shoes last for three days, so that the stock of shoes in the consumers' wardrobes is equal to the sum of the purchases of shoes over the last three days (cf. equation 4.7).

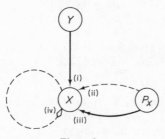

Figure 8

Diagrammatically we could express this as in Figure 8 and algebraically as:

$$X(t) = aY(t-1) + A - bP_x(t) + B + c\{P_x(t) - P_x(t-1)\}$$
$$+ E - d\{X(t-1) + X(t-2) + X(t-3)\} + X(t-3)$$

or

$$X(t) = F - dX(t-1) - dX(t-2) + (1-d)X(t-3)$$
$$+ \alpha Y(t-1) + (c-b)P_x(t) - cP_x(t-1) \ \ldots \ldots \ldots \text{(4.16)}$$

where $F = A + B + E$.

The point to be stressed is simply that the level of X on day t can be expressed as dependent upon the levels of X, Y and P_x on previous days, however complicated may be the combination of negative or positive proportional, derivative, and integral effects influencing X.

The same conclusion can be reached when we allow for the fact that these positive and negative proportional, derivative and integral effects may all operate only after time-lags of various forms and lengths. We will give only one example of this.

Suppose that the equilibrium demand for shoes is shown by the particular combination of the four influences (i) to (iv) mentioned above and expressed in equation 4.16. But suppose that this is subject to the type of time-lag expressed in equation 4.12, that is to say the consumers of shoes on day t raise their demand between day t and day $t-1$ by a fraction (λ) of the shortfall of their actual demand on day $t-1$ below their equilibrium demand on day $t-1$.

Then equation 4.16 would become:

$$X(t) - X(t-1) = \lambda\{F - dX(t-1) - dX(t-2)$$
$$+ (1-d)X(t-3) + aY(t-1) + (c-b)P_x(t)$$
$$- cP_x(t-1) - X(t-1)\}$$

or

$$X(t) = \lambda F + (1-\lambda-d\lambda)X(t-1) - d\lambda X(t-2)$$
$$+ (1-d)\lambda X(t-3) + a\lambda Y(t-1) + (c-b)\lambda P_x(t)$$
$$- c\lambda P_x(t-1) \dots \dots \dots \dots \dots \dots \dots \dots (4.17)$$

Once again, the level of X on day t can be expressed in terms of the levels of X, Y and P_x on previous days.

In this chapter we have up to this point illustrated all these relationships by means of linear equations. That is to say, we have in each case assumed that the affect of one variable upon another could be expressed by multiplying the causal variable by a constant coefficient (the 'a's, 'b's, 'c's, and 'd's of the examples given in this chapter) in order to obtain the value of the variable which it affected. But this is, of course, in many cases unreal.

Let us consider, for purposes of illustration, the negative proportional effect given by the demand curve given in equation 4.2, namely:

$$X(t) = A - bP_x(t).$$

This could be expressed by a straight line demand curve, as in Figure 9, where A would represent the amount of $X(t)$ which would

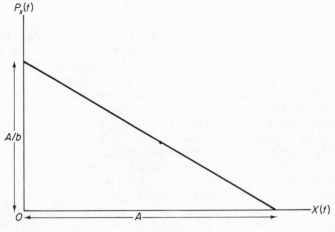

Figure 9

be bought if $P_x(t)$ were zero, and where A/b would represent the price which would be sufficiently high to cause consumers to give up the purchase of X altogether.

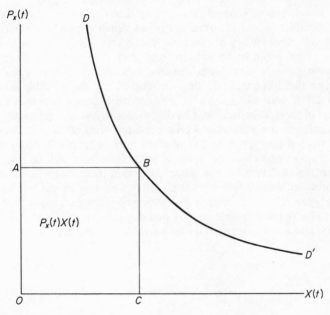

Figure 10

But suppose that the demand curve had a price elasticity equal to unity or, in other words, suppose that when the price fell the amount bought increased by an amount which caused the total expenditure on the product to remain constant.[6] Then we would express the demand curve as in Figure 10, where the demand curve DD' was such that the rectangle $P_x(t)X(t)$, which represents the value of the expenditure on $X(t)$ at the price $P_x(t)$, remains constant. If M represented this constant expenditure, then:

$$P_x(t)X(t) = M$$

or

$$X(t) = M/P_x(t) \dots\dots\dots\dots\dots\dots\dots\dots\dots (4.18)$$

We still have the level of $X(t)$ dependent upon the level $P_x(t)$ and

[6] See *The Stationary Economy*, p. 44.

we still have a negative relationship in the sense that the higher is $P_x(t)$ the lower will $X(t)$ be. But the influence of $P_x(t)$ on $X(t)$ can no longer be expressed as $P_x(t)$ multiplied by minus a constant (i.e. by $-bP_x(t)$ in our previous example). The influence of $P_x(t)$ on $X(t)$ is now represented by the reciprocal of $P_x(t)$ (i.e. by $1/P_x(t)$).

There can clearly be all sorts of non-linear relationships between the variables in an economic system of which the unitary elasticity demand curve shown above is only one very special example. But the general proposition remains true that, if we consider a system moving through time from one atomistic day to another, we can express the influences affecting the level of any one variable on any one day in terms of the levels of other variables on previous days. Some of these influences will be due to identity, some to technological and some to behavioural relationships; some of these influences will work directly, but some will work only indirectly through their effect upon expectations; some of these influences will be proportional, some derivative and some integral in their nature; and some of these influences will work only after time-lags of various forms and types. But the general truth of the proposition remains that the level of any one variable on any one day can be explained in terms of the levels of the other relevant variables on previous days.

CHAPTER V

POSITIVE AND NEGATIVE FEEDBACK

In the last chapter we discussed the many ways in which one economic variable may affect another. The economic system as it moves through time is a network of interconnections by which one variable affects another, which in turn affects another, which in turn affects another, and so on without cessation. In this process it will often happen not only that one variable (say X) will indirectly or directly affect another variable (say Y), but also that this other variable (Y) will itself indirectly or directly affect the first variable (X).

Now if an upward movement in X will directly or indirectly cause a change which itself in turn will tend directly or indirectly to cause an upward movement of X, we have what is known as a case of positive feedback. But if an upward movement in X will directly or indirectly cause a change which in its turn will tend to cause a downward movement in X, we have a case of negative feedback.

In this chapter we intend to give a few very simple economic models of cases of positive and negative feedback in order to show how these relationships may be expressed and the sort of results to which they may give rise.

We will start with a case of negative feedback. Consider the following fairy tale. There is an industry employing a certain type of labour; this labour can earn a given wage (W^*) in occupations outside this industry; labour is attracted into this industry at a rate which is greater, the greater is the excess of the wage rate in the industry (W) over the wage rate outside the industry (W^*) or, alternatively, labour is repelled from the industry at a rate which is greater, the greater is the excess of W^* over W; the demand for labour in the industry (D) depends upon the wage rate ruling in the industry (W), a high W leading to a low D; and finally the wage rate in the industry is bid up (or down) at a rate which depends upon the excess (or deficiency) of the demand for labour (D) over the supply of labour (S) currently available in the industry.

This is a case in which two negative feedback relationships are at work. First, if the wage rate (W) is very high, then the demand (D) will be low; thus the deficiency of demand (D) over supply (S) will be great; thus the wage rate (W) will be bid rapidly in a downwards direction. A high W has led to a rapidly falling W. Secondly, if the wage rate (W) is very high, it will be high relatively to the wage rate that can be earned in alternative occupations (W^*); thus labour will be attracted rapidly into the industry and the supply of labour in the industry (S) will be rising rapidly; thus sooner or later a deficiency of demand (D) over supply (S) of labour will appear; and thus the wage rate (W) will be bid down. Once again there is a set of influences at work which is causing a high W to lead to a fall in W. This story can be expressed in three simple equations:[1]

$$D(t) = A - \alpha W(t) \quad \dots \dots \dots \dots \dots \dots \quad (5.1)$$

$$W(t) - W(t-1) = \lambda\{D(t-1) - S(t-1)\} \quad \dots \dots \dots \quad (5.2)$$

$$S(t) - S(t-1) = \mu\{W(t-1) - W^*(t-1)\} \quad \dots \dots \dots \quad (5.3)$$

Equation 5.1 simply states that the amount of labour which employers in the industry would like to employ during day t depends upon the wage rate at which labour is offered at the beginning of day t. This demand relationship is expressed in the form of a straight-line demand curve, A being the amount of labour which would be demanded if the wage rate were zero and α representing the amount by which the demand for labour is reduced by every unit increase in the wage rate (cf. Figure 9).

But on any one day the amount of labour which employers would like to hire may not be equal to the amount of labour available to be hired. If on day $t-1$, $D(t-1) > S(t-1)$, then there will be unfilled vacancies equal to $D(t-1) - S(t-1)$. If, on day $t-1$, $D(t-1) < S(t-1)$, then there will be unemployed workers equal to $S(t-1) - D(t-1)$.

Equation 5.2 shows how this excess or deficiency of demand may cause the wage rate to go up or down. Thus suppose that the situation is such that the wage rate goes up between the beginning of day $t-1$ and the beginning of day t by an amount of dollars which is equal to half the number of unfilled vacancies, then $\lambda = 0.5$.

Similarly, equation 5.3 shows how quickly the excess of the wage offered in the industry at the beginning of day $t-1$ over the wage offered outside the industry at the same time will attract labour into the industry. If the situation were such that for every dollar excess of the wage rate inside the industry over the wage rate outside the industry at the beginning of day $t-1$, two new workers would be attracted to seek employment in the industry on the following day, then $\mu = 2$.

---

[1] The algebraic expression of this model is treated more extensively in the Note at the end of this chapter.

These relationships can also be expressed in two diagrammatic ways which are shown in Figures 11 and 12.

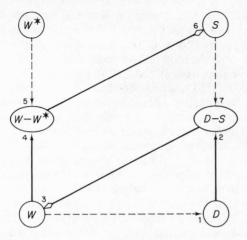

Figure 11

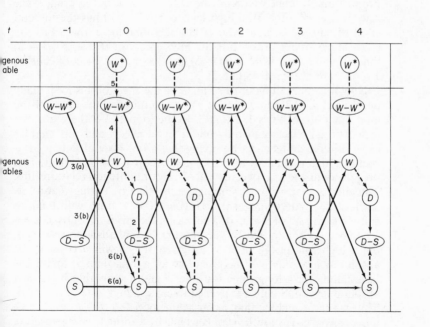

Figure 12

Let us first examine Figure 11. In the diagram the lines numbered 4 and 5 together express the simple identity relationship that at any point of time the excess of W over W^* is positively proportional to W and negatively proportional to W^*. And similarly lines 2 and 7 express the identity that the excess of D over S at any point of time is positively proportional to D and negatively proportional to S.

Consider now the loop of lines numbered 1, 2 and 3. If we follow this loop, we start from W and end up back at W. This is a negative feedback loop. It is a feedback loop because we end where we started; it is a negative loop, because there is an odd number of negative lines in the loop, in this particular case only one, namely the broken line 1. Thus a low W causes a proportionally high D (line 1); a high D causes a proportionally large excess of demand $(D - S)$ (line 2); a high excess of demand $(D - S)$ has the integral effect of causing a rapid rate of rise of the wage rate (W) (line 3). Through this loop, a low W tends to cause a high rate of rise of W.

Consider next the loop of lines 4, 6, 7 and 3. Once more this is a feedback loop because we end where we started; and it is a negative loop because there is an odd number of negative relationships in the loop, in this case the single broken line 7. Thus a low W causes a proportionally high excess of the external over the internal wage rate $(W^* - W)$ (line 4); a high level of $(W^* - W)$ has the integral effect of causing a rapid rate of fall of S (line 6); a low S has the effect of causing a proportionally high excess of D over S $(D - S)$ (line 7); and a high level of $(D - S)$ has the integral effect of causing a rapid rate of rise of W (line 3).

Now it is more difficult to summarize the effect of this loop made up of lines 4, 6, 7 and 3 than it was to summarize the effect of the loop made up of lines 1, 2 and 3. In the loop 1–2–3 there are two proportional effects and only one integral effect; and this enables us to summarize its effect by saying that a low level of W tended to lead to a high rate of rise of W. But in the loop 4–6–7–3 there are two proportional and also two, instead of only one, integral relationships. This means that we must summarize its effect by saying that a low level of W WHICH HAS PERSISTED FOR A LONG time will tend to cause a high rate of rise of W. The reason for this is as follows. Lines 4 and 6 show that a low W will cause not a low absolute level of S, but a high rate of fall of S. Thus, given W^*, S will necessarily be absolutely low only if W has been low for a long time so that S has been falling for a long time. But lines 7 and 3 show that it is a low absolute level of S which is needed to cause a high rate of rise of W. Thus we can conclude that, as far as the loop 4–6–7–3 is concerned, it is a PERSISTENTLY low level of W which, by leading to a low absolute level of S, will cause rapid rate of rise of W. It is clear that even in the simplest models the dynamic relationships can become somewhat complicated.

The method of expression used in Figure 11 is particularly well suited to show up the elements of positive and negative feedback in the system. Starting from any variable in the system there is a feedback of relationships, if one can follow a path along the lines in the direction of the arrows and arrive back at the starting point; and this is a positive or a negative feedback relationship according as one has traversed an even[2] or odd number of negative relationships (i.e. broken lines) in the journey.

This form of depiction is not, however, so useful in drawing attention to the way in which the system would move through time. The same relationships as those depicted in Figure 11 are shown in an alternative manner in Figure 12 which emphasizes their development through time. Each column in Figure 12 shows the level of the variables on the successive days which are numbered at the head of each column. In our present model the only exogenous variable is W^*, the wage rate ruling outside the industry. All the other variables are endogenous, that is to say, are determined by the interplay of supply and demand within the industry. W^* is thus shown on the top line of Figure 12; it may itself be changing from day to day for reasons quite unconnected with developments within the industry under examination; the broken line leading down from W^* into the system of endogenous variables (W, D and S) shows the influence of the 'outside' world on the 'inside' of the system.

All the arrowed lines in Figure 12 correspond exactly to the arrowed lines of Figure 11 and are numbered in the same way as those in Figure 11. There is, however, one outstanding difference. In Figure 11 we distinguished between proportional relationships (lines 1, 2, 4, 5 and 7) and integral relationships (lines 3 and 6). In Figure 12, all lines show proportional relationships. The reason for this is as follows.

Consider the integral relationship shown by lines 3 in Figure 11, namely:

---

[2] Suppose, for example, that a rise in X leads to a fall in Y and that a fall in Y leads to a rise in X. This is clearly a case of positive feedback. But it is made up of two negative relationships, thus:

which means that a high absolute level of excess demand $(D - S)$ causes a rapid rate of rise of the wage rate (W). When we turn to a day-to-day analysis we can express this, as we have done in equation 5.2, as:

$$W(t) - W(t - 1) = \lambda\{D(t - 1) - S(t - 1)\}$$

or

$$W(t) = W(t - 1) + \lambda\{D(t - 1) - S(t - 1)\}$$

The level of the wage rate on day t is equal to what it was on day $t - 1$ plus any increase due to an excess demand on day $t - 1$. In other words $W(t)$ can be expressed as subject to a twofold proportional influence; both $W(t - 1)$ and $\{D(t - 1) - S(t - 1)\}$ have positive proportional effects upon $W(t)$. Thus the integral effect shown by line 3 in Figure 11 can be expressed by the two proportional effects shown by lines 3(a) and 3(b) in Figure 12.[3]

Let us then with the help of Figure 12 consider the movement through time in the particular labour market which we are considering. In order to know what the position will be on days 0, 1, 2, 3, 4 etc., we must know (i) what will be the value of W^* on days 0, 1, 2, 3, 4 etc.; (ii) what were the values of $(W - W^*), W, (D - S)$ and S on day $- 1$; and (iii) what are the forces of the relationships numbered 1, 3(b) and 6(b) (i.e. the values of the parameters in equations 5.1, 5.2 and 5.3). Thus, as can be seen from Figure 12, knowing $(W - W^*)$ and S on day $- 1$ we shall know S on day 0 (lines 6(a) and 6(b)); and knowing W and $(D - S)$ on day $- 1$ we shall know W on day 0 (lines 3(a) and 3(b)); but knowing W on day 0 we shall know D on day 0 (line 1); and knowing W and W^* on day 0 we shall know $(W - W^*)$ on day 0 (lines 4 and 5); and knowing D and S on day 0 we know $(D - S)$ on day 0 (lines 2 and 7). Thus knowing $(W - W^*), W, (D - S)$ and S on day $- 1$, we shall know $(W - W^*)$, $W, (D - S)$ and S on day 0, which, by an exactly similar reasoning, will enable us to know $(W - W^*), W, (D - S)$ and S on day 1; and so on ad infinitum.

While it is clear that, given the three vital pieces of information (i), (ii) and (iii) of the previous paragraph, the system will move in a determinate way through time, it is not at all obvious how it will move. Indeed, generalization is very difficult and it is an outstanding feature of these dynamic problems that the result depends essen-

---

[3] This is, of course, only a particular example of the general principle explained above that, when we use this day-to-day type of analysis, we can show all proportional integral and derivative relationships and all time-lags by expressing the absolute level of a variable on any one day as dependent upon the absolute levels of the relevant variables on previous days, i.e. as a set of proportional relationships.

tially not merely upon the structure of the dynamic relationships (i.e. not merely upon the pattern of the paths of causality shown in Figures 11 and 12), but also upon the particular numerical values of the various influences and time-lags in the system. We will now illustrate this point by taking three different numerical examples of the force of the influences at work in the same structure of relationships as those shown in Figures 11 and 12. It will be seen that a change in the numerical values of the different relationships can have very startling results.

Let us give numerical values to the constants A, α, λ and μ in equations 5.1, 5.2 and 5.3. Let $A = 1,000$ and $\alpha = \lambda = 1$. We will then examine three different values of μ, namely: case (i) with $\mu = 0.2$; case (ii) with $\mu = 0.5$; and case (iii) with $\mu = 1.1$. In all three cases, we will assume that the economy starts in equilibrium with the outside and inside wage rate equal to 100 ($W = W^* = 100$), and that between day 0 and day 1 the outside wage rate (W^*) goes up from 100 to 110 and then stays constant at this higher level.

In all three cases the initial equilibrium of the economy would be one in which W and W^* are constant at 100. It follows from equation 5.3 that S will be constant; there is no wage differential to pull labour into, or to push it out of, this industry. From equation 5.1 it is clear that, with $A = 1,000$ and $\alpha = 1$, the demand for labour when $W = 100$ will be 900. From equation 5.2 it is clear that the wage rate will be constant only if $S = D$, i.e. only if we start with a supply of labour of 900 in the industry.

By an exactly similar process of argument it can be seen that if the outside wage rate goes up from 100 to 110 the industry will regain an equilibrium position with no further changes in the supply of labour, in the demand for labour, or in the wage rate, only if the supply settles down at the reduced level of 890 instead of 900. At the new wage of 110 the demand for labour will now be 890 (equation 5.1 gives $D = 1,000 - 1 \times 110$); if the supply is equal to this demand there will be no further change in the wage rate (equation 5.2); and with the inside wage equal to the outside wage at 110 there will be no further change in the supply.

In brief we start in all our examples with an equilibrium situation which lasts up to day 0 with $D = S$ at 900 and $W = W^*$ at 100. In all our examples on day 1, W^* rises to 110 and stays at that higher level indefinitely, and the new equilibrium position would then be one in which $D = S$ at 890 and $W = W^*$ at 110. This change in the equilibrium situation is shown by the broken line in Figure 13. Our problem now is to see how, if at all, the particular labour market moves from the old to the new equilibrium given the responses and delays in the system represented by the parameters α, λ and μ.

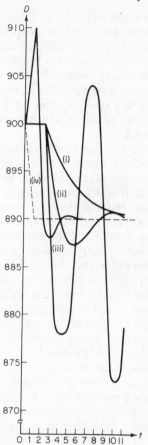

Figure 13

Case (i). With $A = 1,000$, $\alpha = \lambda = 1$ and $\mu = 0.2$, we can write equations 5.1, 5.2 and 5.3 as:

$$D(t) = 1,000 - W(t) \dots\dots\dots\dots\dots\dots\dots\dots (5.4)$$

$$W(t) = W(t-1) + D(t-1) - S(t-1) \dots\dots\dots (5.5)$$

$$S(t) = S(t-1) + 0.2\{W(t-1) - W^*(t-1)\} \dots\dots (5.6)$$

By means of equations 5.5 and 5.6 we can now express the values of W and S on any day in terms of the values of W, S and D on the previous day; and by means of equation 5.4 when we know the value of W on any day we can derive the value of D for that day as well.

Thus we can determine W, S and D on any day if we know W, S and D on the previous day. Case (i) in Table II simply carries out this arithmetic for the numerical value of $\mu = 0.2$. We start on day 0 with the equilibrium values $W = W^* = 100$ and $S = D = 900$; on day 1 W^* rises to 110 giving a deficiency of 10 for the inside wage rate ($W - W^* = -10$) on day 1; and this causes (see equation 5.6) a fall in S from 900 to 898 on day 2. For each future day we now use equations 5.4, 5.5 and 5.6 to calculate the values of W, S and D from their values on the previous day. This is simply the arithmetical calculation of the effect of the arrowed lines of Figure 12 when their forces are given the particular values of $\alpha = \lambda = 1$ and $\mu = 0.2$.

Table II

t		0	1	2	3	4	5	6	7	8	9	10
W^*		100	110	110	110	110	110	110	110	110	110	110
case (i)												
$\mu = 0.2$	W	100	100	100	102	104	105·6	106·8	107·7	108·3	108·8	109·1
	D	900	900	900	898	896	894·4	893·2	891·7	891·2	891·2	890·9
	S	900	900	898	896	894·4	893·2	892·3	891·7	891·2	890·9	890·7
	$D-S$	0	0	2	2	1·6	1·2	0·9	0·6	0·5	0·3	0·2
	$\mu(W-W^*)$	0	-2	-2	$-1·6$	$-1·2$	$-0·9$	$-0·6$	$-0·5$	$-0·3$	$-0·2$	$-0·2$
case (ii)												
$\mu = 0.5$	W	100	100	100	105	110	112·5	112·5	111·2	110	109·4	109·4
	D	900	900	900	895	890	887·5	887·5	888·8	890	890·6	890·6
	S	900	900	895	890	887·5	887·5	888·8	890	890·6	890·6	890·3
	$D-S$	0	0	5	5	2·5	0	$-1·3$	$-1·2$	$-0·6$	0	0·3
	$\mu(W-W^*)$	0	-5	-5	$-2·5$	0	1·3	1·2	0·6	0	$-0·3$	$-0·3$
case (iii)												
$\mu = 1.1$	W	100	100	100	111	122	120·9	107·7	95·7	98·2	113·9	126·9
	D	900	900	900	889	878	879·1	892·3	904·3	901·8	886·1	873·1
	S	900	900	889	878	879·1	892·3	904·3	901·8	886·1	873·1	877·4
	$D-S$	0	0	11	11	$-1·1$	$-13·2$	$-12·0$	2·5	15·7	13·0	$-4·3$
	$\mu(W-W^*)$	0	-11	-11	1·1	13·2	12·0	$-2·5$	$-15·7$	$-13·0$	4·3	18·6
case (iv)												
$\lambda = 1$	W	100	100	110	111	110	109·9	110	110			
$\mu = 1.1$	D	900	910	890	888	890	890·2	890	890			
	S	900	900	889	889	890·1	890·1	890	890			
	$D-S$	0	10	1	-1	$-0·1$	0·1	0	0			
	$Y(W-W^*)$	0	-10	0	1	0	$-0·1$	0	0			
	$\mu(W-W^*)$	0	-11	0	1·1	0	$-0·11$	0	0			

The resulting path of D, the demand for labour, is shown by the continuous line marked (i) in Figure 13. With these particular values of α, λ and μ the labour market moves smoothly towards its new equilibrium and by day 10 has practically settled down in this new equilibrium position.

Case (ii). We keep $\alpha = \lambda = 1$ but raise μ from 0.2 to 0.5. We are assuming, that is to say, that, in otherwise unchanged conditions, workers move in or out of the industry at a considerably more rapid rate when any given discrepancy between the inside and the outside wage appears. Our three equations are now unchanged except that equation 5.6 now becomes:

$$S(t) = S(t-1) + 0.5\{W(t-1) - W^*(t-1)\} \quad \ldots \ldots \quad (5.7)$$

Case (ii) of Table II applies exactly the same arithmetical process as is applied in case (i) of Table II with this one change in the value of μ. The resulting time-path for D is plotted by the line marked (ii) in Figure 13.

The result now is that D falls more quickly than before towards the equilibrium level. This is what one would expect: when the outside wage goes up, labour moves out more quickly; as a result, a large excess demand for labour develops; as a result, the inside wage rises more quickly; as a result, the demand falls more quickly. But in this case the demand falls below the equilibrium level: when the outside wage exceeds the inside wage, labour moves out very quickly (μ is relatively high) causing a deficiency of labour, but with any given deficiency of labour the wage rate is driven up relatively slowly (λ is relatively low) with the result that the supply of labour falls very quickly relatively to the demand and it overshoots the equilibrium mark. In time this deficiency of labour below the new equilibrium level causes the inside wage to rise above the outside wage which both reduces demand below the new equilibrium level but also reverses the flow of labour which now once more flows into the industry. The result is the fluctuating system shown by line (ii) in Figure 13. The demand fluctuates around the new equilibrium level; but in this case these fluctuations become smaller and smaller and the system thus settles down towards its new equilibrium.

Case (iii) Equation 5.6 now becomes:

$$S(t) = S(t-1) + 1.1\{W(t-1) - W^*(t-1)\} \quad \ldots \ldots \quad (5.8)$$

Labour moves still more quickly in or out of the industry as a result of any discrepancy which arises between the inside and the outside wage. The arithmetic is carried out in case (iii) of Table II and the resulting time-path of D is shown by the line (iii) in Figure 13. The result is not only that the fluctuations in the system are greater than before, but also that the fluctuations become larger and larger as time goes on. The system is no longer a stable one; it will no longer of itself settle down to the new equilibrium level.

Theoretically these fluctuations would become bigger and bigger without any limit. In practice, of course, this would not happen. In one way or another the system of relationships given in equations

5.1, 5.2 and 5.3 would break down.[4] It is not our intention at this point to discuss these practical possibilities. But there is one possibility which we will discuss at this point because it emphasizes and illustrates a very important feature of many economic systems, namely the importance of expectations and speculation.

Let us elaborate our model in the following way. Suppose that the employers in the industry in question are producing a durable product. They keep stocks of this product so that their production of the product need not at any time exactly match their sales. They can produce for stock if they **think** that conditions are temporarily peculiarly well suited for production; they can cut down production temporarily and sell from stock if they think that conditions are temporarily peculiarly unfavourable for production. Suppose further that these employers are alive to the fact that the wage at which they can hope to attract labour is closely related to the outside wage (W^*). In consequence they expect the inside wage (W) always to move towards the outside (W^*). In consequence, when $W > W^*$, they expect labour to become cheaper. They cut down their production and their demand for labour in the expectation that they will be able to produce more cheaply in the future. Conversely, when $W < W^*$, they plan to produce more now than they otherwise would have done in order to anticipate an expected rise in their labour costs.

The demand for labour (D) is now made up of two parts: first, the regular demand to meet the current demand for the product which we may still express as $A - \alpha W(t)$ and, secondly, the speculative demand which we may express as $\gamma\{W^*(t) - W(t)\}$. Equations 5.1, 5.2, and 5.3 now become:

$$D(t) = A - \alpha W(t) - \gamma\{W(t) - W^*(t)\} \dots \dots \dots (5.9)$$

$$W(t) = W(t-1) + \lambda\{D(t-1) - S(t-1)\} \dots \dots \dots (5.10)$$

$$S(t) = S(t-1) + \mu\{W(t-1) - W^*(t-1)\} \dots \dots \dots (5.11)$$

Figures 11 and 12 are now replaced by Figures 14 and 15 in which the only change is the addition of the negative proportional relationship, numbered 8, between $W - W^*$ and D. This introduces a new negative feedback loop along the lines 4, 8, 2 and 3. A high level of W (relatively to W^*) (line 4) causes an expectation of a fall in W and so a low speculative D (line 8) which causes an excess of S over D (line 2) which causes a rapid rate of fall in W.

---

[4] One obvious limit is given by the facts that S, D and W cannot fall below zero. Thus if $W(t-1)$ has fallen far below $W^*(t-1)$ and if $S(t-1)$ is already very low, equation 5.8 would require $S(t)$ to fall below zero. But one cannot drain more men out of the industry than there are in it to be drained.

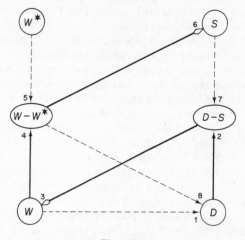

Figure 14

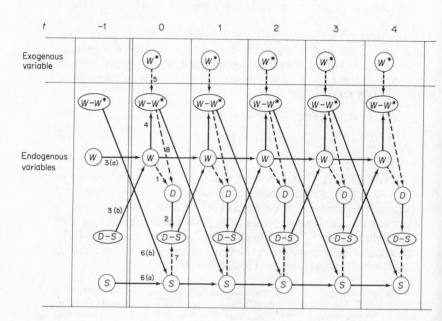

Figure 15

Let us now give a numerical example of this influence. Let us assume, as in all our examples, that $A = 1{,}000$ and $\alpha = \lambda = 1$. We assume, as in Case (iii) of Table II, that $\mu = 1{\cdot}1$, so that in the absence of the new speculative influence we would have the unstable fluctuating system of line (iii) of Figure 13. Let us assume that $\gamma = 1$. We can then write our equations as:

$$D(t) = 1{,}000 - 2\,W(t) + W^*(t) \quad\dots\dots\dots\dots \quad (5.12)$$

$$W(t) = W(t-1) + D(t-1) - S(t-1). \quad\dots\dots\dots \quad (5.13)$$

$$S(t) = S(t-1) + 1{\cdot}1\{W(t-1) - W^*(t-1)\} \quad\dots\dots \quad (5.14)$$

The arithmetic of this case is shown in part (iv) of Table II and the consequential time-path of D is shown by the line marked (iv) in Figure 13.

The result is a very dramatic change. When on day 1 the outside wage rises abruptly from 100 to 110, there is an immediate large speculative demand for labour in anticipation of a future sympathetic rise in the inside wage; in fact D rises dramatically from 900 to 910. But this rise in demand causes a big rise in the inside wage; indeed, in our particular case, the inside wage as a result rises up to the outside wage. Thus, there is an almost immediate stoppage of the drain of labour to the outside world. The system is liable to small and rapidly diminishing fluctuations. But what was an exceedingly unstable system has become one in which adjustment is very rapid but the system remains very stable.[5]

But speculation may not always be of this beneficial variety. Figures 16 and 17 illustrate another type of speculation which may turn a stable system into a very unstable one. Let us suppose that the employers of labour in the industry concerned are quite unaware of the effect of the outside wage (W^*) upon the inside wage (W). When the inside wage rate goes up, they do not know why it has gone up; but once it starts to rise they expect it to go on rising. In this case there will be a speculative demand for labour which will be the greater, the more rapidly the wage rate has gone up in the immediate past. To the non-speculative demand for labour

[5] Table II and Figure 13 show a big upward jump in D between day 0 and day 1—due to the speculative demand to anticipate the upward pressure on wage rates—followed by a rapid fall of D to its new equilibrium level. An examination of Table II shows that the supply of labour (S) moves in an even more satisfactory manner. It changes more or less instantaneously on day 2 from its old to its new equilibrium level and then stays at that level. S moves down to its new equilibrium level on day 2 because of the attraction of the higher outside wage rate on day 1. The excess of D over S on day 1—due to the speculative element in D—raises the inside wage rate to the outside wage rate on day 2. There is in consequence no further loss of labour on day 3; S is now more or less constant at its new equilibrium level.

C*

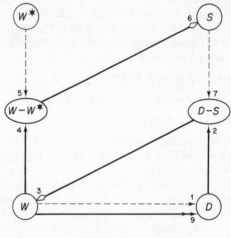

Figure 16

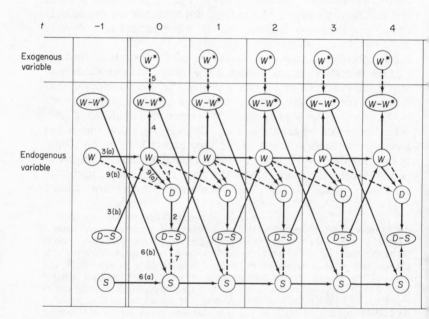

Figure 17

$[A - \alpha W(t)]$, we must now add a speculative demand which can be expressed as $\beta\{W(t) - W(t-1)\}$. Our three equations now become:

$$D(t) = A - \alpha W(t) + \beta\{W(t) - W(t-1)\} \quad \ldots \ldots \ldots \ldots \text{(5.15)}$$

$$W(t) = W(t-1) + \lambda\{D(t-1) - S(t-1)\} \quad \ldots \ldots \ldots \text{(5.16)}$$

$$S(t) = S(t-1) + \mu\{W(t-1) - W^*(t-1)\} \quad \ldots \ldots \ldots \text{(5.17)}$$

This system is represented by Figures 16 and 17. Figure 16 is the same as Figure 11 with the exception that a new positive derivative relationship is added between W and D, numbered 9, which

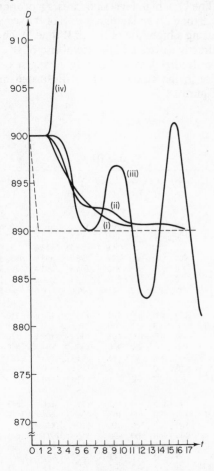

Figure 18

indicates that, for speculative reasons, a high rate of rise of W causes a high absolute level of speculative demand for labour. This speculative demand can, as we have already explained, be expressed as $\beta\{W(t) - W(t - 1)\}$ or $\beta W(t) - \beta W(t - 1)$. In Figure 17, accordingly, this speculative demand is represented as the combination of a positive proportional effect of $W(t)$ on $D(t)$, represented by the continuous line 9(a), and a negative proportional effect of $W(t - 1)$ on $D(t)$ represented by the line 9 (b).

We have now introduced a positive feedback loop into our labour market. This can be seen from the lines 9,2 and 3 in Figure 16. A high rate of rise of W has the positive derivative effect of causing a high level of D (line 9); a high level of D causes a proportionally high excess of D over S (line 2); and a high excess of D over S has the integral effect of causing a high rate of rise of W (line 3). Thus a high rate of rise of W indirectly causes a high rate of rise of W.

If this positive feedback is sufficiently strong it can cause very great disturbance in the system. This is illustrated numerically in Table III and Figure 18.

Table III

	t	0	1	2	3	4	5	6	7	8	
	W^*	100	110	110	110	110	110	110	110	110	1
Case (ii)											
	W	100	100	100	102	105	107·1	107·6	107·4	107·6	10
	$(\alpha - \beta) W$	50	50	50	51	52·5	53·6	53·8	53·7	53·8	5
$\alpha = 1$	βW	50	50	50	51	52·5	53·6	53·8	53·7	53·8	5
$\mu = 0.2$	D	900	900	900	899	896·5	893·9	892·6	892·5	892·5	89
$\beta = 0.5$	S	900	900	898	896	894·4	893·4	892·8	892·3	891·8	89
	$D - S$	0	0	2	3	2·1	0·5	−0·2	0·2	0·7	
	$\mu(W - W^*)$	0	−2	−2	−1·6	−1·0	−0·6	−0·5	−0·5	−0·5	−
Case (iii)											
	W	100	100	100	102	106	109·6	110	106·9	103·4	10
	$(\alpha - \beta) W$	0	0	0	0	0	0	0	0	0	
$\alpha = 1$	βW	100	100	100	102	106	109·6	110	106·9	103·2	10
$\mu = 0.2$	D	900	900	900	900	898	894	890·4	890	893·1	89
$\beta = 1$	S	900	900	898	896	894·4	893·6	893·5	893·5	892·9	89
	$D - S$	0	0	2	4	3·6	0·4	−3·1	−3·5	0·2	
	$\mu(W - W^*)$	0	−2	−2	−1·6	−0·8	−0·1	0	−0·6	−1·3	−
Case (iv)											
	W	100	100	100	102	114	166	363	1080		
	$(\alpha - \beta) W$	400	400	400	408	456	664	1452	4320		
$\alpha = 1$	βW	500	500	500	510	570	830	1815	5400		
$\mu = 0.2$	D	900	900	900	908	946	1092	1623	3505		
$\beta = 5$	S	900	900	898	896	894	895	906	957		
	$D - S$	0	0	2	12	52	197	717			
	$\mu(W - W^*)$	0	−2	−2	−2	1	11	51			

We assume as always that $A = 1,000$ and $\alpha = \lambda = 1$. Let us also assume that $\mu = 0.2$, so that in the absence of this positive speculative feedback (i.e. with $\beta = 0$) we would have the gradual and stable approach to the new equilibrium shown in case (i) of Table II and line (i) of Figure 13. Line (i) in Figure 18 simply reproduces line (i) from Figure 13. With a positive value of β our equations become:

$$D(t) = 1,000 - W(t) + \beta\{W(t) - W(t - 1)\}$$
$$= 1,000 - (1 - \beta)W(t) - \beta W(t - 1) \ldots \ldots \ldots (5.18)$$
$$W(t) = W(t - 1) + D(t - 1) - S(t - 1). \ldots \ldots \ldots (5.19)$$
$$S(t) = S(t - 1) + 0.2\{W(t - 1) - W^*(t - 1)\} \ldots \ldots (5.20)$$

In Table III and Figure 18, case (ii) represents the result when $\beta = 0.5$, case (iii) the result when $\beta = 1$, and case (iv) the result when $\beta = 5$.

With a low speculative effect ($\beta = 0.5$) the effect is merely to cause a small and diminishing fluctuation of the time-path of D around the otherwise steady approach to equilibrium (line ii fluctuates in small and diminishing waves around line i). With a larger speculative influence ($\beta = 1$) these fluctuations are large and ever-increasing

11	12	13	14	15	16	17	18	19	20	21	22
110	110	110	110	110	110	110	110	110	110	110	110
109·3	109·3	109·1	109·1	109·4	109·8	110					
54·7	54·7	54·6	54·6	54·7	54·9	55					
54·7	54·7	54·6	54·6	54·7	54·9	55					
890·8	890·6	890·7	890·8	890·7	890·4	890·1					
890·8	890·8	890·7	890·5	890·3	890·2						
0	-0·2	0	0·3	0·4	0·2						
-0·1	-0·1	-0·2	-0·2	-0·1							
114·8	116·8	111·2	102·2	98·6	105·8	118·9	125·6	117·5	99·5	88·1	96·8
0	0	0	0	0	0	0	0	0	0	0	0
114·8	116·8	111·2	102·2	98·6	105·8	118·9	125·6	117·5	99·5	88·1	96·8
891·8	885·2	883·2	888·8	897·6	901·4	894·2	881·1	874·4	882·5	900·5	911·9
889·8	890·8	892·2	892·4	890·6	888·3	887·5	889·3	892·4	893·9	891·8	887·4
2·0	-5·6	-9·0	-3·6	7·2	13·1	6·7	-8·2	-18·0	-11·4	8·7	
1·0	1·4	0·2	-1·8	-2·3	-0·8	1·8	3·1	1·5	-2·1	-4·4	

(line iii); the system is unstable and never settles down at the equilibrium level. With a sufficiently marked speculative effect ($\beta = 5$) we get the straightforward runaway hyperinflation of demand shown by line iv; in this case, the initial rise in W induced by the rise in W^* causes such a strong speculative demand that W is made to rise still more rapidly, which causes such a large increase in the speculative demand that W rises still more rapidly and so on without end—until the system itself breaks down.

In Figures 11 and 14 there were only negative feedback loops. In Figure 16 there were two negative feedbacks loops (1–2–3 and 4–6–7–3) but one positive feedback loop (9–2–3). Let us close the illustrations in this chapter by considering one economic model in which there are only positive feedback loops. This is provided by the well-known multiplier-accelerator model of the whole economy. We assume that citizens earn their incomes in the form of wages, profits, rents etc. simply from the sale of the goods and services which they produce, so that on any day the income which they receive is equal to the amount spent on goods and services by those who are demanding them. We assume further that this total demand for goods and services in the economy can be divided into three parts: first, an exogenously given demand for investment goods (e.g. amount spent on public works by the government); second, a demand for investment goods by private business, this demand depending solely upon the rate at which the total demand for goods and services is rising, since businessmen simply put in new and additional machines to keep up with the expanding demand for their products; and, thirdly, a demand for consumption goods which depends solely upon the level of consumers' incomes earned on the previous day.

This very simple model can be expressed by the following four equations:

$$D'(t) = I_c^*(t) + I_v(t) + C(t) \dots \dots \dots \dots \dots \dots \dots \dots (5.21)$$

$$I_v(t) = v\{D'(t-1) - D'(t-2)\} \dots \dots \dots \dots \dots \dots (5.22)$$

$$Y(t) = D'(t) \dots \dots \dots \dots \dots \dots \dots \dots \dots \dots \dots \dots (5.23)$$

$$C(t) = cY(t-1) \dots \dots \dots \dots \dots \dots \dots \dots \dots \dots (5.24)$$

Equation 5.21 states that total demand[6] at any time (D') is simply made up of exogenous or constant investment (I_c^*) plus endogenous or variable investment (I_v) plus consumption (C). Equation 5.22 states that variable investment on day t is determined solely by the

[6] We employ D' for net demand (i.e. excluding the demand for capital goods to replace existing capital goods) to distinguish it from D which will be used in Chapter VII for gross demand. See Note A to Chapter VII.

rate at which the total demand for goods and services has risen
between day $t - 2$ and day $t - 1$. Equation 5.23 states that the
income received by consumers on day t is derived solely from the
value of the goods and services which they sell on day t. Equation
5.24 states that consumers spend on day t an amount equal to a
fixed proportion (c) of the income which they earned on day $t - 1$.

This system is depicted in Figure 19 in the form of a feedback loop

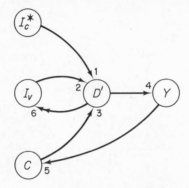

Figure 19

diagram. Lines 1, 2 and 3 represent the proportional effects of I_c^*, I_v
and C in adding up to D' (equation 5.21). Line 4 represents the proportional effect of D' upon Y (equation 5.23). Line 5 represents the
proportional effect of Y upon C (equation 5.24). Line 6 represents
the derivative effect of D' on I_v (equation 5.22). There are two clear
positive feedback loops, namely 3–4–5 and 2–6. The loop 3–4–5 is
the well-known multiplier loop; a high level of D' causes a high
level of Y which causes a high expenditure on C which causes a high
D' which causes a high Y which causes a high C, and so on. The loop
2–6 is the accelerator loop; a high rate of rise of D' causes a high I_v
which causes a high D'.

This model can be shown in the alternative form in Figure 20. In
order to know how the system will behave on day 0 we need to
know (i) the level of D' on the two previous days, namely day -1
and day -2; (ii) the level of Y on the previous day, namely day -1;
(iii) the level of I_c^* on day 0; and (iv) the force of the accelerator (v)
and of the multiplier (c). I_v on day 0 is equal to $vD'(-1) - vD'(-2)$
(see equation 5.22), that is to say, it can be expressed as positively
proportional to $D'(-1)$ (line 6 (a) in Figure 20) and negatively
proportional to $D'(-2)$ (line 6(b) in Figure 20). C on day 0 is equal
to $cY(-1)$ (see equation 5.24), that is to say, it is positively proportional to $Y(-1)$ (line 5 in Figure 20). Given I_c^* on day 0 we now know

D' for day 0, which is simply the sum of I_c^*, I_v and C on day 0 (see equation 5.21 and lines 1,2, and 3 on Figure 20). But Y on day 0 is equal to D' on day 0 (equation 5.23 and line 4 on Figure 20). Since we now know D' and Y for day 0 as well as for day -1, we can go on in a similar manner to calculate all the endogenous variables for day 1, provided that the exogenous variable, namely I_c^* is also known for day 1. And so on for all future days.

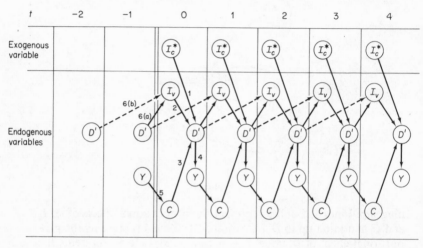

Figure 20

It is to be observed that with the present model, if I_c^* is constant over time, an equilibrium situation can exist at which D', Y and C are also constant over time. We can see this possibility in the following way. If D' were constant, then I_v—which depends solely upon the rate of increase in D'—would be zero (see equation 5.22). But if $I_v = 0$, then from equation 5.21

$$D' = I_c^* + C \dots\dots\dots\dots\dots\dots\dots\dots\dots\dots\dots\dots\dots (5.25)$$

and from equation 5.23 and 5.24 with Y and D constant,

$$C = cD' = cY \dots\dots\dots\dots\dots\dots\dots\dots\dots\dots\dots\dots\dots (5.26)$$

From 5.25 and 5.26 we obtain

$$Y = D' = I_c^* + cD'$$

or $\quad Y = D' = \dfrac{1}{1-c} I_c^*$, so that $C = \dfrac{c}{1-c} I_c^* \dots\dots\dots\dots (5.27)$

These are the well-known multiplier equations. If c were 0.75 (i.e. if consumers always spent three-quarters of their incomes) then $Y = D' = 4I_c^*$ and $C = 3I_c^*$. In other words, if I_c^* were constant, the system would be in equilibrium if C were constant at a level of $c/(1 - c)$ times I_c^*, if I_v were zero, and if Y and D' were constant at a level of $1/(1 - c)$ times I_c^*.

Let us then consider a numerical example in which we start with I_c^* constant at one level and with the system initially in equilibrium

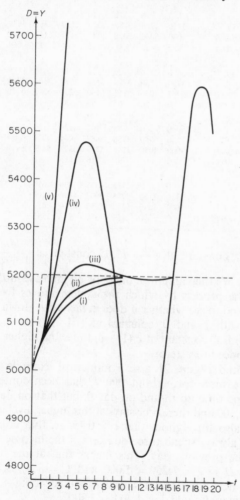

Figure 21

Table IV

	t	0	1	2	3	4	5	6	7	8	9
	I_c^*	1250	1300	1300	1300	1300	1300	1300	1300	1300	130●
Case (i) $v = 0$	I_v	0	0	0	0	0	0	0	0	0	
	C	3750	3750	3788	3816	3836	3852	3864	3873	3880	38●
	$Y = D'$	5000	5050	5088	5116	5136	5152	5164	5173	5180	51●
	$D'(t) - D'(t - 1)$	0	50	38	28	20	16	12	9	7	
Case (ii) $v = 0.1$	I_v	0	0	10	10	7	5	3	2	1	
	C	3750	3750	3788	3823	3850	3867	3879	3887	3892	38●
	$Y = D'$	5000	5050	5098	5133	5157	5172	5182	5189	5193	51●
	$D'(t) - D'(t - 1)$	0	50	48	35	24	15	10	7	4	
Case (iii) $v = 0.5$	I_v	0	0	25	31	27	18	9	2	-2	
	C	3750	3750	3788	3835	3874	3901	3914	3917	3914	39●
	$Y = D'$	5000	5050	5113	5166	5201	5219	5223	5219	5212	52●
	$D'(t) - F'(t - 1)$	0	50	63	53	35	18	4	-4	-7	
Case (iv) $v = 1.1$	I_v	0	0	55	102	128	124	90	29	-45	-1●
	C	3750	3750	3788	3857	3944	4029	4090	4109	4079	40●
	$Y = D'$	5000	5050	5143	5259	5372	5453	5479	5438	5334	51●
	$D'(t) - D'(t - 1)$	0	50	93	116	113	81	26	-41	-104	-1●
Case (v) $v = 2.3$	I_v	0	0	115	351	806	1650				
	C	3750	3750	3788	3902	4164	4702				
	$Y = D'$	5000	5050	5203	5553	6270	7652				
	$D'(t) - D'(t - 1)$	0	50	153	350	717	1382				

with Y and D' constant at $\dfrac{1}{1 - c} I_c^*$, C constant at $\dfrac{c}{1 - c} I_c^*$, and I_v equal to zero. We then assume a once-for-all increase in I_c^*. We wish to observe the process by which the system moves from the old equilibrium and to see whether it does in fact settle down at the new equilibrium with Y and D' constant at $1/(1 - c)$ times the higher level of I_c^*, with C constant at $c/(1 - c)$ times the higher level of I_c^*, and with I_v once more zero.

Table IV and Figure 21 give a numerical example for such a change. We assume throughout that I_c^* has been continuously at 1,250 for some time up to and on day 0, but that on day 1 it rises abruptly to 1,300 and thereafter stays at this higher level indefinitely. We assume also throughout that $c = 0.75$, i.e. that consumers on any one day always spend three-quarters of the income which they earned on the previous day. This means that at the initial equilibrium $Y = D' = 4 \times 1{,}250 = 5{,}000$ and $C = 3 \times 1{,}250 = 3{,}750$, while in the new equilibrium Y and D' would equal $4 \times 1{,}300 = 5{,}200$ and C would equal $3 \times 1{,}300 = 3{,}900$.

We make five different assumptions about the accelerator co-

10	11	12	13	14	15	16	17	18	19	20	21	22
300	1300	1300	1300	1300	1300	1300	1300	1300	1300	1300	1300	1300
0												
889												
189												
4												
0	0											
897	3898											
197	5198											
2	1											
−3	−2	−1	−1	0	0	0	0					
904	3901	3899	3898	3898	3899	3899	3900					
201	5199	5198	5197	5198	5199	5199	5200					
−5	−2	−1	−1	1	1	0	0					
164	−176	−146	−75	20	120	200	239	166	99	1		
889	3769	3670	3618	3632	3714	3851	3963	4126	4194	4195		
025	4893	4824	4843	4952	5134	5351	5502	5592	5593	5496		
160	−132	−69	19	109	182	217	151	90	1	−103		

efficient v of equation 5.22: in case (i), $v = 0$; in case (ii), $v = 0{\cdot}1$; in case (iii), $v = 0{\cdot}5$; in case (iv), $v = 1{\cdot}1$; and in case (v), $v = 2{\cdot}3$. Our object is to see how the jolt of the increase of I_c^* from 1,250 to 1,300 affects the future course of the system with these various derivative or accelerator forces of changes in D' upon the level of I_v and so back upon the level of D'.

The five cases are worked out arithmetically in Table IV. In each case, we start on the assumption that Y and D' have been constant at 5,000 for some time. Between day 0 and day 1, I_c^* rises from 1,250 to 1,300 and then stays at the new and higher level. For each day C is written down as equal to $0{\cdot}75Y$ on the previous day. For each day I_v is written down as v times the increase of D' which took place the previous day.[7] D' and so Y are then calculated for each day as the sum of I_c^*, C and I_v for that day. The resulting time-paths of Y and D' are recorded numerically in Table IV and are shown in Figure 21 for the five different values of v.

Case (i) is the case in which there is no accelerator effect ($v = 0$)

---

[7] That is to say, $I_v(t) = v\{D'(t-1) - D'(t-2)\}$.

and only the multiplier is at work. D' rises smoothly from its initial equilibrium value of 5,000 towards its new equilibrium value of 5,200. Case (ii) adds a very moderate accelerator effect ($v = 0.1$); and in this case the additional demand, due to the accelerator effect so long as D' is rising, has the effect simply of speeding up somewhat the smooth path of D' towards the new equilibrium level. In case (iii), the accelerator effect is somewhat stronger ($v = 0.5$), and this has the effect of making D' overshoot the mark and then turn down again; but these fluctuations in D' about the new equilibrium level become smaller and smaller and the system is still a stable one. In case (iv), with a still higher level of v ($v = 1.1$) these fluctuations in D' become larger and larger as time goes on and the whole system has become unstable. In case (v), with v as high as 2.3, the whole system explodes in a hyperinflation (cf. case iv of Table III and Figure 18 and the earlier discussion of that case).

In the model illustrated in Table IV and Figure 21 all the feedback loops are positive or, in other words, any initial increase in D' (such as that due to the increase in I_c^* which we have examined) will lead to further repercussions which cause a still further increase in D', which will lead to still further repercussions which will lead to a still further increase in D', and so on ad infinitum. But this does not mean that the system is necessarily unstable; in our example, the system is stable in case (i), (ii) and (iii), but unstable in cases (iv) and (v).

Conversely, in the model illustrated in Table II and Figure 13, all the feedback loops were negative; or, in other words, any initial increase in W (such as would have occurred as the indirect result of an increase in W^*) would lead to repercussions—through its tendency to increase the supply and decrease the demand for labour—which would tend in turn to mitigate the rise in W. But this, as we saw, did not mean that the system was necessarily a stable one. In cases (i), (ii) and (iv) it was stable, but in case (iii) it was unstable.

It is clearly important not to confuse positive feedback with instability and negative feedback with stability. Whether feedback is positive or negative in its effect will determine whether there are influences at work which, if the system does reach a new equilibrium, will intensify or mitigate the original change. But it is quite a different matter to consider whether or not the process of change initiated by the original jolt to the system will cause it to settle down at a new equilibrium, i.e. whether the system is stable or not.

There are two further and saddening conclusions that we must draw from these examples, namely (i) that the economic system in its dynamic aspects is a complicated system and (ii) that it is impossible to reach any very general conclusions about the dynamics of an economic system without a great deal of empirical quantitative knowledge about the particular features of that particular system.

Even with the systems which we have illustrated in this chapter the interrelationships are complicated enough; but it is obvious that in fact very many more variables and interrelationships must be involved in any model of the total economic system, if it is to be at all realistic. Moreover, even in the greatly simplified models examined in this chapter we have considered only the effect of a once-for-all change in one exogenous variable. But, of course, there are many exogenous influences and these influences will not be constant at one level and then make a once-for-all change to a new level. In the real world, these exogenous influences will themselves be continuously varying. In this chapter we have done little more than consider the stability or instability of a dynamic economic system by considering what would be the effect of a once-for-all jolt to that system. In fact it is necessary to consider a more complicated set of endogenous dynamic relationships subject to ever changing exogenous influences. We will try to make a little progress in this direction in Parts 2 and 3 of this volume.

But one feature of the problem remains which will not be covered at all in this volume. It should already be very apparent that how any one economy will in fact move through time will depend not only upon the general structure of interrelationships between the variables but, above all, on the numerical importance of the various forces at work. For example, in Table II and Figure 13, different numerical values of μ, and in Table IV and Figure 21, different numerical values of v, give results which are totally different in kind—some fluctuating and some not fluctuating, some stable and some unstable. This makes generalization in drawing conclusions about economic policy very difficult. Each system must be treated on its own merits in view not only of the structure of relationships which is relevant to its study, but also of the numerical importance of the various causal links. In this volume we shall attempt to do no more than discuss some of the main principles involved in considering the best way of controlling a dynamic economic system; we shall not apply these principles to any particular system.

Note to Chapter V

A MATHEMATICAL TREATMENT OF THE MODELS

In this Note we will analyse the equations which are involved in the examples given in Chapter V.

I

Let us start with the model discussed first. The set of difference equations are those given in equations 5.1, 5.2 and 5.3, namely:

$$D(t) = A - \alpha W(t) \dots\dots\dots (5.28)$$

$$W(t) = W(t - 1) + \lambda \{D(t - 1) - S(t - 1)\} \dots\dots (5.29)$$

$$S(t) = S(t - 1) + \mu \{W(t - 1) - W^*(t - 1)\} \dots\dots (5.30)$$

Substituting for $D(t - 1)$ from 5.28 into 5.29 we get:

$$W(t) = \lambda A + (1 - \alpha\lambda) W(t - 1) - \lambda S(t - 1) \dots\dots (5.31)$$

From 5.30 we obtain:

$$S(t - 1) = S(t - 2) + \mu \{W(t - 2) - W^*(t - 2)\}$$

and substituting this value of $S(t - 1)$ into 5·31 we get:

$$W(t) = \lambda A + \lambda\mu W^*(t - 2) + (1 - \alpha\lambda) W(t - 1)$$
$$- \lambda\mu W(t - 2) - \lambda S(t - 2) \dots\dots (5.32)$$

and substituting for $S(t - 2)$ from 5.31 into 5.32 we get:

$$W(t) - (2 - \alpha\lambda) W(t - 1) + \{1 + \lambda(\mu - \alpha)\} W(t - 2)$$
$$= \lambda\mu W^*(t - 2)$$

This is a second-order difference equation in W and the characteristic equation is:

$$w(t) - (2 - \alpha\lambda) w(t - 1) + \{1 + \lambda(\mu - \alpha)\} w(t - 2) = 0 \quad (5.33)$$

The roots of this characteristic equation are:

$$\tfrac{1}{2}\{2 - \alpha\lambda \pm \sqrt{(\alpha\lambda - 2)^2 - 4(1 + \lambda[\mu - \alpha])}\}$$
$$= 1 - \alpha\lambda/2 \pm \sqrt{(\alpha\lambda/2)^2 - \lambda\mu} \dots\dots (5.34)$$

The system will, therefore, oscillate if

$$(\alpha\lambda/2)^2 < \lambda\mu, \text{ i.e. if } (\alpha\lambda/2)^2(1/\lambda) < \mu.$$

The oscillations will be unstable if $1 + \lambda(\mu - \alpha) > 1$, i.e. if $\alpha < \mu$. The oscillations will be damped if $\mu < \alpha$. Damped oscillations are a possible outcome, therefore, only if $(\alpha\lambda/2)^2(1/\lambda) < \mu < \alpha$, i.e. only if $\alpha\lambda < 4$.

The system will not oscillate if $\mu < (\alpha\lambda/2)^2(1/\lambda)$. In this case it can be seen from 5.34 that the dominant root will be the positive root or the negative root according as $\alpha\lambda \lessgtr 2$.

Let us consider first the case of $\alpha\lambda < 2$. In this case, it is clear that the dominant root $1 - \alpha\lambda/2 + \sqrt{(\alpha\lambda/2)^2 - \lambda\mu}$ lies between 0 and

+1. The system will, therefore, be stable. With $2 < \alpha\lambda$ we must consider the negative root which is now the dominant root, namely $1 - \alpha\lambda/2 - \sqrt{(\alpha\lambda/2)^2 - \lambda\mu}$. Since this root is negative it will lead to alternations. These alternations will be explosive or damped according as this root is $\lessgtr -1$, i.e. as

$$\sqrt{(\alpha\lambda/2)^2 - \lambda\mu} \gtrless 2 - \alpha\lambda/2 \quad\dots\dots\dots\dots\dots\dots(5.35)$$

Since the LHS of 5.35 is positive, it will certainly exceed the RHS if the RHS is negative, i.e. if $4 < \alpha\lambda$. The result will then necessarily be explosive alternations. If, however, we consider the case of $2 < \alpha\lambda < 4$, the RHS as well as the LHS of 5.35 is positive. Squaring both sides of 5.35 and rearranging terms, the inequality in 5.35 and thus the condition whether the alternations will be explosive or not becomes $\mu \lessgtr (2/\lambda)(\alpha\lambda - 2)$.

With the numerical example given in the text we have $\alpha = \lambda = 1$, so that $\alpha\lambda = 1 < 2$. In these circumstances, the system will be (i) unstable oscillating if $1 < \mu$; (ii) stable oscillating if $0\cdot25 < \mu < 1$; but (iii) stable non-oscillating if $0 < \mu < 0\cdot25$.

II

In the second model discussed in chapter V, the three difference equations are those given in 5.9, 5.10 and 5.11 namely:

$$D(t) = A - (\alpha + \gamma)W(t) + \gamma W^*(t) \quad\dots\dots\dots\dots(5.36)$$

$$W(t) = W(t - 1) + \lambda\{D(t - 1) - S(t - 1)\} \quad\dots\dots\dots\dots(5.37)$$

$$S(t) = S(t - 1) + \mu\{W(t - 1) - W^*(t - 1)\} \quad\dots\dots\dots\dots(5.38)$$

By a process of substitution exactly similar to that described in Section I of this Note for equations 5.28, 5.29 and 5.30 we can eliminate D and S from equations 5.36, 5.37 and 5.38 and obtain:

$$W(t) - \{2 - \lambda(\alpha + \gamma)\}W(t - 1) + \{1 + \lambda(\mu - \alpha - \gamma)\}W(t - 2)$$
$$= \lambda\gamma\{W^*(t - 1) - W^*(t - 2)\} + \lambda\mu W^*(t - 2)$$
$$\dots\dots\dots\dots\dots\dots(5.39)$$

The characteristic equation now becomes

$$w(t) - \{2 - \lambda(\alpha + \gamma)\}w(t - 1) + \{1 + \lambda(\mu - \alpha - \gamma)\}w(t - 2) = 0$$
$$\dots\dots\dots\dots\dots\dots(5.40)$$

which is exactly the same as equation 5.33, except that α in 5.33 is replaced by $\alpha + \gamma$ in 5.40. The whole analysis of Section I of this Note therefore applies if $\alpha + \gamma$ is substituted for α.

III

The other type of speculation is represented by equations 5.15, 5.16 and 5.17, namely:

$$D(t) = A - (\alpha - \beta) W(t) - \beta W(t - 1) \quad \dots\dots\dots\dots\dots (5.41)$$

$$W(t) = W(t - 1) + \lambda \{D(t - 1) - S(t - 1)\} \quad \dots\dots\dots\dots (5.42)$$

$$S(t) = S(t - 1) + \mu \{W(t - 1) - W^*(t - 1)\} \quad \dots\dots\dots (5.43)$$

By a process of substitution once more exactly similar to that described in Section I for equations 5.28, 5.29 and 5.30 one can eliminate D and S and obtain:

$$W(t) - \{2 - \lambda(\alpha - \beta)\} W(t - 1) + \{1 + \lambda(\mu - \alpha) \\ + 2\lambda\beta\} W(t - 2) - \lambda\beta W(t - 3) = \lambda\mu W^*(t - 2)$$

with the characteristic equation

$$w(t) - \{2 - \lambda(\alpha - \beta)\} w(t - 1) + \{1 + \lambda(\mu - \alpha) \\ + 2\lambda\beta\} w(t - 2) - \lambda\beta w(t - 3) = 0 \quad \dots\dots\dots\dots\dots (5.44)$$

This is a third order system which involves finding the roots of the cubic equation implied in 5.44. Write

$$w^3 - \{2 - \lambda(\alpha - \beta)\} w^2 + \{1 + \lambda(\mu - \alpha) + 2\lambda\beta\} w - \lambda\beta = y$$
$$\dots\dots\dots\dots\dots (5.45)$$

We have to find the roots of this cubic, i.e. the values of w when $y = 0$. Now there must be at least one real root for the cubic equation; for since, as $w \to -\infty$, $y \to -\infty$ and as $w \to +\infty$, $y \to +\infty$, there must be at least one intermediate real value of w at which $y = 0$. With the particular cubic given in 5.45 it can be seen that one real root of w must lie between $w = 0$ and $w = 1$. For with $w = 0$, $y = -\lambda\beta$ and with $w = 1$, $y = \lambda\mu$. Thus, since both λ and μ are positive quantities, there must be some value of w with $0 < w < 1$ which gives a real root of the cubic in 5.45.

With this knowledge, one can find the three roots of the cubic in 5.45 given any arithmetical values of α, λ, β and μ. Let us take as an example the values assumed for case (iii) of Table III and of Figure 18 namely $\alpha = \lambda = 1$, $\mu = 0\cdot2$ and $\beta = 1$. Then the cubic in 5.45 becomes:

$$w^3 - 2w^2 + 2\cdot2w - 1 = y \quad \dots\dots\dots\dots\dots\dots\dots\dots (5.46)$$

We search for that value of w between 0 and 1 at which $y = 0$. Taking values of w by intervals of $0\cdot1$ from 0 to 1 and calculating the resulting values of y, we obtain:

w	0	0·1	0·2	0·3	0·4	0·5
y	$-1·0$	$-0·799$	$-0·632$	$-0·493$	$-0·376$	$-0·275$

w	0·6	0·7	0·8	0·9	1·0
y	$-0·184$	$-0·097$	$-0·008$	$+0·089$	$+0·2$

From this it is clear that one real root of w is found at $w = 0·8$ (approximately). If we divide $w^3 - 2w^2 + 2·2w - 1$ by $w - 0·8$ we obtain:

$$w^2 - 1·2w + 1·24 \text{ (approximately)} \dots\dots\dots\dots\dots\dots (5.47)$$

The roots of 5.47, namely $0·5\{1·2 \pm \sqrt{1·44 - 4·96}\}$, give the remaining two roots of the cubic in 5.46. Since $1·44 - 4·96 < 0$, these roots are conjugate complex and the resulting system will oscillate, and the system will be unstable since $1·24 > 1$. The period of the oscillation will be equal to $2\pi/\theta$ where $\tan\theta = \sqrt{(4·96 - 1·44)}/1·2$. It follows that $\tan\theta = 1·563$ so that $2\pi/\theta = 6·3$. In other words, we have an explosive fluctuation with a period of just over six days.

IV

Finally let us consider the multiplier-accelerator model expressed by the equations 5.21, 5.22, 5.23 and 5.24, namely:

$$D'(t) = I_c^*(t) + I_v(t) + C(t) \dots\dots\dots\dots\dots\dots\dots\dots (5.48)$$

$$I_v(t) = v\{D'(t-1) - D'(t-2)\} \dots\dots\dots\dots\dots\dots (5.49)$$

$$Y(t) = D'(t) \dots\dots\dots\dots\dots\dots\dots\dots\dots\dots\dots\dots (5.50)$$

$$C(t) = cY(t-1) \dots\dots\dots\dots\dots\dots\dots\dots\dots\dots (5.51)$$

Substituting for I_v, C and D' from 5.49, 5.50 and 5.51 into 5.48 we obtain:

$$Y(t) - (v + c)Y(t-1) + vY(t-2) = I_c^*(t)$$

with the characteristic second order equation:

$$y(t) - (v + c)y(t-1) + vy(t-2) = 0 \dots\dots\dots\dots\dots (5.52)$$

with roots

$$\tfrac{1}{2}\{v + c \pm \sqrt{(v + c)^2 - 4v}\}$$

The system is, therefore, oscillating or non-oscillating as $(v + c)^2 - 4v \lessgtr 0$, i.e. as $v^2 + 2(c - 2)v + c^2 \lessgtr 0$. Let:

$$v^2 + 2(c - 2)v + c^2 = z \dots\dots\dots\dots\dots\dots\dots\dots (5.53)$$

The roots of the expression in 5.53 are

$$\tfrac{1}{2}\{-2(c-2) \pm \sqrt{4(c-2)^2 - 4c^2}\}$$
$$= 2 - c \pm 2\sqrt{1-c} = (1 \pm \sqrt{1-c})^2 \quad\ldots\ldots\ldots\ldots(5.54)$$

Since c is always a positive fraction, these roots are both real and both positive; and it follows that for very small and very large values of v the expression in 5.53 is positive and for an intermediate range of values of v the expression in 5.33 is negative, as can be seen from Figure 22.

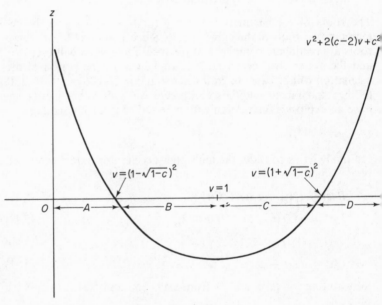

Figure 22

In the ranges of value for v marked B and C in Figure 22, we have $(1 - \sqrt{1-c})^2 < v < (1 + \sqrt{1-c})^2$ and in this range the value of the expression in 5.53 is negative, so that the roots of the characteristic equation in 5.52 are conjugate complex. In these ranges of value for v the system is, therefore, oscillatory. From 5.52 we can see that these oscillations are damped or explosive according as $v \lessgtr 1$. Therefore, in the range marked B in Figure 22 the system has damped oscillations and in the range marked C it has explosive oscillations.

In the ranges of value for v marked A and D, the expression in 5.53 is positive so that the roots of 5.52 are real. It remains to consider whether the system will be stable or unstable in these ranges. The dominant root of 5.52 can be seen to be positive. The system is. therefore, unstable or stable in the ranges A and D according as $\frac{1}{2}\{v + c + \sqrt{(v + c)^2 - 4v}\}$ is $\gtreqless 1$, i.e. as:

$$\sqrt{(v + c)^2 - 4v} \gtreqless 2 - v - c \quad \ldots\ldots\ldots\ldots\ldots\ldots\ldots\ldots\ldots (5.55)$$

Consider first the range A. Since, in this range $v < (1 - \sqrt{1 - c})^2 = 2 - c - 2\sqrt{1 - c} < 2 - c$, it follows that the RHS of 5.55 is positive. Squaring both sides of 5.55 and rearranging terms, the condition in 5.55 becomes:

$$0 \gtreqless 4(1 - c) \quad \ldots\ldots\ldots\ldots\ldots\ldots\ldots\ldots\ldots\ldots\ldots\ldots\ldots\ldots\ldots (5.56)$$

Since $0 < c < 1$, it is clear that the LHS is less than the RHS in 5.56 so that, in the range A in Figure 22, the system is stable and non-oscillatory.

In the range D we have

$$v > (1 + \sqrt{1 - c})^2 = 2 - c + 2\sqrt{1 - c} > 2 - c,$$

so that the RHS of 5.55 is negative. Since the LHS of 5.55 is positive, the LHS is greater than the RHS of 5.55. Thus, in the range D, the system is unstable and non-oscillatory.

In the numerical example given in Table IV and Figure 21, we have $c = 0.75$, so that $(1 - \sqrt{1 - c})^2 = 0.25$ and $(1 + \sqrt{1 - c})^2 = 2.25$. It follows that the system is (i) stable non-oscillatory if $0 < v < 0.25$; (ii) damped oscillatory if $0.25 < v < 1$; (iii) explosive oscillatory if $1 < v < 2.25$; and (iv) unstable non-oscillatory if $2.25 < v$.

PART 2

A DYNAMIC MODEL OF THE ECONOMY

...when we perceive the whole at once,
as in numerical computations, ...

SAMUEL JOHNSON : *Rasselas*

CHAPTER VI

THE INADEQUACY OF THE MULTIPLIER-ACCELERATOR MODEL

In the last two Chapters we have discussed and illustrated some of the basic forms which the interrelationships between the variables in a dynamic economic system may take. It is now necessary to consider what the general structure of these interrelationships will be like in an actual economy. For this purpose we must consider a complete, but simplified, set of relationships which cover simultaneously all the main markets in the economy (i.e. a macro-economic model) rather than the relationships in one single market in isolation from the rest of the economy (i.e. a micro-economic model).

The multiplier-accelerator model discussed in Chapter V constitutes a macro-economic model of this kind, which purports to explain the movements in the total economy, whereas the labour market models were all micro-economic models of one small sector of the economy. But the multiplier-accelerator model is a most inadequate and much too highly simplified model of the whole economy. It was introduced solely to illustrate the sort of problems which can arise when a system includes a positive proportional and a positive derivative feedback relationship.

The basic inadequacy of the multiplier-accelerator model is due to the fact that it is concerned solely with certain broad forces which determine the demand for goods and services, the multiplier determining the demand for consumption goods and the accelerator determining the demand for investment goods. It neglects completely the equally important question of what it is which affects the possibilities of supplying these goods and services when they are demanded. We can start to consider this basic inadequacy by raising the question whether the terms expressing the demand for goods and services in the multiplier-accelerator model,[1] are to be measured (i) as demands expressed in real terms (i.e. as the number of units of goods bought) or (ii) as demands expressed in money terms (i.e. as the number of dollars spent on the goods in question).

---

[1] That is to say, I_c^*, I_t, C and D' in equation 5.21, namely the demands for investment goods, the demand for consumption goods, and the combined total demand for goods for all purposes.

(i) If the demands are measured in real terms, we must assume that there is always unemployed labour and productive capacity available to meet any increase in demand. For it is assumed that the real demand for goods and services (expressed by D' in equation 5.21) is equal to the real income which consumers have available to spend (expressed by $Y = D'$ in equation 5.23). But real income can be earned only by actually producing real goods and services; and if an increase in demand is always to lead to an equivalent increase in real income, this implies that any increase in demand can always be met by increased production of real output which will lead to the earning of an equivalent increase in real income. This clearly implies that there is always sufficient spare capacity to meet any increase in demand. But if there is always unlimited spare capacity in the economy, the logic of the accelerator (see equation 5.22) becomes very questionable. For why should businessmen always decide to adjust the demand for new machines to the amount needed to satisfy the current increase in the demand for their products, if there is always an adequate amount of idle capacity already available to meet any increase in demand?

(ii) Suppose however that the demands for goods and services (the terms I_c^*, I_v, C and D' in equation 5.21) are expressed in money terms. Then an increase in demand may lead to an increase in output at constant prices so long as there is idle capacity and unemployed labour; but it must lead to a rise in prices when there is full employment of labour and/or of productive capacity and, in consequence, the increased money expenditure must be spent on the same number of goods. But there is little reason to believe that consumers will react in their decisions to spend on consumption goods, or that businessmen will react in their decisions to spend on machines, in the same way, whether a rise in money incomes and money demands is due to a rise in real incomes or merely to a rise in prices. But the relationships between incomes and expenditures in the multiplier-accelerator model (see equations 5.22 and 5.24) make no such distinctions.

This basic inadequacy of the simple multiplier-accelerator model can be seen in a different way. We have already concluded that it implies a static equilibrium with D', C and Y constant and I_v zero, if I_c^* is constant. The system (if in equilibrium) will grow through time only if the exogenous variable I_c^* is growing for some exogenous reason. In other words, the system does not carry within it the seeds of economic growth; it is a purely static system. This inadequacy is also due to the neglect by the multiplier-accelerator model of the factors on the supply side which determine whether output can be increased or not.

As we have seen in *The Growing Economy*, equilibrium growth depends upon growth in productive capacity due to population growth, technical progress, and the accumulation of new capital equipment. In order to ensure that good use is in fact made of this growth potential, the maintenance of demand, of course, is of vital importance; for this reason, we can perhaps best look on the problem of stable economic growth in the following way. The real factors—such as population growth, technical progress, and capital accumulation—set a constraint on the total amount that can be produced. The demand factors (many of which are proportional or derivative relationships of the kind examined in the multiplier-accelerator model) determine how large the demand will be. There may result an excess of total demand or an excess of total potential supply. Various markets in the economy will then react in various ways to such an excess demand or excess supply situation; these reactions will then determine the further development of the economy both on the demand side and on the supply side. Growth can take place as the real factors on the supply side ease up the supply constraints and enable an increase in real demand (if it occurs) to be satisfied. A central problem of policy is then to keep real demand in line with the growing potentiality of real supply.

It is on these lines we shall proceed, namely by considering the causes and effects of tensions between demand and supply in the main sectors of the economy and by considering the interactions between these main sectors. The economy is in fact a much more complicated system than is suggested by the simple multiplier-accelerator model; and although, as we have already seen, it is necessary drastically to simplify things before any dynamic model of the economy can be constructed, the simple multiplier-accelerator model undoubtedly goes much too far in this direction and 'tips out the baby with the bath water'.

In the model which we will now proceed to construct, we have tried to include all the main influences which will be found in the discussion by the main authorities of the problems involved in stabilizing a macro-economic system.[2] This makes it inevitable that the system should be fairly complicated. In fact, for operational purposes in the real world any system would almost certainly have to be further simplified by the omission of whatever relationships were considered to be the least influential in that particular economy. But subject to our attempt to display all the most important macro-economic influences which have been stressed by

[2] There is one most important exception: we shall be considering a closed economy with no commercial or financial relations with the outside world and, therefore, with no balance of payments problems.

D

various authorities, we have simplified the model as far as is possible.

In the result, we shall consider the interrelationships between the following seven main sectors or divisions of the total economy: (1) the production system; (2) the balance between the demand and supply of products; (3) the labour market; (4) money prices, costs and profitability; (5) the market for consumption goods; (6) the financial markets—(a) the budget, (b) the money and capital markets.

These divisions are necessarily somewhat arbitrary. Indeed, a major purpose of our discussion will be to show that the economic system constitutes a single whole and that the division of the economy into different sectors is merely a device for convenient exposition of the manifold interconnections.

CHAPTER VII

A SEVEN-SECTOR MODEL

(1) THE PRODUCTION SYSTEM

Let us start with a consideration of the production system. We will treat this as it was treated in Chapter XV of *The Growing Economy*. There are a large number of processes of production—*a*, *b*, *c*, *d*, etc. Each process of production for its operation on a given unitary scale needs a fixed input of labour and of various man-made intermediate products, and it produces a fixed output of various products either for use as intermediate products or for final consumption. Thus process *a* requires for its operation on a unitary scale inputs of L_{1a} units of labour of type 1, L_{2a} units of labour of type 2, and inputs of X_{1a} units of product 1, X_{2a} units of product 2, etc.; and process *a* then produces $\overline{X}_{1a}$ units of product 1, $\overline{X}_{2a}$ units of product 2 and so on.[1]

On day t the various processes are operated on various scales, namely $S_a(t)$, $S_b(t)$, $S_c(t)$, etc. It follows that the total input into the production system at 8 a.m. on day t of labour of type 1 is expressed by

$$L_1(t) = L_{1a}S_a(t) + L_{1b}S_b(t) + L_{1c}S_c(t) + \ldots.$$

Similarly the total input of product 1 at 8 a.m. on day 1 is expressed by:

$$X_1(t) = X_{1a}S_a(t) + X_{1b}S_b(t) + X_{1c}S_c(t) + \ldots$$

and the total output of product 1 at the end of day t, available to be used at 8 a.m. on day $t + 1$ is expressed by:

$$\overline{X}_1(t) = \overline{X}_{1a}S_a(t) + \overline{X}_{1b}S_b(t) + \overline{X}_{1c}S_c(t) + \ldots$$

---

[1] There are two minor ways in which this formulation differs from that used in Chapter XV of *The Growing Economy*. In the first place, in the earlier volume we used X and Y to denote consumption goods and K and J to denote intermediate products (K and J being inputs and $\overline{K}$ and $\overline{J}$ outputs of these products). We now use X_1, X_2, X_3 to cover all inputs of all products and $\overline{X}_1$, $\overline{X}_2$, $\overline{X}_3$, to cover all outputs of all goods whether they be used as consumption goods or as intermediate products. In the second place, in the earlier volume we assumed that there was only one type of labour, L; but we now assume that there may be many different types of labour (e.g. labour trained with different skills), namely L_1, L_2, L_3, etc.

We shall treat technical progress exactly as it was treated in Chapter XV of *The Growing Economy*. A technical improvement introduces the possibility of using a new process of production in which the same amount of some output can be obtained for a smaller amount of some inputs (cf. pp. 348–50 of *The Growing Economy*). Formally we can treat the problem in the following way. We can assume that the technical ideas behind every process that will ever be invented already exist in some heavenly workshop; but there is a constraint which makes $S = 0$ for every process which has not yet been invented; technical progress then removes this constraint on the scale of the various processes as they are 'invented'.

This productive system is displayed diagrammatically in Figure 23. Thus the scales on which the various processes are operated on any day will determine the total outputs of the various products at the end of the day (line 1), the total inputs of the various intermediate products needed at the beginning of the day (line 2), and the total inputs of the various types of labour needed at the beginning of the day (line 3). The three effects illustrated by lines 1, 2 and 3 are all positive proportional influences in the sense that an increase in the scale of any process cannot in itself cause any $\overline{X}$, X, or L to fall but will involve a corresponding rise in some $\overline{X}$, X, and/or L.

In its turn the state of technical knowledge which we will denote by T^{*2} will affect the scale on which the various processes are operated by removing the constraints on the scale of the processes which had not previously been invented. Technical progress (i.e. a higher level of technical knowledge) will thus operate by causing some new improved process to replace some old outdated process. Thus a higher level of technical knowledge will cause some processes to be operated on a higher and some on a lower scale. This is basically a proportional effect, but the effect will be negative on the scales of some processes and positive on the scales of other processes. We have used a continuous line to show a positive, and a broken line to show a negative, influence; we now introduce a dotted line to show the influence which may be positive or negative which T^* will exert on the various 'S's (line 4).

Lines 1, 2, 3 and 4 represent the technological relationships in our system (see Chapter III). The implications of this way of depicting the production system have been discussed at length in Part 2 of *The Growing Economy*, but it may be useful here to mention very briefly some of the most relevant points. In particular it is to be

---

[2] Throughout this model we will express environmental factors with a single asterisk (e.g. T^*) and governmental controls with a double asterisk (e.g. G_1^{**}, the government's demand for product 1).

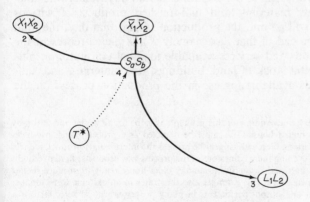

Figure 23

noted that all decisions in the production system can be expressed in terms of decisions about S, i.e. about the scales on which the various processes shall be operated. A general rise in total economic activity can be depicted as the consequence of decisions to raise the scales on which all the processes at present in use are being operated. Decisions to produce more of one product and less of another can be depicted as decisions to increase the scale of processes which are intensive in the output of the former product and to decrease the scale of processes which are intensive in the output of the latter product. Decisions to produce any given output by a different technique (e.g. to substitute a cheap input for a more expensive one) can be depicted as decisions to increase the scale of processes which are intensive in the cheap input and to reduce the scale of processes which are intensive in the expensive input. Technical progress, as we have seen, can be depicted as the expansion of a newly invented improved process at the expense of an existing outmoded process.

There is one feature of this method of depicting the production system which is of basic importance in what follows. Both the inputs (X_1, X_2, etc.) and the outputs ($\overline{X}_1$, $\overline{X}_2$, etc.) are expressed in the grossest possible form. Thus, consider a factory producing some product. The inputs at the beginning of any day into that factory include not only the labour and the raw materials but also the factory buildings themselves; the outputs at the end of the day include not only the finished products and the half-finished products, but also the factory buildings themselves (cf. pp. 287–8 of *The Growing Economy*). Thus the total inputs of products into the production system at the beginning of any one day (namely X_1, X_2, etc.) represents also the total stock of productive capital that is used in the productive system at the beginning of that day, namely the land, buildings, raw materials, and half-finished products of various kinds which will go into the production system that day; the total outputs at the end of that day (namely $\overline{X}_1$, $\overline{X}_2$, etc.) represent the output of goods and services available for final consumption plus the total capital stock of land, buildings, raw materials, and half-finished goods available for use in the production process on the next day.[3]

[3] The most extreme example of this principle is to be found in the habitation by any family of a rented house. This must be depicted as a process which produces shelter. Each morning there enters into the process the intermediate product, namely the house; each evening there comes out of the process two products: first, overnight shelter for the family and, secondly, a one-day-older house ready to produce shelter during the following day. This example also illustrates in an extreme form the fact that many input and output coefficients in many processes will be zero. Here is a case in which there is no labour input but only one intermediate product input and in which there are only two very specific outputs, namely shelter and a house.

(2) THE BALANCE BETWEEN THE DEMAND
AND SUPPLY OF PRODUCTS

So much for the depiction of the actual production system. As we explained in the previous chapter, a central feature of the dynamic development of the economy is the balance between the total potential supply of the products of industry and the total effective demand for these products. Accordingly, we turn next to the depiction of the balance between the total demand and supply of the products of industry. In Figure 24 we add to the relationship already given in Figure 23 some of the basic relationships which arise in the markets for the outputs of the production system.

As we have already explained, $\overline{X}_1$, $\overline{X}_2$, etc., represent the actual output of products 1, 2, etc., from the production system. We now let D_1, D_2, etc., represent the total demand for products 1, 2, etc. If demand is not equal to total supply, there may result either (i) a change in stocks or else (ii), what may be called, a frustration of demand or supply.

(i) Suppose that, in the case of a durable product, 100 units of the product are produced during day t to be sold on the morning of day $t + 1$. If on the morning of day $t + 1$, buyers in the market purchase only 90 units, there will be an addition to stocks of 10 units; but if buyers purchase 110 units there will be a reduction of 10 in the stocks of the product.

(ii) But there is another type of reaction resulting from a deficient or an excess demand for a product, a reaction which must occur if the product is perishable and which may occur even if it is durable. In the case of a deficient demand some of the supply may just be wasted. This is a phenomenon which must occur in the case of a perishable service. For example, a house produces shelter; but if it is uninhabited for a day the shelter which it produces for that day is just wasted; it is not used, but it cannot be added to a stock of shelter available for use later on.[4] Or, to take another example, perishable food which finds no immediate buyer must be thrown away; it cannot be added to a stock for future use. Similarly, in the case of an excess demand the wishes of some buyers may simply be frustrated; there will be shop shortages and some consumers must just go without. Their demands cannot (or for some other reason are not) satisfied by the running down of a stock of the item.

The way in which markets develop in a dynamic economy may be greatly affected by the answer to the question whether the balance between demand and supply is adjusted by method (i) or by method

---

[4] This is exactly comparable to the phenomenon of unemployed labour. The work which might have been done by today's unused labour cannot be added to a stock for later use.

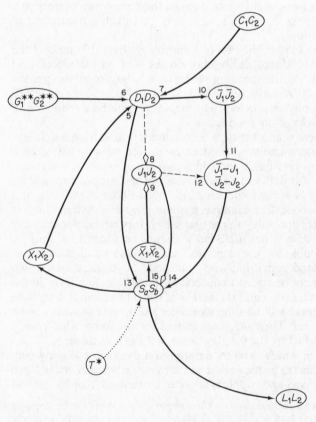

Figure 24

(ii) above. For if an excess supply, for example, is simply frustrated, then the output is lost and will not directly affect future market conditions; but if it is added to a stock which overhangs the market, today's excess supply may cause a cut-back in tomorrow's decisions to produce in order that the excess stock may be sold off. The subsequent dynamic reactions to an initial excess supply may this be very different in the two cases.

Solely for purposes of simplification we will proceed as if all adjustment of demand and supply were by method (i). We assume, that is to say, that there are stocks of all products which we will denote by J_1, J_2 etc., and that an excess demand causes a reduction in stocks and an excess supply an increase in stocks.

But in a world of uncertainty, in which stocks constitute the buffer between demand and supply, some level of unused stocks will be desirable. Retailers and wholesalers will wish to hold stocks of consumption goods, raw materials, etc., so that fluctuations in demand can be met. Equally important is the fact that producers will want to possess some spare capacity of machinery, factory space, etc., so that they can meet an unexpected increase in the demand for their products. In our model, in which the inputs (X) and the outputs ($\overline{X}$) include the daily inputs and outputs of fixed capital equipment, such spare capacity must be treated as an unused stock of idle machines and factories. In Figure 24 we depict as $\overline{J}_1$, $\overline{J}_2$, etc., the level of unused stocks of the various products, which traders and producers would like to be holding to meet unexpected fluctuations in demand or supply.

In Figure 24 lines 5, 6 and 7 show that the demand for the various goods is composed of X_1, X_2, etc. (the demands for intermediate products for use as inputs into the production system) plus G_1^{**}, G_2^{**}, etc. (the demands for the various products by the government for public purposes), plus C_1, C_2, etc. (the demands by private citizens for the satisfaction of their needs as consumers). Lines 8 and 9 show the fact that the balance between these demands (D_1, D_2, etc.) and the available supplies ($\overline{X}_1$, $\overline{X}_2$, etc.) will determine the rate at which the unused stocks (J_1, J_2, etc.) change. Thus the higher is the level of supply and the lower is the level of demand in the case of any one item, the higher will be the rate of increase in the unused stock of that commodity.

Line 10 states that the level of unused stocks which traders and producers aim at holding is related to the level of the demand for that product. Thus if a producer wished always to have spare capacity of some machine which was equal to 5% of the machinery which he was actually using for production purposes, then in his case (assuming this machine to be product 1) $\overline{J}_1$ would be 5% of

D*

that part of D_1 which represented his demand for the machinery as an input (X_1) into his productive process. Lines 11 and 12 simply define $\overline{J}_1 - J_1$, $\overline{J}_2 - J_2$, etc., i.e. the deficiency of the actual stocks below their desired level (or the excess of actual stocks if $\overline{J} - J$ is negative).[5]

Lines 5, 6, 7, 8, 9, 11 and 12 all represent identity relationships, which are employed merely to define certain terms including those which, like stocks in our present model, are the balancing items. Line 10, however, introduces a behavioural relationship, namely the decision of traders and producers as to the size of the stocks which they will aim at holding in any given state of demand for the goods concerned. Lines 13, 14 and 15 introduce further behavioural relationships, namely those decisions which producers take about the scale of their productive operations and which depend not upon prices, costs and profits (which we will discuss later) but upon the amounts demanded relatively to the supplies.

The basic relationship of this kind is that which is represented by line 13. The producers of goods will naturally take into account the level of the demand for their products when they decide how much to produce. Line 13 simply states that the higher is the level of the demand for any product, the higher will be the scale of the productive processes which produce that product.

But goods may be produced not only to meet a current final demand, but also to add to the stock of that product if the stock is considered to be dangerously low. Thus line 14 represents this fact that one factor which will encourage a high level of activity in a particular line of production is an undesirably low level of stocks of that product. If the level of the stock of shirts in the shops and warehouses (J_1) is much below what is considered a normal amount ($\overline{J}_1$) in view of the level of the demand for shirts (D_1), then this will encourage a relatively high scale of the productive operations which are intensive in the output of shirts (X_1). But, in our model, line 14

[5] In the construction of the dynamic economic model in this chapter, we shall make frequent reference to discrepancies between demand and supply or between the desired and the actual level of some variable. We shall show these as the absolute difference between the two quantities (e.g. as $\overline{J} - J$) although in many cases it might be preferable to show them as the ratio between the two quantities (e.g. $\overline{J}/J$). For example, when we come to state that an excess of desired over actual stocks may cause prices to be raised (line 32 of Figure 26 below), it might be more reasonable to say that the higher was $\overline{J}$ relatively to J, the higher would be the percentage rise of prices per period of time than to say that the higher was the absolute excess of $\overline{J}$ over J, the higher would be the absolute rate of increase of prices. The choice between these modes of expressing discrepancies between desired and actual levels and their effects may be of great importance in the interpretation of an actual economic system. In this chapter we aim at no more than giving a very general 'bird's eye view' of what the general pattern of interrelationships may be like.

represents not only the influence of a low level of stocks of this kind on the level of production, but also the influence of a low level of productive capacity on the production of additional capacity. Thus if the amount of idle looms (J_2) which the producers of shirts have in their mills is small relatively to the spare capacity ($\overline{J}_2$) which they would like to have in view of the current level of the demand for looms ($D_2 = X_2$) as an input into the shirt-making processes, then their desire to invest in more looms will lead to an increase in the scale of operations of those processes which produce looms ($\overline{X}_2$). Line 13 and 14 thus represent the ways in which producers may desire to bring outputs into line with the demands (including the demand for planned idle stocks or capacity). But the scale on which various processes can be operated may be affected by the availability of the inputs of the products required for those processes. This constraint on the side of the available supplies of inputs is represented by line 15. If the actual stocks of raw cotton (J_3) are very low, then it may be difficult to build up quickly the scale of operations of a process which requires a large input of raw cotton (X_3) in order to produce shirts ($\overline{X}_1$). Thus high levels of stocks of intermediate products may enable the relevant productive processes to be expanded rapidly, whereas low levels of such stocks may reduce the rate at which such processes can be expanded. A high level of J_1 thus has a positive integral effect upon those processes which are intensive in the input of X_1 (line 15).[6]

(3) THE LABOUR MARKET

The productive system requires labour of different kinds as well as intermediate products as inputs, and a scarcity of labour can impede the building up of a productive process just as effectively as a shortage of intermediate products. Accordingly, in Figure 25, we add certain labour market relationships to the relationships shown in Figure 24.

Let N^* be the total exogenously given amount of manpower available in the economy. However, labour is not in fact a simple undifferentiated mass, but is required with different trainings and

---

[6] The demand for products as inputs into the productive process (line 5) is the basic relationship which lies behind the accelerator (discussed on pp. 66–72). In our present model we are treating demand and supply in the grossest possible way, that is to say, as including in each day's input and output the total stock of capital equipment. This necessarily complicates the expression of the accelerator relationship which expressed the relationship between the net demand for new investment in capital goods and the rate of increase in the net demand for all purposes (consumption and net additions to capital stock). The way in which this accelerator relationship is embedded in the gross relationships of Figure 24 is discussed in Note A at the end of this chapter.

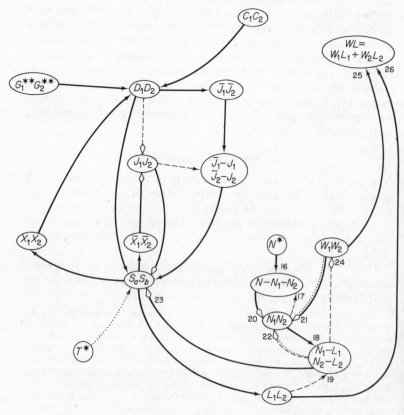

Figure 25

skills in different occupations. We assume, therefore, that there are a number of different, but interconnected, labour markets, numbered 1, 2, 3, etc. These differentiations are of skill, training, etc. Let L_1, L_2, etc., be the total number of workers of these different kinds actually in employment; let N_1, N_2, etc., be the total number of workers of each kind available for employment, that is to say with the necessary skill, training, and so on. Then lines 16, 17, 18 and 19 in Figure 25 simply define certain relevant variables in the labour market. Lines 16 and 17 state that the amount of as yet undifferentiated manpower will be equal to the total available (N^*) less the amounts which are already differentiated and attached to the particular subsidiary labour markets (N_1, N_2, etc.). Lines 18 and 19 then express the fact that the amount of unemployed labour available in each market is equal to $N_1 - L_1$, $N_2 - L_2$, etc. The higher these levels, the less the tension (i.e. the scarcity of labour) in those particular labour markets.

Lines 20, 21 and 22 express the forces at work affecting the rates at which the manpower attached to particular labour markets can be built up. Line 20 expresses the simple fact that the larger is the mass of unattached labour, the more quickly will it be likely that labour (by training, etc.) can be attracted and attached to any particular labour force. Let W_1, W_2, etc, represent the wage rates offered in labour markets 1, 2, etc. Then lines 21 and 22 represent the pulling power to particular markets of high wages and of good employment prospects respectively. In general, the higher the wage rate and the lower the unemployment in any labour market the more quickly is the labour force in that market likely to be built up.[7] Line 21 is, therefore, shown basically with a continuous line as a positive integral effect and line 22 basically with a broken line as a negative integral effect. But the build-up of labour in any one market will be affected not only by the absolute level of wages and the absolute level of unemployment, but also by the relative wage rates and employment opportunities in the different labour markets. Thus a high wage or a low unemployment situation in market 1 may attract labour to market 1 from market 2 and may thus REDUCE the rate at which N_2 is built up as well as increasing the rate at which N_1 is built up. This phenomenon is indicated by the dotted line components which are shown for lines 21 and 22. Basically, high

[7] Whether labour is attracted mainly by high earnings or by good employment prospects is a matter of fact which may differ from community to community; and whether, in consequence, line 21 or line 22 exerts the more powerful influence may be a very important factor in the dynamic characteristics of the economy. The fact that we have included both influences in our model is merely an example of our intention, mentioned above, to build a model which includes all the most important hypotheses which have been advanced in the relevant literature.

wages and low unemployment attract undifferentiated labour into particular markets (the basic relationship shown by the continuous line component of 21 and the broken line components of 22). But since relative wages and employment opportunities are important, a low level of one particular wage rate or a high level of unemployment in that particular labour market may increase the rate at which the labour force can be built up in some other market.

Line 23 allows for the difficulties of expanding particular processes of production if there is a market scarcity of the particular type of labour required for that process. If the unemployment percentage is very low in a particular labour market, that will reduce the rate at which particular employers are able to acquire the labour necessary to expand their particular processes of production which rely heavily on that type of labour. Thus line 23 expresses for labour shortages the same sort of restraint on the expansion of production which line 15 (in Figure 24) expressed for shortages of intermediate products.

Finally the degree of tension in the various labour markets may affect the rates at which the corresponding wage rates are bid up. Thus if there is much shortage of labour in market 1 (i.e. $N_1 - L_1$ is low), bargaining power among workers in that market is likely to be high and the corresponding wage rate (W_1) is likely to be rising quickly. These effects of low unemployment leading to rapid rates of rise of wage rates[8] are indicated by line 24.

Finally the total wage bill in the economy is simply the sum of the wage bills (i.e. the wage rate times the level of employment) in each of the individual labour markets. The derivation of the total wage bill (WL) from the particular wage rates (W_1, W_2, etc.) and the particular levels of employment (L_1, W_2, etc.) is shown by lines 25 and 26.

(4) MONEY PRICES, COSTS, AND PROFITABILITY

Up to this point we have not considered at all the influence which the relationships between the money selling prices of outputs and the money costs of inputs, and so the profitability of production, may have upon the expansion or contraction of various industries. We have allowed for the facts that the expansion or contraction of various firms may be affected by the quantities of the outputs which are being sold (line 13), by a desire to add to the quantities held in stock (line 14), by a physical shortage of necessary intermediate products (line 15), or by the absence of any unemployed labour (line 23). But we have made no reference to the relationship between

[8] The relationship expressed in the well-known Phillips curve.

selling prices and costs and to the simple fact that entrepreneurs will wish to expand the profitable and to contract the unprofitable lines of production. We make allowances for these factors in the lines which are introduced in Figure 26.

Let us consider the profitability of operating any particular process—say, process a—on a unitary scale on day t. This gross profit will not be realized until the product is sold at the beginning of day $t + 1$. Accordingly, the gross profit obtained in respect of the operations of day t (i.e. the excess of money receipts for the sale of the outputs over the money payments made for the inputs of intermediate products and of labour) will be denoted by $q_a(t + 1)$ and is given by the following expression:

$$
\begin{aligned}
q_a(t + 1) = {}& P_1(t + 1)\overline{X}_{1a} + P_2(t + 1)\overline{X}_{2a} \\
& - \{P_1(t)X_{1a} + P_2(t)X_{2a}\} \\
& - \{W_1(t)L_{1a} + W_2(t)L_{2a}\} \quad\ldots\ldots\ldots\ldots\ldots\ldots (7.1)
\end{aligned}
$$

The output of product 1 produced by the operation of process a on a unitary scale—namely $\overline{X}_{1a}$—if it is produced on day 1 will be available on the morning of day $t + 1$ for sale at a price, $P_1(t + 1)$. On the other hand, the input of product 1 needed for this same operation of process a on a unitary scale—namely X_{1a}—must be purchased on the morning of day t at a price, $P_1(t)$; similarly, the labour of type 1 required for this purpose—namely L_{1a}—must be paid the wage rate which is fixed on the morning of day t—namely $W_1(t)$. The expression 7.1 thus describes the gross profit made on the operation of process a on a unitary scale on day t.

It will be observed from 7.1 that, given the physical input and output coefficients for any given process, its gross profitability depends simply upon the relationship between the prices of inputs (including the wage rates of various types of labour) and of outputs. We can make the following generalizations.

(i) The lower are the wage rates, the higher will be the profitability of any one process.

(ii) Given the wage rates, then, on average, high prices mean high profitabilities for the various processes. For processes of production to be in any meaningful sense productive outputs of products must on average be greater than inputs of products, the whole purpose being to produce a net surplus of output. Thus if all product prices were 10% higher, wage rates remaining the same, general profitability would increase. There is a general positive proportional influence of prices on profit margins.

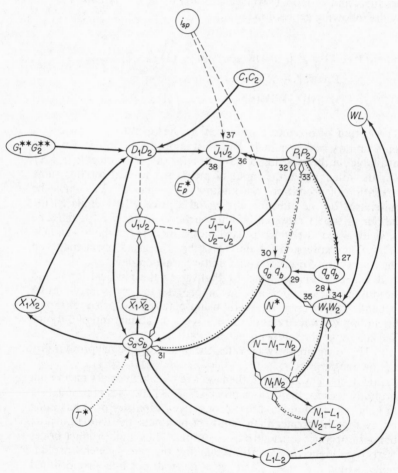

Figure 26

(iii) But while a high level of all product prices will give a high level of profitability all round, it does not of course follow that a high level of one particular price will lead to a high level of profitability in every productive process. If the product in question is an intermediate product, it will increase the profitability of those processes which produce it but will decrease the profitability of those processes which use it as an input.

(iv) Profitability depends not only on the level, but also on the rate of change of product prices. Thus the higher the rate of rise of product prices, the greater the level of profitability. Inputs for day t are bought at prices $P(t)$: the outputs of day t are sold at prices $P(t + 1)$. In other words, profits as we have defined them include capital gains as well as profit margins available at constant prices.[9]

These price-cost relationships are shown in lines 27 and 28 of Figure 26. Influence (i) is shown by the negative proportional effect which wage rates exercise on gross profit margins, represented by line 28. Influence (ii) is a basic positive proportional effect, and influence (iv) a basic positive derivative effect, of prices on gross profit margins and these are shown by the continuous line 27.[10] Influence (iii) expresses the importance of relative prices on the profitability of different processes and, since a rise in one price may raise the profitability of some processes but reduce the profitability of others, it is represented by the dotted component of line 27.

The gross profit margins q_a, q_b, etc., do not allow for the cost of interest payments. Since inputs of intermediate products are financed at the biginning of day t, but outputs become available only at the end of day t for sale on the morning of day $t + 1$, it is necessary to borrow money to finance the purchase price of the intermediate products for one day.[11]

Let $i_{sp}(t)$ represent the rate of interest payable at 8 a.m. on day $t + 1$ on the money borrowed for a day from the banks at 8 a.m. on day t to finance the purchase of intermediate products at 8 a.m. on day t. We can now modify equation 7.1 so as to show net profit margins (q') as contrasted with gross profit margins (q). The net profit (i.e. gross profit less interest payment) made on the operation of process a on a unitary scale during day t may be expressed as

---

[9] See pp. 301–2 of *The Growing Economy*.

[10] Line 27 combines the sign for a proportional effect ($\rightarrow$) with the sign for a derivative effect ($\rightarrow\!\!\!\rightarrow$).

[11] We assume, as in *The Growing Economy*, that while the wage rate for labour employed during day t is fixed on the morning of day t, the wage is not actually paid till the morning of day $t + 1$, so that no interest is payable by the employer on the wage bill. (See pp. 32–3, 290–91 of *The Growing Economy*).

follows:

$$q'_a(t + 1) = P_1(t + 1)\overline{X}_{1a} + P_2(t + 1)\overline{X}_{2a}$$
$$- \{1 + i_{sp}(t)\}\{P_1(t)X_{1a} + P_2(t)X_{2a}\}$$
$$- \{W_1(t)L_{1a} + W_2(t)L_{2a}\} \quad \ldots \ldots \ldots \ldots \ldots \ldots \ldots \quad (7.2)$$

Thus the net profit margins are equal to the gross profit margins less the short-term rate of interest on the value of the capital goods invested in the process. A high rate of interest will tend to reduce all net profit margins relatively to gross profit margins; this is shown by lines 29 and 30 in Figure 26, which shows net profit margins as being raised by a rise in gross profit margins but reduced by a rise in the short-term interest rate. A rise in the short-term interest rate, while it will reduce all net profit margins, will not affect all such margins equally. Capital-intensive processes will be more adversely affected than labour-intensive processes.

Line 31 then expresses the fact that entrepreneurs are likely to expand the scale of operation of those processes on which the net profit margins are high and to reduce the scale of those processes on which it is negative or low. This relationship is shown basically as a positive integral effect: the higher is the net profit margin on any one process, the more rapidly is that process likely to be expanded. But once again there is an effect due to relative net profit margins on different processes. Thus even if the net profit margin on process a is positive and unchanged, a rise in the net profit margin on process b may induce an entrepreneur to shift his attention and resources from process a to the more profitable process b. Thus a rise in the net profit margin on one process may lead to a reduction in the scale of operation of another process. This relative profitability effect is shown by the dotted component of line 31.

So much for the effect of profit margins on production and for the determination of profit margins in terms of interest rates, wage rates, and product prices. We must now consider what determines the level of product prices.

An obvious influence upon the money prices of a product is the market balance between the supply and the demand for that product. We have assumed that this market balance is in all cases shown by a change in the idle spare capacity stocks of the product (J). If producers and traders adjust the selling prices of products to the market situation, we can in this stock adjustment model assume that they will put up the price of a product if the stock is undesirably low and lower the price if the stock is undesirably high. Line 32 accordingly shows the price of each product as being raised the more rapidly, the higher is the deficiency of the actual stocks below the desired stock level.

But producers of a product in setting the prices which they charge may consider not only the state of the market demand but also the cost of production of the product. They may be more prepared to put up the price of their product if the cost has gone up as well as the demand being good, than if the cost has not gone up in the same market demand conditions. This influence is shown by line 33 which expresses the fact that the lower is the net profit margin on a process which produces a particular product, the more quickly will the price of that product be raised (or the more slowly will it be reduced) to correspond with its cost of production in any given market conditions. This influence must be predominantly a negative effect. Since the value of product outputs exceeds the value of product inputs, low profit margins are on the average to be raised by pushing up product prices and not by holding them down. But once again there is a relative effect. A particularly low profit margin can be raised by beating down the price of an input as well as by pushing up the price of the outputs. Thus it is possible that to a limited extent certain low profit margins may reduce the rate at which certain prices can be raised. This is shown by the dotted component in line 33.

But in addition to these conditions of current demand conditions (line 32) and current cost conditions (line 33), there is another set of considerations which will be very important in determining the market prices of durable products, namely the expectation of the future usefulness of such durable products. Consider the market value of a dwelling-house. This will be affected not only by the current cost of production of a house (line 33) and by the current demand-supply position as shown by the number of empty houses offered for sale or renting on the market (line 32), but also by the present discounted value of the future rents which may be expected on a house in the more distant future. A long-term investor in house property will obviously be greatly affected by consideration of the long-term yield which he can expect to obtain on such property.

This consideration will be of importance in the case of all very durable assets. The current market value of the looms in a textile mill will be affected not only by their current cost of production and by the current level of spare capacity in the textile industry, but also—perhaps, above all—by the expected yield over the long run of investment in the looms, which will depend upon the prospect of future profits from their use.

These considerations affecting the price of durable products are so closely connected with the factors determining prices, yields and interest rates on various forms of asset that we will leave their intro-duction into our model until we come to a general discussion of the capital and money markets.

We may now depict on Figure 26 some of the effects of product prices in addition to their direct effects upon the profitability of different productive processes (line 27).

In the first place, the cost of living may affect the money wage rate. In so far as workers, in setting the money wage rate which they demand, are thinking in real terms and not merely in money terms, a rise in the cost of living, i.e. in the price of consumption goods, will cause money wage rates to be higher than they would have been in otherwise similar market conditions. This influence is shown by the positive proportional effect of the '*P*'s upon the '*W*'s depicted in line 34.

Incidentally, it is convenient at this point to complete our account of the factors which may affect the level of money wage rates. We have already shown the effect of a scarcity of labour (line 24 on Figure 25) and of the cost of living (line 34 of Figure 26) on wage rates. But it is possible that there is a third main influence, namely the profitability of industry. When profits are high, employers may offer less resistance to wage claims and workers may demand increases in wages more insistently. This influence is shown in line 35 which suggests that the higher are the net profit margins on the various productive processes, the more rapid will be the rate of rise of the wage rates of the labour employed in those processes. Line 35 is the complement of line 33; the lower are profit margins, the more insistent will producers be on putting up the prices of their outputs and in resisting increases in the prices of their inputs, including the wages of their employees.

Another very important influence of price changes is shown in line 36. The willingness to hold idle stocks of goods will be much influenced by the expectation as to whether their price is likely to go up or down. If a product is bought today and sold tomorrow, a profit is made equal to the rise in the price of the product less the interest which must be paid on the money borrowed for the day to invest in the stock. It is the expected rate of capital gain (i.e. the expected proportionate rate of rise in the price of the product) less the rate of interest payable on the cost of the product which determines the net rate of profit expected from holding the stock.[12] If we confined our attention to the simplest speculative behaviour in which speculators always operated on the assumption that the current rate of change of prices would continue, we could simply show the speculative motive for holding stocks as being positively proportional to the difference between the current rate of rise of prices and the current rate of interest on the cost of the stocks (lines

[12] See pp. 38–9 of *The Growing Economy*.

36 and 37) of Figure 26. But price expectations are so much influenced by exogenous influences—e.g. wars and rumours of wars—that we have introduced in line 38 an additional factor, namely the influence of outside events upon price expectations (E_p^*) and so upon the speculative motive to hold stocks.

(5) THE MARKET FOR CONSUMPTION GOODS

We turn next to a consideration of the principal factors which determine the level of private consumption of the various goods available on the market. These factors are illustrated in the numbered lines on Figure 27.

A first major set of factors which determine the level of consumption is the level of money incomes available for expenditure on consumption goods. In our model, we will distinguish between expenditure out of wages and expenditure out of other personal incomes, i.e. out of incomes from property.

We have already (see lines 25 and 26 of Figure 25) considered the factors which determine the level of money wage incomes. Money incomes from property are obtained in Figure 27 as the difference between the total money national income and that part which is paid out in wages. The total money national income generated by the productive operations of day t will be realized only at the beginning of day $t + 1$ when the output of day t is sold. We shall, therefore, call $Y(t + 1)$ the income earned in respect of the trading and production operations of day t, and we can express it in the following way:

$$Y(t + 1) = \{\overline{X}_1(t) + J_1(t)\}P_1(t + 1) + \{\overline{X}_2(t) + J_2(t)\}P_2(t + 1)$$
$$- \{X_1(t) + J_1(t)\}P_1(t) - \{X_2(t) + J_2(t)\}P_2(t)$$
$$= \{\overline{X}_1(t) - X_1(t)\}P_1(t + 1) + \{\overline{X}_2(t) - X_2(t)\}P_2(t + 1)$$
$$+ K_1(t)\{P_1(t + 1) - P_1(t)\} + K_2(t)\{P_2(t + 1) - P_2(t)\} \quad . . (7.3)$$

where $K_1(t) = X_1(t) + J_1(t)$ and $K_2(t) = X_2(t) + J_2(t)$.

When we are considering the total income (including capital gains) accruing from the whole productive and trading apparatus, we must not forget the existence of idle or spare capacity stocks. The 'input' of product 1, for example, is $X_1 + J_1$, i.e. the input for productive purposes plus the idle stock carried during the day. The 'output' is $\overline{X}_1 + J_1$, namely the output from the productive process plus the idle stock which is still available at the end of the day.

The first form of the expression in 7.3 shows the value added during day t. $\{\overline{X}_1(t) + J_1(t)\}P_1(t + 1)$ is the market value at the beginning of day $t + 1$ of the amount of product 1 then available for all uses;

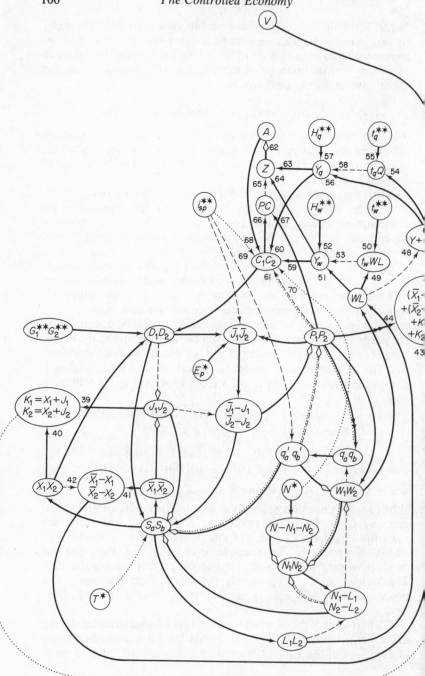

Figure 27

while $\{X_1(t) + J_1(t)\}P_1(t)$ is the cost of the inputs (including the idle stock $J_1(t)$) needed to make $\overline{X}_1(t) + J_1(t)$ available at the end of the day. The total gross money receipts from the outputs of day t less the total money expenditure on the inputs of intermediate products needed to produce these outputs is the net income available for the payment of wages, interest and rent, and for the residual receipt of profits, inclusive of capital gains.[13]

The second form of the expression in 7.3 shows that this total income can also be formulated as the value at current prices of the net outputs of the various products plus the capital gain made in the productive and trading system through the rise in price over the course of the day of the total capital stocks held either for productive purposes or as spare capacity stocks.

It can be seen that the net national money income thus derived from the productive and trading system will be the greater (i) the greater are the net outputs $(\overline{X}_1 - X_1, \overline{X}_2 - X_2,$ etc.); (ii) the higher are the product prices;[14] (iii) the more rapidly prices are rising and thus the greater are the capital gains; and (iv) if prices are rising, then the higher the amount of capital on which capital gains are made; but if prices are falling, then the smaller the amount of capital on which capital losses are made.

These relationships are shown in lines 39, 40, 41, 42, 43, 44 and 45 of Figure 27. Lines 39 and 40 simply define K_1 and K_2 as $X_1 + J_1$ and $X_2 + J_2$. Lines 41 and 42 simply define the net outputs $\overline{X}_1 - X_1,$ $\overline{X}_2 - X_2,$ etc. Line 43 expresses condition (i) above. Line 44, showing both a positive proportional and a positive derivative effect, expresses conditions (ii) and (iii). Line 45 expresses condition (iv) and is represented by a dotted line, since a high K will lead to high capital gains and so a high income if prices are rising, but to high capital losses and so a low income if prices are falling.

We shall in due course introduce a national debt into our model. Citizens then receive as income from property not only the interest, rents and profits from industry and trade, but also interest on government debt. Let us denote by V the interest on the national debt, inclusive of capital gains, i.e. inclusive of any appreciation in the value of government bonds. We are now in a position to distinguish between wages and income from property.

---

[13] See pp. 290–91 and 301–2 of *The Growing Economy*.

[14] So long as $\overline{X}_1 - X_1 > 0$ we can say that the higher is P_1, the greater is the net national income. In general, outputs must be greater than inputs of products in any truly productive system. But if techniques are changing, inputs may exceed outputs in the case of intermediate products which are going out of use. In the particular case of such products, a high P would lead to a low national income; the price would be more important as a cost than as a receipt.

Let us denote incomes from property, inclusive of any interest on national debt owned by private individuals and inclusive of their capital gains, by Q. Q is then equal to $Y + V - WL$ and this is shown by lines 46, 47 and 48.

We now proceed to derive from total wage incomes and total incomes from property the corresponding figures of net disposable wage and property incomes (i.e. income after the deduction of tax payments and the addition of any transfer payments—e.g. social security benefits—received from the state). Let us denote net disposable incomes from wages and from property as Y_w and Y_q respectively; the rates of tax payable on wage incomes and property incomes as t_w^{**} and t_q^{**} respectively;[15] and the transfer incomes received from the state by wage earners and owners of property as H_w^{**} and H_q^{**} respectively.

Then lines 49 and 50 show that the total tax payments of wage earners is $t_w WL$, and lines 51, 52 and 53 show that the net disposable income from wages is gross wages plus transfer incomes minus tax payments. Similarly, lines 54 and 55 show the total of taxes paid out of property incomes, while lines 56, 57 and 58 show that the net disposable income from property is gross property income plus transfer incomes minus tax payments. Lines 59 and 60 then depict the fact that the higher are net disposable wage incomes and property incomes, the higher will be the expenditure on consumption goods,[16] and so given the price of consumption goods, the greater will be the amounts (C_1, C_2, etc.) of such goods which are demanded.

Y_w and Y_q are expressed in money terms, while C_1, C_2, etc., are in real terms. Given the disposable money incomes, the quantities of consumption goods which will be bought will be the greater, the lower are the prices at which such goods can be bought. This basic negative proportional effect of the price level upon the amount bought is shown by the broken-line component of line 61. But a reduction in the price of a particular product, while it will cause an increase in the purchase of some product or products, may cause a reduction in the purchase of some other particular product. If the product whose price has fallen is very inferior, it may even cause a fall in the amount of that same product which consumers will purchase.[17] But a more probable case is where the price elasticity of demand for a particular product is numerically greater than unity so that, when its price falls, a greater total amount of money is

[15] In this model, we assume that there are only direct taxes on wages and on property incomes. There are no indirect taxes and no taxes on wealth or inheritance.

[16] This effect, like the other causal effects discussed in this chapter, is likely to operate only after a time lag as illustrated on pp. 38–44.

[17] See p. 45 of *The Stationary Economy*.

spent on it. In this case, less may be spent on other products, so that smaller amounts of these other products are purchased. The dotted component of line 61 indicates that, while the basic relationship is one in which low prices enable greater quantities to be bought, yet a low price for a particular product may lead to either a higher or a lower consumption of other particular products.

Lines 59, 60 and 61, which we have just discussed, express the fact that a major determinant of the amounts of consumption goods demanded is the current levels in terms of consumers' spendable incomes, i.e. of their money spendable incomes deflated by the cost of living. The higher are their real incomes, the greater will be the level of their purchases. But this does not, of course, imply that they spend the whole of their spendable incomes. Some part of their incomes they may save, and the amount which they save will also depend upon the level of their incomes. But this choice between saving and spending will be influenced by other factors besides the level of their real incomes, and in the remaining lines of Figure 27 we depict three of these possible influences, namely (i) the amount of existing property which individual savers already possess; (ii) the rate of interest which they can obtain on their savings; and (iii) the size of the population of citizens between whom the total incomes must be shared.

(i) The greater is the value of the property which savers have already accumulated, the smaller will be their need to save in order to accumulate still more property and the greater, therefore, will by their expenditure on current consumption. The value of the assets which people already hold (which we will depict as A) is the sum of all past savings—if we include capital gains in income and so in savings (which we will depict as Z). Line 62 shows this identity relationship; the higher is Z, the greater will be the rate of increase of A. But savings are disposable incomes less the amount spent on consumption so that $Z = Y_q + Y_w - PC$ where $PC = P_1 C_1 + P_2 C_2 + \ldots$. These identity relations are shown by lines 63, 64, 65, 66 and 67. Finally, in line 68, we show the behavioural relationship which states that the greater is the existing value of the property already accumulated by savers, the lower will be their savings and the higher, therefore, their purchases of consumption goods.

(ii) The choice between consumption and savings may also be affected by the rate of interest and this influence is depicted by line 69, where we have assumed that the anticipated rate of interest is that which rules in the market for short-term private bills (i_{sp}). This influence may, however, work in either of two directions. A high rate of interest is likely to make people plan for a higher rate of growth of their consumption levels over their life time. But since a high rate of interest, if it is expected to continue in the future, will bring a higher future return on their savings, a high rate of interest will enable them to combine a slightly higher current level of consumption with a slightly more rapidly growing rate of consumption. If, however, it is desired as a result of a high rate of interest to raise the rate of growth of consumption very appreciably, then a lower current level of consumption and a higher current level of savings will be required to bring about the desired future increase in consumption. Line 69 is, therefore, a dotted line, indicating that the influence of the rate of interest upon consumption may be positive or negative.

(iii) Consumption functions will depend upon real income per head and real property per head rather than simply upon total real income and total real property. For this reason, the size of the total population will also be a factor affecting the level of consumption (line 70). But the way in which this factor will work is uncertain. An increase in the number of citizens will, in itself, reduce real income per head (which may raise the proportion of income spent on consumption), but it will also reduce the amount of real property per head (which may raise the incentive to save). We have, therefore, shown the influence of N^* on C_1, C_2, etc., by a dotted line.

The influences of the level of real income per head, of the size of existing holdings of property per head, and of the rate of interest on the level of consumption have been discussed at length and in a more sophisticated manner in Chapters XII and XIII of *The Growing Economy*. It is not intended to repeat that analysis here. The lines 59, 60, 68, 69 and 70 in Figure 27 do not claim to do more than give a rough, and in many ways inadequate, summary of the influences at work.

There is one way, however, in which the method of Figure 27 is particularly inadequate and which needs, therefore, to be underlined. The division of the national income as between wages and income from property does not, in fact, imply a division of recipients of income into wage earners and property owners unless one assumes that the economy is a Plantcap, in which one class of persons does all the work, owns no property and does not save, while another class of persons does no work, owns all the property and does all the savings.[18]

Figure 27 is strictly accurate only for such an economy. In this case, lines 59, 61 and 70 would be relevant for wage earners. They spend the whole of their incomes on consumption goods at current prices. Lines 60, 61, 68, 69 and 70 would be relevant to property owners. They own all the assets (line 68) and they alone are concerned

[18] Cf. Chapter III of *The Growing Economy*.

with the rate of interest on savings (line 69). They determine their consumption of various products in the light of their incomes, the prices of the various goods, the existing level of their assets and the rate of interest.

A much more satisfactory distinction to make would be between different types of income recipients, some rich, some poor, some relying mainly on wages and some mainly on property incomes, but all receiving some wages and some property incomes. The factors determining the distribution of income in such a Propcap have been considered in Chapter XIV of *The Growing Economy*. But to depict them on our present model, which would involve depicting the distribution of the ownership of A through past accumulation, would involve very great complication.[19]

The simple division into wage incomes and incomes from property is maintained in Figure 27 largely on the grounds that it is made in much of the current discussion of the problems involved in the control of the economy. There is some justification for this usage. Property incomes consist largely of profits and profits are made largely by corporative bodies. Such corporations are often subject to special corporation duties, so that it is desirable to be able to make a distinction between the taxation of wages and the taxation of profits.[20] Moreover, the directors of such corporations can control the amount of profits which are distributed in dividends to shareholders and the amount which is saved and ploughed back into the development of the corporations's capital equipment. Thus the factors affecting savings out of profits may be different in kind from those affecting savings out of wages.[21] If, in addition, the community is rather like a Plantcap in the sense that there is one class which in fact relies mainly on wages and owns little property,

[19] A very easy way to simplify Figure 27 would be to assume the conditions for a Propdem in which every citizen is a representative wage earner and property owner and has the same total income and wealth as every other citizen. In this case, no distinction between wages and property incomes need be made and only one class of spendable incomes need be considered. This simplification is adopted in the next chapter (see Figure 31).

[20] In the real world, a distinction is also made between net income and capital gains for tax purposes. This could be introduced into our model by distinguishing between that part of Q which consisted of capital gains on real property and on government bonds. We have avoided this complication.

[21] It should, however, not be forgotten that if profits are ploughed back into a business concern, the value of the shares owned by the individual shareholders is likely to be enhanced. To the extent that this enhancement of value is exactly equal to the profits ploughed back and to the extent that shareholders treat these capital gains in exactly the same way as they treat their income from dividends, the decisions of the directors to save out of the corporation's profits would be offset by the decision of the shareholders to spend out of their capital gains.

and another richer class which relies mainly on income from property, a model—such as that depicted in Figure 27—which makes a simple division between wage incomes and property incomes may be useful. But, let it be stressed, it is not in fact an accurate description of the normal Propcap.

(6) THE FINANCIAL MARKETS

We can now complete our model by introducing financial markets into the economy. In a number of instances in the preceding parts of our model we have already introduced the rates of interest on various forms of loan or asset as causal factors affecting various decisions by private decision makers. We have assumed that there is a short-term rate of interest at which private producers and traders can borrow money from the banks and which will affect the profitability of their productive operations and the incentive to hold spare capacity stocks (lines 30 and 37 in Figure 26). We have assumed that this same short-term rate of interest on private borrowings represents the rate of interest which private individuals expect to obtain on their savings (line 69 of Figure 27). Above all, we have referred to the importance of the investor's valuation of durable capital assets in influencing the market price offered for the production of such durable instruments. We have assumed that, at any one time, there is a market valuation of the totality of all assets privately held which will affect the decisions of private individuals as to how much they will save and how much they will spend on consumption (line 68 of Figure 27). We have included interest received on the government debt in the incomes of property owners (line 47 of Figure 27). Finally, we must allow for the fact that the government must borrow money from the banks or from private citizens in order to finance any budget deficit which may result from its fiscal policy, i.e. from the level of expenditure on goods and services (G_1^{**}, G_2^{**}) and on transfer payments (H_w^{**}, H_q^{**}) and from the rates of tax (t_w^{**}, t_q^{**}) which it may set.

All these variables—the rates of interest on various forms of asset or of debt, the current valuation of all privately held assets, the total of interest payable on the national debt, and the amount which the government must borrow to finance its budget—will interact on the markets on which money is borrowed and lent and on which stocks and shares and capital assets in general are bought and sold. In order to complete our model we must introduce such a market for capital assets of all kinds.

In the real world, capital assets can take myriad forms: coins, notes, current deposits and time deposits with commercial banks and with other financial institutions such as building societies, short-term and long-term government debt of an indefinite variety of terms of interest payment and of redemption, long-term and short-term debts of private business, preference shares and ordinary shares of business concerns with different rights to participate in profits and in voting, shares in investment trusts, participations in professional partnerships, mortgages, insurance policies, hire-purchase loans, and actual physical assets such as land, houses, machinery, stocks of raw materials, etc.

Different persons and concerns have different needs and tastes as to the amounts which they should borrow or lend and as to the forms in which they should do so. Many financial intermediaries exist in order to match these varying needs and tastes of borrowers and lenders. Thus a building society is an institution which enables the lenders to hold their assets in a fairly liquid form (deposits with the building society which can be withdrawn on fairly short notice) and the borrowers to incur their debts in a form in which repayment is spread over a long period (mortgages on their houses). In such financial intermediaries, the total liabilities of the institution balance its total assets, though the form (as to risk and maturity, for example) of the liabilities differs from that of the assets. The total net assets to be held by private property owners must add up to the total value of the real assets in the community (the land, houses, machinery, stocks of goods, etc.) plus the total value of the net national debt of the government (i.e. of the total debt which it has issued in the past to cover its budget deficits less any of the real assets of the community which it owns in, for example, nationalized industries). Thus the money and capital markets can be regarded as institutions through which the real assets of the community plus the government's net national debt are held by private property owners, the forms of the assets being modified by the various forms of paper debt or money which the various financial intermediaries issue—for example, houses being backed by mortgages which are backed by building society deposits owned by private citizens or, to take another example, government debt covered by Treasury Bills held by the banks against which deposit liabilities are owed by the banks to private citizens.

The different forms of asset and of debt will in the capital market offer different yields or expectation of yields. Given the structure of financial intermediaries, one must envisage the amounts issued of the various forms of paper asset and debt and the yields on them tending always to settle down at levels such that no individual property owner or financial intermediary would wish to issue more or less debt of any kind or to hold more or less assets of any kind, given the total net capital owned by the individual or institution in question, its distribution between various assets and debts, and the relative yields and expected yields on these various assets and debts. There will be some interrelationships between these yields, since borrowers will always tend to shift to the lower yield type of debt and lenders towards the higher yield type of asset; but differences of tastes and needs as regards risks and the time structure of future payments will mean that yields are never completely equalized.

It is clear that, in reality in a highly developed economy, the money and capital markets are very complex institutions; these matters will be discussed somewhat more fully at a later stage in this volume (see Chapter XXI). For our present purposes we must make extreme simplifying assumptions. We shall assume that there are only five types of asset, each with its own yield or rate of interest.

(1) We assume that there is MONEY on which no interest is paid. This money is issued as a liability by the banking system either to the government in the purchase of government debt (short-term bills or long-term bonds) or else to private concerns in the form of short-term loans to such private customers. Whether this money takes the form of coin, notes or bank deposits is a matter of indifference to us. We may regard it all as being in the form of $1 banknotes. It is, in any case, the completely liquid asset in terms of which all debts and tax payments can be settled and it earns no interest. We will denote by $M(t)$ the amount of money issued at the beginning of day t.

(2) We assume that there is SHORT-TERM GOVERNMENT DEBT which takes the form of one-day bills issued by the government. These bills are all in denominations of $1. The government sells them at the beginning of day t for $1 each and repays them at the beginning of day $t + 1$ in the form of $1 in money plus the relevant rate of interest for one day on the money. We will denote the number of government bills so issued to the private sector at the beginning of day t as $F_{sg}(t)$ and the rate of interest to be paid on them, together with the repayment of principal at the beginning of day $t + 1$, as $i_{sg}^{**}(t)$.

(3) We assume also that there is LONG-TERM GOVERNMENT DEBT which takes the form of the issue of an irredeemable bond on which $1 a day is paid in interest in perpetuity. We denote by $F_{lg}(t)$ the value of such bonds held by the private sector. We will write i_{lg}^{**} as the long-term rate of interest on such bonds so that $F_{lg} i_{lg}$ measures the total interest payable daily on the outstanding bonds; and since we define a bond as a promise to pay $1 a day, $F_{lg} i_{lg}$ also measures the number of bonds outstanding. If $i_{lg}(t)$ is the long-term rate of interest ruling at the beginning of day t, then $\$1/i_{lg}(t)$ will represent the price of one bond in the capital market at the beginning of day t.

For the rate of interest on a perpetual bond is the amount of daily interest paid on it, divided by its price; or, in other words,

$$\frac{\$1}{\${1/i_{lg}(t)}} = i_{lg}(t).$$

(4) We assume that there is SHORT-TERM PRIVATE DEBT which takes the form of one-day bills for \$1 each issued by private borrowers. The number of such bills issued at the beginning of day t we shall denote as $F_{sp}(t)$ and the rate of interest payable on them at the beginning of day $t + 1$ as $i_{sp}^{**}(t)$. We shall assume that such bills are held only by the banking system. In other words, F_{sp} represents the amount of bank lending to the private sector and takes the form of short-term debt on which a given short-term rate of interest is paid.

(5) Finally, we allow for the existence of REAL ASSETS (i.e. houses, land, machinery, stocks of raw materials, etc.). These are held entirely by private property owners (i.e. neither by the banks nor by the government) and we make no distinction between the ownership of such assets and the ownership of an ordinary share which represents a participation in the ownership of such assets through a business concern. The total value of such real assets at the beginning of day t we denote by $A_r(t)$. We will write $\hat{i}_{lp}(t)$ as the rate of the yield which at the beginning of day t is expected on these real assets.

In this very simple model, we have the government issuing bonds and bills to finance the budget deficit and the private sector of the economy accumulating real assets. There is only one form of financial intermediary, namely the banking system, which takes up some of the government debt and lends some money on short-term to private individuals to finance the ownership of some real assets, and against this bank holding of government debt and of private short-term debt issues money. Private individuals are left with the choice of investment of their property as between money, government bills, government bonds or real assets, and they can supplement such investments by borrowing short-term from the banks.

We shall proceed in our present very simple model as if the whole banking system were concentrated in the hands of a single bank. For our present purpose it would be just as satisfactory to assume that there was a structure of competing commercial banks, controlled by a single Central Bank, provided that the Central Bank's control was completely effective over the combined operations of the commercial banks. But, for purposes of simple exposition, we will talk of the banking authorities as if there were a single unit for all operative purposes.

In this financial structure there are still two controlling authorities, the government and the banking authorities, with two types of policy decision to take—on the structure of the national debt and on the liquidity of the monetary system. When the government has decided (as in Figures 24 and 27) on the fiscal controls G_1^{**}, G_2^{**}, t_w^{**}, t_q^{**}, H_w^{**} and H_q^{**}, the budget deficit will be given. The amount of new debt which it must incur will no longer be under its control. But it can still decide whether to issue bills or bonds to finance the debt. The government having decided how many bills and how many bonds in total should be issued, the banking authorities can then decide how many such bills and bonds they will purchase with newly issued money and on what terms they will issue new money in the form of new short-term loans to the private sector.

But, in a modern economy, these two sets of decisions are not taken separately. We shall assume that one co-ordinated set of decisions is taken by the controllers of the national debt and the banking authorities (which we will call in combination simply the financial authorities) which results in a decision as to how much money and how many government bills and bonds will be issued to the private sector and at what rate of interest bank loans will be offered to private citizens.

We shall therefore proceed as if there were one financial authority which determined the structure of the national debt and the amount of money issued against government debt and loans to the private sector. For this purpose it is convenient to consider a consolidated balance sheet of the government and of the banking system; this is done in Table V.

As far as the banks are concerned (Part I of Table V), they hold as assets part of the government issue of bills—namely $_bF_{sg}$ (item 3) —part of the government issue of bonds valued at their current price—namely $_bF_{lg}$ (item 4)—and the whole of the short term debt of private concerns—namely F_{sp} (Item 5). Against this, they have as a liability the amount of money issued to the private sector—namely M (item 1). Although all their assets have been acquired dollar for dollar by the issue of money, yet there are two reasons why, at any one point of time, the value of the bank's assets may differ from the amount of money issued by the banks. In the first place, the banks may have made a capital loss or a capital gain on any long-term securities which they hold. Thus if the long-term rate of interest (i_{lg}) goes up, the price of government bonds $(1/i_{lg})$ will go down. The banks will make a capital loss on any bonds which they have bought in the past at the old price and which they now hold at the lower valuation. Secondly, the banks will have received interest in the past on the various assets which they hold but they will not be paying any interest on the money which they have issued. If we neglect the expenses of running the banking system, they will be making a current profit on their operations which they can use to invest in new assets without issuing new money. There must, therefore, be a balancing item on the banks' balance sheet which we have called the 'net worth of the banks'—namely item (2) on Table V.

Table V

Consolidated Balance Sheet of the Government and of the Banks

I. *Balance Sheet of the Banks*

Liabilities	Assets
(1) M	(3) $_bF_{sg}$
	(4) $_bF_{lg}$
(2) Net Worth of Banks	(5) F_{sp}

II. *Balance Sheet of the Government*

Liabilities	Assets
(6) $_tF_{sg}$	(8) National Debt
(7) $_tF_{lg}$	

III. *Consolidated Balance Sheet of the Financial Authorities*

Liabilities	Assets
(9) M	(12) F_{sp}
(10) $_tF_{sg} - {_bF_{sg}} = F_{sg}$	(13) R = the National Debt—Net Worth of Banks = Net National Debt
(11) $_tF_{lg} - {_bF_{lg}} = F_{lg}$	

The government's balance sheet (Part II of Table V) is extremely simple. On the liabilities side is the current value of the total government bills and bonds which have been issued, which we denote as $_tF_{sg}$ (item 6) and $_tF_{lg}$ (item 7) respectively. Against this is the balancing item 8, namely the value of the national debt.

In Part III of Table V, the banks' and the government's balance sheets are consolidated so that only the net liabilities of the combined financial authorities to the private sector and the net assets (i.e. liabilities of the private sector to the combined financial authorities) are shown. These net liabilities are then the amount of money (M) issued to the private sector (item 9), the value of the net amount of government bills issued to the private sector—namely $_tF_{sg} - {_bF_{sg}}$ which we denote simply as F_{sg} (item 10)—and the current value of the net amount of government bonds issued to the private sector—namely $_tF_{lg} - {_bF_{lg}}$ which we denote simply as F_{lg} (item 11). The assets are simply the loans made to the private sector—namely F_{sp} (item 12). The balancing item, then, is the value of the total national debt less the net worth of the banking system which we will call the 'net national debt' (item 13) and denote by R.

We can now use this combined balance sheet of the financial authorities to consider the way in which a budget deficit may be financed. At the beginning of day $t + 1$ the financial authorities can raise funds (1) by increasing the supply of money from $M(t)$ to $M(t + 1)$; (2) by increasing the value of government bills outstanding from $F_{sg}(t)$ to $F_{sg}(t + 1)$; (3) by increasing the value of the bonds issued to the private sector by an amount $F_{lg}(t + 1) - F_{lg}(t)$; and (4) by reducing the amount lent to the private sector from $F_{sp}(t)$ to $F_{sp}(t + 1)$. The sum of these four items must be equal to the budget deficit which needs to be financed at the beginning of day $t + 1$. If we write $\Delta M = M(t + 1) - M(t)$ and similarly for the other terms, we express the relationship for the finance of the budget deficit (B) as:

$$B = \Delta M + \Delta F_{sg} + \Delta F_{lg} - \Delta F_{sp} \dots \dots \dots \dots (7.4)$$

Item 3 above can be split into two elements, thus:

$$F_{lg}(t + 1) - F_{lg}(t) =$$

$$\text{(i) } \{F_{lg}(t + 1)i_{lg}(t + 1) - F_{lg}(t)i_{lg}(t)\} \frac{1}{i_{lg}(t + 1)}$$

$$\text{(ii) } + F_{lg}(t)i_{lg}(t)\left\{\frac{1}{i_{lg}(t + 1)} - \frac{1}{i_{lg}(t)}\right\} \dots \dots \dots \dots (7.5)$$

Element (i) on the RHS of 7.5 is the increase in the number of bonds issued as between the beginning of day $t + 1$ and the beginning of day t (i.e. the number of new bonds issued at the beginning of day $t + 1$) multiplied by the price of a bond at the beginning of day $t + 1$. This element (i) measures, therefore, the amount of new money raised through new bond issues and available for the finance of other governmental expenditures. Element (ii) on the RHS of 7·5 is the increase between the beginning of day t and the beginning of day $t + 1$ in the value of the bonds already outstanding at the beginning of day t. This measures the capital gains made by the existing holders of government bonds. We have included such capital gains in the incomes of the private sector from property and in the gross interest on government debt (see Q, V, and line 47 in Figure 27). Since we have included these capital gains in the gross interest received by the owners of the national debt (V), we must define a gross budget deficit (B in equation 7.4) as including the capital appreciation on the outstanding government bonds. Element

(ii) of 7.5 is, therefore, an offsetting item in the accounts of the financial authorities. It represents both a way of raising money in so far as the private sector is willing to hold an increased value of government bonds, and, at the same time, it represents a need for additional finance to cover the increased 'liability' to the private sector represented by the increased value of the outstanding government bonds.

Thus interest plus capital gains payable at the beginning of day $t + 1$ on government bonds outstanding at the beginning of day t is

$$F_{lg}(t)i_{lg}(t) + F_{lg}(t)i_{lg}(t)\left\{\frac{1}{i_{lg}(t + 1)} - \frac{1}{i_{lg}(t)}\right\}$$

$$= F_{lg}(t)\left\{i_{lg}(t) + \frac{i_{lg}(t) - i_{lg}(t + 1)}{i_{lg}(t + 1)}\right\} = F_{lg}(t)\hat{\imath}_{lg}(t)$$

where $\hat{\imath}_{lg}(t)$ stands for the yield on government bonds including both interest and capital gains.[22]

We can now build the capital market in to our diagrams. This is done in two stages. In Figure 28 we add the lines which show the way in which the budget deficit is financed, and in Figure 29 we show the factors which will then determine the prices and yields of the various assets on the capital market.

(a) The Budget

The gross budget deficit or the increase in the value of the net national debt is made up of (i) government expenditure on goods and services; (ii) government payment of interest to the private sector plus any appreciation in the value of existing debt; (iii) government expenditure on transfer payments to wage earners and property owners; less (iv) tax payments to the government by wage earners and property owners.

The contribution of government expenditure on goods and services to the budget deficit is shown by lines 71, 72 and 73 in Figure 28.

Interest payments by the government to the private sector include interest on government bills ($i_{sg} F_{sg}$) plus the yield, i.e. interest and capital gains, on government bonds ($\hat{\imath}_{lg} F_{lg}$) minus interest payments by the private sector to the banks ($i_{sp} F_{sp}$), shown by the lines 74, 75, 76, 77, 78 and 79. Line 80 then shows the total effect of these interest payments (including the change in the capital value of outstanding bonds) on the gross budget deficit.

---

[22] If the long-term rate of interest falls by 1% of itself, then the price of bonds rises by 1%, giving a rate of capital gain of 1%.

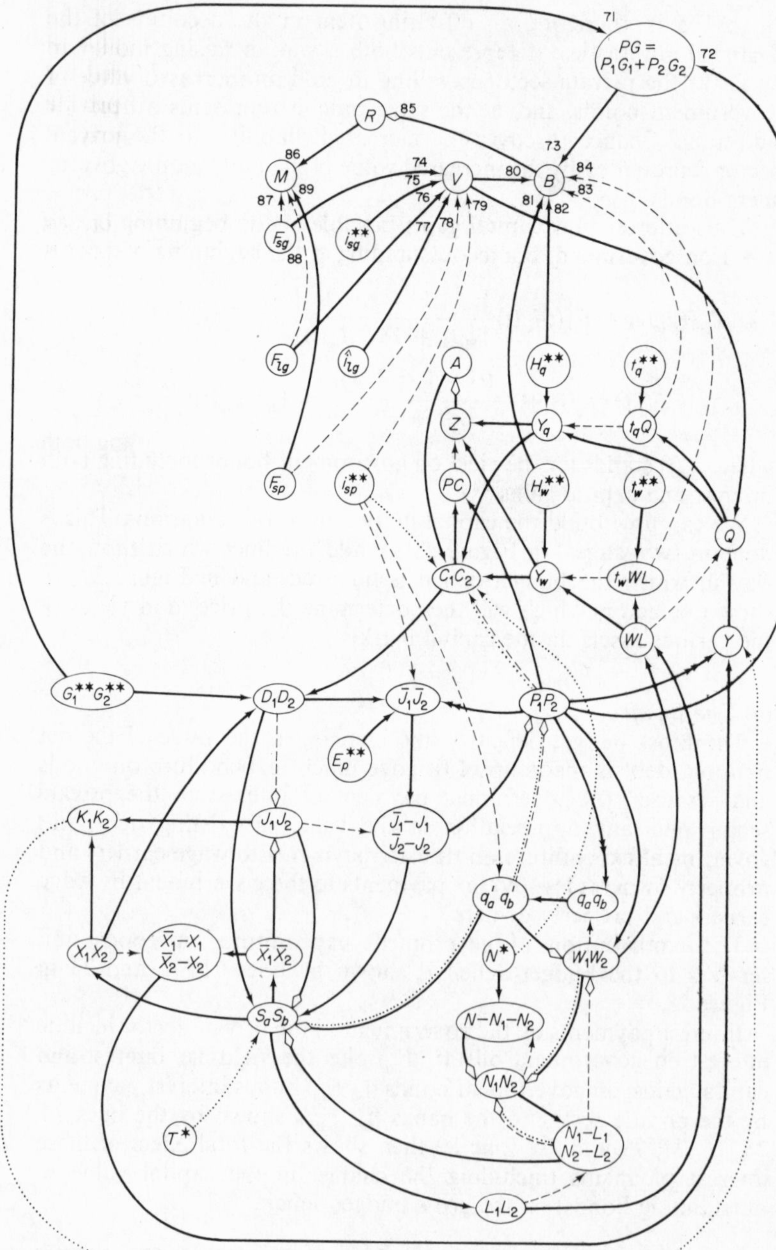
71
$PG = P_1G_1 + P_2G_2$
72
R
85
86
M
74
75
V
80
B
73
84
83
87
89
76
79
81
82
F_{sg}
i_{sg}^{**}
77
78
88
F_{lg}
$\hat{i}_{lg}$
A
H_q^{**}
t_q^{**}
Z
Y_q
t_qQ
F_{sp}
i_{sp}^{**}
PC
H_w^{**}
t_w^{**}
Q
C_1C_2
Y_w
t_wWL
WL
Y
$G_1^{**}G_2^{**}$
D_1D_2
$\bar{J}_1\bar{J}_2$
P_1P_2
E_p^{**}
K_1K_2
J_1J_2
$\bar{J}_1 - J_1$
$\bar{J}_2 - J_2$
$q_a'q_b'$
q_aq_b
X_1X_2
$\bar{X}_1 - X_1$
$\bar{X}_2 - X_2$
$\bar{X}_1\bar{X}_2$
N^*
W_1W_2
S_aS_b
$N - N_1 - N_2$
N_1N_2
T^*
$N_1 - L_1$
$N_2 - L_2$
L_1L_2

Figure 28

Lines 81 and 82 then show the effect of transfer payments on the budget deficit, while lines 83 and 84 show how tax revenue reduces the budget deficit.

R denotes the value of the total net national debt of the public sector to the private sector, so that line 85 simply states the identity that the gross budget deficit is the increase in the value of the total net national debt.

From section III of Table V, we know that

$$M = F_{sp} + R - F_{sg} - F_{lg} \dots\dots\dots\dots\dots\dots\dots\dots\dots (7.6)$$

and this relationship is expressed by lines 86, 87, 88 and 89 of Figure 28.

(b) The Capital Market

We can now complete our picture by considering the factors which determine the values and yields of the various assets. For this purpose, we first introduce into Figure 29 the remaining form of assets which we include in our model, namely the total value of all real assets, A_r. Now $A_r = K_1 P_1 + K_2 P_2$, i.e. the amount of each real asset multiplied by its market price, and this is shown by lines 90 and 91. The expected yield on these real assets we denote as $\hat{i}_{lp}$. This in turn depends upon the expected future profits, including capital gains,[23] to be made in the processes in which the durable assets will be used and upon the current cost price of those assets. The higher is the expected future profitability of the relevant processes of production and the lower is the current price of the durable asset, the higher is the expected yield on current investment of property in that asset.

Now the expected future profitability of the relevant processes of production will probably be higher, the higher and the more rapidly rising are the present profitability of those processes, and this is shown by the positive proportional and derivative effect of line 92. But there are a great number of exogenous events which will affect businessmen's optimism or pessimism about future profitabilities and these we have denoted by E_q^* and the line 93. The line 94 completes the determination of $\hat{i}_{lp}$ by stating that, giving the expected future profitabilities, the yield of the asset will be higher the lower is its present cost price.

The yield on government bonds $(\hat{i}_{lg})$ depends upon (i) the rate of interest on these bonds (i_{lg}) and (ii) the rate of capital gains on the bonds which, as we have seen, is equal to the proportional rate of fall in the long-term rate of interest. Line 95 shows the positive

---

[23] The profit margins, q_a and q_b, are already defined as inclusive of any capital gains on the capital goods employed. See equation 7.1.

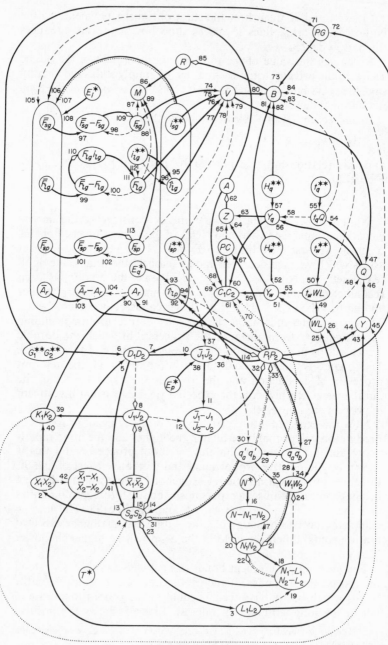

Figure 29

proportional effect (i) and line 96 the negative derivative effect (ii) of the rate of interest (i_{lg}) on the yield ($\hat{i}_{lg}$).

We now have a column of the values of the various assets owned or owed by the private citizens (M, F_{sg}, F_{lg}, F_{sp} and A_r) and a column of the rates of interest or expected yields on these assets (i_{sg}, $\hat{i}_{lg}$, i_{sp} and $\hat{i}_{lp}$). The basic problem of the capital market is to consider whether citizens would want to hold this particular portfolio of assets, given these yields, and what happens if the market is out of equilibrium in the sense that they would prefer another portfolio of assets and decide to exchange one type of asset for another.

We proceed (top left of Figure 29) by denoting by $\bar{F}_{sg}$, $\bar{F}_{lg}$, $\bar{F}_{sp}$, and $\bar{A}_r$ the values of their property which they would like to hold in these forms of asset in the given market conditions.[24] We can then introduce a series of terms showing the degree of disequilibrium in each asset market, i.e. the excess of the desired over the actual amount of property held in each form. This is done by means of lines 97, 98, 99, 100, 101, 102, 103 and 104. We have then first to consider what determines the values of the desired portfolio of assets and then what investors do to correct any discrepancy between the desired and the actual composition of their portfolio of investments.

As to the determination of the desired composition of their portfolio, this is shown in lines 105, 106, 107 and 108. Line 106 simply suggests that the higher is the total value of the property to be invested (A), the greater, other things being equal, will be the amount which it is desired to hold invested in each form of property. Line 105 expresses the need to hold money as a liquid means of payment. If Y, the net national income, is taken as a good index of the total of money transactions in the economy, then line 105 states that the higher is the volume of such transactions, the greater is the amount of money which people will desire to hold and the less, therefore, the part of their property which they will choose to hold in the non-monetary assets, namely $F_{sg} + F_{lg} - F_{sp} + A_r$.

But there is no rigid relationship between the amount of money which must be held and the volume of transactions to be financed,

[24] Private citizens have a given value of property, namely A, to invest. If they would like to invest $\bar{F}_{sg} + \bar{F}_{lg} - \bar{F}_{sp} + \bar{A}_r$ in a non-monetary form, then the difference between these two totals must be equal to the amount which they would wish to hold in the form of money. In other words, $\bar{M} = A - \bar{F}_{sg} - \bar{F}_{lg} + \bar{F}_{sp} - \bar{A}_r$. We show in Note B at the end of this chapter that $M = A - F_{sg} - F_{lg} + F_{sp} - A_r$. It follows that, by bringing their actual holdings of F_{sg}, F_{lg}, F_{sp} and A_r into equilibrium, they will necessarily bring their monetary holdings into equilibrium. We need consider only the disequilibrium in the markets for four out of our five assets; the budget constraint that the total invested in all five assets must equal A will then look after the equilibrium in the fifth market.

and the solid component of line 107 suggests that the higher are the yields on non-monetary assets, the more will people be persuaded to choose the non-monetary assets rather than money. Line 105 and the solid component of 107 thus express the familiar relationship that the demand for money will be greater, (i) the greater the volume of transactions to be financed and (ii) the lower are the yields on non-monetary assets.

The dotted component of line 107, together with line 108, is intended to allow for the very important and manifold relationships between the demand for different forms of non-monetary asset and the relative yields on these various assets. The first general principle is straightforward: the higher is the yield on one asset relatively to that on another, the more attractive will the former asset be for the investor relatively to the latter asset. Thus if i_{sg} goes up, government bills become more attractive and this might be expected to raise $\bar{F}_{sg}$ and $\bar{F}_{sp}$ and to lower somewhat $\bar{F}_{lg}$ and $\bar{A}_r$. This explains the dotted line component of line 107: a rise in the yield on a particular form of asset is likely to raise the demand for that asset but to reduce the demand for other assets or increase the supply of other liabilities.

There are, however, some rather special relationships between the yields on certain assets. One of these is the relationship between short-term and long-term pure rates of interest (i_{sg} and i_{lg}) which has been discussed at length in pages 314–8 of *The Growing Economy*. In equilibrium, the long-term rate must be an amalgam of future expected short-term rates. If short-term rates are expected to fall, then the long-term rate should be lower than the short-term rate; and vice versa. Expectations of future levels of interest rates depend upon all sorts of exogenous factors (which we depict by E_i^* and line 108). But these expectations are not held with certainty and we can say that investors will want to hold a higher ratio of $\bar{F}_{sg}$ to $\bar{F}_{lg}$ (i) the higher is the short-term rate relatively to the long-term rate and (ii) the greater are the expectations that the short-term rate will rise in the future.

Finally, we must ask how people react to disequilibrium in their holdings of assets. As far as government bills and bonds are concerned, we can say that, at the given interest rates, people will increase their holdings at a rate which depends upon the existing deficiency of their actual below their desired holdings and this is shown by the two positive integral lines 109 and 110. Then, with the number of bonds outstanding determined in this way (F_{lg} i_{lg}) and with the bond rate of interest given (i_{lg}^{**}), we will have the value of bonds (F_{lg}) determined and this is shown by the two lines 111 and 112.

A similar mechanism can be assumed to be at work for private borrowing from the banking system. The amount of private bills sold to the banks will rise at a rate dependent upon the deficiency of the existing borrowing below the desired borrowing (line 113).

As far as real assets are concerned, the greater is the excess demand for the given physical amounts (K_1, K_2), the more quickly will their prices be bid up by investors and this is shown by line 114.

This last relationship is of crucial importance. Its importance, and indeed the whole mechanism of the capital market, may be illustrated by means of a particular example. Suppose that the government decides to fund some short-term debt, and in order to tempt the private sector to switch from bills to bonds reduces i_{sg}^{**} and raises i_{lg}^{**}. At the new level of i_{lg} there will be a rise in $\hat{i}_{lg}$ (line 95). This rise in $\hat{i}_{lg}$ will make A_r less attractive relatively to F_{lg} and will thus reduce $\bar{A}_r$ (dotted line component of 107). This causes an excess supply of A_r (line 103). This causes a fall in the price of durable assets (line 114). This makes the production of such durable assets less profitable (line 27). Thus we have shown how a funding of government debt by causing a rise in long-term interest rates could lead to a reduced incentive to invest in durable capital equipment.

This completes our description of the financial markets in our model of the economy. One or two comments may be useful.

We have depicted monetary policy as taking the form of the financial authorities setting, from time to time, rates of interest (l_{sg}^{**}, l_{lg}^{**} and l_{sp}^{**}) at which they are prepared to deal in unlimited amounts in the securities concerned. An alternative form of monetary policy would be for the financial authorities to determine the amounts of the government assets which they would issue—namely F_{sg}^{**} and $(F_{lg}\ i_{lg})^{**}$—and the amount of private assets which they would hold—namely F_{sp}^{**}—and then to let the corresponding rates of interest be determined by market forces. In this case, we could assume that the rates of interest on government bills and bonds would fall the more quickly, the greater were the deficiency of the actual below the desired holdings of these securities by the private sector, and that the rate of interest on private bills would rise the more quickly, the greater were the deficiency of actual below desired private borrowings. In this case lines 109, 110 and 113 of Figure 29 would have to be deleted and replaced by lines 109′, 110′, and 113′ of Figure 30a.

But whichever form monetary policy might take, we have in Figure 29 depicted the supply of M as a residual item. Once the government has decided upon its fiscal controls (G_1^{**}, G_2^{**}, t_w^{**}, t_q^{**}, H_w^{**} and H_q^{**}) the budget deficit will be determined. And once it has decided upon the amount of the other assets which it will issue or hold (F_{sg}^{**}, $[F_{lg}\ i_{lg}]^{**}$ and F_{sp}^{**}) or alternatively once it has

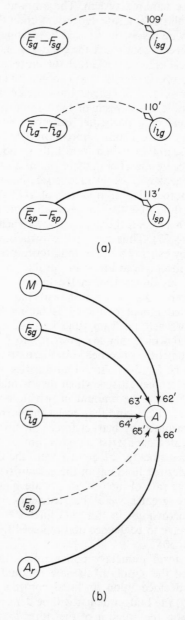

(a)

(b)

Figure 30

fixed upon the terms on which it will issue or hold these assets in amounts then to be decided by the private sector (l_{sg}^{**}, l_{lg}^{**} and l_{sp}^{**}), the funds which it can raise by means other than the issue of new money will be determined. The inevitable result is that the supply of money (M) is treated as a residual item. We have also expressed the demand for various assets by the private sector in such a way that the demand for money is treated as the residual item, i.e. as the form in which they hold that part of their total assets which they do not hold in other non-monetary forms. Let it be once more emphasized that this does not imply that the authorities are necessarily indifferent to the level of the supply of money. They may alter F_{sg}^{**}, $(F_{lg}\ i_{lg})^{**}$ and F_{sp}^{**} in order to affect M,—e.g. sell government securities on the open market or call in loans to the private sector in order to reduce M. Alternatively, they can alter l_{sg}^{**}, l_{lg}^{**} or l_{sp}^{**} in order to induce the private sector to demand more or less money. Nor does it imply that the private sector is indifferent to the amount of money which they are holding. They may decide to reduce $\bar{F}_{sg}$, $\bar{F}_{lg}$ or $\bar{A}$ or to increase $\bar{F}_{sp}$, because they want to hold more money. This treatment of M as the residual item in both the supply and the demand functions for assets is shown in Figure 29 by the fact that while there are four arrowed lines (86, 87, 88 and 89) leading into the circle enclosing M, there are no arrowed lines leading from M to other variables. M is an effect and not a cause.

It follows that if we had no interest in the levels of M, R, B, or PG in and for themselves, we could in fact eliminate these four variables and the thirteen lines 71, 72, 73, 80, 81, 82, 83, 84, 85, 86, 87, 88 and 89 from Figure 29 without in any way impairing the complete picture of the causal interrelationships in the economy. If the fiscal controls (G_1^{**}, G_2^{**}, t_w^{**}, t_q^{**}, H_w^{**} and H_q^{**}) and the financial controls (i_{sg}^{**}, i_{lg}^{**} and i_{sp}^{**}) are given, then the calculation of the budget deficit and of the amount of finance to be raised in other ways simply determines how much money must be issued. We could in fact dispense with the whole of section 6(a) of this chapter, since the actual display of the budget deficit is needed only to calculate the supply of money. The sizes of the budget deficit, of the national debt, and of the supply of money need not be displayed explicitly in order to understand the causal relations in the rest of the economy; they are, of course, implied in the workings of the rest of the economy.

The way in which they are implied by the rest of the economic relationships is discussed in Note B at the end of this chapter. In that Note it is shown that A measured as the accumulation of past savings (i.e. through lines 62, 63, 64, 65, 66 and 67) is identically equal to A measured as the sum of the various assets held by the private sector (i.e. as the sum $M + F_{sg} + F_{lg} - F_{sp} + A_r$). If we

were not interested in what happened to Z or PC, we could, therefore, maintain M, R, B and PG and the thirteen lines 71, 72, 73, 80,
81, 82, 83, 84, 85, 86, 87, 88 and 89, but instead delete Z and PC and
lines 62, 63, 64, 65, 66 and 67 from Figure 29. In their place we
would have to insert the lines $62'$, $63'$, $64'$, $65'$, and $66'$ as in Figure
30b. This would show A as the sum of the various types of asset
whose supply was determined by the finance of the budget deficit,
by monetary policy and by investment in real assets, instead of as
the result of the accumulation of past savings. As is shown in
Note B, the one type of measurement implies the other. We could
fully explain the development of the economy in either way.

(7) THE COMPLETE MODEL

Figure 29 incorporated the money and capital markets into the
rest of the model already constructed in Figure 28 and we thus
obtained a complete picture of the dynamic relationships in our
much simplified model. The reader may now amuse himself by
making any number of feedback tours of the economy. All he has
to do is to start at any point and follow the arrows along any lines,
wandering about until he returns to his starting point. He will then
have obtained a particular self-contained theory about the dynamic
factors affecting growth, fluctuations and stability in the economy.
Some of the theories which he can thus construct will be more
convincing than others but none of them will have involved in-
conceivable or, indeed, very improbable relationships. In so far as
the many influences which we have described in the various sectors
of the economy in the previous parts of this chapter are all in fact
at work to a greater or lesser extent, all the particular theories will
be correct but each one will represent only a partial aspect of
reality. The way in which the system will in fact react will depend
upon the simultaneous interaction of all these influences, the
outcome depending above all upon the relative magnitudes and the
relative time lags of each reaction.

The most obvious moral to be drawn from this is that it is not
possible to obtain by *a priori* reasoning any single simple explanation of the dynamic behaviour of a modern economy. Empirical
econometric work is essential in order to determine which influences
work most powerfully and most quickly and in order thus to decide
which influences can be neglected in any simplification of the
complete model. *A priori* reasoning of the kind in which we have
indulged in this chapter has its purpose in suggesting the sort of
hypotheses which it is worthwhile testing.

It may be of some interest to close this chapter by taking one or two strolls around the economy. In each case we will start from the level of demand, $(D_1, D_2,$ etc.) assuming that it has been affected by some exogenously given factor such as an increase in government demand (G_1^{**}, G_2^{**}).

The path 13-3-26-51-59-7 brings us back to D. This is a simple multiplier relationship. The increased demand for products makes people produce more which increases the demand for labour which increases the wage bill which increases the workers' demands for consumption goods.

The path 13-2-5 brings us back to D. This is an accelerator effect[25]; the increased demand has led to increased production which has led to an increased demand for machinery, raw materials, etc.

These expansionary effects of the initial increase in demand on production could be reached by other routes such as (i) 10-11-14; (ii) 8-12-14; and (iii) 10-11 (or 8-12)-32-36-11-32-36-11-32-27-29-31; where (i) expresses the fact that the higher level of demand may make people want to hold larger stocks, the ordering of which leads to increased production; (ii) expresses the fact that the higher level of demand causes a reduction of actual stocks the replacement of which leads to increased production; and (iii) expresses the fact that the increased demand causes a rise in selling prices (exaggerated by a speculative demand in anticipation of continuing price rises) which makes production more profitable, which encourages expansion. This expansion can then lead back onto D by the multiplier (3-26-51-59-7) or the accelerator (2-5) which we have already discussed.

There are many other possible repercussions of quite different kinds. Thus

$$\begin{Bmatrix} 10\text{-}11 \\ 8\text{-}12 \end{Bmatrix}\text{-}32\text{-}44 \text{ (derivative element)-}46\text{-}56\text{-}60\text{-}7$$

shows the effect of increased demand causing a price rise which causes capital gains which increases the demand for consumption goods by property owners. Or, if we assumed the sort of monetary policy depicted in Figure 30a,

$$13\text{-}\begin{Bmatrix} 1\text{-}41 \\ 2\text{-}42 \end{Bmatrix}\text{-}43\text{-}105\text{-}\begin{Bmatrix} 97\text{-}109' \\ 99\text{-}110'\text{-}95 \end{Bmatrix}\text{-}107\text{-}103\text{-}114\text{-}27\text{-}29\text{-}31\text{-}2\text{-}5$$

expresses the possibility that the increased demand causes an increase in net output and so in the volume of transactions which,

---

[25] The reader is referred to Note A at the end of this chapter for a discussion of the way in which the accelerator is expressed in our model in which D includes the gross demand for all capital goods.

by increasing the demand for money and decreasing the demand for non-monetary assets, causes interest rates to go up, which reduces the demand for durable assets, which makes the production of such goods less profitable, which reduces the demand for the intermediate products to produce these goods.

Alternatively, though

$$\begin{Bmatrix} 10\text{-}11 \\ 8\text{-}12 \end{Bmatrix}\text{-}32\text{-}44 \text{ (proportional element)-}105\text{-}\begin{Bmatrix} 97\text{-}109' \\ 99\text{-}110'\text{-}95 \end{Bmatrix}\text{-}107\text{-}103$$
$$-114\text{-}27\text{-}29\text{-}31\text{-}2\text{-}5.$$

this same effect of a rising rate of interest due to an increased demand for money is brought about by the price rises due to the initial increase in the demand for goods, so that the value of transactions is increased, which also means that larger cash balances will be wanted.

Many further repercussions could occur through the effects of the increased demand for labour on the wage rate (13-3-19-24). This might make industry less profitable if the wage rate rose more quickly than prices' (i.e. if 13-3-19-24-28 outweighed $\begin{Bmatrix} 10\text{-}11 \\ 8\text{-}12 \end{Bmatrix}$ -32-27), so that the expansion was damped down through 29-31. Alternatively, through 25-$\begin{Bmatrix} 51\text{-}59 \\ 48\text{-}56\text{-}60 \end{Bmatrix}$-7, if wage rates rose more quickly than profits, the consequential shift from profits to wages might cause an increased demand for consumption goods, and this expansionary effect might outweigh the contractionary effect of lower profit margins on productive processes.

But enough is enough. The reader can be left to spend many pleasant hours illustrating his own pet theories by choosing carefully his route around Figure 29. Exercises of this kind will, it is hoped, give him a feel of the sort of repercussions which may occur in the actual world in which he lives.

Note A to Chapter VII

THE EXPRESSION OF THE INVESTMENT ACCELERATOR
IN FIGURES 23 AND 24

In equation 5.22 above the investment accelerator was represented as a relationship between the net demand for additional capital equipment (I_v) and the rate of rise in the net demand for all goods and services (D'). In equation 5.22 the amount spent on investment on day t—namely $I_v(t)$—was designed to install machinery to catch up with the recent increase in the demand for the products of machinery—namely $D'(t-1) - D'(t-2)$. But with perfect foresight producers would install equipment today to meet tomorrow's demand for the output of the machinery. In this case, if v represented the amount of capital equipment required (with the techniques at present in use) to produce one unit of net output, $v\{D'(t+1) - D'(t)\}$ would represent the amount of additional capital equipment which must be installed during day t (namely $I_v(t)$) in order to produce the additional output on day $t+1$. If total demand was made up of an exogenous demand (I_c^*), consumption (C), and productive investment (I_v), then in conditions of perfect foresight we would have:

$$D'(t) = I_c^*(t) + C(t) + v\{D'(t+1) - D'(t)\} \dots\dots\dots\dots (7.7)$$

Part of the level of demand is thus to be ascribed to the rate of increase in demand. This is the essence of the accelerator.

How does this appear in Figures 23 and 24? In order to bring out the most elementary relationship, let us interpret Figures 23 and 24 as if there were only one product which was used as an intermediate product (an input X) as well as for government consumption (G^{**}), for private consumption (C), and for holding in a spare capacity stock (J).

From lines 1 and 2 of Figure 23 we can derive the productive relationship:

$$X(t) = \mu\{\overline{X}(t) - X(t)\}$$

or $\quad X(t) = \{\mu/(1 + \mu)\}\overline{X}(t) \dots\dots\dots\dots\dots\dots\dots\dots (7.8)$

where μ represents the ratio of capital equipment used—$X(t)$—to the net output produced—$\overline{X}(t) - X(t)$—on the basis of the existing techniques, i.e. of the process of production at present selected for use.

From lines 5, 6 and 7 of Figure 24 we have the definition of gross demand:

$$D(t) = G^{**}(t) + C(t) + X(t) \dots\dots\dots\dots\dots\dots\dots\dots (7.9)$$

From lines 8 and 9 we have the definition of idle spare capacity stocks, namely:

$$J(t+1) = J(t) + \overline{X}(t) - D(t+1) \dots\dots\dots\dots\dots (7.10)$$

since the idle stocks of day $t+1$ are those taken over from day t plus what is added to them by the output which appears at the end of day t minus the amount which is required to satisfy the gross demand at the beginning of day $t+1$.

Finally, let us assume that line 10 of Figure 24 takes the form:

$$\overline{J}(t) = \lambda D(t) \dots\dots\dots\dots\dots\dots\dots\dots\dots\dots\dots\dots (7.11)$$

namely that producers and traders would like to hold an idle spare capacity stock equal to a constant proportion of the total daily gross demand for the product. From 7.8 and 7.9 we obtain:

$$D(t) = (1 + \mu)\{G^{**}(t) + C(t)\} + \mu\{\overline{X}(t) - D(t)\}$$

which from 7.10 becomes:

$$D(t) = (1 + \mu)\{G^{**}(t) + C(t)\} + \mu\{D(t + 1) - D(t) + J(t + 1) - J(t)\}$$

and from 7.11 becomes:

$$D(t) = (1 + \mu)\{G^{**}(t) + C(t)\} + \mu(1 + \lambda)\{D(t + 1) - D(t)\} - \mu\{[\bar{J}(t + 1) - J(t + 1)] - [\bar{J}(t) - J(t)]\} \ldots\ldots\ldots (7.12)$$

Now we may write

$$D(t) = (1 + \mu)D'(t) \ldots\ldots\ldots\ldots\ldots\ldots\ldots\ldots\ldots\ldots\ldots (7.13)$$

where $D(t)$ is gross demand and $D'(t)$ net demand, since gross demand is made up of net demand plus the amount of capital needed to produce the net output required to satisfy that net demand.

From 7.12 and 7.13 we obtain

$$D'(t) = G^{**}(t) + C(t) + \mu(1 + \lambda)\{D'(t + 1) - D'(t)\} - \{\mu/(1 + \mu)\}\{[\bar{J}(t + 1) - J(t + 1)] - [\bar{J}(t) - J(t)]\} \ldots (7.14)$$

Equation 7.14 is the accelerator equation in the form given in equation 7.7, provided that with perfect foresight output is successfully adjusted so that stocks are in fact kept at their desired level, i.e. $\bar{J}(t + 1) = J(t + 1)$ and $\bar{J}(t) = J(t)$. μ in equation 7.14 is the same as v in equation 7.7, namely the ratio of capital to net output in the productive process; and the factor $(1 + \lambda)$ which appears in 7.14 but not in 7.7 allows for the fact that in the former, but not in the latter case, demands for government consumption, for private consumption and for production purposes are supplemented by a demand for idle stocks.

The accelerator relationship in 7.14 is complicated by the stock adjustment factor; and the dynamic properties of the system (e.g. whether it is stable or not) will depend, in ways such as those discussed in Chapter V, upon many factors including the manner in which output is in fact changed as a result of divergences between the desired and the actual levels of idle stocks (line 14 of Figure 24).

Note B to Chapter VII

THE EQUALITY BETWEEN SAVINGS AND INVESTMENT

In Figures 27 and 30 we have derived the value of the total property owned by private citizens in two apparently independent ways. In Figure 27 in lines 62, 63, 64 and 65 we have shown A as the result of the accumulation of past savings (including capital gains). In Figure 30 we referred to the fact that the total property owned by individuals must be equal to the sum of the various kinds of property which they hold, namely $M + F_{sg} + F_{lg} - F_{sp} + A_r$. But these items seem to be determined in quite different ways: M by the residual supply of money needed to finance the budget deficit and A_r by the level of K and P, for example. Is there any reason to believe that these two ways of measuring A will lead to the same result?

In fact, they are merely different ways of expressing the same identity relationships. This can be seen in the following way.

If we start with the method shown on Figure 27, we may write:

$$A(t + 1) - A(t) = Y_w(t + 1) + Y_q(t + 1) - PC(t + 1) \quad ..(7.15)$$

or the increase in the value of private property owned between the beginnings of days t and $t + 1$ is equal to the disposable incomes earned in respect of the operations of day t, available to be spent at the beginning of day $t + 1$ less the amount which is so spent.

From lines 49, 50, 51, 52, 53, 54, 55, 56, 57 and 58 of Figure 27, (reproduced in Figure 29), we have

$$Y_w(t + 1) = WL(t)(1 - t_w) + H_w(t + 1)$$

and

$$Y_q(t + 1) = Q(t + 1)(1 - t_q) + H_q(t + 1) \dots\dots\dots\dots (7.16)$$

or disposable income earned during day t and realized at the beginning of day $t + 1$ is income earned during day t less the tax liable on it (and paid to the government at the beginning of day $t + 1$) plus the transfer payments received from the government at the beginning of day $t + 1$.

But from lines 46, 47 and 48:

$$Q(t + 1) = Y(t + 1) - WL(t) + V(t + 1) \dots\dots\dots\dots (7.17)$$

or property incomes accruing in the course of day t are total net income produced during day t (including capital gains) less wages payable in respect of work done during day t plus interest (including capital gains) on government bonds accruing to property owners in the course of day t.[26]

Using 7.16 and 7.17 in 7.15 we obtain:

$$A(t + 1) - A(t) = V(t + 1) + H_w(t + 1) + H_q(t + 1)$$
$$-t_w WL(t) - t_q Q(t + 1) + Y(t + 1) - PC(t + 1) \quad \ldots (7.19)$$

But from 7.3 (see lines 39, 40, 41, 42, 43, 44 and 45 of Figure 29):

$$Y(t + 1) = \{\overline{X}(t) + J_1(t)\} P_1(t + 1) + \{\overline{X}_2(t) + J_2(t)\} P_2(t + 1)$$
$$- \{X(t) + J_1(t)\} P_1(t) - \{X_2(t) + J_2(t)\} P_2(t) \quad \ldots (7.20)$$

Furthermore, we also have (lines 5, 6, 7, 8 and 9 of Figure 29):

$$\overline{X}_1(t) = C_1(t + 1) + G_1(t + 1) + X_1(t + 1) + J_1(t + 1)$$
$$- J_1(t)$$

and

$$\overline{X}_2(t) = C_2(t + 1) + G_2(t + 1) + X_2(t + 1) + J_2(t + 1)$$
$$- J_2(t) \ldots\ldots\ldots\ldots\ldots\ldots\ldots\ldots\ldots\ldots\ldots\ldots (7.21)$$

since the gross outputs of day t are available at the beginning of day $t + 1$ to be consumed by private individuals, purchased by the government, ploughed back into industry, or added to idle stocks. Also (lines 66 and 67):

$$PC(t + 1) = P_1(t + 1)C_1(t + 1) + P_2(t + 1)C_2(t + 1) \ . (7.22)$$

From 7.19, 7.20, 7.21 and 7.22 we obtain:

$$A(t + 1) - A(t) = B(t + 1) + A_r(t + 1) - A_r(t) \ldots\ldots\ldots (7.23)$$

where

$$B(t + 1) =$$

$$V(t + 1) + H_w(t + 1) + H_q(t + 1) + P_1(t + 1)G_1(t + 1)$$
$$+ P_2(t + 1)G_2(t + 1) - t_w WL(t) - t_q Q(t + 1)$$

and

$$A_r(t + 1) = P_1(t + 1)\{X_1(t + 1) + J_1(t + 1)\}$$
$$+ P_2(t + 1)\{X_2(t + 1) + J_2(t + 1)\}.$$

[26] The wage rate and the level of employment relevant to the operations of day t are both fixed at the beginning of day t and result in $WL(t)$. The income and profits accruing from the operations of day t are realized only when the product is sold at the beginning of day $t + 1$ and result in $Y(t + 1)$ and $Q(t + 1)$. The net interest payable on government bills and bonds in respect of day t is fixed at the beginning of day t, but the gross interest includes capital appreciation on bonds held during day t and is realized only when the price of bonds is determined at the beginning of day $t + 1$, so that such gross interest is expressed by $V(t + 1)$.

This last equation expresses the identity equality between savings and investment, since we start in 7.15 with $A(t + 1) - A(t)$, defined as the gross savings of individuals (including capital gains), and we now find in 7.23 that it is equal to the gross budget deficit (including the capital appreciation of government stocks) plus gross investment (including the capital appreciation of real assets). By deducting capital gains from both sides of the equation this relationship can readily be translated into the equality between net savings and the net budget deficit plus the value of net real investment.

If we now turn to the alternative method of calculating A, from equation 7.6 we obtain:

$$\{M(t + 1) - F_{sp}(t + 1) + F_{sg}(t + 1) + F_{lg}(t + 1)\}$$
$$- \{M(t) \quad - F_{sp}(t) \quad + F_{sg}(t) \quad + F_{lg}(t)\}$$
$$= R(t + 1) - R(t) = B(t + 1), \quad \dots\dots\dots\dots\dots (7.24)$$

since $R(t + 1) - R(t)$ is the increase in the national debt between the beginning of day t and day $t + 1$ and is, therefore, equal to $B(t + 1)$, the gross budget deficit needing to be financed at the beginning of day $t + 1$. But, eliminating $B(t + 1)$ from 7.23 and 7.24 we obtain:

$$A(t + 1) - A(t) =$$
$$\{M(t + 1) - F_{sp}(t + 1) + F_{sg}(t + 1) + F_{lg}(t + 1) + A_r(t + 1)$$
$$-\{M(t) \quad - F_{sp}(t) \quad + F_{sg}(t) \quad + F_{lg}(t) \quad + A_r(t)\}$$

Since this equation must have been satisfied from the beginning of time, we have:

$$A = M + F_{sg} + F_{lg} - F_{sp} + A_r \quad \dots\dots\dots\dots\dots (7.25)$$

The two ways of estimating A, by the accumulation of savings or by the summation of different forms of asset, are in fact identical. We started with A being accumulated out of savings (equation 7.15) and we showed that this accumulation was equal to investment plus the budget deficit (equation 7.23); we have now shown that the total so accumulated is the same as the sum of the various assets which are available on the market to be held.

CHAPTER VIII

A SIMPLIFIED ONE-PRODUCT MODEL

It would be illuminating if we could express Figure 29 in the form used in Figures 12, 15, 17 and 20 in Chapter V, that is to say, in a way which would enable one to visualize the various interrelationships as they operate through time. Unfortunately the complete model in Figure 29 is much too complicated to be usefully treated in this way. In this chapter we will greatly simplify the model shown in Figure 29. This we will do for two reasons. First, it will enable us to show it in the alternative form which brings out the movement of the variables through time. Secondly, it will enable us to show the simplest dynamic form of the one-product economic model presented in Part I of *The Growing Economy*.

The simplifications which we make to the model in Figure 29 are as follows.

(1) We assume that there is only one output, $\overline{X}$. This product has four uses: (i) it can be consumed by consumers, C; (ii) it can be used for governmental purposes, G; (iii) it can be used as an input, X, like seed corn, to help in the production of a further output; or (iv) it can be carried in an idle stock, J.

(2) There is only one form of labour, L. Different processes of production a, b, c, etc., consist solely in different ways of using X and L to produce $\overline{X}$, the differences being due either to differences in the labour and capital intensities of the techniques or differences between outmoded inefficient, and newly invented efficient, processes.

(3) There are thus only two prices in the market, the prices of the product, P, and the wage rate of labour, W. Both the product market and the labour market have the same type of dynamic quality. Movements of the product price are determined solely by the demand—supply tension in the product market, and this is measured by the excess of desired over actual idle stocks $(\overline{J} - J)$. Movements in the wage rate are determined solely by the demand—supply tension in the labour market, and this is measured by the amount of unemployment, i.e. by the excess of the available manpower over the volume of employment $(N - L)$.

(4) The scale, S, at which each process of production is carried

out is influenced solely by its profitability, q', any process being expanded the more rapidly, the higher is its profitability.

(5) We live in a Propdem so that every citizen is a representative wage earner and a representative property owner with the result that the distribution of income between wages and profits does not affect the distribution of income between persons.

(6) The amount of output being purchased for current consumption is determined solely by the level of total spendable money incomes and the price of the good available for consumption. In other words, consumers plan to spend a fixed proportion of their money incomes on consumption, so that the amount of consumption goods purchased is the higher (i) the higher is the total disposable money incomes and (ii) the lower is the price level of consumption goods, but is unaffected by the rate of interest, the amount of accumulated property, or the size of the population.

(7) There are only three forms of asset—money, one-day bills, and the real product. The monetary authority sets a rate of interest for money for one day, namely i^{**}, at which it will buy bills both from the government and from private citizens.

(8) The government purchases some supplies of the economy's product for governmental purposes, G^{**}, and it raises taxation (or subsidizes spendable incomes) simply by a system of lump sum poll taxes (or transfer payments), H^{**}, of the same absolute amount taken from (or paid to) each individual citizen.

This extremely simple economy is depicted in Figure 31. Lines 1 to 12 are exactly the same as lines 1 to 12 in Figure 29 with the sole exception that there is now only one product and only one form of labour, so that different processes of production a, b, c, etc., simply show different ways of combining inputs of labour and of the product to produce still more of the product.

Lines 13 and 14 define the volume of unemployment, i.e. the excess of the exogenously given available supply of manpower (N^*) over the volume of employment (L). Line 15 (the Phillips curve) then states that the money wage rate rises the more rapidly, the lower is the volume of unemployment.

Lines 16, 17, 18 and 19 define the profitability of various processes of production.

We are assuming that the selling price of the product is adjusted solely in line with the stock position, rising (or falling) the more rapidly, the greater is the deficiency (or the excess) of actual stocks as compared with desired stocks (line 16). But given P, W and i^{**}, the profitability of each process of production will be determined. Thus if $\overline{X}_a$, X_a and L_a are the output of the product, the input of the product, and the input of labour needed to operate process a on a unitary scale ($S_a = 1$), then:

$$q_a'(t + 1) = P(t + 1)\,\overline{X}_a - \{1 + i^{**}(t)\}\,P(t)\,X_a - W(t)\,L_a$$

expresses the net money profit realized by the sale at the beginning of day $t + 1$ of the output produced during day t. This profitability will be the greater, (i) the lower is W (line 17); (ii) the lower is i^{**} (line 19); and (iii) the higher and more quickly rising is P (line 18).

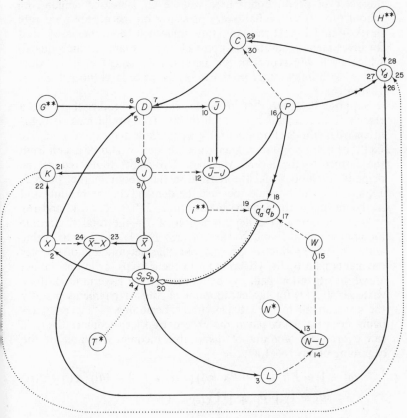

Figure 31

The unbroken component of line 20 then states that in general the greater is the profitability of any process of production, the more rapidly will its scale be expanded, while the dotted component of the line expresses the fact that a relative rise in the profitability of one process may attract resources from, and thus contract the scale of, alternative processes.

It is through this mechanism that, in our present very simple model, both the general inflationary/deflationary influences and also the relative shifts from one technique of production to another display themselves.

Thus suppose that for some reason or another (a reduction in i^{**} and/or a reduction in W and/or a rise in P) all processes become more profitable. Then (line 20) there will be a general expansion in the scale of production. There will be an increased demand for labour (line 3) with inflationary pressures on the money wage rate (lines 14 and 15). At the same time there will be an increased need for investment in additional inputs of intermediate products (line 2) which itself will represent an increased demand for the product (line 5) with inflationary pressures on the price level (lines 8, 10, 11, 12 and 16).

Suppose, however, that for some reason or another there was a rise in W accompanied by a fall in i^{**}. This would make labour-intensive methods of production less profitable and capital-intensive methods more profitable. Then (line 20) there would be a shift from the former to the latter processes. This shift would reduce the demand for labour and the tension in the labour market (lines 3, 14, and 15). But it would increase the demand for the product and so the tension in the product market (lines 2, 5, 8, 10, 11, 12 and 16).

We turn next to the determination of Y_d—the total disposable money income available to the citizens. This is equal to the value added in the productive process plus the net amount of transfer payments paid by the government to the citizens (or minus the net amount of taxation paid by the citizens to the government). If we write $H^{**}(t + 1)$ for the net amount of transfer payments paid by the government to the citizens at the beginning of day $t + 1$ (H being negative if tax payments exceed transfer incomes), then we can express the amount of disposable incomes available at the beginning of day $t + 1$ as:

$$Y_d(t + 1) = H(t + 1) + P(t + 1)\{\overline{X}(t) + J(t)\} - P(t)\{X(t) + J(t)\}$$
$$= H(t + 1) + P(t + 1)\{\overline{X}(t) - X(t)\}$$
$$+ K(t)\{P(t + 1) - P(t)\}$$

where $K(t) = X(t) + J(t)$. Apart from the element $H(t + 1)$ this expression is merely the one-product version of equation 7.3. It is clear that disposable income will be the higher (i) the higher is H (line 28); (ii) the higher is $\overline{X} - X$ (lines 23, 24, and 26); (iii) the higher is $P(t + 1)$ (the proportional component of line 27); (iv) the higher is $P(t + 1) - P(t)$ (the derivative component of line 27); and

(v) the higher is K, if $P(t + 1) - P(t) > 0$, and the lower is K, if $P(t + 1) - P(t) < 0$ (lines 21, 22, and 25).

We can then complete the figure depicting our very simple economic model with lines 29 and 30 which make the level of total consumption depend solely upon the level of the total real disposable income of the community.

It will be observed that, in this model, we have been able to assume away the whole of the budgetary and capital market relationships except for the three control variables H^{**}, G^{**} and i^{**}. The amount of money is automatically adjusted to whatever amounts the citizens desire to hold by the purchase or sale of bills for money by the banking authorities at the fixed rate of interest, i^{**}. Since consumption is not affected by the amount of property held by the citizens, we are not concerned with the level of A as in Figure 29. We are, of course, indirectly concerned with the amount of interest received by the citizens on any outstanding national debt (the level of V in Figure 29) since this will affect the level of disposable incomes (Y_d) and so consumption (C). But by assuming that all taxes are lump sum taxes we can subsume V in H; in other words, each day the government decides on a level of lump sum taxes which, after the payment of any contractual interest which it owes to citizens on the national debt, will leave them with a net transfer income (inclusive of interest on the national debt) of H. It is this net payment out of, or into, the budget which the government uses as its fiscal control. Since there is only one product, corn, which can be used for consumption or as an intermediate product, we are not concerned with the evaluation of the long-term prospects of profit on durable instruments of production. We are concerned only with the expectation of the rise or fall in the selling price of the product over the immediate future, which we have assumed to depend solely upon the current rate of rise or fall in the price level.

This model is translated into the alternative form in Figure 32 on the assumption that all time lags are of the simplest one-day-long form. If we consider the position on day 1 (the middle column of the figure), the scale of the various processes on day 1 will determine the inputs of labour and of product (lines 3 and 1) and the output of the product (line 2) on day 1. The demand for the product at the beginning of day 1 is the sum of the productive inputs needed at the beginning of day 1 plus the governmental and the private consumption demands at the beginning of day 1 (lines 5, 6 and 7). The level of the idle spare capacity stock carried during day 1 is the amount carried during day 0 (line marked 8b and 9b) plus the output produced at the end of day 0 (line 9a) minus the demand for the product at the beginning of day 1 (line 8a). The amount of idle

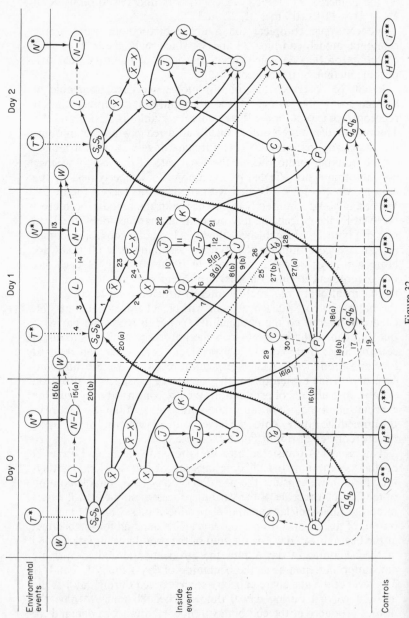

Figure 32

spare capacity stocks that producers and traders would like to have been left to carry during day 1 depends upon the level of demand at the beginning of day 1 (line 10), there being a possible discrepancy between the desired and the actual level of such stocks (lines 11 and 12). The price charged for the product at the beginning of day 1 will be the price already ruling for day 0 plus or minus an adjustment depending upon the deficiency or excess of the stocks carried during day 0 (lines 16a and 16b). The unemployment level of day 1 is the excess of the available over the actually employed manpower of day 1 (lines 13 and 14); the wage rate ruling at the beginning of day 1 will be that ruling during day 0 plus or minus an adjustment depending upon whether the unemployment experienced during day 0 was exceptionally low or high (lines 15a and 15b). The profitability of the various processes of production if they were operated during day 0 would be realized by the sale of the product at the beginning of day 1; and these profitabilities would be the greater, the higher the selling price of the product at the beginning of day 1, the lower the purchase prices of the inputs of the product and of labour at the beginning of day 0, and the lower the rate of interest at which money could be raised for the purchase of the inputs at the beginning of day 0 (lines 17, 18a, 18b and 19). The various processes of production would be operated on day 1 on the same scales as on day 0 subject to adjustments due to (i) the invention of new processes (line 4) and (ii) the expansion of profitable processes and contraction of unprofitable or of less profitable processes (lines 20a and 20b). The level of disposable income realized at the beginning of day 1 will be the greater, (i) the greater is the net transfer payment to individuals from the government (line 28); (ii) the higher is the net output produced during day 0 (lines 23, 24 and 26); (iii) the higher the price at which the net output is sold at the beginning of day 1 (line 27a); (iv) the higher is the capital gain (or the lower the capital loss) realized on the capital stock engaged at the beginning of day 0, this capital gain being the greater, the greater the rise in price (lines 27a and 27b); and (v) the higher (or lower) the capital stock engaged according as a price rise (or fall) is realized (line 25). The capital stock itself on day 1 includes both the capital actively engaged in production and the idle spare capacity stock (lines 21 and 22). Finally, consumers spend at the beginning of day 1 an amount of money which is a given fraction of the disposable incomes which they realized at the beginning of day 0. This means that they purchase at the beginning of day 1 an amount of goods for consumption which is the greater (i) the greater their disposable money incomes realized at the beginning of day 0 (line 29) and (ii) the lower the selling price of the product at the beginning of day 1 (line 30).

We now have a system in which there are two environmental events—technical progress and demographic change (T^* and N^*)—in which there are three governmental controls—budgetary expenditure on goods and services, net transfer payment to or from the citizens, and the ease or tightness of monetary credit (G^{**}, H^{**} and i^{**})—and in which there are a number of inside events related to each other, to the outside events, and to the controls in the specific dynamic manner depicted in Figure 32. Clearly the level at which the controls are set on any one day will affect the inside events of that day, which in turn will affect the inside events of the next day, and so on ad infinitum. Each day's controls will set in motion a series of repercussions which in principle will mean that at no future date will the position be quite the same as it would have been if the controls on the day in question had been set at some other levels. But tomorrow's inside events will, of course, depend not only on today's controls; they will depend also on tomorrow's outside events and tomorrow's controls. It follows that in order to decide what is the best level at which today's controls should be set, one must (1) know what future courses of the economy one prefers; (2) forecast what will happen to the environmental events; (3) know what the interconnections are between the environmental events, the controls, and the inside events; and (4) have a programme for the future controls without which one cannot foresee the result of today's controls.

The last of these four considerations means that in order to set today's controls at their optimum level, one must have already an idea about what one will consider to be the optimum level for the controls tomorrow, the next day, and so on. In order to set today's controls at the optimal level, one must today construct a programme for the optimal levels of the controls stretching into the distant future. This is the essence of the control problem to which we shall turn our attention in Part 4 of this volume.

PART 3

THE THEORY OF INDICATIVE FORECASTING

The causes of good and evil, answered
Imlac, are so various and uncertain, so
entangled with each other, so
diversified by various relations, and so
much subject to accidents which
cannot be foreseen, that he who would
fix his condition upon incontestable
reasons of preference, must live and
die inquiring and deliberating.

SAMUEL JOHNSON : *Rasselas*

CHAPTER IX

FORECASTING IN THE ABSENCE OF ENVIRONMENTAL UNCERTAINTIES

In Part 2 of this volume we have outlined the main dynamic inter-relationships which may be expected to exist in a modern developed economy. We ended with a structure in which there are certain environmental events and certain governmental controls continually affecting a number of economic variables (inside events) which in turn affect each other as they move through time. The problem of optimal control of this system is to devise that movement of the governmental controls through time which, given the expected future movements of the outside events and given the interrelationships between the various events, will make the system move through time in what the policy-makers judge to be the socially most desirable way. We will consider this problem of the optimal use of governmental controls in Part 4 of this volume. There is, however, a preliminary question of governmental policy to be considered, namely whether governmental action can be taken to improve the institutional framework in which economic decision-makers attempt to foresee future developments.

Accordingly, let us first consider conditions in which no governmental controls would be needed if it were not for the problems which arise from the development of the economy through time and the inevitable uncertainties which are connected with such development. Suppose that our economy were a Propdem with perfect intergenerational altruism and that it contained no externalities and no indivisibilities. In a Propdem with perfect intergenerational altruism we would not be concerned with governmental action to redistribute income and wealth either between the members of one generation or between one generation and another (cf. *The Growing Economy*, pp. 44-6, 220-21). If there were no externalities and no indivisibilities, there would be no call in a static economy for governmental expenditure or taxes or subsidies or other similar interventions; the forces of actual or of potential perfect competition in free markets would, as we have seen (cf. *The Stationary Economy*, pp. 184-98), lead to a fully efficient economic system.

Moreover, we have also seen (cf. *The Growing Economy*, pp.

147

475–88) that if these conditions of absence of externalities and indivisibilities are combined with perfect foresight of future events then the forces of actual or of potential perfect competition will suffice to cause a dynamic economy to move on a fully efficient path through time. It is not our intention to repeat here the analysis which leads to the conclusion that if each private decision-maker could foresee accurately the future course of all prices and other relevant market conditions, the private profit motive would cause him to act in a way which was fully efficient.

One may conclude that even in a dynamic economy, provided that it was a Propdem with perfect intergenerational altruism and without any externalities or indivisibilities, there would be no need for any controls at all if foresight of all relevant market conditions were perfect.[1] In these circumstances, the question immediately arises whether, and if so how, is it possible to improve, if not to perfect, foresight of future market conditions.

This is in fact a question of the utmost importance. In Part 1 of this volume we stressed the importance of expectations in determining people's decisions. But we argued that as expectations can be formed only in the light of past experience we could at one remove say that people's decisions were determined by past experience. It was in this way that we were led to the formulation of a model in Part 2 in which the level of any one variable was determined solely by the past or present values of other variables. This procedure tends to obscure the importance of expectations. If the way in which expectations are formed can be changed, then the interrelationships between the variables in the economic system will themselves be changed. If the formation of expectations is improved (in the sense that people come to expect more nearly that which does in fact come to pass), then the behavioural relationships inside the economic system will themselves be changed in a way which makes the system move through time in a more efficient manner even without any governmental controls.

Our subject matter in Part 3 of this volume is, therefore, to consider the means by which in conditions of uncertainty forecasting of future events by economic decision-makers can be

---

[1] In Part 2 we have included certain rates of interest or certain supplies of liquid assets by the financial authorities among the controls. If we are to do without all controls, we must specify some completely uncontrolled conditions on the capital and money markets. We may, for example, assume that people use ounces of gold as their money, i.e. as their numeraire for measuring relative prices and as their ultimate means of settling debts, and that the supply and demand for gold are determined in a completely free market. Lending and borrowing in all forms is also free of all governmental intervention and various rates of interest are freely determined for various kinds of loan.

improved. For this purpose we will start with an extremely simple model based upon a number of extreme simplifying assumptions, which will be modified as the argument is developed. These initial simplifying assumptions may be grouped under four heads.

(1) First, as already stated, there is perfect competition throughout the economy.

(2) Second, as already stated, there are no externalities or public goods; no indivisibilities, monopolies, or increasing returns to scale; and no inequities in the distribution of income and wealth between citizens of different classes or of different generations. In short, there is no call at all for state intervention in the economic sphere except in so far as it may be able to help private economic agents (i.e. individuals as consumers, merchants, entrepreneurs, investors or producers) to plan to meet the future more efficiently.

(3) Third, the world will last for a definite period and will then come to an end at a known date in the future which we will call 'Kingdom Come'. Thus every individual economic agent knows precisely what future time span there is to be covered by his plan.

(4) Fourth, every private economic agent who will transact any business at all between now and 'Kingdom Come' is already alive and transacting business; and, on the other hand, every economic agent now alive will live until 'Kingdom Come'. This means that there are to be no births or deaths between now and 'Kingdom Come', and also that all citizens are already adult and do not age so as to become senile before 'Kingdom Come'. We shall not be concerned with many of the implications of this strange demographic assumption. What is needed for our present simplified model is to be able to assume that the whole of any plan covering the period from now to 'Kingdom Come' will be relevant for every economic agent now alive and for no one else.

Apart from these four groups of far-reaching assumptions, the economy can be extremely complicated, covering markets for lending and borrowing, and for insurance and betting; production and trade carried out by joint stock companies, co-operatives, partnerships, private businesses; men and women at work with different skills in many occupations; and innumerable types of consumption good and service, of capital goods and intermediate products, and of natural resources. An essential feature, however, is that all concerned are faced with an uncertain future.

We shall distinguish between two types of uncertainty which will be called 'market' uncertainty and 'environmental' uncertainty respectively. A homely example may serve to explain the difference. A manufacturer of sunshades and umbrellas in forming his plans this year as to how many sunshades and how many umbrellas he

F

will produce now to put on the market next year does not know whether next year will be wet or fine; in fact, nobody knows whether it will be wet or fine and this is an environmental uncertainty. The manufacturer also does not know what the market demands for umbrellas and for sunshades will be if it is wet nor what the demands will be if it is fine; but the consumers of sunshades and umbrellas may know very well how many of these objects they will buy next year at given market prices for these objects if it is wet and how many they will buy at given prices if it is fine. This lack of knowledge by the producer is a market uncertainty; and, to anticipate the argument, it is the sort of uncertainty which can be removed by a system of forward markets or of indicative planning. Forward markets and indicative planning are in fact information systems which reduce uncertainty by passing to producers the knowledge which consumers have about future demand conditions and passing to consumers the knowledge which producers have about future supply conditions. But no one has any certain knowledge to pass on about future environmental uncertainties.

Environmental uncertainties cover a very wide class of events. Some are obvious exogenous events. The future state of the weather may affect the harvest or the demand for bathing dresses; or, in the case of a single economy, the future state of economic activity and of price inflation or deflation in the outside world may affect the demand for a country's exports. In other cases, it is the parameters in production or consumption functions which are basically uncertain. Future technical progress may affect the real input cost of nuclear power and the course of such progress may not be known with certainty even to the experts most closely concerned; or future changes in fashion may affect the demand for mini-skirts in ways which at present are still obscure to the consumers themselves.

This distinction between market uncertainties (about things which some people know for certain and others do not know at all) and environmental uncertainties (about things which nobody knows) should not in reality be drawn too sharply. There are some things which are relevant to the plans of many individual agents, which are not known for certain by anyone, but about which some agents can form a much better opinion than others. An obvious example is the difference in knowledge between the producers and consumers of a product about the probable effect of technical progress on the future cost of the product. A consumer's choice between an electric and a gas heating installation will depend upon his estimate of the probable future course of relative costs of electricity and of gas; but this may depend upon whether or not some expected technological breakthrough is successfully carried out in the production of electricity. No-one may know for certain whether and, if so, when this will happen. But the producers of electricity may be able to estimate the probabilities much better than the consumers. A diffusion of knowledge from producers to consumers about their estimates of probabilities of environmental change is thus important. But, for the time being, a rather sharp distinction will be drawn between those things about which one group is pretty certain while another group is very uncertain, and those things about which everyone is inevitably very uncertain; these will be called market and environmental uncertainties respectively.

Let us first consider what the position would be in such an economy if there were no environmental uncertainties. It may at first sight appear that since the absence of environmental uncertainties implies the absence of uncertainties about changing fashions and changing technical knowledge and since we are making the strange demographic assumption of no births or deaths, there would in fact be no change going on in the economy at all. But this is not so for two reasons. First, it is conceptually possible to imagine a state of affairs in which technical progress is taking place but in which it is precisely and exactly known in advance when each particular bit of increased technical knowledge will occur. In this case there would be technical progress without any uncertainty about its occurrence. But if it seems too unreal to imagine that the precise date and form of a future invention can be known without the invention having already been made, we can fall back on the second reason for change, namely savings, investment and capital accumulation. We have not ruled these out and as the amount of man-made capital equipment of various kinds changes per head of the population and per acre of natural resources, so market conditions will change. Rates of wages and rents will probably rise; the rate of interest will probably fall; some goods will become more costly to produce relatively to other goods; and some goods will be in greater demand relatively to others as the real incomes of consumers rise. Producers and consumers will be faced with all sorts of market uncertainties about the future course of the prices of their inputs and outputs, of their incomes and of the prices of their final consumption goods and services.

In order that our competitive economy should move efficiently through time, it is necessary that every decision-maker should be able to foresee correctly the future prices that will rule for the goods and services in which he is interested. Whether or not it is economic to set up a new steel mill will depend upon the future prices of the inputs of labour and of the outputs of steel which will be associated with that mill if it is installed. But the future demand for steel will depend upon the future plans of the users of steel to make machine tools, the worthwhileness of which will depend upon the still more distant prices of the inputs and outputs associated with the use of the machine tools, and so on. The economic system is a general system of interrelationships in which every price is directly or indirectly related to every other price, prices of steel to prices of labour and—the point which is most pertinent for our present enquiry—present prices to future prices.

Now if, as we are assuming, all future decision-makers are already alive and operating in the market and there are no unforeseen changes in technical knowledge or tastes, we can imagine a comprehensive set of forward markets which would remove all remaining market uncertainties. By one once-for-all gigantic market 'higgle-haggle' everyone could buy and sell forward for all periods of time from now to 'Kingdom Come' everything in which he or she is interested, including the hire of his or her own labour and the purchase or sale, and the lending or borrowing, of different forms of property. When the market had settled down, everyone would know precisely the future course of his income, the prices of what he would buy and sell, the future level of his consumption of every good and service, the amounts of capital equipment of various kinds he would instal at every future date, and so on and so on. Future prices and quantities would only settle down at levels at which competitive supply was equal to competitive demand at every point of time. No expectations would ever be disappointed and as time passed there would be no need to supplement in spot markets the obligations already entered into in past forward contracts. Relative prices of different products and of the same product at different points of time would in the free competitive forward markets measure both the marginal rates of substitution in any one citizen's consumption plan and the marginal rates of transformation in any one citizen's production plan. Thus we would have an efficient system in the sense that we would achieve a development of the economy through time such that it would be impossible to make one citizen better off without making someone else worse off.[2]

There are two different ways in which one can imagine the money payments being made in such a comprehensive set of forward markets. One must, in any case, imagine that the forward markets cover not only the prices of goods and services at each future date, but also the rate of interest at which money can be lent or borrowed at each future date. If people were uncertain about the market rate of interest which they could get on their savings at future dates, they would be uncertain about the market offers which they could afford

[2] See *The Growing Economy*, pp. 479–88.

to make for various goods at different dates. Market uncertainties would not be eliminated. Consider a three-day future of the kind shown in Figure 33.

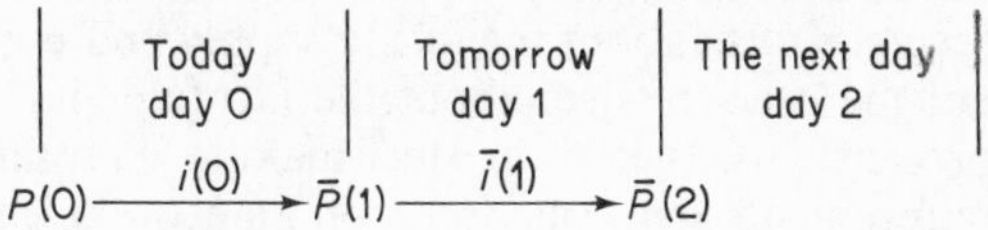

| Today day 0 | Tomorrow day 1 | The next day day 2 |

$$P(0) \xrightarrow{\;i(0)\;} \bar{P}(1) \xrightarrow{\;\bar{i}(1)\;} \bar{P}(2)$$

Figure 33

Suppose that we stand now at 8 a.m. on day 0. The market has already determined the spot prices at which goods and services are actually being bought and sold at 8 a.m. on day 0, these prices being represented by $P(0)$. The market for loans will also already have determined a spot rate of interest, $i(0)$, at which money is actually being lent and borrowed for day 0. If the great and glorious forward market 'higgle haggle' has also taken place at 8 a.m. on day 0, the forward prices at which goods will exchange hands at 8 a.m. on days 1 and 2 and the rate of interest at which money will be lent from 8 a.m. on day 1 to day 2 will also have been determined; and these forward prices are represented by $\bar{P}(1)$, $\bar{P}(2)$ and $\bar{i}(1)$ respectively.

Suppose that as part of this 'higgle-haggle' Mr A purchases forward from Mr B 1 unit of steel to be delivered on day 2 at a price of $\bar{P}(2)$. Then the contract may take the form either that on day 2 A pays B $\bar{P}(2)$ in money and B gives A one unit of steel or else that A pays B today $\bar{P}(2)/(1 + i(0))(1 + \bar{i}(1))$ units of money and B gives A one unit of steel on day 2. Let $\tilde{P}(2) = \bar{P}(2)/(1 + i(0))(1 + \bar{i}(1))$. If the latter form of contract is used, B can (i) today lend the $\bar{P}(2)/(1 + i(0))(1 + \bar{i}(1))$ at an interest of $i(0)$ and receive $\bar{P}(2)/(1 + \bar{i}(1))$ tomorrow and (ii) at the same time today lend this sum of $\bar{P}(2)/(1 + \bar{i}(1))$ at interest $i(1)$ in the forward market for loans from tomorrow till the day after tomorrow, thus receiving $\bar{P}(2)$ the day after tomorrow. It is a matter of indifference which form of contract is used. Thus we can envisage either a once-for-all payment of money from buyers to sellers on day 0 of prices like $\tilde{P}(2)$, in which case all that happens as time passes is that the sellers have to provide the goods and services at the appropriate dates or else a once-for-all fixing of contracts which require buyers to pay prices like $\bar{P}(2)$ at the future appropriate dates for the goods and services then to be supplied. With a comprehensive set of forward markets covering interest rates as well as commodity prices, the difference is a formal one. But it will prove a useful distinction later on when we come to consider environmental uncertainties.

Whichever form of contract was used, prices would provide a fully efficient signalling system horizontally over time as well as vertically between one product and another. The price of steel in the future markets would thus bring together the specialized knowledge of the producers of steel about the future supply and the specialized knowledge of the users of steel about the future demand in such a way that present investments in steel-making equipment and in steel-using equipment were consistent, on an economically efficient scale, and in an economically efficient form.

It should be observed that if all future prices both for goods and for loans could somehow be foreseen accurately and for certain, then exactly the same results could be achieved without any forward contracts of either of the two kinds which we have described. Thus suppose that the actual spot rate of interest ruling for a day's loan today is $i(0)$, that it is known for certain that the rate of interest tomorrow will be $i(1)$, and that it is known for certain that the price of a unit of steel the day after tomorrow will be $P(2)$. Then Mr A can invest $P(2)/(1 + i(0))(1 + i(1))$ today to get $P(2)/(1 + i(1))$ tomorrow. He knows that he will be able to invest this $P(2)/(1 + i(1))$ tomorrow so as to get $P(2)$ the day after tomorrow; and he knows that $P(2)$ will then buy him a unit of steel.

It is precisely this forecasting of future market conditions which one can try to achieve by a mimicry of forward markets through a form of governmental indicative planning. Let us caricature the procedure by considering it in a complete, ideal, but patently absurd form. The government summons to a meeting in the Albert Hall every citizen in the country. At this meeting every citizen is provided with a list of prices of every conceivable good and service, including, of course, wage rates, rates of interest, security prices, etc., for every day in the future from now till 'Kingdom Come'; these prices being initially, if you like, simply the current market prices of everything. Every citizen is then required to write down for every day in the future how much he or she would buy or sell of every good or service at these prices, including, of course, the amounts which he or she would wish to borrow or lend on any future day at the stated rates of interest. There is then a coffee break, during which the bureaucrats add up the total supplies and demands of every good and service for every future day. They then prepare a revised schedule of forward prices, having put up the prices for which demand exceeded supply and having put down the prices for which supply exceeded demand. The citizens are then recalled, confronted with the new price lists, and asked to revise their schedules of amounts supplied and demanded. This process is repeated until hopefully a series of price lists, one for every future day, is found at which the supply–demand position is balanced for every good and service at every future point of time.

It can be shown that the particular process described in the preceding paragraph for groping towards the equilibrium set of prices which will bring all supplies and demands simultaneously into balance cannot be relied upon to converge onto that equilibrium solution except in the rather special circumstances in which every good is a substitute for every other good. This is because of the interaction of one market on another. The reason for this may be suggested intuitively in the following way.

Suppose that the process has succeeded in making aggregate demand equal to aggregate supply, but that it has not yet succeeded in bringing equilibrium to all particular markets, so that while some goods are in excess supply, others are in excess demand. Suppose these two classes of goods to be good substitutes for each other, such as white bread which is in excess supply and brown bread which is in excess demand. Then putting down the price of white bread which is in excess supply will help not only to increase the demand for white bread but also to reduce the demand for brown bread which is in excess demand. Conversely putting up the price of brown bread because it is in excess demand will not only reduce the demand for brown bread but will also stimulate the demand for white bread which is in excess supply. Each price adjustment will thus help to restore equilibrium in both markets.

But suppose that the two groups of commodities were complementary. Petrol is in excess supply and motor cars are in excess demand. Putting down the price of petrol decreases the cost of motoring, increases the demand for cars, and thus increases the excess demand for cars. Putting up the price of cars reduces the demand for cars, but by so doing reduces also the demand for petrol and thus increases the excess supply of petrol. Complementarity in production can lead to a similar perverse result. Suppose that wool is in excess supply and mutton in excess demand. A fall in the price of wool reduces the profitabilty of rearing sheep which reduces the supply of mutton and accentuates the excess demand for mutton. The appropriate price adjustment for the market directly concerned worsens the position in the other related market. In this case the process cannot be relied upon to lead to an equilibrium.

In such cases, more subtle processes for finding the equilibrium set of prices would be necessary. In this volume we shall, however, neglect this problem and simply assume that some modified form of the simple process already described can be relied upon to find the equilibrium set of prices which balances supplies and demands for all goods at all points of time. For the sake of simplification, we shall treat this as if it were the actual simple process described above for the Albert Hall meeting.

If this process is successfully carried out, the result will be the same as that achieved by a comprehensive set of actual forward markets. Both procedures indicate what set of spot prices at each given date in the future will in fact clear all markets and if all the citizens really make their plans in the expectation of these prices, then these prices will in fact result in balanced supply and demand positions. Both procedures are mechanisms for forecasting balanced market conditions and this is the essence of the matter. The difference of form is simply that with a set of forward markets, actual contracts will have been entered into, these contracts being of a kind which no one will wish to alter when the time comes to fulfill them, whereas with the indicative plan citizens will have undertaken no contractual obligations in advance, but will in fact have planned freely to enter into these same contracts when the time comes. In the case both of the comprehensive set of forward markets and of the comprehensive indicative plan, no revision is ever needed. The forward market 'higgle-haggle' or the Albert Hall meeting takes place once-for-all and covers all future transactions.

The essence of the matter then, so far, is to find a procedure which will give citizens a foresight of future market prices so that they can make their present plans in the knowledge of what future costs of inputs, selling prices of outputs, and so on will in fact be. Now there is a third way, in addition to the methods of forward markets and of indicative planning, of trying to make such a forecast, namely the building of an econometric model of the economy and its use to forecast future market developments. If one knows all the technological and behavioural relationships in the economy—that is to say, what outputs can be produced with what inputs and how citizens as entrepreneurs, workers, savers, consumers, etc., react to changes in prices, costs, incomes, interest rates, etc—if one knows the starting point of the economy—that is to say, the existing capital equipment and so on—and, finally, if one knows how the future exogenous variables will behave—and we are in fact assuming that there are no environmental uncertainties—then, theoretically, since one thing necessarily leads to another according to the known technological and behavioural relationships, one should be able to forecast the future course of all prices and quantities in all markets.

Consider the use of this method by envisaging the situation of an individual producer of steel in the absence of forward markets or of an indicative plan. He must make his decisions on the basis of his own unaided best guess about the future. The economic system is a general system in which the price of any one particular thing at any one particular time is related to the price of every other thing at every other point of time. The future price obtainable by our citizen for his output of steel will, for example, depend upon the price of alternative materials which will depend upon the price of the inputs used to produce those materials which will depend upon the future demand for those inputs in alternative uses to produce, say, equipment to produce in the more distant future some range of consumption goods. Thus, in principle, each individual business would need to have its own economic section to study the future development of the whole economy in order to consider its impact upon the particular business concerned.

It would obviously be very inefficient for every citizen to build his own econometric model in order to improve his own knowledge of future developments. Apart from the obvious duplication of effort, not every citizen would be as good as every other citizen in building comprehensive economic models. If some central organization, such as a governmental statistical office, constructed such an economic model calling on the specialist knowledge of, for example, steel producers in constructing that part of the model which dealt with the supply of steel and of steel users in constructing the demand schedules for steel, a better model might hopefully be achieved at a lower cost which, if published, could be used as a forecasting tool by all private decision makers.

But the construction of an econometric model for forecasting —quite apart from the very great statistical and econometric problems of estimation involved—raises one issue which differentiates it sharply from the methods of forward markets and of indicative planning. Economic behaviour depends in part on economic expectations. Thus the present demand for durable goods is likely to be higher if purchasers expect their cost to go up than if they expect them to go down. In constructing an econometric model it is not possible to measure expectations directly; we cannot measure the effect of past events on present expectations and then the effect of present expectations on present decisions. One can only take the short cut of observing the indirect effect of past events on present decisions, observing perhaps that if prices of durables have been going up in the past, people buy more of them now and merely surmising that this is because a recent rise of price makes buyers expect a future rise of price. In the absence of forward markets, of an indicative plan, and of an econometric forecast, citizens will form their expectations somehow in the light of past experience; and it is virtually certain that they will not foretell the future correctly. Expectations will be disappointed and the economy will move in a disequilibrium way through time.

F*

Introduce now an econometric forecast on the scene. Suppose it correctly estimates the effects of the existing method of formation of expectations. It will then predict the future disequilibrium path for the economy. If its forecasts are now believed by the citizens, they will see that their former expectations are going to be disappointed. If they now believe the predictions of the econometric forecast, they will alter their expectations and so alter the behavioural relations on which the econometric forecast is built. The predictions of the econometric forecasts will be falsified and perhaps they will not be believed in the future. In any case the econometric model-builders must revise the behavioural relationships making the predictions of the model themselves explanatory variables in the explanation of the citizens' behaviour. There is, of course, nothing conceptually impossible in this; and if the predictions of the econometric forecast do come to be more and more trusted. and if the econometric model-builders can introduce the forecasts which result from the econometric model as explanatory variables into the behavioural relations of the model and if they thus succeed gradually in improving the fit of their behavioural relationships to the changed formation of expectations, one might perhaps in due course hope to converge on to the point at which all private decision-makers expected the predictions of the model to be true and the econometric model-builders simultaneously correctly estimated the effect of this on the behaviour of the private decision-makers. One could then hope to achieve the same final equilibrium result as through a comprehensive system of forward markets or of indicative planning.

But the process would, at the very best, be a prolonged and unreliable one. Econometric forecasting involves both estimating indirectly the formation of expectations and their effect on behaviour and also altering the way in which expectations are formed. Forward markets and indicative planning kill both birds with one stone. They find out directly how private decision-makers will behave if they expect prices to move in the way in which they will in fact move.

CHAPTER X

FORECASTING IN CONDITIONS OF ENVIRONMENTAL UNCERTAINTY

In the preceding chapter we discussed forward markets, indicative planning, and econometric forecasting in the absence of any environmental uncertainties. Let us now introduce such uncertainties, retaining for the time being the four sets of outrageous simplifying assumptions made on page 149. The situation becomes much more complicated. But we will discuss it in terms of one very simple example of an economy with environmental uncertainties. It is hoped that this simple example does adequately illustrate the principles involved and that it is intuitively clear that the conclusions could be generalized to cover the more complicated forms of the problem.

Let us suppose then that the only environmental uncertainty is whether from day to day it will be wet or fine and that the world will last only for three days, today, tomorrow, and the day after tomorrow, or—to be sophisticated—day 0, day 1 and day 2, coming to a certain end at midnight between day 2 and day 3. The BBC tells us at 7.45 each morning whether the day is wet or fine, but we do not know until 7.45 tomorrow whether tomorrow will be wet or fine. We stand then at 8 a.m. on day 0, knowing already for certain whether day 0 is wet or fine, but confronted with the four possible future environmental paths shown in Figure 34. The future two days may be WW, WF, FW or FF and these weather paths are numbered 1, 2, 3 and 4 respectively. There are seven environmental points: today, we are on all four paths and we will call this point 1234; tomorrow, if it is wet, we shall know that we are on either path 1 or 2 and we will call this point 12; and so on for the other points.

What a citizen does today may depend very much upon his expectations about the environmental paths. Thus an umbrella may be reasonably durable, and if it is wet today he may think of replacing his already shabby and worn umbrella. If he knew that he was on path 1 and that it would also be wet tomorrow and the next day, he would certainly do so. He would be somewhat less inclined to do so if he knew that he was on path 2, i.e. that while it would be wet tomorrow it would be fine the next day. He would be still less inclined to do so, if he knew that he was on path 3, i.e. that it would be fine tomorrow and wet the next day, so that his investment in an umbrella would lie idle for one fine day though it would still be useful the day after that. He would be least inclined to do so if he knew that he was on path 4, so that a new umbrella would have no use after today. But he does not know and *ex hypothesi* cannot know for certain which path he is on. He can only make his own assessments of the probabilities of the four possible weather paths.

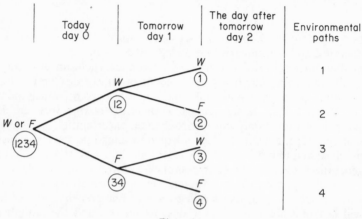

Figure 34

The example of the choice between sinking one's capital in an umbrella or in a sunshade is a frivolous one but the underlying problem is far from frivolous. In the real world, it is of the greatest importance. Whether the community should sink durable resources on a vast scale in producing equipment to promote travel by air or by a renewed railway system, or to produce electrical power from coal-fired or nuclear stations, are questions which may depend in large measure upon the assessment of the probabilities of important future and uncertain technological advances. These issues are merely exemplified by the choice between umbrellas and sunshades in view of the uncertainty of the weather.

There are conceivable types of forward markets which could in theory cope with the tractable parts of the problems raised by environmental uncertainties. We can see the possibilities best by realizing that not only is an umbrella tomorrow a different good from an umbrella today, but equally well an umbrella-tomorrow-if-it-is-wet-tomorrow is a different good from an umbrella-tomorrow-if-it-is-fine-tomorrow. We will call these goods 'contingency' goods.

Thus there are seven different 'contingency' umbrellas, one at each of the seven points on the weather paths in Figure 34. Suppose now that there was today a market in all contingency goods; that is, suppose, for example, that by paying a definite sum of money to Mr B today, Mr A put Mr B under an obligation to give to Mr A an umbrella-at-point-1, i.e. an umbrella on day 2 if, but only if, it is wet on day 1 and wet on day 2. This sum of money may be called today's contingency price for an umbrella to be delivered at point 1 and we will represent such a price by $\tilde{P}_1$. This price is a price paid for certain now in return for a good which will be provided in the future and then only if some defined environmental event occurs. It is, therefore, in some way an amalgam of the value of an umbrella at point 1, the rates of interest at which this future value must be discounted to obtain its present value, and of the allowance for the risk involved in the fact that Mr A may never get his umbrella because the economy may never reach point 1. These relations between spot prices, interest rates, and allowances for risk are of central importance, and it is as well to get them clear at once.

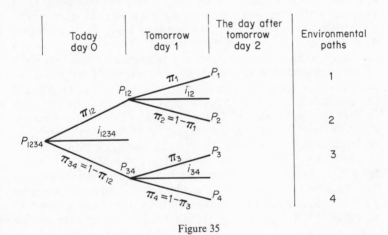

Figure 35

The prices and money transactions of one day are now bound to the prices and money transactions of the next day by two links. In the first place, there is the tie of the rate of interest. We are at point 1234 on Figure 35. At this point there will rule a rate of interest— call it i_{1234}—at which a citizen can lend money for one day at 8 a.m. today and receive principal and interest at 8 a.m. tomorrow. But at 8 a.m. tomorrow the economy may be at point 12 or at point 34;

that is to say, it may be wet or it may be fine, and the rate of interest which will rule tomorrow if the economy is at point 12—call it i_{12}— is not necessarily the same as the rate which will rule if the economy is at point 34—which we will call i_{34}. That this is so is obvious if, for a moment, we suppose that the difference between points 12 and 34 is not whether it is wet or fine, but whether some very extensive technological invention making it profitable to borrow huge sums of capital for some vast new developments has taken place or not. Thus we can imagine a rate of interest for a day's loan of money, ruling at 8 a.m. on every day, the level of the rate depending among other things upon the environmental conditions ruling at that point of time.

But the prices and money transactions of one day must now be regarded as being bound to the prices and money transactions of the next day not only by the rate of interest but also by an insurance or betting market on which one can cover the risk of movement from any given point on any one day on the environmental time paths to any feasible point on the following day. On day 0 the economy is at point 1234 and on day 1 it may move to point 12 or to point 34. We suppose for the time being that all risks are insurable so that for the payment of a premium (say $\$\pi_{12}$) Mr A can insure $1 against the risk of moving from point 1234 to point 12 (i.e. Mr A can insure today against the risk that tomorrow will be wet). Such a contract is made at 8 a.m. on day 0 (i.e. at point 1234) but the actual premium is payable at 8 a.m. on day 1. Thus at 8 a.m. on day 1 if the economy is at point 12 Mr A pays the premium of $\$\pi_{12}$ but receives the insured sum of $1, a net receipt of $\$(1 - \pi_{12})$; whereas, if at 8 a.m. on day 1 the economy is at point 34, he pays the premium of $\$\pi_{12}$ and receives nothing. Thus we can also think of the contract as a bet entered into at 8 a.m. on day 0 such that Mr A will receive $\$(1 - \pi_{12})$, if tomorrow is wet, but will pay $\$\pi_{12}$ if tomorrow is fine. Thus we can talk of $\$\pi_{12}$ as the rate of insurance premium payable to insure against a movement from point 1234 to point 12 or we can talk of $(1 - \pi_{12})/\pi_{12}$ as the betting odds as between moving to point 12 or to point 34 from point 1234. We suppose that at 8 a.m. every future day there will be a similar insurance or betting market which will enable anyone to insure against, or to bet as between, its being wet or fine on the subsequent day, though the rate of premium or betting odds which will have to be paid may well depend upon the environmental conditions as well as the date of the transactions. Thus we envisage in Figure 35 that at point 12 there will be rates of premium of π_1 and π_2 respectively for insurance against the next day being wet and fine respectively, and that at point 34 these rates will be π_3 and π_4.

Now if by some means or another Mr A could foresee precisely and exactly what these spot interest rates, insurance premiums and commodity prices would be at each future point on the environmental paths in Figure 35, then he would know exactly how much he must set aside today in order to be in a position to purchase any given commodity at any given future point on the environmental paths. Suppose P_1 is what the price of an umbrella will be at point 1. Then if he sets aside $P_1\pi_{12}\pi_1/(1 + i_{1234})(1 + i_{12})$ today and invests this sum at the current rate of interest, he will have $P_1\pi_{12}\pi_1/(1 + i_{12})$ tomorrow. If today he has undertaken to pay an insurance premium of $P_1\pi_{12}\pi_1/(1 + i_{12})$ tomorrow against its being wet tomorrow (i.e. against the economy reaching point 12), he will receive $P_1\pi_1/(1 + i_{12})$ tomorrow if the economy does reach point 12. But this sum he will be able to invest at point 12 at a rate of interest i_{12} to get $\pi_1 P_1$ at 8 a.m. the day after tomorrow; and if he has undertaken at point 12 to pay a premium of $\pi_1 P_1$ on the following day as an insurance against wet weather (i.e. against reaching point 1), he will receive P_1 if the economy does reach point 1, with which sum he can purchase his umbrella at point 1. Thus we may write:

$$P_1 = P_1\pi_{12}\pi_1/(1 + i_{1234})(1 + i_{12}). \quad \ldots \ldots \ldots \ldots \ldots (10.1)$$

if $\tilde{P}_1$ is today's price for the contingent commodity, namely an umbrella-at-point-1, and if individuals can correctly foresee the future loan, insurance and commodity markets. For in these conditions it is a matter of indifference to Mr A whether (i) he operates today's contingent forward market and pays down $\tilde{P}_1$ to someone today who in return promises to give him an umbrella if and when point 1 is reached or (ii) he puts aside $P_1\pi_{12}\pi_1/(1 + 1_{1234})(1 + i_{12})$ and undertakes the necessary operations on the day-to-day loan and insurance markets as described above, so as to obtain the price which he will have to pay for an umbrella if and when the economy reaches point 1. Arbitrage should imply that the two ways of acquiring today an umbrella-at-point-1 should cost the same.

The question then arises whether there are any means whereby Mr A can accurately foresee what the relevant future rates of interest, rates of insurance premiums and commodity prices will be. One possibility would be through a system of what may be called conditional forward markets.

At point 1234, i.e. at 8 a.m. on day 0 where the economy now stands, there will be an actual loan market which will determine the rate of interest (i_{1234}) for a loan for the duration of day 0. This we can call today's spot loan market. But let us envisage also the existence of what we may call a conditional forward loan market in which at 8 a.m. today Mr A can enter into the following sort of contract with Mr B: 'At 8 a.m. tomorrow I (Mr A) will lend you (Mr B) \$1 and in return you (Mr B) will pay me (Mr A) $\$(1 + \bar{\imath}_{12})$ at 8 a.m. the day after tomorrow; but this bargain is on only if it is wet tomorrow (i.e. only if we are then at point 12); otherwise no payment will be made in either direction.' Similar conditional loan markets must be available for every other day in the future, in each of which anyone can today undertake to lend or borrow money at a stated rate of interest at the stated date if, but only if, the economy is then at a stated point on the environmental time paths.

At point 1234, i.e. at 8 a.m. on day 0 where the economy now stands, there will also be an actual insurance market which will offer rates of insurance premia (π_{12} and π_{34}) payable to insure against movements to points 12 and 34 respectively. This we can call today's spot insurance market. But let us envisage also the existence of what we may call a conditional forward insurance market in which it would be possible for Mr A at 8 a.m. on day 0 to make the following sort of contract: 'At 8 a.m. on day 2 I (Mr A) will pay you (Mr B) $\$\bar{\pi}_1$, if, but only if, the economy has been at point 12 on day 1. In return you (Mr B) will pay me (Mr A) \$1 at 8 a.m. on day 2 if, but only if, we are then at point 1.' This is simply a forward contract to insure against a movement from point 12 to point 1. If the economy never reaches point 12, the whole contract is inoperative.

We can also envisage a conditional forward market for commodities in which Mr A can enter into a deal of the following kind: 'I (Mr A) undertake now at 8 a.m. on day 0 that I (Mr A) will pay you (Mr B) $\bar{P}_1$ at 8 a.m. on day 2 if, but only if, we are then at point 1 and in return you (Mr B) will provide me (Mr A) with an umbrella at 8 a.m. on day 2 if, and only if, we are then at point 1. If we are not then at point 1, the whole contract lapses.'

These conditional forward markets would simply be mechanisms whereby the future spot prices, including interest rates and insurance premiums as well as commodity prices, were fixed in advance; and if all future transactions were on day 0 once and for all settled in such markets in conditions in which all possible environmental developments were taken into account, the result would correspond to a state of affairs in which all equilibrium spot prices were accurately foreseen along all possible environmental paths. Equation 10.1 would now become:

$$\tilde{P}_1 = \bar{P}_1 \pi_{12} \bar{\pi}_1 / (1 + i_{1234})(1 + i_{12}) \quad \ldots \ldots \ldots \ldots \quad (10.2)$$

i_{1234} and π_{12} would be the actual rates ruling in today's spot markets for loans and insurance, while i_{12}, $\bar{\pi}_1$ and $\bar{P}_1$ would be an interest rate, an insurance premium, and a commodity price at which Mr A could make suitable firm contracts now in the relevant conditional forward markets. Thus he would know for certain how much money he must put aside now in order that, by fulfilling his contracts in the relevant conditional forward markets as and when the conditions arose, he might obtain his umbrella at point 1.

Theoretically, future spot prices along each environmental path could be accurately forecast, and thus precisely the same results achieved, by a suitable development of the method of indicative planning.

The planning procedure would now have to be modified in the following way. The government, as before, summons all the citizens to a meeting in the Albert Hall. In the absence of environmental uncertainty, it issued to everyone merely a single questionnaire, showing a price for every good and service and an interest rate for loans for every day from now until 'Kingdom Come', and asking each citizen to write down for each day how much of each good or service he would buy or sell and how much capital he would lend or borrow if these prices in fact ruled. Now it must issue not merely a single questionnaire, but as many questionnaires as there are environmental paths, each such questionnaire suggesting a course which might be taken along that particular path by the prices of every good and service, by the rates of interest for the loan of a day's money, and by each day's insurance premiums or betting odds on moving from that day's point on that path to the next day's point on that path.

Each citizen must now write down how much of each good he would buy or sell, how much capital he would borrow or lend, and how much he would bet on or against moving from one point to the next on each particular path, if the prices, interest rates, and betting odds in the market did move in the specified way. The government officials must then add up the total demands and supplies for goods and services, loans and bets along each environmental path. They must then put up the price, interest rate, or insurance premium at any point on any environmental path where the demand for goods, the loan, or the insurance exceeded the supply; and vice versa. The procedure is then repeated and this process goes on until, hopefully, there is a balance between supply and demand in every market at every point on every environmental path.

The result is, as it were, as many indicative plans as there are environmental paths—one plan for each path. If the game has been played properly, that is to say, if each decision-maker has truthfully stated how he would behave on each path if prices moved as indicated along that path, then in fact supplies and demands will balance at those prices along each path and the prices will, therefore, in fact behave as indicated in the plan. The conditional future spot prices will have been accurately forecast and all market uncertainties will have been eliminated.

For the reasons already given, the result will in theory be exactly the same as would be achieved from a comprehensive set of competitive contingency markets. If this is so, then, it follows—and this is the crucial point—that one can remove all market uncertainties even in the presence of environmental uncertainties by any one of the following three mechanisms. First, one can have a single gigantic once-for-all forward 'higgle-haggle' in which all contingent goods and services (i.e. all goods and services at each possible time-cum-environmental condition) are bought and sold once and for all now for money payments made now. Second, one can have a single gigantic once-for-all forward market 'higgle-haggle' in which what we have called conditional forward contracts for loans, bets and goods are settled once and for all. Third, one can rely on a mechanism analogous to the indicative planning procedures already outlined for the case of no environmental uncertainties, which will reveal what future spot prices, interest rates and insurance premiums will in fact balance supplies and demands for goods and services and for loans and bets from one day to the next at every future date in every possible environmental condition. Theoretically, all three methods should lead to the same results and it is to be observed that, in the assumed conditions in which all environmental paths are fully covered for all time, the forward market 'higgle-haggle' or the Albert Hall planning process would need to be carried out only once. The contracts reached in the forward markets or the price paths forecast in the Albert Hall would never need revision.

It would also be possible to use an econometric model for the purpose of forecasting in conditions of environmental uncertainty. It would be necessary for the econometric model-builders to estimate the causal relationships, of the kind illustrated in Figure 32 above, which explained the inside events in the economy in terms of past inside and environmental events—many of these relationships having their effect through the moulding of expectations. The model could then be used to predict how the various inside events would develop along each of the possible environmental paths, i.e. with each of the possible combinations of future environmental events being fed into the model.

We would then be faced once more with the complication discussed on pages 157–8. If the predictions of what would happen on each of the environmental paths were published and came to be believed, then this would alter the way in which expectations were formed; the behavioural relationships in the economy would be changed, and the economy would as a result move in a different way along each environmental path. It would be necessary, in the way discussed earlier, to attempt to revise the behavioural relationships, making them depend where necessary upon the forecasts of the economic model itself. The principle is the same but the application of the principle would be much more complicated.

Consider the demand for a durable commodity which may be increased if purchasers expect a rise in its price. Suppose that the econometric model forecasts different rates of rise or of fall of the price of this commodity along each of the four environmental paths in Figure 35. Suppose that a rapid rate of rise is predicted on path 1, but no rise or a fall is predicted on paths 2, 3 and 4. Whether or not this will cause a strong speculative demand for the commodity will depend upon the subjective probability with which the potential purchasers of the commodity expect the environmental conditions to move along path 1—and, of course, different purchasers may have different assessments of this probability. To discover by trial and error how the model's predictions of events on the various environmental paths will on balance affect behavioural patterns presents no easy problem to the economic model-builders.

Note to Chapter X

DIFFERENT FORMS OF FORWARD CONTRACT

In this chapter we have confined our attention to two particular types of forward market: (1) a contingency forward market in which it is agreed today that a given sum of money is paid for certain today for a good or service to be provided at some specified date in the future if, but only if, some specified condition has been fulfilled and (2) a conditional forward market in which it is agreed today that a certain sum of money will be paid at some date in the future for a good or service to be provided at that same date in the future, both the payment of the money and the delivery of the good or service being made if, but only if, some specified condition has been fulfilled. We have represented contingency forward prices with $\tilde{P}$ and conditional forward prices with $\bar{P}$; the relationship between the two was illustrated by equation 10.2 derived in the way explained earlier. We can also derive in a similar manner:

$$\tilde{P}_{12} = \bar{P}_{12}\pi_{12}/(1 + i_{1234}) \quad \dots \dots \dots \dots \dots \dots \quad (10.3)$$

and

$$\tilde{W}_{12} = \bar{W}_{12}\pi_{12}/(1 + i_{1234})(1 + i_{12}) \quad \dots \dots \dots \dots \quad (10.4)$$

The expression for $\tilde{W}_{12}$ is in form exactly the same as the expression for $\tilde{P}_{12}$, except that, whereas $\overline{P}_{12}$ is paid at the beginning of day 1, $\overline{W}_{12}$ is fixed at the beginning of day 1 when the labour is hired but paid at the beginning of day 2. It follows that, while to fulfil a conditional forward contract for the purchase of a unit of a product at point 12, the whole price $\overline{P}_{12}$ will be needed at point 12, to fulfil a conditional forward contract to hire a unit of labour at point 12, only $\overline{W}_{12}/(1 + i_{12})$ will be needed at point 12, since this sum can be invested at an interest rate of i_{12} for one day in order to meet the obligation to pay the wage $\overline{W}_{12}$ at the beginning of day 2.

But there are in fact an infinite variety of forms of possible forward contracts of which our contingency and conditional forward contracts are very special cases. Let us confine our attention to contracts entered into on day 0 where a certain sum of money is to be provided by the one party in return for a unit of some specified good by the other party. We may represent the amount of money contracted to be paid in return for a unit of the good or service by

$$_b^a P_d^c$$

where a specifies the date at which the money is to be paid, b specifies the condition on which the money is to be paid, c specifies the date at which the unit of the good in question is to be handed over to the purchaser, and d specifies the condition on which the good is to be supplied. Thus this symbol could specify the rather bizarre contract entered into today (say, Sunday) whereby the purchaser will pay P next Saturday ($=a$) if it has been wet on Monday and Tuesday ($=b$) (otherwise paying nothing) in return for which the supplier will supply one unit of the good next Wednesday ($=c$) if it is fine on Wednesday ($=d$) (otherwise supplying nothing.) The only restrictions on such contracts are that the time (a) should not be earlier than the period covered by the condition (b), since to make the payment one must already know whether the conditions for the payment is satisfied or not; similarly the time (c) must not be earlier than the period covered by the condition (d).

In fact, if there were a complete set of perfectly competitive forward markets in which arbitrage transactions could be freely undertaken, all possible forward contracts could be expressed in terms of the prices ruling in the various conditional forward markets, including the day-to-day conditional forward markets for loans and insurance. Consider, for example, in terms of the points on Figures 34 and 35 the peculiar forward price $_{12}^2 P_{1234}^1$, i.e. the price which the buyer undertakes to pay on day 2, if, but only if, the economy passed through point 12 on day 1, in return for which the seller will provide the good on day 1 in any case. One can compare (1) the present sum of money which would be necessary in order, by operations in the conditional forward markets, to obtain a sum of money $_{12}^{2}P_{1234}^{1}$ at 8 a.m. on day 2 if the economy passed through point 12 and (2) the present sum of money which would be needed to purchase the good for certain on day 1 by operations in the conditional markets. These two sums will be equated by arbitrage operations.

(1) The first sum is $\left[_{12}^{2}P_{1234}^{1}\right]\pi_{12}/(1 + i_{1234})(1 + i_{12})$. The buyer invests this sum now for one day at the interest rate of i_{1234}. He contracts now a bet of $\left[_{12}^{2}P_{1234}^{1}\right]\pi_{12}/(1 + i_{12})$ that on day 1 the economy will be at point 12, thus receiving $_{12}^{2}P_{1234}^{1}/(1 + i_{12})$ on day 1 if at point 12; and he undertakes now to lend this on day 1 in the conditional market at a rate of interest i_{12} thus ending up with $_{12}^{2}P_{1234}^{1}$ if the economy has passed through point 12.

(2) The second sum is $(\pi_{12}\bar{P}_{12} + \pi_{34}\bar{P}_{34})/(1 + i_{1234})$ which he invests now for one day receiving $\pi_{12}\bar{P}_{12} + \pi_{34}\bar{P}_{34}$ on day 1. He undertakes now a bet of $\pi_{12}\bar{P}_{12}$ on the economy being at point 12 on day 1 and $\pi_{34}\bar{P}_{34} = (1 - \pi_{12})\bar{P}_{34}$ on its being at point 34, thus acquiring $\bar{P}_{12}$ if at point 12 and $\bar{P}_{34}$ if at point 34. These sums enable him to purchase now one unit of the product in both conditional markets 12 and 34, so that he receives one unit of the product tomorrow in any case.

Sum (1) must equal sum (2) so that

$$_{12}^{2}P_{1234}^{1} = (1 + i_{12})\{\bar{P}_{12} + \bar{P}_{34}(1 - \pi_{12})/\pi_{12}\}$$

which expresses this peculiar forward price in terms of the conditional commodity prices, rates of interest, and betting odds.[1]

In Chapter X we have not mentioned what may be called ordinary forward markets, i.e. markets in which a **contract** is entered into today, i.e. on day 0, by which, at a certain specified date in the future, a given amount of money will be paid in return for a given good or service, whatever the environmental conditions may be at that time. Let us represent such prices by $\bar{\bar{P}}(t)$, where t represents the day on which the good or service is to be delivered.

Let us start with the derivation of $\bar{i}(1)$. One way of obtaining \$1 for certain on day 2 is to invest $\$1/[1 + i_{1234}][1 + \bar{i}(1)]$ on day 0 which will amount to \$ $1/[1 + \bar{i}(1)]$ on day 1, and to invest this sum in the ordinary forward market for day 1 at an interest rate $\bar{i}(1)$, so that \$1 results on day 2. Another method is to invest $\${\pi_{12}/(1 + i_{12}) + \pi_{34}/(1 + i_{34})}/(1 + i_{1234})$ on day 0, to bet

---

[1] Forward contracts may be of a composite kind. Thus a contingent contract which involved paying a price now for a good to be delivered on day 2 if it were wet on day 2 (regardless of the weather on day 1) would be a contract to supply the good if at point 1 or if at point 3. This could be treated as the sum of the contingent price for a good-if-at-point-1 plus the contingent price for a good-if-at-point-3. Composite forward contracts can always be broken down into a combination of separate forward contracts.

$\pi_{12}/(1 + i_{12})$ on point 12 and $\pi_{34}/(1 + i_{34})$ on point 34, thus obtaining $1/(1 + i_{12})$ if point 12 is reached and $1/(1 + i_{34})$ if point 34 is reached, and to invest these sums at interest i_{12} and i_{34} on the conditional loan markets for 12 and 34, thus obtaining \$1 on day 2 whether the economy passes through point 12 or point 34 on day 1. Thus:

$$\frac{1}{1 + \bar{\imath}(1)} = \frac{\pi_{12}}{1 + i_2} + \frac{\pi_{34}}{1 + i_{24}} \dots \dots \dots \dots \dots (10.6)$$

From this one can obtain:

$$\bar{\imath}(1) = \frac{i_{12}\pi_{12}/(1 + i_{12}) + i_{34}\pi_{34}/(1 + i_{34})}{\pi_{12}/(1 + i_{12}) + \pi_{34}/(1 + i_{34})} \dots \dots \dots (10.7)$$

so that $\bar{\imath}(1)$ can be expressed as a weighted average of i_{12} and i_{34}.

The same principle could be used for the derivation of $\bar{\imath}(2)$. The present discounted value of \$1 on day 3 is

$$\frac{1}{1 + i_{1234}} \frac{1}{1 + \bar{\imath}(1)} \frac{1}{1 + \bar{\imath}(2)}.$$

One can also obtain \$1 on day 3 by investing

$$\frac{1}{1 + i_{1234}} \left\{ \frac{\pi_{12}}{1 + i_{12}} \left(\frac{\bar{\pi}_1}{1 + i_1} + \frac{\bar{\pi}_2}{1 + i_2} \right) \right.$$
$$\left. + \frac{1}{1 + i_{34}} \left(\frac{\bar{\pi}_3}{1 + i_3} + \frac{\bar{\pi}_4}{1 + i_4} \right) \right\}$$

for one day, placing a bet of

$$\frac{\pi_{12}}{1 + i_{12}} \left(\frac{\bar{\pi}_1}{1 + i_1} + \frac{\bar{\pi}_2}{1 + i_2} \right)$$

on point 12, investing

$$\frac{1}{1 + i_{12}} \left(\frac{\bar{\pi}_1}{1 + i_1} + \frac{\bar{\pi}_{12}}{1 + i_2} \right)$$

on the conditional loan market 12, placing a bet of $\bar{\pi}_1/(1 + i_1)$ on point 1, and investing $1/(1 + i_1)$ on the conditional loan market 1, so as to obtain \$1 on day 3 if one passes through point 1, together with similar transactions for points 2, 3 and 4. One thus gets:

$$\frac{1}{1 + \bar{\imath}(1)} \frac{1}{1 + \bar{\imath}(2)} = \frac{\pi_{12}}{1 + i_{12}} \left(\frac{\bar{\pi}_1}{1 + i_1} + \frac{\bar{\pi}_2}{1 + i_2} \right)$$
$$+ \frac{\pi_{34}}{1 + i_{34}} \left(\frac{\bar{\pi}_3}{1 + i_3} + \frac{\bar{\pi}_4}{1 + i_4} \right) \dots \dots \dots \dots (10.8)$$

and using the expression for $1/(1 + \bar{\imath}(1))$ obtain in equation 10.6 one obtains $\bar{\imath}(2)$ as a weighted average of i_1, i_2, i_3, and i_4, where the weights are

$$\frac{\pi_{12}}{1 + i_{12}}\frac{\bar{\pi}_1}{1 + i_1}, \frac{\pi_{12}}{1 + i_{12}}\frac{\bar{\pi}_2}{1 + i_2}, \frac{\pi_{34}}{1 + i_{34}}\frac{\bar{\pi}_3}{1 + i_3},$$

and

$$\frac{\pi_{34}}{1 + i_{34}}\frac{\bar{\pi}_4}{1 + i_4}$$

respectively.

$\bar{P}(1)$ is the price which is pledged to be paid in any case for a specified good tomorrow and the sum of money which, if invested today at interest i_{1234}, will give this price tomorrow, is $\bar{P}(1)/(1 + i_{1234})$. An alternative method of obtaining the good for certain tomorrow is to invest $\{\pi_{12}\bar{P}_{12} + \pi_{34}\bar{P}_{34}\}/(1 + i_{1234})$ for one day at interest of i_{1234}, to bet $\pi_{12}\bar{P}_{12}$ on point 12 and $\pi_{34}\bar{P}_{34}$ on point 34, so that $\bar{P}_{12}$ is obtained if point 12 is reached and $\bar{P}_{34}$ if point 34 is reached. In either case one unit of the good can then be purchased on day 1. Thus:

$$\bar{P}(1) = \pi_{12}\bar{P}_{12} + \pi_{34}\bar{P}_{34} \dots\dots\dots\dots\dots\dots\dots (10.9)$$

$\bar{P}(2)$ is the price which is pledged for payment in any case for the good on day 2, and the present discounted value of this sum is $\bar{P}(2)/[1 + i_{1234}][1 + i(1)]$. This sum invested on day 0 at interest i_{1234} and in the ordinary forward market for day 1 at interest $\bar{\imath}(1)$ will produce $\bar{P}(2)$ on day 2. An alternative method of acquiring the good in any case on day 2 is to invest

$$\frac{1}{1 + i_{1234}}\left\{\pi_{12}\frac{\bar{\pi}_1\bar{P}_1 + \bar{\pi}_2\bar{P}_2}{1 + i_{12}} + \pi_{34}\frac{\bar{\pi}_3\bar{P}_3 + \bar{\pi}_4\bar{P}_4}{1 + i_{34}}\right\}$$

on day 0, to bet $(\bar{\pi}_1\bar{P}_1 + \bar{\pi}_2\bar{P}_2)\pi_{12}/(1 + i_{12})$ on point 12, to invest $(\bar{\pi}_1\bar{P}_1 + \pi_2\bar{P}_2)/(1 + \bar{\imath}_{12})$ in the conditional loan market 12, to bet $\bar{\pi}_1\bar{P}$ on point 1, with similar transàctions for points 2, 3 and 4.

Thus, using the expression for $1/(1 + \bar{\imath}(1))$ given in equation 10.6 we obtain

$$\bar{P}(2) = \frac{(\bar{\pi}_1\bar{P}_1 + \bar{\pi}_2\bar{P}_2)\pi_{12}/(1 + i_{12}) + (\bar{\pi}_3\bar{P}_3 + \bar{\pi}_4\bar{P}_4)\pi_{34}/(1 + i_{34})}{\pi_{12}/(1 + i_{12}) + \pi_{34}/(1 + i_{34})}$$

It may be observed that, provided that there are only two possible conditions for the environment (e.g. the weather will be either wet or fine tomorrow and there are no other environmental uncertainties), then a combination of conditional and of ordinary forward markets is sufficient to enable any desired betting or insurance operation to be carried out. This can be seen by showing that the betting odds as between wet and fine tomorrow (π_{12}/π_{34}) can be derived from the ordinary forward market price $(\bar{\bar{P}}(1))$ and the conditional forward market prices $(\bar{P}_{12}$ and $\bar{P}_{34})$ for any given commodity.

Thus remembering that $\pi_{34} = 1 - \pi_{12}$ and assuming $\bar{P}_{12} \neq \bar{P}_{34}$, i.e. that the state of the weather will affect the price of the product, we can derive from equation 10.9,

$$\pi_{12} = \frac{\bar{\bar{P}}(1) - \bar{P}_{34}}{\bar{P}_{12} - \bar{P}_{34}} \text{ and } \pi_{34} = \frac{\bar{P}_{12} - \bar{\bar{P}}(1)}{\bar{P}_{12} - \bar{P}_{34}}$$

so that:

$$\frac{\pi_{12}}{\pi_{34}} = \frac{\bar{\bar{P}}(1) - \bar{P}_{34}}{\bar{P}_{12} - \bar{\bar{P}}(1)} \quad \dots\dots\dots\dots\dots\dots\dots\dots\dots(10.11)$$

Thus by appropriate transactions at the prices $\bar{\bar{P}}(1)$, $\bar{P}_{12}$ and $\bar{P}_{34}$, a man can bet as between wet and fine weather tomorrow. This was the case examined and the formula obtained on page 466 of *The Growing Economy*.

CHAPTER XI

ECONOMIC EFFICIENCY IN CONDITIONS OF ENVIRONMENTAL UNCERTAINTY

We have seen in the previous chapter that one can obtain the same results through (1) a comprehensive set of contingency markets, (2) a comprehensive set of conditional forward markets, and (3) an ideal form of indicative planning which led to perfect foresight of all the market conditions (including rates of interest and of insurance premiums) which would rule along each environmental path. All three institutional arrangements would lead to the same results.

Let us consider some of the implications of the results which would be reached. We will do so in terms of the simple model depicted in Figures 34 and 35 and we will consider the results in terms of a complete set of contingency markets. The conclusions can, of course, be applied to the results of either of the other two institutional arrangements, since the results will be the same in all three cases. Suppose then that Mr A personally feels virtually certain that it will be fine. He is free to sell his labour in the wet weather markets and to buy his sunshades in the fine weather markets, i.e. to sell labour at points 12, 1 and 3 and to purchase sunshades at points 34, 2 and 4. In these circumstances, he receives now a given price for undertaking to work on days 1 and 2 if, but only if, it is wet on those days; and he uses this money to pay now to a sunshade manufacturer who undertakes to provide him with sunshades on days 1 and 2 if but only if it is fine on those days. If his expectations are correct and it turns out fine, then he can take a perpetual holiday in the sun parading up and down with a fine collection of sunshades; but if it turns out wet, he must toil away without receiving any sunshades or umbrellas in return. If everybody felt like him, then the current price of future labour-if-wet would be very depressed and the current price of future sunshades-if-fine would be much pushed up; and conversely the current price of future labour-if-fine would be pushed up and of future umbrellas-if-wet would be depressed. At some point those who were not quite so sure that it would be fine would sell labour-if-fine (thereby enabling entrepreneurs to plan to produce some sunshades-if-fine) and would purchase umbrellas-if-wet (thereby giving some employment opportunities for the many offers of labour-if-wet). The contingency prices would settle at levels which cleared the contingency markets.

But would there be any virtue in this state of affairs? Is there any sense in which it is an economically efficient outcome? In the case in which there were no environmental uncertainties we argued that a comprehensive set of competitive forward markets would lead to an efficient solution in the sense that it would be impossible to change the use of the community's resources in such a way as to make one citizen better off over the period from now to 'Kingdom Come' without making any other citizen worse off. We cannot any longer apply this criterion without modification. For suppose that the community's resources are being used today partly to prepare for the production of sunshades in case it turns out to be fine and partly to prepare for the production of umbrellas in case it turns out to be wet. If it turns out fine, then everyone could have been better off if today none of the community's resources had been devoted to the production of umbrellas. But to say that today's use of resources is inefficient because in fact no umbrellas turn out to be wanted would be comparable to saying that it is inefficient to have insured one's house except in the years in which it turns out to have been actually burned down.

But suppose that every citizen today has a preference ordering between different collections of contingent goods. That is to say, suppose that Mr A can say as between two different sets of goods, X and Y, which he has the prospect of receiving if and when he passes through the points 12, 34, 1, 2, 3, and 4 on Figure 34 whether he prefers prospect X or prospect Y. Then one can conclude that a comprehensive set of competitive contingent markets will lead to an efficient state of affairs today in the sense that no citizen could today look forward to a preferred set of possibilities without someone else having to look forward to a less preferred set of possibilities for himself.

The argument is exactly similar to that used in Chapter XII of *The Stationary Economy*. In today's comprehensive contingency markets there will be uniform market prices quoted for every good and service at every future date-cum-environment point. Each consumer can today trade these contingent goods and services for each other freely at these uniform market prices in order to move as far as possible up his own preference ordering of future prospects for the various environmental outcomes. Thus the economy will achieve the Optimization of Trade in Contingent Products (cf. p. 185 of *The Stationary Economy*).

At the same time, entrepreneurs can arrange today to purchase inputs of various resources at each future time-cum-environment point to produce various outputs at each such time-cum-environment point in such a way as to maximize today's net receipts or profits from the prices which they receive today for these contingent outputs less the prices which they pay today for these contingent inputs. If it were possible for any entrepreneur to change his plans so as to obtain a larger value of contingent outputs from a given value of contingent inputs, he would do so. Thus the economy will achieve the Maximization and the Optimization of the Production of Contingent Goods (cf. pp. 185–8 of *The Stationary Economy*).

It is important to note two features of the outcome in the very simple conditions which we are at present assuming.

First, it is not assumed that all citizens must form the same assessment of the probabilities of the different environmental paths. On the contrary, Mr A may expect fine weather and sell labour-if-wet and purchase sunshades-if-fine, while Mr B expects wet weather and sells labour-if-fine and purchases umbrellas-if-wet. Different assessments of the probabilties of different environmental outcomes will affect different people's demand for different contingent goods; they have the same effect as differences of tastes in the ordinary analysis of consumers' demand functions. But given these differences of 'taste' for wet-weather and for fine-weather goods, the competitive contingency markets will ensure that no individual's prospects can be improved without someone else's prospects being made worse.

Second, entrepreneurs as such bear no risks. They purchase and sell for fixed and known prices now all their future contingent inputs and outputs. They can thus make their future production plans for each of the various environmental paths in such a way as to maximize today's riskless net value of these plans and they can then, as ordinary consumers, spend this net sum on the purchase of contingent goods and services for their own personal future use. In this respect they, like all other citizens, do face risks. Just as any citizen, if he sells all his labour in the markets for wet weather and spends all the resulting income on sunshades in the markets for fine weather, stands to fare badly if it turns out in fact to be wet so the generality of citizens as earners of income and as consumers of goods and services (including leisure) must bear risks. It may be wet or it may be fine. This is a risk which must be faced, though any gains or losses from the risk may, of course, be spread or otherwise traded through contingency deals. The risk-bearing function of entrepreneurial activity must wait on the modification of some of the far-reaching assumptions made on page 149. In the conditions which we are at present assuming, entrepreneurs make the best certain profit they can by producing for wet-weather or fine-weather conditions according to the consumers' choice between wet-weather and fine-weather products as expressed by the prices offered by them for these contingent goods; in deciding what to do with this profit they, like any other citizen, must face the risks of wet and fine weather.

The sort of way in which entrepreneurs' decisions may be determined is illustrated by the three following simple examples, all of which are based on the simplifying assumptions that entrepreneurs have certain decisions to take today which will affect their outputs tomorrow, that the only environmental uncertainty is whether it will be wet or fine tomorrow, and that what happens after tomorrow is irrelevant for today's decisions.

As a first example, let us suppose that because tomorrow's weather is uncertain it is uncertain whether sunshades or umbrellas will be most needed. But let us suppose that the production programme for umbrellas and sunshades for tomorrow's use has to be decided today. The producer must, therefore, decide today how many umbrellas and how many sunshades he should produce for tomorrow's use. In conditions in which there were comprehensive contingency forward markets his decision would in principle be simple; and the solution of his problem is illustrated in Figure 36.

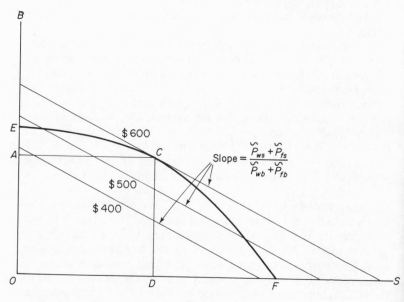

Figure 36

Let the curve *ECF* represent the combinations of sunshades (*S*) and umbrellas (*B*) that he can produce with any given amount of resources which he has at his disposal. Each sunshade which he produces he can sell forward tomorrow both as a sunshade-to-be-provided-if-fine (i.e. as S_f) for a firm price $\tilde{P}_{fs}$ and also as a sunshade-to-be-provided-if-wet (i.e. as S_w) for a firm price $\tilde{P}_{ws}$. He receives the price $\tilde{P}_{fs}$ and the price $\tilde{P}_{ws}$ whatever the weather may be. Thus the firm price which he can get today for each sunshade that he produces for sale tomorrow will be $\tilde{P}_{fs} + \tilde{P}_{ws}$. Similarly, the firm price which he can get today for each umbrella that he produces for sale tomorrow will be $\tilde{P}_{fb} + \tilde{P}_{wb}$. For him there is no uncertainty left. He will determine his outputs just as any competitive producer will do when faced in conditions of certainty with selling prices equal to $\tilde{P}_{fs} + \tilde{P}_{ws}$ and $\tilde{P}_{fb} + \tilde{P}_{wb}$ for the two commodities *S* and *B*. In the case illustrated in Figure 36, he will use his given resources to produce *OD* units of *S* and *OA* units of *B* because this brings him at the point *C* (where the ratio between the marginal costs of *S* and *B* equals the ratio between their selling prices), onto his highest possible revenue line of \$600.[1]

But let us now consider a rather more subtle sort of decision which our producer of umbrellas and sunshades may have to take today. We no longer assume that he must decide today the actual number of umbrellas and sunshades which will be produced for sale to consumers tomorrow. He can tomorrow decide to produce umbrellas or sunshades. But today he must decide what sort of plant to install. (1) If he installs one sort of plant, he will be able to produce umbrellas easily but sunshades only with difficulty. (2) If he installs another sort of plant, he will be able to produce sunshades easily but umbrellas with difficulty. (3) There may be yet a third sort of plant—the flexible, unspecialized sort of plant—which will not enable him to produce umbrellas as easily as the first plant nor sunshades as easily as the second plant, but which will enable him to produce umbrellas more easily than the second plant and sunshades more easily than the first plant. These three plants are illustrated in Figure 37. We assume for simplicity that each plant costs the same to build and to operate. The choice which the entrepreneur has to make today is which plant to install. Tomorrow he can use each plant to produce either umbrellas (*B*) or sunshades (*S*) in any combination which lies on the production possibility curve—i.e. the curve passing through the points *A* and *C*—shown in the north-eastern quadrant of each section of the diagram.

Consider the position which the entrepreneur will be in if he has

[1] Cf. Figure 39 on p. 129 of *The Stationary Economy*.

installed any one of these plants—for example, plant 2. Measure the contingency prices for umbrellas— i.e. $\tilde{P}_{wb}$ for umbrellas-if-wet and $\tilde{P}_{fb}$ for umbrellas-if-fine—to the left from the origin O; and measure the contingency prices for sunshades ($\tilde{P}_{ws}$ and $\tilde{P}_{fs}$) downwards from the origin O. The entrepreneur could undertake to sell OB_w umbrellas-if-wet and OS_w sunshades-if-wet because he could tomorrow deliver these quantities by producing tomorrow at the point A on his production possibility curve. OB_w and OS_w are then quantities which he will be under an obligation to produce tomorrow only if it turns out to be wet tomorrow. He can, therefore, simultaneously undertake to produce another combination—say at the point C— of OB_f umbrellas-if-fine and OS_f sunshades-if-fine. The nature of

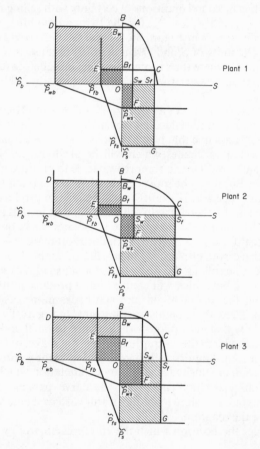

Figure 37

these contingency forward markets is such that he will get a firm and certain revenue (namely $\tilde{P}_{wb}B_w + \tilde{P}_{ws}S_w$) from his sales if it is wet. His total firm revenue, therefore, from undertaking to produce and supply at the point A if it turns out to be wet and at the point C if it turns out to be fine is:

$$\tilde{P}_{wb}B_w + \tilde{P}_{ws}S_w + \tilde{P}_{fb}B_f + \tilde{P}_{fs}S_f$$

i.e. the sum of the four rectangles

$$O\tilde{P}_{wb}DB_w + O\tilde{P}_{fb}EB_f + O\tilde{P}_{fs}GS_f + OP_{ws}FS_w$$

i.e. once the single cross-hatched areas and twice the double cross-hatched areas in Figure 37.

How should he choose the points A and C, i.e. the amounts of goods-if-wet and goods-if-fine which he will undertake today to produce tomorrow, so as to maximize his revenue and so—on the simplifying assumption that his total costs are given—maximize his profit? To answer this question, draw the straight lines $\tilde{P}_{wb}\tilde{P}_{ws}$ and $\tilde{P}_{fb}\tilde{P}_{fs}$ in the south-west quadrant of the diagrams. Then he should choose the point A in such a way that the slope of the production curve at the point A is the same as the slope of the line $\tilde{P}_{wb}\tilde{P}_{ws}$ and he should choose the point C at that point on the production possibility curve at which its slope is equal to the slope of the line $\tilde{P}_{fb}P_{fs}$. The reason for this can be seen from Figure 38. Given the plant which he has to operate, the entrepreneur will wish to maximize his receipts from sales-if-wet and from sales-if-fine independently of each other, since what he commits himself to do tomorrow if tomorrow turns out to be wet in no way affects what he can commit himself to do tomorrow if tomorrow turns out to be fine. Consider then how he will choose the point A so as to maximize his revenue from sales-if-wet. Suppose he is considering a commitment at point A' but wishes to compare the result with a commitment at point A. If he moves from A' to A he will increase his sales of umbrellas-if-wet by ΔB_w and will reduce his sales of sunshades-if-wet by ΔS_w. He will, therefore, increase (decrease) his revenue from sales-if-wet if $\Delta B_w \tilde{P}_{wb}$ is greater (less) than $\Delta S_w \tilde{P}_{ws}$, i.e. according as $\Delta B_w/\Delta S_w \gtrless \tilde{P}_{ws}/P_{wb}$. In other words, he will maximize his revenue from sales-if-wet by moving the point A from A' up to the production possibility curve until the slope of that curve is the same as the slope of the price line $\tilde{P}_{ws}/\tilde{P}_{wb}$.

To choose between the three plants shown in Figure 37 it is necessary, therefore, (1) to draw in the three production possibility curves, (2) to draw in the two contingency price lines—i.e. the ratios $\tilde{P}_{ws}/\tilde{P}_{wb}$ and $\tilde{P}_{fs}/\tilde{P}_{fb}$, (3) to choose the points A and C at which the slopes of the production possibility curves are equal to the slopes of these price lines, and (4) to choose that plant for which the total revenue, represented by the sum of the four cross-hatched rectangles in the south-east and north-west quadrants, is greatest. Which plant will turn out to be the most profitable will depend both upon the technical production possibilities (i.e. the relevant production possibility curves) and upon the four contingency prices. The reader must be left to consider the many possibilities for himself. We will give only one obvious example.

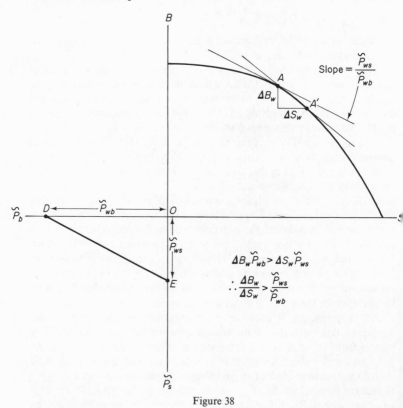

Figure 38

Suppose the majority of consumers come strongly to expect wet weather rather than fine weather so that $\tilde{P}_{wb}$ and $\tilde{P}_{ws}$ are both doubled. The effect of this will be to double the rectangles $O\tilde{P}_{wb}DB_w$ and $O\tilde{P}_{ws}FS_w$. The really substantial effect of this will be the doubling of the large rectangle $O\tilde{P}_{wb}DB_w$, and this will clearly increase the profitability of the plant where $O\tilde{P}_{wb}DB_w$ is in any case largest, i.e. plant 1. We reach the not altogether surprising conclusion that the more consumers expect wet weather, the more likely is it to prove profitable for the producers to install plants which specialize in the production of umbrellas.[2]

The two examples which we have so far examined are both cases in which the uncertainty (namely whether tomorrow will be wet or fine) affects the tastes of consumers (namely for umbrellas and sunshades). Let us now consider a case in which the uncertainty concerns not the tastes of consumers, but the productive possibilities of producers. The most important case of this is, of course, uncertainty about the future course of technical progress which is a main reason for not knowing how much one will produce tomorrow from a given amount of inputs. But we can illustrate exactly the same uncertainty by considering the effect of the weather upon a farmer's output. If the weather is fine, the harvest will be good; but if the weather is wet, the same inputs of ploughing, sowing, reaping, etc., will produce a much smaller output. However, it may be possible by choice of seed to affect the influence of the weather upon the output. Suppose there are three types of seed. In all three cases the harvest will be greater if the weather is fine. But seed 1 is a fine-weather seed in the sense that the harvest will be very good if the weather is fine but very bad if it is wet. Seed 2 is a wet-weather seed in the sense that, while the harvest will be a good deal worse than with seed 1 if the weather is fine, it will be a good deal better than with seed 1 if the weather is wet. Seed 3 is of an intermediate variety. Which seed should the farmer sow?[3]

The answer is shown in Figure 39. On the two axes we measure the amount of corn which will be harvested if the weather is fine (H_f) and the amount which will be harvested if the weather is wet (H_w). The combinations of wet weather and fine weather amounts harvested from a given expenditure of inputs will be OC_1 and OA_1 if seed 1 is planted, OC_2 and OA_2 if seed 2 is planted, and OC_3 and OA_3 if seed 3 is planted. The farmer can sell these amounts in the forward contingency markets for corn according as to which seed he chooses to

[2] The fact that a producer will prepare to produce umbrellas rather than sunshades does not necessarily mean that he expects wet weather. In the absence of contingency markets he will prepare to produce sunshades if he expects fine weather and, therefore, expects that his customers will go for sunshades rather than umbrellas when the time comes. But with contingency forward markets he will follow the expectations of his customers and will prepare to produce umbrellas if they bid high for umbrellas in the contingency market. He may, of course, himself simultaneously as a consumer use his income from profits to purchase sunshades-if-fine and thus as a user of goods to bet on fine weather.

[3] The analogy to this question in the case of uncertainty about technical progress is: Should an entrepreneur invest in a form of plant which assumes that a particular piece of research and development will be successful or in the form of plant which assumes that this piece of technical progress will not occur?

sow. Which will bring him the most revenue will depend upon the ratio of the contingency price for corn if it is wet to the contingency price of corn if it is fine. If (1) consumers expect fine weather and (2) don't mind going rather foodless if the weather should be wet, the contingency price for corn-if-fine will be relatively high and farmers may find it profitable to sow seed 1. If (1) consumers expect wet

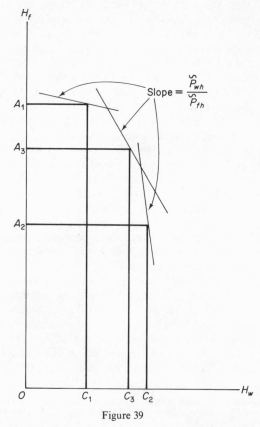

Figure 39

weather and/or (2) are extremely anxious to ensure a substantial subsistence level of food whatever may happen to the weather, the price of corn-if-wet will be high; the farmers will find it profitable to sow seed 2.

The systems which we have examined in this and the preceding chapter have contained two conceptually separate elements, namely (1) a comprehensive system of forward markets or of indicative planning which will enable all economic decision-makers to foresee accurately the development of market conditions along each environmental path and (2) a comprehensive set of insurance or betting markets which will enable decision-makers to exchange income with each other as between one environmental path and another. These two elements do not necessarily go together.

When environmental uncertainties are so numerous that they cannot all be considered—a possibility which we will consider at length later—or, what comes perhaps to much the same thing, when any particular environmental risks are so hard to define and to distinguish from each other that it is impossible to base a firm betting or insurance contract upon the occurrence or non-occurrence of any one of them, then for this reason alone it is impossible to have a system of contingency or of conditional forward markets. In terms of equation 10.2 given above; namely:

$$\tilde{P}_1 = \bar{P}_1 \pi_{12} \bar{\pi}_1 / (1 + i_{1234})(1 + i_{12})$$

it is impossible to make a contract involving $\tilde{P}_1$ or $\bar{P}_1$, simply because one will not on day 2 be able to decide precisely enough for the purposes of a firm legal contract whether or not one is in fact at what each party to the contract considers to be point 1.

There is, however, another possible state of affairs in which it would be possible to make a contract in terms of the conditional forward price $\bar{P}_1$ but not in terms of the betting odds or insurance premiums (i.e. the π_{12} and $\bar{\pi}_1$) and thus not in terms of the contingency forward price P. This is the case where what is known as the 'moral hazard' rules out insurance and betting, even though the risk can be precisely defined. Let us take an example. An entrepreneur is undertaking research into a new technological process. If his research is successful, the result will be of great value. It may be quite possible to lay down an exact criterion as to whether or not the new process has been found by next year to perform in a precisely defined manner. But the entrepreneur will not necessarily be able to lay a bet of $1 million that he will not discover the process by next year. He might be too much tempted to relax his inventive endeavours and take a year's rest.

In this sort of case, it may be quite possible to develop a system of conditional forward markets. Our entrepreneur, for example, may quite well be able to make forward contracts in the form that he will sell to a particular customer Q_1 units of his product at a price $\bar{P}_1$ if he is successful in his invention but Q_2 units at a price $\bar{P}_2$ if he is unsuccessful. This will remove some degree of market uncertainty for him as well as for his customer and this may well affect his behaviour, including perhaps the nature of his research activities. But if the quantities Q_1 and Q_2 and the prices $\bar{P}_1$ and $\bar{P}_2$ correspond more or less to what he thinks they would be in any case in the two possible eventualities of the outcome of his research, his incentive to research will not be basically blunted.

What he cannot do without seriously affecting his incentives is to sell Q_1 for $\tilde{P}_1$ and Q_2 for $\tilde{P}_2$ in the contingency market, since this means that he will receive $Q_1\tilde{P}_1 + Q_2\tilde{P}$ for certain now, but will have to provide Q_1 if the research is successful and only Q_2 if the research is unsuccessful. If $Q_2 < Q_1$ this will introduce some element of disincentive for his inventive efforts. This simply corresponds to his inability to bet that he won't succeed in his research.

One may conclude that where environmental uncertainties can be reasonably well defined but where the moral hazard rules out insurance or betting, one can still have a set of indicative sub-plans, one for each well defined environmental path. These sub-plans will help to predict what will actually happen in the future to spot prices including interest rates (i.e. the P_{12}, P_{34}, P_1, P_2, P_3, P_4, i_{12} and i_{34} of our simple example). But there will be no betting odds or insurance premiums to predict (the π_{12}, π_{34}, π_1, π_2, π_3 and π_4 of Figure 35). The planning procedure must aim at discovering what will be the course of prices and interest rates along each environmental path when the individual economic agents are unable to place bets on or to ensure against these environmental uncertainties.

For the ordinary citizen as worker, saver and consumer this means in theory that he will be able to foresee his future along each environmental path, but will be unable to transfer by betting or insurance his resources from one such path to another. Previously, to repeat our previous extreme but homely example, Mr A could sell his labour in wet-weather markets and buy his sunshades in fine-weather markets, thereby working if, and only if, it was wet and consuming if, and only if, it was fine. He had only one budget constraint covering all contingencies; what he earned in wet-weather markets limited his purchases in fine-weather markets. With a reliable indicative plan, but in the absence of betting markets, he would know what he could earn by his labour or gain in interest on his savings on each weather path and he would know at what prices he could purchase goods on each weather path; but what he earned on each weather path would limit his consumption on that weather path; he would be subject to a separate budget constraint for each weather path; he would have to earn in fine weather in order to be able to spend in fine weather. It would be impossible for someone who expected fine weather to exchange income-if-wet for income-if-fine with someone who expected wet weather.

But while there would now no longer be a straightforward market in which resources-if-wet could be traded directly for resources-if-fine, there would still exist limited possibilities on the production side of transforming resources-if-wet into resources-if-fine, just as a farmer who is precluded from trading corn for clothes can start to produce his own clothes as well as his own corn. In our homely example, a person who expects fine weather can concentrate on producing sunshades for which there will be a high price if it is fine, while a person who expects wet weather can concentrate on the production of umbrellas. By shifting from the production of umbrellas to the production of sunshades, an entrepreneur is shifting from profits-if-wet to profits-if-fine.

Thus the entrepreneur of production now starts to have to take risks. Previously, with a complete comprehensive set of contingency markets or—as we saw, what comes to the same thing—with a comprehensive indicative plan with comprehensive betting markets, the entrepreneur as such took no risks. He could plan his operations so as to get now a certain revenue for all his contingency outputs and to pay now a certain cost for all his contingency inputs; he could maximize the excess of certain revenue over certain cost; and as an individual he could then lay out his maximized certain net resources through the betting markets or contingency markets as he thought best in view of his own (and not his customer's) expectations of wet or fine.

This is no longer possible to him. He cannot produce sunshades at a high and certain price because other citizens are foolish enough to expect fine weather and use the proceeds to purchase for himself umbrellas at a certain low price because he and he alone knows that it will be wet. To make a big income if it is wet he must now produce umbrellas, however much other people may think that it will be fine, simply because if it is in fact wet he will get a low price for any sunshades he produces and a high price for any umbrellas. The entrepreneur must now bear the risk. It is in these conditions that the great entrepreneurial function of judging what the future market and technological developments will be comes into its own. The successful entrepreneur is now the one who is best at judging what the future market-cum-environmental paths will be and is, therefore, more likely than others to plan to produce what will in fact turn out to be wanted. The ordinary citizen as consumer will no longer determine in the contingency and betting markets through his own expectations the eventualities for which the entrepreneur should plan; the entrepreneur takes over from the run of citizens this function of assessing the probabilities of the various environmental paths.

But cannot the ordinary run of citizens share in this entrepreneurial function of assessing the probabilities of the various outcomes? With the existence of joint stock companies with equity shares and with a well-organized stock exchange, an ordinary citizen can invest his savings in a company producing sunshades which will declare a high dividend if it is fine or in a company producing umbrellas which will declare a high dividend if it is wet. He is in fact participating in the entrepreneurial risk-bearing function by choosing, as it were, to use some of his productive resources to produce a fine-weather product or a wet-weather product. By a judicious mix of his portfolio he can vary the extent to which he is thereby betting on wet weather or on fine weather.

But, for two basic reasons, this provides only a very partial substitute for a straightforward betting or insurance market on which one might exchange directly income-if-wet for income-if-fine. The first reason is that it can be operated only by the use of an individual's property and property income. It cannot be operated by the use of his labour and his wages. With a stock exchange, a citizen can without too much cost spread his capital over many uses and thus to some extent place bets of various sizes on many different environmental outcomes. But he cannot without intolerable cost work part of the day in a sunshade factory, part of the day in an umbrellas factory, and so on. Nor is it easy for him to shift from day to day from one occupation to another. He cannot, therefore, readily as a worker distribute his productive effort in whatever parcels he chooses over the various environmental outcomes, whereas with comprehensive betting or insurance markets he could so distribute his wage income. And if he owns little or no property he will not in fact be able to raise the funds to speculate on the stock exchange. The entrepreneurial alternative to betting and insurance markets is broadly speaking open to property and not to work.

The second reason is that productive techniques may be such that it is impossible to use shifts of production instead of shifts of trade to exchange income-if-wet for income-if-fine. This would be so if umbrellas and sunshades were for technical reasons joint products. Let us again illustrate from a homely but simple example. Let us suppose that the only physical difference between a sunshade and an umbrella is that the former object is covered with a bright material whereas the latter is always covered in sombre black. Let us then suppose that the whole of the population is smitten with colour blindness. There is now no relevant physical difference between a sunshade and an umbrella, so that we may call the resulting single object a sunbrella. Suppose, however, that the consuming population is divided into those who expect fine weather and have skins which are exceptionally liable to blister if exposed to the sun and those who expect wet weather and are exceptionally liable to catch cold if exposed to the rain. There will be all the difference in the world to both groups between a sunbrella-if-fine and a sunbrella-if-wet. The two groups would dearly love to exchange

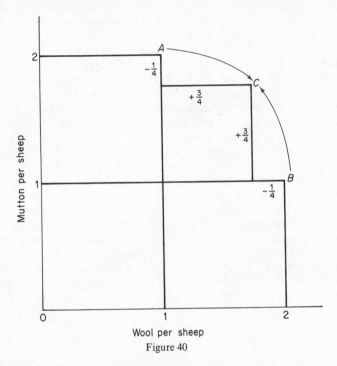

Figure 40

sunbrellas-if-wet for sunbrellas-if-fine; that is to say, both would expect a higher utility if it could be so arranged that the sunbrellas all went to the first group if it were fine and to the second group if it were wet, but there are no contingency markets or betting or insurance markets in which this trade can directly take place. And, as far as the productive side is concerned, producers can produce today for sale tomorrow only sunbrellas; that is to say, for every sunbrella-if-wet produced there will be one sunbrella-if-fine produced. People cannot purchase ordinary shares in companies producing sunbrellas-if-fine as opposed to companies producing sunbrellas-if-wet.[4]

[4] Just as in the theory of international trade, there are conditions of production in which the movement of productive factors is not a complete substitute for trade in the products of the factors.

A less extreme, though still very simple example, may be useful. Suppose mutton to sell well in fine weather (because it is a good picnic food) and wool to sell well in wet weather (because it makes good raincoats). Suppose that one can invest in three types of sheep—type A which produces 2 units of mutton + 1 unit of wool, type B which produces 1 unit of mutton + 2 units of wool, and an intermediate type C which produces $1\frac{3}{4}$ units of both products as shown in Figure 40.

One can now have two independent farms, one producing with sheep of type A and the other with sheep of type B. Those who wish to bet on fine weather can invest their money in farm A and those who wish to bet on wet weather in farm B. This enables some betting on the environmental outcome to take place, but only at the expense of productive efficiency. For if farm A and farm B both exchanged one of their sheep for a type C sheep, there would be a net gain of $\frac{1}{2}$ unit of both wool and mutton. The change in farm A would cause an increase of wool of $\frac{3}{4}$ and a loss of mutton of only $\frac{1}{4}$, but the change in farm B would cause a fall in wool of only $\frac{1}{4}$ but an increase in mutton of $\frac{3}{4}$. The flocks may properly be concentrated on types A and B on the different farms in order to be able to place different bets against weather risk. But this is a second-best arrangement. If people could use a betting or insurance market to make direct exchanges of income-if-wet for income-if-fine while all farmers concentrated on producing that type of sheep which provided the highest certain income when consumers had made their bets, everyone could be better off.

CHAPTER XII

THE PLANNING OF FUTURE ACTION

In the discussion of forward markets and of indicative planning in the previous chapter of this part, we have so far ignored some of the basic problems which will confront the individual decision-maker. We have spoken of systems of contingency markets, of conditional forward markets, and of comprehensive indicative planning, as if each private decision-maker would have little or no difficulty in deciding what his future programme of purchase and sales should be along each possible environmental path provided only that (i) he knew by means of the contingency prices, of the conditional forward prices, or of the future prices revealed by the indicative plan what market conditions he must assume to be associated with each environmental time-path and (ii) was free to make his own subjective estimate of the probability of each environmental time-path. In other words, we have assumed away the difficulties which any individual private decision-maker might find in making up his mind how much to buy or sell forward of each good and service at each point of time in the future conditional forward markets, once he knows the conditional forward prices quoted in the market. Similarly, in the case of the formation of an indicative plan we have assumed away the difficulties which a private decision-maker might find in reporting to the governmental planners how much of each good and service he would expect to buy and sell at each future point of time along each environmental time-path on the assumption that the course of future market prices along each path would be that which was indicated by the planners.

But there are certain basic difficulties to be confronted in the formation of these individual programmes for future conditional transactions. Let us illustrate these by considering any one citizen who, during the Albert Hall planning meeting described on page 165 is being asked to fill in the four questionnaires, the first stating how much of everything he will buy and sell at each point on path 1 on Figure 34 (i.e. at points 1234, 12 and 1) given the prices assumed on the questionnaire, the second asking for the same information for the points on path 2 (i.e. for points 1234, 12 and 2) and so on. The point 1234 is common to all four questionnaires; the point 12 is common to the first two questionnaires; and the point 34 is common

189

to the last two questionnaires. In filling up his information for point 1234 on questionnaire 1, our citizen must declare not what he would do today if he knew he was on path 1, but what he would do today in the absence of any knowledge about which path he is on. In filling up his information for point 12 on questionnaire 1, our citizen must declare not what he would do tomorrow if he knew that he was on path 1, but what today he thinks he would do tomorrow if he did not know today what path he was on, but tomorrow found that he was either on path 1 or path 2. And so on.

In describing the Albert Hall meeting on page 165, we spoke of the ideal type of indicative planning as if it consisted of the construction of a set of separate plans, one for each future possible environmental path. In a sense this is a fair description of the end result of the process but it is clear that in their construction this set of plans makes a single interdependent whole.[1] A farmer, for example, cannot properly decide today how much of one particular sort of equipment to purchase and how much of another type until he has decided how much he is likely to need of each kind of equipment along each of the four possible environmental paths, and this will obviously depend upon how much of each crop he plans to produce at each point on each path. It appears that he cannot start on the calculation of any one of his separate programmes until he has finished the calculation of all of them. The whole set of programmes presents a problem in interdependence which requires the solution of a set of simultaneous interrelationships.

This problem is particularly acute in conditions of uncertainty illustrated by our farmer's programming problems. But it exists also in conditions of certainty. Suppose that our farmer was faced with a programme covering many days but that he knew that the weather (with its associated market prices) was certain to move on a particular weather path. What he best decides to do today will depend upon what he will best decide to do tomorrow, but what is best for him to do tomorrow will depend both on what he has done today (e.g. whether he has installed one kind of equipment or another) and also on what it will be best for him to decide to do the day after tomorrow (e.g. whether the day after tomorrow it will be best for him to go in for one particular crop or for another). But what it will be best for him to decide to do the day after tomorrow will depend not only on what he has done today and tomorrow but

---

[1] The separate plans for the different environmental paths in fact form such an interrelated whole that we may refer to them as a single plan; and in what follows when we talk of 'a plan' we mean a set of plans covering the various possible environmental paths, and when we wish to refer to the action planned along only one of the possible environmental paths we will use the term 'a sub-plan'.

also what it will be best for him to do on still more distant days. The optimum programme for his future purchases and sales is a single interdependent whole.

In this chapter we will discuss how an economic decision-maker might try to cope with the problem of constructing a plan for future economic action on the assumption that there is a comprehensive system of conditional forward markets or of indicative planning so that the prices, including the day-to-day interest rates and insurance premiums, which will go with each point on each weather path are known precisely in advance. But the principles involved would be the same even if there were market uncertainties as well as environmental uncertainties. If the prices were not known in advance, then the same principles could be used in individual decision-making but with a much greater number of paths for the exogeneous events. To the individual competitive decision-maker prices, like the weather, are something which happen to him and which he cannot control and are, therefore, to be treated by him as exogenous events. He is concerned with the probabilities of different weather-cum-price paths. If through indicative planning or conditional forward markets, each weather path is associated with one price path, then the number of weather-cum-price paths is greatly reduced. But if wet can occur on day 1 with either a high price or a low price for a good, then instead of the single channel

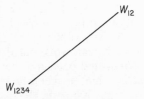

of Figure 34, we must have the double channel

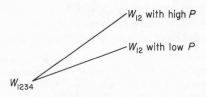

and so on.

One way in which an individual citizen might attempt to formulate an acceptable plan would be (1) to start with any reasonable feasible plan and (2) then to consider a series of adjustments to the plan, accepting any adjustment which improved the outcome and rejecting any adjustment which made the outcome worse. If we assume that his objective is to maximize the expected utility which he can obtain from the future consumption of various goods (including leisure as a good), then he will accept any adjustment to his plan which increases the present expectation of the total utility to be derived from the planned levels of consumption at each and every future point on all the possible environmental paths.[2]

Let us consider first the case in which there are no betting or insurance markets available.

(1) To devise a feasible plan, our citizen must plan his consumption at a sufficiently low level, and the amount of work which he will undertake in order to earn income at a sufficiently high level at points 1234, 12 and 34 on Figure 34 to make sure that, given his initial resources, he has sufficient money from earnings or from past savings at each of the points 1, 2, 3 and 4 to be able to finance some consumption during day 2—the last day of his existence on earth. He must take account in this initial feasible plan of the amounts, if any, which as an entrepreneur he plans to produce of each good at points 1234, 12 and 34, since this will determine his expenses on paying for hired labour and for intermediate products and his receipts from the sale of outputs at the price and wages ruling at the various points on the environment paths. The basic point is a simple one. If he determines his levels of consumption, the amount of work he will do, and the scale on which he will enter into productive operations at points 1234, 12 and 24, and if, as we assume to be the case, he knows the prices and wage rates which rule at every point, then he can work out the implications of this plan along each environmental path and thus calculate how much money will be available to him to spend on consumption on day 2 at the end of each environmental path. His planned outgoings must be sufficiently low and his planned receipts sufficiently high for points 1234, 12 and 34 to ensure that something is left over for consumption expenditure at points 1, 2, 3 and 4.[3]

(2) Starting with some such feasible plan there are four types of marginal adjustment to the plan which can be considered.

[2] In the absence of increasing returns to scale in his productive operations and with diminishing marginal utility from the extra consumption of any good at any point, the series of small marginal improvements in the plan, if carried out relentlessly until there was no more scope for improvement, would lead ultimately to the best possible plan. There would be only one mountain with a smooth ascending slope available to climb; if one moved continuously uphill so long as that were possible, one would ultimately reach the one and only summit—though not necessarily by the easiest or quickest route.

[3] The budget constraints are formulated precisely in equations 11.3 below.

(i) At any one point he might buy more of one good and less of another, spending the same total amount of money on consumption. He can improve his position by planning to buy more X and less Y at that point, so long as the ratio of the marginal utility of good X to the marginal utility of good Y is greater than the ratio of the price of X to the price of Y. This is a familiar result of static analysis.[4]

(ii) At any one point he might be able to substitute one input for another input in his production arrangements for that day in such a way as to leave unchanged his outputs available for sale on the succeeding day. He will improve his position if he can thereby save money, i.e. if he plans at any point to use more of input X and less of input Y in his production plans so long as the ratio of the marginal product of X to that of Y is greater than the ratio of the price of X to the price of Y. This also is a familiar result of static analysis.[5]

(iii) When he is considering adjustments which involve the planned scales of his productive operations, he must take into account the risks which he is running. Thus he may consider the possibility of planning at point 12 to take on one more unit of labour in order to produce an additional output of X ready for sale on day 2—i.e. at point 1 or point 2. Let $\Delta \overline{X}_{12}$ be the additional output. The additional cost to him on day 2 will be the wage of the unit of labour which will then become payable, namely W_{12}. His additional receipts will be $P_{1x}\Delta \overline{X}_{12}$ if point 1 is reached and $P_{2x}\Delta \overline{X}_{12}$ if point 2 is reached, that is to say he will obtain a net receipt of $P_{1x}\Delta \overline{X}_{12} - W_{12}$ at point 1 or of $P_{2x}\Delta \overline{X}_{12} - W_{12}$ at point 2. Should he make the adjustment?

Of course, if both net receipts are positive he will gain for certain, and if both net receipts are negative he will lose for certain. But suppose X to be a good for which the demand price will be high in environmental conditions 1, but very low in environmental conditions 2. Then the net receipt might be positive at point 1, but negative at point 2. Is the adjustment then to be considered an improvement or not?

This depends upon three things: (a) the sizes of the net receipt and of the net loss; (b) the importance to him of having more or less money to spend at points 1 and 2, i.e. the marginal utility of money to him at points 1 and 2 which we will call μ_1 and μ_2 respectively; and (c) the probability with which he expects movements from point 12 to point 1 and to point 2 which we will call ε_1 and $\varepsilon_2 = 1 - \varepsilon_1$ respectively. The expectation of additional utility at point 1 if he does make the adjustment is $\varepsilon_1\mu_1(P_{1x}\Delta \overline{X}_{12} - W_{12})$.

[4] Cf. *The Stationary Economy*, p. 40.
[5] Cf. *The Stationary Economy*, p. 131.

He will thus have an improvement in expected utility if

$$\varepsilon_1\mu_1(P_{1x}\Delta\overline{X}_{12} - W_{12}) + \varepsilon_2\mu_2(P_{2x}\Delta\overline{X}_{12} - W_{12}) > 0$$

i.e. if

$$W_{12} < \Delta\overline{X}_{12}(\varepsilon_1\mu_1 P_{1x} + \varepsilon_2\mu_2 P_{2x})/(\varepsilon_1\mu_{12} + \varepsilon_2\mu_2)$$

He should make the adjustment to his plan if the wage rate is lower than the marginal product of labour valued at a weighted average of the prices for which it may sell, these weights being the marginal utilities of income at each point multiplied by the probability with which the outcome is expected.

(iv) Finally, our citizen must consider whether he should adjust his plan by cutting down his consumption at one point in order to be able to consume more at a later point. If he plans to cut down his consumption by \$1 at point 12 he loses μ_{12}, the marginal utility of income at that point. He can invest this at interest i_{12} to obtain \$$(1 + i_{12})$ by day 2. This will have a marginal utility of $\mu_1(+ 1 i_{12})$ at point 1 or of $\mu_2(1 + i_{12})$ at point 2. $\mu_1(1 + i_{12})$ is expected with probability ε_1 and $\mu_2(1 + i_{12})$ with probability ε_2. The expected additional utility is, therefore $(\varepsilon_1\mu_1 + \varepsilon_2\mu_2)(1 + i_{12})$. He should make the adjustment if $\mu_{12} < (\varepsilon_1\mu_1 + \varepsilon_2\mu_2)(1 + i_{12})$.[6]

Let us now consider the case in which our citizen is able to insure against all environmental risks. For example, at point 12 he can insure for \$1 against a movement to point 2 for a premium of π_2. He now need run no risks as an entrepreneur. Consider adjustment (iii) examined above. If he plans to take on one more unit of labour at point 12 his net receipts will be $(P_{1x}\Delta\overline{X}_{12} - W_{12})$ at point 1 but $(P_{2x}\Delta\overline{X}_{12} - W_{12})$ at point 2. Suppose that he plans to pay an insurance premium of $\pi_2(P_{1x} - P_{2x})\Delta\overline{X}_{12}$ against moving to point 2, where $\pi_2 = 1 - \pi_1$. Then if point 1 is reached he receives net from his productive activities $(P_{1x}\Delta\overline{X}_{12} - W_{12})$ but has to pay out the premium of $\pi_2(P_{1x} - P_{2x})\overline{X}_{12}$, a net receipt of $(\pi_1 P_{1x} + \pi_2 P_{2x})\Delta\overline{X}_{12} - W_{12}$. But if point 2 is reached, he receives net from his productive activities $(P_{2x}\Delta\overline{X}_{12} - W_{12})$, he has to pay the premium of $\pi_2(P_{1x} - P_{2x})\Delta\overline{X}_{12}$, but he now receives the insured sum of $(P_{1x} - P_{2x})\Delta\overline{X}_{12}$ so that once again his net receipts are $(\pi_1 P_{1x} + \pi_2 P_{2x})\Delta\overline{X}_{12} - W_{12}$. He is faced with no uncertainty and should make the adjustment if $W_{12} < (\pi_1 P_{1x} + \pi_2 P_{2x})\Delta\overline{X}_{12}$, i.e. if the wage rate is less than the value of the marginal product of labour, the valuation being made at the certain insured return.[7]

But while our citizen can now avoid all entrepreneurial risks so

---

[6] The implications of this formula are considered on pp. 259–60 below.

[7] It is to be observed that the certain price of X, namely $\pi_1 P_{1x} + \pi_2 P_{2x}$, corresponds to the price in the ordinary forward market as derived in equation 10.9. (p. 171).

that adjustment (iii) is modified in the above way, he is able, if he so desires, through insurance or betting operations to transfer purchasing power from one environmental path to another. For example, suppose that at point 12 he undertakes (apart from any hedging of his entrepreneurial risks) to pay a premium of $\$\pi_2\hat{B}$ to insure for $\$\hat{B}$ against a movement to point 2. Then if point 1 is reached he loses the premium $\$\pi_2\hat{B}$. While, if point 2 is reached, he loses the premium $\$\pi_2\hat{B}$ but gains the insured sum $\$\hat{B}$, a net receipt of $\$(1 - \pi_2)\hat{B} = \$\pi_1\hat{B}$. By such means he can devise an initial feasible plan under (1) which enables consumption at point 2 to be increased by $\$\pi_1$ for every $\$\pi_2$ decrease in consumption at point 1. Having started with any feasible plan he must now consider a fifth type of adjustment to his initial plan, namely adjustments through changes in the amount of insurance.

(v) Should our citizen, for example, by increasing his insurance against a movement from point 12 to point 2 add an additional $\$\pi_1$ to his income at point 2 at the expense of subtracting an additional $\$\pi_2$ from his income at piont 1? The change in net expected utility will be $-\varepsilon_1\mu_1\pi_2 + \varepsilon_2\mu_2\pi_1$. He should make the change if this expression is positive, i.e. if $\varepsilon_2\mu_2/\varepsilon_1\mu_1 > \pi_2/\pi_1$, i.e. if the ratio between the expected additional utility of income at point 2 to its value at point 1 is greater than the cost in the insurance market of shifting income from point 1 to point 2.

Note to Chapter XII

THE SOLUTION OF THE PLANNING PROBLEM BY LAGRANGIAN MULTIPLIERS

In this Note we will consider rather more formally the problems confronting a representative citizen in deciding his plans for future action along each of the four environmental paths in Figures 34 and 35. We assume that by one means or another (i.e. either by a system of conditional forward markets or by a system of comprehensive indicative planning) our citizen knows what the future course of commodity prices, interest rates, and wage rates will be along each environmental path. We will start with the assumption that there are no betting or insurance markets, but will introduce such markets later in this Note. Our citizen's problem is how to devise an optimum programme for his future decisions about consumption, savings, working, production, and so on.

We assume that there are only two commodities, X and Y, which can be used either for final consumption or as intermediate or capital goods as inputs into the productive system in order to produce still more X and Y. The only other input into the productive system is labour, L.

Our representative citizen is simultaneously a consumer of X and Y, a worker who hires out his own labour, and a risk-bearing entrepreneur who at 8 a.m. on any day hires labour and purchases inputs of intermediate products (i.e. of X and Y) in order to produce goods (i.e. X and Y) for sale in the market at 8 a.m. on the following day. In the course of these operations he saves and invests, either lending his excess savings to, or borrowing for his excess investment from, the capital market. He thus represents all types of decision.

We assume that either by a comprehensive system of forward markets or by a comprehensive indicative plan our citizen can accurately foresee the future course of all relevant market prices such as P_{12x}, P_{1x}, π_1, i_{12}, etc.

We assume that our citizen expects a movement from point 1234 to point 12 on Figures 34 and 35 with a probability ε_{12} (and, therefore, a movement from point 1234 to point 34 with probability $\varepsilon_{34} = 1 - \varepsilon_{12}$), a movement from point 12 to point 1 with probability ε_1 (and, therefore, a movement from point 12 to point 2 with probability $\varepsilon_2 = 1 - \varepsilon_1$) and similarly for ε_3 and $\varepsilon_4 = 1 - \varepsilon_3$.[8]

We will first consider our citizen as a worker and consumer. For this purpose we assume that, given his tastes, he can attach a chance-utility index (of the kind discussed at length on pages 419–27 of *The Growing Economy*) to his situation at any point, this utility depending simply on the amounts of X and of Y consumed and the amount of work done (i.e. leisure forgone) at that point. Finally let us assume that his purpose at point 1234 is to make decisions then which will maximize his total expected utility over the three-day period ahead of him.[9]

Table VI illustrates these assumptions.[10] The object of our citizen at 8 a.m. on day 0 (i.e. at point 1234) will be to plan his future consumption and work (i.e. to select values for $\hat{C}$ and $\hat{L}$) so as to maximize his expected total utility (i.e. the value of $\mathscr{E}(\hat{U})$ as given at the bottom of Table VI), given the constraints of his budget equation (i.e. given his initial capital resources, the wage rates and

---

[8] It follows that he expects the four paths of the environmental events in Figures 34 and 35 with probabilities $\varepsilon_1\varepsilon_{12}$, $\varepsilon_2\varepsilon_{12}$, $\varepsilon_3\varepsilon_{34}$ and $\varepsilon_4\varepsilon_{34}$ respectively.

[9] This analysis depends upon the simplifying assumptions made in *The Growing Economy*, pp. 198–202.

[10] Table VI is constructed on exactly the same principles as Table XXI on page 426 of *The Growing Economy* with which it should be compared in order to comprehend the application of the analysis of pages 419–27 of *The Growing Economy* to our present problem. The different policies shown in the left-hand column of Table XXI in *The Growing Economy* correspond to different choices of values for $\hat{C}_x$, $\hat{C}_y$ and $\hat{L}$ in Table VI above.

interest rates he can earn on his labour and his savings at different points, and also his opportunities to make money as the entrepreneur of a productive business).

Table VI

	1234	12	34	1	2	3	4
	Points on the Environment Paths						
	with subjective probabilities of expectation						
	1	ε_{12}	ε_{34}	$\varepsilon_1\varepsilon_{12}$	$\varepsilon_2\varepsilon_{12}$	$\varepsilon_3\varepsilon_{34}$	$\varepsilon_4\varepsilon_{34}$
	where $\varepsilon_{12} + \varepsilon_{34} = \varepsilon_1 + \varepsilon_2 = \varepsilon_3 + \varepsilon_4 = 1$						
Amount of X to be consumed at each point	$\hat{C}_{1234x}$	$\hat{C}_{12x}$	$\hat{C}_{34x}$	$\hat{C}_{1x}$	$\hat{C}_{2x}$	$\hat{C}_{3x}$	$\hat{C}_{4x}$
Amount of Y to be consumed at each point	$\hat{C}_{1234y}$	$\hat{C}_{12y}$	$\hat{C}_{34y}$	$\hat{C}_{1y}$	$\hat{C}_{2y}$	$\hat{C}_{3y}$	$\hat{C}_{4y}$
Amount of labour to be performed at each point	$\hat{L}_{1234}$	$\hat{L}_{12}$	$\hat{L}_{34}$	$\hat{L}_1$	$\hat{L}_2$	$\hat{L}_3$	$\hat{L}_4$

| Total Expected Utility | $\begin{aligned}\mathscr{E}(\hat{U}) = {}& \hat{U}(\hat{C}_{1234x}, \hat{C}_{1234y}, \hat{L}_{1234}) \\ &+ \varepsilon_{12}\hat{U}(\hat{C}_{12x}, \hat{C}_{12y}, \hat{L}_{12}) + \varepsilon_{34}\hat{U}(\hat{C}_{34x}, \hat{C}_{34y}, \hat{L}_{34}) \\ &+ \varepsilon_1\varepsilon_{12}\hat{U}(\hat{C}_{1x}, \hat{C}_{1y}, \hat{L}_1) + \varepsilon_2\varepsilon_{12}\hat{U}(\hat{C}_{23}, \hat{C}_{2y}, \hat{L}_2) \\ &+ \varepsilon_3\varepsilon_{34}\hat{U}(\hat{C}_{3x}, \hat{C}_{3y}, \hat{L}_3) + \varepsilon_4\varepsilon_{34}\hat{U}(\hat{C}_{4x}, \hat{C}_{4y}, \hat{L}_4)\end{aligned}$ ...(11.1) |

Our citizen's productive business is based on a production function which may be represented on any day t as

$$L(t) = L\{\overline{X}(t), \overline{Y}(t), X(t), Y(t)\} \quad \ldots\ldots\ldots\ldots\ldots\ldots\ldots (11.2)$$

where $\overline{X}(t)$ is the amount of X which he decides at 8 a.m. on day t to produce ready for sale at 8 a.m. on day $t + 1$ and $X(t)$ is the amount of X which he purchases at 8 a.m. on day t as an input into this productive process. Similarly for $\overline{Y}(t)$ and $Y(t)$. Since $\overline{X}$ and $\overline{Y}$ will be produced with labour as well as with the capital goods X and Y, a certain amount of labour—namely $L(t)$—will have to be hired. We assume some substitutability between all inputs and outputs so that $L(t)$ will be the greater, the higher are $\overline{X}(t)$ and $\overline{Y}(t)$ and the lower are $X(t)$ and $Y(t)$.

We are now in a position to describe our citizen's budget constraints which are expressed in the seven equations in 11.3. For this

$$\hat{M}_{1234} = \hat{K}_{1234} - P_{1234x}(\hat{C}_{1234x} + X_{1234})$$
$$- P_{1234y}(\hat{C}_{1234y} + Y_{1234})$$

$$\hat{M}_{12} = M_{1234}(1 + i_{1234}) + W_{1234}\{\hat{L}_{1234}$$
$$- L_{1234}(\overline{X}_{1234}, \overline{Y}_{1234}, X_{1234}, Y_{1234})\}$$
$$+ P_{12x}(\overline{X}_{1234} - \hat{C}_{12x} - X_{12})$$
$$+ P_{12y}(\overline{Y}_{1234} - \hat{C}_{12y} - Y_{12})$$

$$\hat{M}_{34} = M_{1234}(1 + i_{1234}) + W_{1234}\{\hat{L}_{1234}$$
$$- L_{1234}(\overline{X}_{1234}, \overline{Y}_{1234}, X_{1234}, Y_{1234})\}$$
$$+ P_{34x}(\overline{X}_{1234} - \hat{C}_{34x} - X_{34}) +$$
$$+ P_{34y}(\overline{Y}_{1234} - \hat{C}_{34y} - Y_{34})$$

$$(\hat{M}_1 =)\,0 = \hat{M}_{12}(1 + i_{12}) + W_{12}\{L_{12}$$
$$- L_{12}(\overline{X}_{12}, \overline{Y}_{12}, X_{12}, Y_{12})\} + P_{1x}(\overline{X}_{12} - \hat{C}_{1x})$$
$$+ P_{1y}(\overline{Y}_{12} - \hat{C}_{1y})$$

$$(\hat{M}_2 =)\,0 = \hat{M}_{12}(1 + i_{12}) + W_{12}\{\hat{L}_{12}$$
$$- L_{12}(\overline{X}_{12}, \overline{Y}_{12}, X_{12}, Y_{12})\} + P_{2x}(\overline{X}_{12} - \hat{C}_{2x})$$
$$+ P_{2y}(\overline{Y}_{12} - \hat{C}_{2y})$$

$$(\hat{M}_3 =)\,0 = \hat{M}_{34}(1 + i_{34}) + W_{34}\{\hat{L}_{34}$$
$$- L_{34}(\overline{X}_{34}, \overline{Y}_{34}, Y_{34})\} + P_{3x}(\overline{X}_{34} - \hat{C}_{3x})$$
$$+ P_{3y}(\overline{Y}_{34} - \hat{C}_{3y})$$

$$(\hat{M}_4 =)\,0 = \hat{M}_{34}(1 + i_{34}) + W_{34}\{\hat{L}_{34}$$
$$- L_{34}(\overline{X}_{34}, \overline{Y}_{34}, X_{34}, Y_{34})\} + P_{4x}(\overline{X}_{34} - \hat{C}_{4x})$$
$$+ P_{4y}(\overline{Y}_{34} - \hat{C}_{4y})$$

$$..(11.3)$$

purpose we use $\hat{K}_{1234}$ to express the amount of money which our citizen will have at his free disposal at 8 a.m. on day 0 available to spend on consumption, on intermediate products, or to lend at interest till 8 a.m. on day 1. Thus $\hat{K}_{1234}$ is reckoned after the settlement of wage and debt contracts entered into at 8 a.m. on day −1 (i.e. day before day 0) and after the receipt of money for the goods produced during day −1 but sold on day 0, but before any money is spent on the purchase of consumption goods or intermediate products at 8 a.m. on day 0. When he is formulating his plan at 8 a.m. on day 0, $\hat{K}_{1234}$ is already out of his control. It depends entirely upon decisions which he has already made on day −1 or on market conditions which are outside his control.

The first equation in 11.3 expresses $\hat{M}_{1234}$, the amount of money which he will have over to lend out at interest at 8 a.m. on day 0. It is simply $\hat{K}_{1234}$ less the amount which he spends on buying X and Y, either for his personal consumption or as intermediate products for his productive operations.

The second equation in 11.3 expresses $\hat{M}_{12}$, the amount of money which he will have available to lend at interest at 8 a.m. on day 1 if the economy is then at point 12. This can be regarded as the result of three items: (i) he will have the principal and interest on what he lent out at 8 a.m. on the previous day; (ii) he will be able to add to this the excess of his receipt of wages for the work he did during day 0 over his payment of wages to any labour which he hired for day 0; and (iii) he will also be able to add the excess, at prices ruling at point 12, of his receipts for the sale of goods produced during day 0 over his purchases of goods for personal consumption or for productive operations during day 1. The third equation in 11.3 shows an exactly similar expression for $\hat{M}_{34}$.

The last four equations in 11.3 simply express the fact that, since the world is known to be coming to an end at midnight between day 2 and day 3, there is no point in saving money to lend at interest at 8 a.m. on day 2 for receipt on day 3 (i.e. $\hat{M}_1 = \hat{M}_2 = \hat{M}_3 = \hat{M}_4 = 0$). Nor is there any point in using money available at 8 a.m. on day 2 to purchase intermediate products for the production of goods which will be available for use on day 3 (i.e. $X_1 = Y_1 = X_2 = Y_2 = X_3 = Y_3 = X_4 = Y_4 = 0$).[11] All available money at 8 a.m. on day 2 will be used to purchase goods for personal consumption during day 2.

If we eliminated the three terms $\hat{M}_{1234}$, $\hat{M}_{12}$ and $\hat{M}_{34}$ between the seven equations in 11.3, we would be left with four budget equations, one for each environmental path; and since we are assuming that our citizen has no access to a betting or insurance market to transfer income from one environmental path to another, he is in fact confronted with four separate budget constraints, one for each environmental path. We shall, however, maintain the budget constraints in the form of the seven equations in 11.3, which gives a budget constraint for each of the seven points on the environmental paths of Figures 34 and 35 and thus enables us to distinguish clearly between the marginal utility derived from an additional unit of purchasing power at each of the seven points on the four environmental time paths.

Our citizen now has to consider the level at which he will set 32 variables over the course of his plan for days 0, 1, and 3, namely (i) the three amounts of money which he will lend on the capital markets at points 1234, 12 and 34, i.e. $\hat{M}_{1234}$, $\hat{M}_{12}$, $\hat{M}_{34}$; (ii) the seven amounts of X which he will consume at each of the seven environmental points, i.e. $\hat{C}_{1234x}$, etc.; (iii) the seven similar amounts for Y, i.e. $\hat{C}_{1234y}$, etc.; (iv) the three amounts of X which he will

---

[11] It will also be true that no work will be done and no goods produced during day 2 so that $\hat{L}_1 = \hat{L}_2 = \hat{L}_3 = \hat{L}_4 = L_1 = L_2 = L_3 = L_4 = \overline{X}_1 = \overline{X}_2 = \overline{X}_3 = \overline{X}_4 = \overline{Y}_1 = \overline{Y}_2 = \overline{Y}_3 = \overline{Y}_4 = 0$.

purchase for productive inputs and the three amounts of $\overline{X}$ which he will produce at points 1234, 12 and 34, i.e. X_{1234}, $\overline{X}_{1234}$, etc.; (v) the six similar amounts for Y and $\overline{Y}$, i.e. Y_{1234}, $\overline{Y}_{1234}$, etc.; and (vi) the three amounts of labour which he will himself undertake at points 1234, 12 and 34, i.e. $\hat{L}_{1234}$, etc.

He must choose the values of these decision variables subject to the seven budget constraints in 11.3 in such a way as to maximize his expected total utility as expressed in 11.1. This can be done by maximizing the Lagrangian expression in 11.4 where $\mathscr{E}(\hat{U})$ has the value expressed in 11.1 and where Z_{1234}, Z_{12}, etc., represent the RHS of the seven budget constraint equations in 11.3:

$$\left. \begin{aligned} \mathscr{L} = \mathscr{E}(\hat{U}) &+ \mu'_{1234}(Z_{1234} - \hat{M}_{1234}) + \mu'_{12}(Z_{12} - M_{12}) \\ &+ \mu'_{34}(Z_{34} - \hat{M}_{34}) + \mu'_1 Z_1 + \mu'_2 Z_2 + \mu'_3 Z_3 \\ &+ \mu'_4 Z_4 \end{aligned} \right\} \quad ..(11.4)$$

An inspection of the budget constraint equations in 11.3 indicates that μ'_1, expresses the addition to expected total utility at 8 a.m. on day 0 from having one more unit of purchasing power on day 2 if the economy is then at point 1. If μ_1 measures the marginal utility of income at point 1 then $\mu'_1 = \varepsilon_1 \varepsilon_{12} \mu_1$; and similarly for the other 'μ''s in 11.4 so that we have:

$$\left. \begin{aligned} \mu'_{1234} &= \mu_{1234} \\ \mu'_{12} &= \varepsilon_{12}\mu_{12} \quad \mu'_{34} = \varepsilon_{34}\mu_{34} \\ \mu'_1 &= \varepsilon_1\varepsilon_{12}\mu_1 \quad \mu'_2 = \varepsilon_2\varepsilon_{12}\mu_2 \\ \mu'_3 &= \varepsilon_3\varepsilon_{34}\mu_3 \quad \mu'_4 = \varepsilon_4\varepsilon_{34}\mu_4 \end{aligned} \right\} \dots\dots(11.5)$$

If we differentiate 11.4 partially in respect of the thirty-two decision variables, using 11.1, 11.3 and 11.5 and equate the resulting expressions to zero we obtain the thirty-two equations[12] in 11.6, 11.7, 11.8, and 11.9.

$$\left. \begin{aligned} \mu_{1234} &= (\varepsilon_{12}\mu_{12} + \varepsilon_{34}\mu_{34})(1 + i_{1234}) \\ \mu_{12} &= (\varepsilon_1\mu_1 + \varepsilon_2\mu_2)(1 + i_{12}) \\ \mu_{34} &= (\varepsilon_3\mu_3 + \varepsilon_4\mu_4)(1 + i_{34}) \end{aligned} \right\} \quad ..(11.6)$$

$$\left. \begin{aligned} \mu_{1234} &= \frac{\hat{U}'_{1234x}}{P_{1234x}} = \frac{\hat{U}'_{1234y}}{P_{1234y}} = -\frac{\hat{U}'_{1234l}}{W_{1234}}(1 + i_{1234}) \end{aligned} \right.$$

with similar expressions for μ_{12} and μ_{34}

$$\mu_1 = \hat{U}'_{1x}/P_{1x} = \hat{U}'_{1y}/P_{1y}$$

with similar expressions for μ_2, μ_3, and μ_4.

$\left. \begin{aligned} & \\ & \\ & \\ & \\ & \end{aligned} \right\} \dots(11.7)$

[12] These thirty-two equations plus the seven budget equations in 11.3 together provide the solution for the values of the thirty-two decision variables and the seven 'μ's in the optimal plan.

$$\left. \frac{W_{1234}}{1 + i_{1234}} = -P_{1234x}\frac{\partial X_{1234}}{\partial L_{1234}} = -P_{1234y}\frac{\partial Y_{1234}}{\partial L_{1234}} \right\} \quad ..(11.8)$$

with similar expressions for $W_{12}/(1 + i_{12})$ and $W_{34}/(1 + i_{34})$

$$\left. \begin{aligned} W_{1234} &= \frac{\varepsilon_{12}\mu_{12}P_{12x} + \varepsilon_{34}\mu_{34}P_{34x}}{\varepsilon_{12}\mu_{12} + \varepsilon_{34}\mu_{34}}\frac{\partial \overline{X}_{1234}}{\partial L_{1234}} \\ &= \frac{\varepsilon_{12}\mu_{12}P_{12y} + \varepsilon_{34}\mu_{34}P_{34y}}{\varepsilon_{12}\mu_{12} + \varepsilon_{34}\mu_{34}}\frac{\partial \overline{Y}_{1234}}{\partial L_{1234}} \end{aligned} \right\} \quad .....(11.9)$$

with similar expressions for W_{12} and W_{34}.

Equations 11.6 express the ultimate goal of adjustments (iv) mentioned on page 194. Equations 11.7[13] express the ultimate goal of adjustments (i).[13] Equations 11.8 express the ultimate goal of adjustments (ii).[14] Equations 11.9 express the ultimate goal of the adjustments (iii).

Let us turn to the effect of the introduction of a comprehensive betting or insurance market. Suppose that there were such markets with rates of insurance premiums as indicated by π in Figure 35. Then, for the reasons explained on page 195, our citizen, by insuring for the sum of $\hat{B}_{12}$ against a movement from point 1234 to point 12, would add $\pi_{34}\hat{B}_{12}$ to his purchasing power at point 12 at the cost of subtracting $\pi_{12}\hat{B}_{12}$ from his purchasing power at point 34. If he undertook such an insurance, we would have to add $\pi_{34}\hat{B}_{12}$ to the RHS of the expression for $\hat{M}_{12}$ in 11.3 and subtract $\pi_{12}\hat{B}_{12}$ from the RHS of the expression for $\hat{M}_{34}$ in 11.3. In order to express the resulting effects of similar insurances on spendable incomes at points 1, 2, 3 and 4 we could add $\pi_2\hat{B}_1$, $-\pi_1\hat{B}_1$, $\pi_4\hat{B}_3$ and $-\pi_3\hat{B}_3$ respectively to the RHS of each of the last four equations in 11.3. If we add these terms, our citizen has three more decision variables, namely $\hat{B}_{12}$, $\hat{B}_1$ and $\hat{B}_3$ to determine.[15] If we differentiate the expression in 11.4 with these additions to the elements in the 'Z's of the constraints in respect to the thirty-five decision variables which now exist and equate the resulting terms to zero, we obtain exactly the same results as in equations 11.6 to 11.9 with two exceptions:

[13] $\hat{U}'_{1234x} \equiv \partial\hat{U}_{1234}/\partial\hat{C}_{1234x}$ and $\hat{U}'_{1234l} \equiv \partial\hat{U}_{1234}/\partial\hat{L}_{1234}$ and similarly for the other '$\hat{U}$'s.

[14] The wage rate W_{1234} is fixed at point 1234 but not payable until the next day. The cost at point 1234 of the unit of labour employed at point 1234 is therefore $W_{1234}/(1 + i_{1234})$.

[15] If we now eliminated the six variables M_{1234}, M_{12}, $\hat{M}_{34}$, $\hat{B}_{12}$, $\hat{B}_1$ and $\hat{B}_3$ from the seven budget constraint equations in 11.4, we would obtain the single budget constraint which would bind our citizen when he can transfer income from one environmental path to another.

(1) we have to add the three equations:

$$\frac{\varepsilon_{12}\mu_{12}}{\varepsilon_{34}\mu_{34}} = \frac{\pi_{12}}{\pi_{34}}, \quad \frac{\varepsilon_1\mu_1}{\varepsilon_2\mu_2} = \frac{\pi_1}{\pi_2}, \quad \frac{\varepsilon_3\mu_3}{\varepsilon_4\mu_4} = \frac{\pi_3}{\pi_4} \dots\dots\dots\dots (11.10)$$

and (2) we can replace equations 11.9 with:

$$W_{1234} = (\pi_{12}P_{12x} + \pi_{34}P_{34x})\partial \overline{X}_{1234}/\partial L_{1234}$$
$$= (\pi_{12}P_{12y} + \pi_{34}P_{34y})\,\partial \overline{Y}_{1234}/\partial L_{1234} \dots\dots\dots\dots (11.11)$$

with similar expressions for W_{12} and W_{34}.

Equations 11.10 express the ultimate goal of the adjustments of type (v), while equations 11.11 express the ultimate goal of the adjustments of the revised type (iii) discussed on pages 193–195.

By a simple manipulation we can replace the six equations in 11.6 and 11.10 with six equations which express the expected marginal utility of income at each of the six points 12, 34, 1, 2, 3 and 4 in terms of the marginal utility of income at point 1234:

$$\varepsilon_1\varepsilon_{12}\mu_1/\mu_{1234} = \pi_{12}\pi_1/(1 + i_{1234})(1 + i_{12})$$

and $\quad \varepsilon_{12}\mu_{12}/\mu_{1234} = \pi_{12}/(1 + i_{1234}) \dots\dots\dots\dots\dots (11.12)$

with similar expressions for μ_{34}, μ_2, μ_3 and μ_4. These expressions are all concerned with the transfer of income from one point to another on the environmental paths in Figure 35 through a combination of the capital markets (to carry income from one point of time to another) and of insurance or betting markets (to carry income from one environmental path to another). It is to be observed that the expressions in 11.12 correspond exactly to the expressions for contingency prices shown in equations 10.2 and 10.3 in Chapter X. The contingency price, $\tilde{P}_1$, is the amount of money which must be paid for certain on day 0 to obtain a good worth P_1 on day 2 if one reached point 1 on day 2. $P_1/\tilde{P}_1$ which, from equation 10.2, equals $\pi_{12}\pi_1/(1 + i_{1234})(1 + i_{12})$ measures, therefore, the amount which must be paid at point 1234 to obtain \$1 at point 1. To obtain the greatest possible expected utility, our citizen will transfer income from point 1234 to point 1 until the expected marginal utilities of income at the two points are in the same ratio as this market exchange ratio, i.e. until $\varepsilon_1\varepsilon_{12}\mu_1/\mu_{1234} = \pi_{12}\pi_1/(1 + i_{1234})(1 + i_{12})$.

CHAPTER XIII

SOME PROBLEMS IN INDICATIVE PLANNING

Up to this point in Part 3 of this volume we have argued as if, apart from the planning problems of the individual decision-makers discussed in the preceding chapter, all market uncertainties could be readily removed by a comprehensive set of forward markets or by an ideal indicative plan. But this result depends upon the extreme simplifying assumptions made on page 149 and when they are modified a number of serious complications and difficulties arise. We will discuss these under five main headings in the present chapter.

THE DEMOGRAPHIC TURNOVER AND THE REPRESENTATION OF INDIVIDUAL DECISION-MAKERS

Let us start by relaxing the strange demographic assumption that there are no births or deaths or ageing between now and 'Kingdom Come'. If new citizens are still to be born or existing children are to grow up, then there will in the future be new economic agents buying and selling, lending and borrowing, taking and making bets in the future, who just do not enter the market now. This means that there cannot now be a comprehensive set of future markets covering all transactions from now till 'Kingdom Come'; the transactions of those who are at present infants or are as yet unborn cannot now be expressed in today's forward markets. The demographic turnover of economic decision-makers thus makes a quite fundamental difference to the situation. It is one, though as we shall see it is not the only, sufficient reason why a market price mechanism cannot be used in a system of forward markets to signal market information horizontally over time as it can be used to signal market information at any one time vertically as between one good and another.

This demographic situation thus provides an argument for supplementing the market mechanism with some procedures for indicative planning or forecasting. But it implies, of course, that in any such procedures the infants and the unborn, who cannot be present in the Albert Hall themselves, should be represented by someone else. Perhaps a governmental statistical office might undertake this task. In order to do so it will have to insist on the introduction of some additional demographic environmental paths into the set of indicative plans, since nobody knows for certain now what will happen to future fertility, mortality and nuptiality. And it is not only the size and the sex and the age composition of future generations which constitute environmental uncertainties for the indicative planners. No one can say for certain what the inborn capabilities or psychological preferences of the future citizens will be, and these things could clearly have important market implications.

In shouldering this task of representing future generations in the formation of an indicative plan, the governmental statistical office would have to employ some econometric techniques. In trying to estimate how much individual citizens would work, save, spend on this good and on that good in future years given the ways in which incomes, prices, wealth, interest rates, family size and structure, etc., may develop along the various environmental paths, the statisticians would have to start by fitting parameters to past changes in these variables and extrapolating the results.

There are, in fact, further practical problems, which mean that, quite apart from the unborn citizens of the future, not all existing individual economic decision-makers could possibly take part directly in the formation of an indicative plan. Limitations on the size of the Albert Hall, quite apart from anything else, would prohibit a town meeting of all the United Kingdom citizens and the mind boggles at the problems involved in trying to carry out the Albert Hall iterative planning procedure by post. Many citizens must in fact have their future market transactions expressed in an aggregative way by representatives who, in many cases, will have to rely on some form of econometric estimation to formulate their representations of their constituents' probable future transactions at future dates in the various market conditions and environmental backgrounds as stated in the plan.

In the construction of an indicative plan, some economic agents may take part individually. Thus all the individual firms producing steel or cars or aeroplanes might be present. In other cases, they might be represented by, for example, a trade association which did not itself have to rely on econometric estimation but could consult each of its constituent members individually in order to form an aggregative picture of the future transactions of the whole industry. In other cases, for example in the case of the purchases of consumption goods by the individual housewives, the representation of total consumers' demands for various goods in different future situations would have to be undertaken on the basis of econometric studies of demand functions by some body like a governmental statistical office.

One must then imagine the indicative plan being formed not in the Albert Hall but in the committee rooms of Whitehall, where this limited number of individual decision-makers or their representatives are gathered together. But in principle the same procedure of indicative planning can be applied. The governmental planners start the dialogue by saying: "Suppose market conditions to be such and such on each of the various environmental paths, how would each of you expect your constituents to behave on each of those paths?" The representatives reply: "In this and that manner." The planners then adjust appropriately their market assumptions and the dialogue is renewed until market consistency between the transactions suggested by the representatives of the different sectors of the economy is obtained. The total plan, containing one sub-plan for each environmental path, is then published in order to enable each individual decision-maker to formulate his own plans and decisions with a better guess as to what the future holds in store for him.

From what has been said, it is clear that no hard and fast dividing line can be drawn between the method of forecasting by means of an indicative plan and forecasting by means of an econometric model. The pure indicative plan outlined earlier can be regarded as an iterative duet between the soloist planning body and the chorus of citizens, the planning body singing out some prices and the citizens, one hopes, replying with some rather less dissonant quantities, the whole performance ending in a glorious finale of prices proclaimed by the planning soloist and an exultant harmony of quantities by the triumphant chorus of individual citizens.

We can imagine an econometric model being produced by the central planning department with just such an iterative duet between the head of the central planning department and the heads of his subordinate sections. Each variable in the economy which needed to be forecast would be allotted to one subordinate section; the head of the planning department would start by suggesting a future course for every variable in the economy; each subordinate section would then take as given the movement of all the variables except those which had been allotted to it for explanation; each subordinate department would then, on the basis of the special econometric studies which it had made of its particular section of the economy, report to the head of the planning department how it estimated that its own particular variables would behave, given the previously announced movements in the other variables; the head of the planning department would then revise his announced future movements of all the variables in the light of the report from each subordinate section about the movements which it predicted for the particular variables for which it was responsible; each section would then once more estimate the future behaviour of the variables for which it was responsible, in the light of the revised estimates of the movements of the other variables.[1]

We can also have mixed choirs. There is no reason why some sections of the economy should not be represented by individuals (e.g. the limited number of steel producers), some by private trading organizations, and others by various statistical sections of a central planning department. The basic procedure is the same: an initial suggestion of a course of development for all the variables concerned prepared perhaps by means of an econometric model developed by some central planning body; the calculation by each separate individual citizen or member of a representative trading organization or statistical section of what the future course of the variables for which he was responsible would be if all other variables behaved in the announced fashion; a revision by the central forecasting agency of the announced movements of all the variables; recalculation by each participant of the future course of the particular variable for which he is responsible; and so on.

THE MULTIPLICITY OF ENVIRONMENTAL PATHS: RESIDUAL UNCERTAINTY

A further complexity in indicative planning arises in the enormous multiplicity of environmental time paths. In the simple example in Figures 34 and 35 with two future days on each of which it might be wet or fine, there were four such paths. Let us first be quite clear that there are four separate relevant paths. Figure 35 indicated that there were four possible price constellations on day 2—namely

---

[1] To take one example from Figure 29, one subordinate section (the labour market section) might be given the responsibility of determining N_1, N_2, W_1, W_2 and WL. For this purpose it would have to make econometric studies of the determinants of the wage rate (lines 24, 34 and 35) and of the determinants of labour supplies of various kinds (lines 20, 21, and 22). It would take the movements of L_1, L_2 (i.e. the demands for labour from industry), N^*, q'_a, q'_b, P_1 and P_2 as announced by the head of the planning department and would report back the resulting estimates of N_1, N_2, W_1, W_2 and WL. Other main subordinate sections might be a production section, a price formation section, a consumers' behaviour section, a budgetary section, and a capital and money market section—each with its own collection of variables to be explained, all such variables being allotted to one or other of the sections.

P_1, P_2, P_3 and P_4. At first sight, it might appear that there are in fact only two price constellations to be considered. On day 2 it will be either wet or fine. Can we not be satisfied with a wet-weather set of prices for umbrellas and sunshades and a fine-weather set of prices for these objects? Can we not assume $P_1 = P_3$ and $P_2 = P_4$? Alas, no. P_1 occurs in wet following wet and P_3 in wet following fine. If day 1 has been wet, the umbrella producers may have made production arrangements on day 1 in order to make it easier to produce umbrellas on day 1 and these arrangements may carry over in part till the next day making it easier to produce umbrellas on day 2. Moreover, if umbrellas are at all durable, consumers may have a stock of umbrellas on day 2 which they have bought on day 1, because day 1 was wet. Thus wet following wet may imply a day 2 in which umbrellas are cheap to produce and the demand is low as compared with wet following fine, which may imply for day 2 a productive apparatus not so well suited to produce umbrellas and a set of consumers with fewer umbrellas already in their possession. P_1 may be very different from P_3.

These interconnections between events in different years make the planning procedure very complicated in fact. Suppose there were only three uncertain exogenous variables; for example, the rates of growth of the size of the population, of the foreign demand for the country's exports and of technical progress in industry. Suppose each of these variables could have one of three values in each year, namely high, medium and low. Suppose that there were only five periods in the plan, e.g. a five-year plan. Then instead of the four weather time-paths of Figures 34 and 35, there would be $3^{3 \times 5} = 14,352,807$ different time-paths for the environmental uncertainties; and it is, of course, a gross simplification of reality to assume that there are only three factors about which one is basically uncertain. The implications of this are far-reaching. A set of 14,352,807 interdependent indicative sub-plans would have to be worked out and in making use of them each private decision-maker would have to consider the various paths and express, in 14,352,807 fractions which added up to unity, his subjective assessment of their probabilities. In fact the task might not be as difficult as it appears because no one would have any time to do anything but to consider the probabilities of future events and to calculate, so that all actual transactions at every point in every sub-plan might be written down as zero. But this would simply mean that the cost of constructing any such indicative plan would clearly be prohibitive.

It is obvious that if an indicative plan is in reality to be constructed to cope with conditions of environmental uncertainty there must be a process of gross simplification. This can take two forms.

In the first place, it is clear that only a very limited number of possible time-paths for the environmental uncertainties can be taken into account. Two possible time-paths for the external demand conditions for the country's exports plus two possible time-paths for the course of general labour productivity plus two possible time-paths for the growth of the population would alone necessitate a set of 2^3 or eight indicative sub-plans.

The implications of limiting in this way the number of environmental paths in an indicative plan are very far-reaching. Clearly the planners should try to choose for consideration one or two representative possible time-paths which are typical of likely developments, but of developments which are unlike each other. But having chosen these environmental time-paths for consideration, what should be the rules of the game? Suppose, by way of illustration, that the planners have chosen to consider only two such possible time-paths. At the Albert Hall meeting or in the committee rooms of Whitehall they must explain to the assembled economic decision-makers or their representatives exactly what are the assumptions about future environmental change on which the two paths are based. They must then, as before, start by enunciating two patterns of market prices which are to be assumed to rule along the two environmental paths which are being considered and, as before, they must ask each economic agent to report how much of everything he would buy or sell along each path if the stated prices in fact ruled along each path. In the light of the replies, they must revise appropriately the price-paths along each environmental path.

But, in making their replies, what are the private citizens to assume about the probabilities of the two environmental paths? If the purpose of the indicative plan is really to discover how people would react along various environmental paths, then, as before, each citizen must be free to ascribe his own subjective probability to each of the two paths under consideration. Each private citizen will realize that the two paths are merely typical and do not by any means exhaust the possibilities. If there are really only two paths under consideration, then there can be only one environmental variable (say, the foreign demand for the country's exports) which is being allowed to take two different courses. For all the other environmental variables (such as the growth of population, the rate of technical progress, and so on) there must be only one single path assumed in the plan. But many citizens whose situation may be much affected by these other variables will want to plan their activities on the assumption that some of these other environmental variables (for example labour productivity) may develop in a more or less favourable way than that assumed by the planners.

The rules of the planning game could be so devised as not to allow the private citizens to take these other possibilities into account. They might be asked by the planners to say how they would react along each path if they were certain that either the one path or the other would in fact develop. Perhaps they could be persuaded to play this unreal hypothetical game and give accurate answers. But in that case the answers would not correspond to what they would in fact do along either of these paths if it did in fact materialize. To return to our earlier frivolous example, the two paths might refer to two different developments of the rate of technical progress in the sunshade and umbrella industry, but in this case there could be only one assumption made about the future course of the weather. If the producers of sunshades and umbrellas had to say what they would do if they were certain that this would be the actual course of the weather, they might report quite properly the installation of some very expensive, specialized, technically efficient, long-lasting plant to produce sunshades and umbrellas in rigid proportions exactly suitable for that one weather path. But this is not what they will in fact do, since they realize that it may be much wetter or much finer than is assumed in the single weather path for the plan, and they may well therefore install much less specialized, cheaper, shorter-lived but flexible plant which can be used to produce either sunshades or umbrellas.

An indicative plan based on a limited number of environmental paths must, therefore, leave a large amount of what may be called 'residual uncertainty'. The planners must ask the private citizens how in fact they would act along each of the representative environmental paths when they are free to make their own assessment of how probable these paths are and of the possibilities that the environment may in fact develop along other paths. Along these other paths the private citizens will, of course, be left with market uncertainties as well as with environmental uncertainties. On weather paths not covered by the plan, the manufacturers of sunshades and umbrellas will not be told what prices for these objects will rule on these unconsidered paths. The manufacturers will have to make their own guesses about the possibilities of different price-paths being connected with each unconsidered weather path.

But while an indicative plan which covers only a very few environmental paths cannot remove such market uncertainties, it may well reduce them very considerably. If the producers of sunshades and umbrellas learn from the indicative plan the market prices which will rule for these objects in the particular weather conditions covered by the plan, they have, as it were, a bench mark from which they can make for themselves more accurate guesses as to what the prices

would be if the weather were so much wetter or so much finer than
the plan assumed. The indicative plan will no longer eliminate, but
it can still hope greatly to reduce, market uncertainties.

In trying to cover these residual uncertainties, each private
economic agent will in turn be left with a vast number of possible
future courses of the market and environmental factors which are
relevant for his own operations. He, in turn, in drawing up his own
individual plans for the future, cannot hope to calculate meticu-
lously what it will be best for him to do along each of the possible
paths. He may himself take one or two additional representative
paths for more detailed consideration. For example, the producer
of sunshades and umbrellas might take one typical weather path
which was wetter by a given amount than the single path considered
in the plan and one typical path which was finer by a given amount
than that considered in the plan. We may call these his representative sub-paths. For these sub-paths he might make his own carefully
calculated guesses about the associated price-paths. But there would
always remain some large measure of residual uncertainty which he
would find it too laborious or indeed quite impossible to cover by
any form of detailed calculation. He would have to form his plans
in the light of the market conditions which he thought would be
associated with these typical sub-paths as well as with the path
assumed in the indicative plan, but always making some allowance
for the fact that things might work out differently in quite uncalculated ways.

The inevitability of much residual uncertainty is due not only to the
mere multiplicity of environmental paths, but also to the fact that
the very possibility of some future environmental developments
may not even occur to anyone today. For example, someone in the
future may think of some entirely new product to satisfy some
entirely new activity, the very idea of which is conceived by no one
today; indeed, if anyone had conceived the idea today, the product
would already have been invented. There is thus residual uncertainty
because of possible developments which no one has even imagined,
as well as because of possible developments about which one has
not had the time to think and calculate precisely. Every economic
decision-maker must make allowance for the unexpected.

This explains the well-known phenomenon that every economic
agent desires to remain liquid in order to be ready for anything
which may turn up. In particular, the private economic agent will
want his capital resources to be in general more flexible and liquid
than would be the case if he knew that every possibility was covered
by the representative sub-paths which he had considered in detail
and in view of which he could have made his betting, insurance and

other hedging arrangements to meet each calculated risk. He will want his real capital equipment to be more diversified, more flexible between uses, and less long-lived than would otherwise be the case, and he will wish to keep more of his total capital resources in forms (of which money is, of course, the extreme example) which can readily, at short notice and at small transactions' cost, be used in the market to meet all sorts of eventualities. We shall return to this aspect of the situation in Part 5 of this volume.

The planners will have to cultivate the art of selecting a number of environmental paths which are typical and yet sufficiently limited to be practicable. It is possible indeed that the right number of environmental paths to consider will turn out to be one.

Indicative planning has been severely criticized on the grounds that the formation of such a plan necessarily involves the formulation of a common view about the probable course of future events in order that a single indicator of the probable future course of prices, incomes, employments and so on may be provided to guide and to make consistent the plans of all the individual participants. This is held to be very undesirable. Surely, it is argued, it is better in a free competitive system that different individuals should be free to form different opinions about the probabilities of different outcomes rather than that all should be persuaded to act on a single view. Is it not a basic virtue of the competitive system that we do not put all our eggs in one basket, that different economic agents can bet on different outcomes, and that the risk-taking agents who best foresee the outcome can thrive and take over more and more decision-making at the expense of those who are not so successful in their speculations?

A single 'most-likely' time-path to cover all the environmental variables is not necessarily open to this criticism. It could be so devised as to be useful in giving a bench mark for market developments from which private individuals could make measurements for their own market and environmental sub-paths and thus for the construction of their own plans. But it would be of use in this indicative way only if the planners did not require the private citizens to assume that the path used for the plan was the only environmental path which could actually materialize. If the private citizens are all left free to say how they would behave on this one environmental path if they made their plans and decisions on their own estimates of the probability of this one path and of any other representative sub-paths which they cared to construct and consider for themselves, then a one-path indicative plan could have a real, though limited, use in removing market uncertainties.

THE MULTIPLICITY OF ENVIRONMENTAL PATHS: THE TIME HORIZON

Besides the limitation of an indicative plan to a small number of representative environmental time-paths, there is a second consequence of the great multiplicity of environmental possibilities which we must now consider. It is clear that the time period of the plan must be limited. We can now drop our assumption that the world will come to end with a loud bang at a definite moment in the future called 'Kingdom Come'. If 'Kingdom Come' is a far distant date, it will be certain that to cover the whole period from now till 'Kingdome Come' by a meaningful indicative plan would be impossible because of the multiplicity of environmental paths. To avoid impossible complexity, the indicative plan must cover a shorter time period. In settling on such a time period, two conflicting influences must be borne in mind.

On the one hand, the longer the period of the plan, the more do the environmental uncertainties multiply. This means that the cost of planning becomes rapidly inflated as the time period is extended, since it becomes more and more meaningless to plan in terms of only one or two limited time-paths for the environmental uncertainties. After a limited period, uncertainties become so great that numerical estimates become really meaningless; the cost of extending the period of the plan has become more or less infinite.

On the other hand, since, as we have already argued, the economic system is a general equilibrium system, ideally an indicative plan should cover the quantities and prices of every good and service for every future day until 'Kingdom Come'. In any case, so long as the decisions which one would rationally take today are at all sensitive to what may reasonably happen after the end of the time period of the plan, there is much to be gained by extending the planning period. We need, therefore, to consider whether the extension of the period of the plan to cover, say, the next six years instead of only the next five years will have much effect upon what one would decide to do this year. This is a question of fact which depends upon such matters as whether the plant and equipment which one installs this year is very long-lasting or very short-lasting, whether it is flexible or inflexible in the uses to which it can be put, and so on. It depends also in a crucial way upon the extent to which the decision-makers discount future utilities; if we do not really care much about the welfare of the next generation, we need not worry too much about the state in which we leave the economy in the distant future.

The optimum time horizon for a plan is that at which the improvement in today's decisions achieved by adding another unit of time to the period covered by the plan is just offset by the additional cost of that extension of the time covered by the plan. If conditions are such that today's decisions are sensitive to far distant future events, but, at the same time, the cost of planning as a result of environmental uncertainties mounts very quickly as the time period of the plan is extended—that is just too bad. It simply means that planning will be difficult and that today's decisions will not be much improved by formal attempts at planning. But there is nothing much that one can do about it.

The limitation of the period covered by the indicative plan means, of course, that the private economic agents will have no indication of what market conditions will be after the close of the plan period. In some cases, this will be an important source of remaining market uncertainty even for the period and the representative environmental paths covered by the plan. An entrepreneur who is installing a steel mill now will want to know the demand for steel, say, three years hence. This future period may be covered by the plan; but the demand for steel three years hence may contain, as an important element, the demand for steel to produce machines to produce products for sale six years hence—a later date which is not covered by the plan period. The reports given to the planners for the demand for steel three years hence may thus depend upon private, unaided guesses by the purchasers of the steel about market and environmental developments after the end of the plan period. It is, of course, quite possible that these purchasers of steel three years hence will revise their demands for steel because they have revised their guesses about the market and environmental conditions which will rule in yet another three years time. Thus, in a plan with a limited time-span, even the market conditions which will be associated with the representative environmental path or paths considered in full detail in the plan cannot be estimated with certainty. Some market uncertainty remains attached even to these paths.

There is, however, one extremely important lesson to be learned from this situation, namely that any indicative plan should be subject to continual revision. We argued that when an ideal comprehensive set of indicative sub-plans could be formed covering all environmental paths over the whole period from now to 'Kingdom Come', a once-for-all planning procedure was all that was needed. No revision need ever be made in the total plan because all eventualities had been covered for all time. But this is no longer so. Consider the simple three-day four-weather-path model of Figures 34 and 35. Suppose we are restricting our plan to cover only three days not, as was previously assumed, because 'Kingdom Come' will occur for certain at the end of day 2, but because we cannot cope with more than four environmental paths. Today we are at point 1234, with four paths possible up to the end of day 2. But tomorrow we shall know for certain whether we are at point 12 or point 34 and we can then add another day to the planned period without increasing the number of weather-paths above four. It should thus never be forgotten that, in conditions of environmental uncertainty, the sole purpose of today's indicative plan is to enable one to take wiser decisions today. Tomorrow, the plan should be extended to cover another day and should be revised in view of all additional available information, but solely in order to enable tomorrow's decisions to be more wisely based. And so on until 'Kingdom Come'.

A NETWORK OF PLANS

There is yet another source of complexity to be examined. We have argued so far as if only one single national indicative plan was being prepared, this being comprehensive in the sense that, even if it could not cover every possible environmental path, yet it did cover in full and separate detail every industry, every region, every product, every quality of labour, and so on. And this is as it should be ideally since, as we have argued, for general equilibrium purposes the price and quantity of every good and service is directly or indirectly related to the price and quantity of every other good and service. But if every commodity, every industry, every occupation, every use of a product, every locality, every type of consumer, in short every possible relevant variable were to be expressed separately, the system of interrelationships in the economic model would become impossibly complicated. It would be impossible to cope with it for at least two reasons. First, the number of independent variables in each relationship would become so great relatively to the number of observations or of other pieces of information about that relationship that it would be impossible to obtain reliable values for the parameters of the system. Second, even if reliable estimates of the relationships could be obtained, the number of relationships and their complexity would be so great that even with the most sophisticated techniques and equipment for simulation and calculation the system could not be handled. Thus no worthwhile forecasts could be obtained from such a system.

This means that the national indicative plan must be a plan for a much simplified model of the whole economy in which groups of relevant variables are consolidated into statistical aggregates and in which simplifying assumptions are made about the relationships between these various aggregates. Thus products may be broken down simply into agricultural products and manufactured products;

income recipients into wage earners and owners of property: uses of products into consumption, investment and government use; workers into skilled, semi-skilled and unskilled; the capital market into banks and other financial institutions; and so on. Even with very broad categories such as these, the number of variables of prices and quantities in an economic model soon becomes surprisingly large.

But, it may be asked, if this is the best that can be expected of a national indicative plan, is it really any use? After all, the individual farmer is interested in forecasts of the markets for particular agricultural products—wheat, beef, butter, cheese, etc.—and in the availability and price of labour of particular agricultural trainings and skills, not in general indices of the price of agricultural goods as a whole or of skilled or semi-skilled labour as a whole. The answer is that a general aggregative plan will reduce some of the market uncertainties, and against this background other less aggregated organizations or indeed particular individuals can make their own subsidiary forecasts and plans.

Let us continue the agricultural example. On the basis of a national framework plan, a more detailed agricultural indicative plan could be formulated. Such an agricultural plan would take as exogenous variables (i.e. as already determined data) many of the variables which were endogenous (i.e. as needing to be determined) in the framework plan. Thus, the total purchasing power of consumers and the price of manufactured consumption goods as a whole, the competing wage levels offered by industry for labour of various general grades and many other relevant factors which were outputs of the framework plan would be taken by the agricultural planners as given exogenous inputs into the agricultural plan. The agriculturalists could then break down their agricultural products into many more detailed categories and still have a manageable number of endogenous variables within their own plan. They would be making detailed forecasts for their particular agricultural products on the assumption that the general trends of the framework plan were correct.

There could then be a feedback from the agricultural plan to the framework plan. To take the clearest example, suppose that there was not only a subsidiary agricultural indicative plan but also subsidiary steel industry, textile industry, car industry plans and so on for all the main industries. Each industry takes as exogenous to it the main relevant indices produced by the framework plan. Each industry from this builds up its own particular demand for labour, for example. But the future demands for labour estimated by the sum of the separately planned industrial demands may not tally with the future demand for labour resulting from the framework plan. Clearly something is wrong with the aggregative behavioural or technical relationships assumed for the framework plan, and these must be altered at the next revision of the framework plan to take account of the discrepancy. But this in turn will affect the results of the framework plan so that the general indices which each individual industry takes as exogenous data for its plan will be changed. This will affect the results of the industry plans which will feed back once more in due course into the framework plan.

Nor are industrial plans the only possible form of subsidiary plan. Another obvious example is regional planning. An indicative plan could be formed for one region taking as exogenous variables many of the general indices resulting from the framework plan and also perhaps some of the results of some of the subsidiary industrial plans. For example, the general national activities likely in a particular industry may be a very relevant datum for indicative planning for a region which was particularly dependent upon that industry. The combined results of a number of regional plans could then well lead to a modification of the relationship assumed in the framework plan.

Nor are there necessarily only two layers in the hierarchy of indicative plans. Thus in the framework of a general national indicative plan a more detailed plan for agriculture as a whole may be worked out; and then in turn, in the light of this agricultural plan, a still more detailed plan for dairy farming in a particular region of the country may be prepared; and then in turn, in the light of this plan, the individual dairy farmer can construct his own plan for his own particular farm.

The system of indicative planning has been presented rather as if it were something novel and *sui generis*. But this is really not so. Even if the government does nothing about it, academic economists and financial journalists are likely on the basis of the more or less explicit assumptions of more or less sophisticated models to make general forecasts about the general future course of the economy in its broad aggregates, based partly upon forecasts made by particular trade associations or particular business concerns about the future of their particular markets. But these particular forecasts will often have been influenced by the results of the more general forecasts of the academics and journalists. An unorganized iterative feedback mechanism will be at work building up an interrelated network of indicative forecasts between a large number of planners ranging from the individual plans of the individual decision-makers to the sophisticated generalized econometric model of the high powered academic research institution. All this can itself be regarded as a partial substitute for a comprehensive system of formal indicative planning; it does help to confront the anticipated future transactions of different sectors of the economy. In this sort of case we may say that national indicative planning is informal rather than formal; and, as we shall see later, arguments can be made in favour of preserving the informal nature of indicative planning.

INDICATIVE PLANNING WITH MONOPOLISTS AND OLIGOPOLISTS

There is another fundamental reason which we have not so far considered why, in indicative planning, great reliance must in fact be placed upon econometric model-building. Up to this point, the whole analysis has been based upon the assumption of perfect competition. It is our intention to postpone as far as possible any discussion of monopolistic conditions for a later volume in this series. In fact, of course, much private enterprise is monopolistic or oligopolistic and this makes so fundamental a difference to the analysis of indicative planning that some reference to the problem must be made here. In perfect competition, the only market conditions which are relevant for any one economic decision-maker are prices. No individual producer, consumer, worker, saver, insurer, etc., can affect the prices of his inputs or outputs or of his purchases for final consumption or the wage rate he can obtain from his work or the rate of return he can get on his property or the insurance premium for any particular risk. It is for this reason that the indicative planning procedure could take the form of a duet between the planning authority and the private citizens in which the planning authority simply states a set of prices, the private citizens reply with a set of quantities, the planning authority replies with a revised set of prices aimed at bringing the quantities into balance, the citizens reply with a revised set of quantities, and so on.

Where competition is not perfect, this procedure just will not work. Consider the simplest classical theory of monopoly pricing. It is not sufficient to tell a monopolistic producer what the market price for his product will be and then ask him how much he will produce. The market conditions relevant for the sale of his product are described not by a demand price but by a demand curve. Consider then the possibility that the planning authority should open the planning duet by saying, as before, to the PURCHASERS of the product: "How much of this product would you purchase at each point on each environmental path if its price moved in such and such a way?" but saying to the PRODUCER: "How would you behave at each point on each environmental path if the demand schedule for your product were such-and-such at each point?" The producer, if he was a price-taker, could answer with the quantities he would put on the market or, if he was a price-maker, with the prices which he would charge; given the assumed demand schedule, the quantity put on the market implies the price and vice versa, so that in either case the planning authority could estimate the market disequilibrium involved in its first guesses. Moreover, the statements of the consumers, as to how much they would purchase at each point at the price announced by the planning authority, would inform the planning authority about one point on the demand curve at each point on the various environmental paths. At its next round in the planning dialogue, the planning authority could revise the prices announced to the purchasers in a direction which would help to close any gaps between supplies and demands and it could revise the demand schedules announced to the monopolistic producer in a way which would make them consistent with the new information obtained from the purchasers in the first round of the dialogue.

This sort of procedure would obviously be much more complicated than that which was relevant in conditions of perfect competition when only market prices need to be announced by the planning authority. But let us leave these practical complications on one side for the moment. The procedure is in any case much less reliable than the perfect competition procedure. Suppose that every participant plays the game according to the rules and suppose that the procedure does converge on to a set of sub-plans and that at every point on every environmental path the quantity which the monopolist will produce and the price which he will charge are equal to the quantity which the consumers will purchase at that price. 'Playing the game according to the rules' means that the producer must truthfully report what he would do if the demand schedule were as announced by the planning authority, but he may not in fact believe that the demand schedule is truly estimated by the planning authority. The only firm estimate which the planning authority will have is of certain points on the demand curve and if the producer is not convinced that the demand curve is properly estimated, then he will not in future behave as he quite truthfully reported that he would have behaved if the demand schedule were as announced. The moral of this is that it would not be sufficient for the planning authority simply to announce its own revisions of the demand curve, though it is sufficient in conditions of perfect competition for it simply to announce its own revisions of the market price. It would now be necessary to discuss and agree its revision of the demand curve with the monopolist.

These difficulties are multiplied a thousandfold when one allows for the fact that one has not got to cope just with a classical mono-polist but with a whole range of oligopolistic activities. The general analysis of oligopolistic behaviour must be postponed to a later volume in this series, but the sort of problems which arise are as follows. In the first place, the oligopolist will be able to affect his sales by advertisement and other selling expenditures and the levels of advertisement expenditure must be added to the planning picture. Theoretically, this means, of course, that the consumers must now be asked in the planning procedure not merely how much they would buy at given prices but how much they would buy from each oligo-polist at given combinations of prices charged by the different oligopolists and of levels of informative and of 'bamboozling' advertisement by each oligopolist; and the question immediately arises whether, in the nature of things, consumers can foretell their own degree of 'bamboozlement'. The oligopolist in his turn has to consider not simply how his customers will react directly to a change in the prices he charges or in his advertisement and other selling expenses. He must also consider how his closest competitor or competitors will react in their prices and selling expenditures to any changes in his own marketing policies, which depends, of course, upon how they think that he will react to their reactions. We are in the realm of the theory of games, of bargaining, of conventional good behaviour among potential and powerful rivals, of letting sleeping dogs lie, of tacit or open collusion, and so on. In such conditions, it is clearly not sufficient for the planning authority to announce an assumed demand schedule for the product of an oligopolist in order to find out what the oligopolist would do in various situations. The market conditions facing an oligopolist have to be described in a much more complicated fashion which include such matters as the assumed reactions of his closest competitors to changes in his own marketing policies.

In these circumstances, there is only one possible promising line of procedure, a procedure which, in certain respects, is probably much more like what actually happens in the real world in the formation of an indicative plan. The planning authority must start by constructing its own econometric model whereby, on the best estimations it can make from past statistical information and other evidence, it states how it expects prices, quantities, loans, interest rates, bets, betting odds, advertisement expenditures, etc., etc., to develop along each specified environmental path. The planning dialogue now takes the form of showing the econometric forecasts to the various economic agents or their representatives and asking for their answers to questions of the following rather general charac-ter: "If the different variables in the economy, in so far as they are outside your control or direct influence but are relevant to your own actions, behaved in the way suggested by our econometric forecasts, would you behave as we have said you would behave and would you expect those whose actions are most closely affected by your own action to behave as we have said they would behave? If not, please tell us how you would behave, and how you would expect those most closely affected by you to behave, if the other general conditions behaved as we forecast?"

The answers to questions of this kind would all be of a form which suggested revisions in the structure of relationships or in the parameters in the existing relationships of the planning authority's econometric model. The model could be revised and resubmitted with the same sort of question. Theoretically, one might apparently hope to converge on to a solution such that everyone agreed that the forecast did show accurately how he would behave if everyone else behaved as forecast along each specified environmental path.

But this hides a basic difficulty. Consider two duopolists A and B, the only two producers of motor-vehicles in the economy. Suppose the planning authority to produce at some stage a forecast on which A comments: "Yes, that is how I would behave if I thought that B was going to behave like that, but I don't think he would" and on which B similarly comments: "Yes, that is how I would behave if I thought that A was going to behave like that, but I don't think he would." A and B must have misjudged each other's market strategies, since if each did think that the other would so behave, each would in fact so behave. But in fact neither A nor B will base their plans on these forecasts since neither believes that the other will so behave.

What should the planning authority do? There is in fact a remaining market uncertainty—namely, how B will in fact react to A is unknown to A and vice versa. Could not this market uncertainty be removed in the process of forming the indicative plan? Should not the planning authority get A and B together so that they could inform each other of their reactions to each other's strategies or, failing that, might not the planning authority reveal to B what it has learned during the planning process about A's reactions and vice versa?

This suggestion presents us with a dilemma. In an oligopolistic situation there are many trade secrets which a particular producer will not want to reveal to his rivals, such as his marketing strategy or the probability of his achieving a particular technological breakthrough in the near future. Surprise may be an important weapon in achieving commercial success. It is naive, therefore, to expect that the planning authority will readily obtain unbiassed information from big private concerns about their future prospects of cost reductions, introduction of new products, commercial strategies, and so on, where this information might serve to inform their competitors of their future plans and prospects. Or, alternatively, the provision of such information might depend upon the formation of collusive monopolistic arrangements between the competing concerns which made innocuous the sharing of trade secrets among the producers concerned. Indeed there may be a serious risk that the dialogue between the government, on the one hand, and trade associations or other representative bodies of industrial and commercial groups, on the other, might encourage the formation of open or tacit monopolistic arrangements. Sharing of information about their investment plans by all the producers of a particular product may help to make their plans more consistent, but it might also encourage them jointly to make quite sure that the market was not oversupplied with their product.

This is a real dilemma. Individual decision-makers should certainly be able to make better decisions if, through something corresponding to a comprehensive set of forward markets, they are given information about the supply/demand situations likely to be caused by the decisions of their competitors as well as of their customers. But, for reasons which we have examined at length, such a forward market mechanism does not and cannot exist. Any official, formalized planned exchange of information instituted to take the place of a forward market mechanism is difficult to separate from monopolistic restrictive collusion. It can be argued that, for this reason, we should rely not upon formal, but upon informal, indicative planning, where unofficial bodies are left to make forecasts which will naturally interact on each other. There are dangers as well as gains in officially instituted indicative planning if it is desired to promote competitive behaviour in a free enterprise market economy.

H*

PART 4

GOVERNMENTAL CONTROL PLANNING

I will confess, said the Prince, an indulgence more dangerous than yours. I have frequently endeavoured to image the possibility of a perfect government. . . . . This thought produced innumerable schemes of reformation, and dictated many useful regulations and salutary edicts.

Whosoever has many to please or to govern, must use the ministry of many agents, some of whom will be wicked and some ignorant.

Both conditions may be bad, but they cannot both be worst.

SAMUEL JOHNSON : *Rasselas*

CHAPTER XIV

THE NATURE OF A GOVERNMENT CONTROL PLAN

Measures taken by the government to influence the course of economic events can be divided into two broad categories. On the one hand, the government can take steps to influence the expectations of private decision-makers. It is this range of measures which we have discussed at length in Part 3 of this volume. In the absence of forward markets, the government can organize a system of indicative planning in order to reduce market uncertainties and to enable private decision-makers to anticipate more correctly what will in fact be the market conditions which will accompany the various possible future courses of the outside events. The consequential improvement in anticipations will affect present decisions and will make them less liable to future regret.

But the government can, and in the modern economy for a number of social reasons which we will consider, later it does, take many more direct measures to influence and control the development of the economy. By the imposition of taxes and subsidies of various kinds, by influencing the supply of money and the terms on which dealings take place on the capital market, by the purchase of goods and services for direct public purposes, and by direct prohibition or regulation of private economic activities, it exercises an extremely powerful and pervasive direct effect upon economic decisions in the modern economy. The government then needs to have some control plan if it wishes to attempt to get the best results over time from the controls which it has introduced for various basic social purposes. The purpose of a governmental control plan is thus different from that of an indicative plan. It is not designed to enable private decision-makers to make better informed or more consistent decisions. It is designed to enable the authorities to set their own controls at levels which will more effectively attain the social objectives of the politicians. But while the two sorts of plans are conceptually distinct, there are, of course, certain very close connections between them.

Clearly a government cannot formulate a sensible control plan without taking into account how the private sector of the economy is likely to develop on various assumptions about the levels of its own controls; and this means that a control plan cannot be formulated without there being some governmental forecast of the future development of the economy derived either from an indicative plan or else from a governmental econometric model of the economy.

On the other hand, it is impossible to formulate a comprehensive indicative plan without there being something in the nature of a governmental control plan and without this control plan being in large measure revealed to the public.

It is obvious that governmental expenditure programmes, as well as private demands, must be considered by the indicative planners in estimating future market excess demands and supplies. It is equally true that private decision-makers in announcing their future plans and intentions to the indicative planners must make assumptions about future levels of tax rates, subsidies, interest rates, etc.; and to get the most rational and consistent plans would involve the revelation to the private sector of the government's expectations about the future course of those controls.

An indicative plan is, as we have seen, a process whereby a number of decision-makers can inform each other about their expectations of market conditions and about their own plans, so that their plans and market expectations can be made consistent. In fact the government can be regarded simply as one decision-maker—albeit, of course, an immensely important one—whose expectations and plans must be put, like everyone else's, into the pool for the formation of a consistent indicative plan.

In short, while it is possible, in the absence of any formal indicative plan, for the government to have a control plan based on its own econometric model of the economy, it is not possible to have a useful formal indicative plan in the absence of a control plan. We will return later (in Chapter XVIII) to the problems involved in integrating a governmental control plan into a formal indicative plan. For the present, we will concentrate our attention on the basic problems of governmental control planning by making the simple assumption that there is no formal indicative planning. Private decision-makers simply have to make their own best guesses with the help of any private forecasting agencies that may exist. Indicative planning is, as we have expressed it already, informal and not formal.

Many of the problems which face a government in planning the use of its controls are analogous to those which face a private decision-maker and which we have already discussed in Chapter XII. In particular, in order to decide what is the best use of its controls today, the government must consider the future course of events, including the future use of its own controls. The government's controls today (its expenditures, tax rates, interest rates, etc.) will affect the situation tomorrow. Thus the optimum level of today's controls will depend upon what is expected to happen tomorrow, but a large part of what happens tomorrow will depend upon tomorrow's governmental controls and these in turn should presumably also be set at their optimum levels. Thus the optimum level of today's controls will depend upon the optimum level of tomorrow's controls which will depend upon the optimum level of the controls of the day after tomorrow, and so on in a continuous series till 'Kingdom Come'. This is the problem of optimum dynamic control. The problems which arise can be seen to be of the same nature as those discussed for the private decision maker in Chapter XII. One or two illustrations may serve to make the point.

A government may have a policy of social services and benefits and of direct taxes and subsidies on income and wealth in order to affect the distribution of income and property. If so, one of the matters with which it will be concerned will be the distribution as between present and future generations. To what extent, for example, should it take steps to raise the current standard of living of the poorest members of the community if this necessarily implies some reduction in current savings and thus some reduction in the resources available to next year's citizens? The optimum present fiscal policy will be that which achieves the best available balance between this year's standards and next year's standards. But next year's standards will depend among other things upon next year's fiscal policy, which in turn will hopefully be set at its optimum level. Thus this year's optimum fiscal policy will depend, among other things, upon what is decided to be the optimum fiscal policy for next year, which in its turn will depend upon what is decided to be the optimum fiscal policy for the year after next, and so on far into the future. Thus the choice of an optimum fiscal policy cannot be reduced simply to finding separately the optimum policy for each year as it comes along. It must take the form of finding an optimum plan for the development of a fiscal policy over time.

Moreover, just as in the case of the private decisions discussed in Chapter XII, if there are important environmental uncertainties which the government cannot resolve, then this optimum fiscal policy should take the form of a set of optimal fiscal sub-plans rather than of a single fixed optimum fiscal plan. Thus there may be basic uncertainties about the future course of the size and age composition of the population, and also about the future course of productive technology and thus about the future output per head of the future working population. The smaller is the future ratio of dependent citizens to working population and the higher is the production effectiveness of each worker, the higher will be the standard of living available to future generations out of their own resources. And the higher the resources of future generations relatively to those of the present generation, the less need is there to keep down present standards in order to boost future standards. Thus the government in considering this year's optimal fiscal policy must assess the different probabilities of the future courses of population growth and of technological progress and must devise a set of optimal fiscal sub-plans in the sense of considering what would be the best way for its fiscal policy to develop in the future along each of the possible future paths of population growth and technological progress. For reasons analogous to those discussed for private decision makers in Chapter XII, it is only through devising a set of optimal fiscal sub-plans that it can decide what is the best present fiscal policy.

We may take another example from a different branch of economic activity. Motor roads are large indivisible units. There cannot be a large number of perfectly competitive contractors building a large number of perfectly competitive motor roads between London and Birmingham. One single motor road or network must be designed, built and operated as a single indivisible whole. For this reason, the road network will either be constructed and operated by a public authority or, at the very least, will be subject to strict public control. At the same time, the motor-vehicles which use the roads create very important external effects—congestion, noise, poisonous fumes, danger to life and limb and the cost of doctors, hospitals and undertakers. These are costs for which they will not be charged if the use of the roads is free, unless some public authority intervenes by means of taxation or other regulation.

What, then, should be the government's optimum policies of road-building and of motor-vehicle taxation? Clearly what it is best to do in the one sphere depends upon what is being done in the other. Thus there is no sense in reducing motor-vehicle taxation if its essential effect is merely to encourage more traffic on an unchanged network of already overcrowded and congested roads. Even more important for our present purpose is the fact that the optimum present road-building programme depends upon the future density of traffic which will depend not only upon current motor-vehicle taxation (since the present demand for new cars will affect the future stock of cars in existence) but also upon future roadbuilding and upon future levels of road taxation. But if, as is to be hoped, these future road-building programmes and the future levels of motor-vehicle taxation will be at their optimum levels, we reach once more the conclusion that the present optimum levels of road-building and of motor-vehicle taxation depend upon next year's optimum road-building and motor-vehicle taxation, which depend upon the following year's optimum levels, and so on. An optimum plan for future road-building and motor-vehicle taxation is required.

But all this must be designed in terms of future environmental uncertainties. The governmental planners will not know how technological progress in industry in general will affect the total output of goods and so the demand for goods' traffic on the roads nor how technological progress may affect real incomes and so the demand for passenger cars. There may also be important, but uncertain, technical possibilities for alternative means of transport by air or rail. Once again, it is clear that what is wanted is not simply an optimum control plan for road-building and motor-vehicle taxation, but a set of optimal control sub-plans which consider the best alternative ways in which road-building and motor vehicle taxation should be developed over the coming years on the various assumptions about the different paths along which the various possible technological and other relevant uncertainties may themselves move. Such a consideration of alternative possible paths is, for the reasons discussed in Chapter XII, in principle necessary in order to decide what is the best set of policies to adopt today.

For reasons which we will discuss later, the government may wish to control the level of effective demand in the economy. If so, this provides another example of the need for a dynamic optimal control plan.

The government might, for example, attempt to offset fluctuations in private demand by raising income tax and thus reducing tax-free spendable incomes when private demand threatened to be excessive and lowering income tax when private demand threatened to be deficient. But, once again, it would not be satisfactory simply to consider what current level of tax was necessary to maintain current demand at the desired level. It would once more be necessary to have a plan for the future level of taxation for stabilization purposes.

One obvious reason for this could be due to time-lags in the effect of changes in taxation on private expenditure. Suppose that a rise in this year's rate of tax with a consequential reduction in this year's spendable income will cause only a moderate reduction in this year's spending, but will cause a much larger reduction in next year's demand as consumers have time to adjust th ir expenditure habits. Suppose, then, that the government at the beginning of year 0 foresees a moderate deficiency in demand for year 0. If it attempts completely to offset this, then a large reduction in taxation in year 0 may be required so that the moderate immediate effect of this large tax reduction in stimulating demand during year 0 will restore the moderate deficiency of demand in year 0. But the delayed large effect in year 1 of the large reduction of tax in year 0 might cause a threat of a large excess demand in year 1. To offset this, a very large rise of tax is required in year 1 so that the moderate immediate effect of this very large rise in restraining demand in year 1 may be sufficient to offset the large inflation in year 1 caused by the large tax reduction of year 0. But this very large rise of tax in year 1 might threaten a very large slump in year 2 which might be offset by a very, very large reduction of tax in year 2 which will threaten a very, very large boom in year 3, which must be offset by a very, very, very large rise in tax in year 3, and so on.

Clearly ever-increasing swings in tax rates of this kind must be avoided. This means, of course, that this year's tax rates must be set with a view to their effects not only this year but also next year. But the effect which will be needed next year will depend among other things upon next year's tax rates, which will also be having an effect upon demand the year after next. Thus the optimum level of this year's tax depends upon the planned level of next year's tax which, if it is to be planned at its optimum level, must take into account the planned level of tax for the year after next, and so on. Moreover, since there are inevitable uncertainties about the future course of private expenditures due to basic uncertainties about the future course of many environmental events (such, for example, as the incentive to spend money on new investment in newly invented machinery or other capital equipment), it is not sufficient to have a single tax stabilization plan. It is necessary to devise a set of tax stabilization sub-plans which determine how tax policy should evolve along the different possible environmental paths.

In the light of these considerations we may enumerate the basic requirements of a governmental control plan under seven heads.

(1) The government must have some ECONOMETRIC MODEL of the technological and behavioural causal relationships in the economy, in order to be able to assess how the use of its controls will affect the development of the economy.

(2) The government must also have some information about the current STARTING POINT; that is to say, about the current position of the economy from which the future developments will take place as the result of its use of its controls.

(3) The government must make some estimates of the PROBABLE DEVELOPMENT OF THE ENVIRONMENTAL OUTSIDE EVENTS which will affect the future course of the economy, events which it cannot itself control and which are also uninfluenced by the private decision makers.

(4) Given items (1), (2) and (3) above the government controls will

themselves determine how the economy will in fact develop.[1] The government must have some set of value judgements—call it a SOCIAL WELFARE FUNCTION to determine its own preference between one development of the economy and another.

(5) In particular, since (for reasons analogous to those given earlier for private decision-makers) the government's plans can cover only a limited future period, the government must judge the social value of the TERMINAL CONDITIONS in which any particular control strategy will leave the economy at the end of the plan period.

(6) The government must have made a CHOICE OF THE WEAPONS OF CONTROL which it will use.

(7) The government must have some METHOD FOR DECIDING UPON THE OPTIMUM USE OF THE CONTROLS which it has selected (item 6) in order to maximize its expectation of social welfare (items 4 and 5) in the light of the way in which the controls will cause the economy to develop given the technological and behavioural relationships in the economy (item 1), the present starting point of the economy (item 2), and the various possible developments of the environmental events (item 3).

---

[1] See Figure 3 in Chapter II.

CHAPTER XV

THE BASIC COMPONENTS OF A GOVERNMENT CONTROL PLAN

In this chapter we will discuss briefly in turn each of the seven basic components of a governmental control plan which were enumerated at the end of the last chapter.

(1) THE ECONOMETRIC MODEL

If the government intends to develop a comprehensive control strategy in the absence of an indicative plan, it must build an econometric model of the dynamic relationships in the economy. The nature of these relationships has been discussed in Part 2 of this volume. The construction of a dynamic econometric model of this kind presents a most formidable task of statistical investigation. But it is not proposed in this volume to discuss these problems. One particular aspect of this problem must, however, be borne in mind, namely the treatment of expectations and their effect upon the actions of private decision makers. In so far as present actions depend upon expectations about the future and in so far as present expectations are moulded by past experience, one must include in the econometric model behavioural relationships which make present actions depend in this indirect manner on past experience.

(2) THE STARTING POINT

Given the behavioural and technological interrelationships estimated under (1), the government must have statistical and other information about the present position of the economy in order to know how the economy will develop. Where one will arrive on one's journey depends not only upon one's future speed and direction, but also upon one's starting point. The starting point of the economy depends, however, not only upon the current level of the stock of capital goods, the size of the working population, and similar physical factors, but also upon the current state of expectations. If, therefore, as we have suggested under (1) above, current expectations depend upon past events, then the starting point of the

233

economy must be taken to comprise these past events. In order to forecast how the economy will develop, one must in fact know how it has been developing over the relevant past period, which can be a long stretch of time. Thus the current and immediate future demand for consumption goods may depend upon whether consumer's incomes and the prices of durable consumer's goods have been rising or falling in the past; the current demand for capital equipment may depend upon whether the demand for the products of that equipment has been rising or falling in the past; and so on.[1]

(3) THE ENVIRONMENTAL PATHS

In order to assess the probable future course of events, the government must consider the possible future paths of the environmental events and it must make its own assessment of the probabilities of each such path. The problems which arise in this connection are similar to those which arise in the case of the private decision-makers and which we have already discussed at length in Chapter XIII.

In the first place, it is clear that governmental control plans cannot possibly be formulated so as to cover all possible environmental developments. This means that the government must cope with a lot of residual uncertainty. Like those who plan fixed capital investments in the private sector, it also, in its own plans for fixed capital investments in the public sector, must put an additional emphasis upon general flexibility of use. But there is in this connection one rather special implication for governmental control planning. All sorts of unexpected environmental events may directly or indirectly cause fluctuations in the total demand for goods and thus threaten to put into operation a cumulative positive feedback cycle of inflation or of deflation and unemployment. Just as private citizens must carry cash to meet many uncalculated contingencies, so the government must be ready with what may be called a stabilization programme, namely with some set of fiscal and/or monetary control weapons with which it can rapidly react so as to stimulate total demand when an unexpected decline occurs and vice versa. A calculated governmental control plan is needed to shape the general structure of governmental policies over the coming years. In addition to this, a stabilization programme for quick reaction to wholly unpremeditated instabilities is needed. The two types of control plans or programmes are separate, but complementary, entities. We will return to this problem in Part 5 of this volume.

[1] Thus in the very simple model shown in Figure 20 we had to consider events in days -2 and -1 in order to know how the economy would behave on day 0.

Secondly, it is also clear that, just as in the case of private decision-makers, the government will have to limit the period of future time covered by its plans for the reason that the environmental uncertainties after a time become too manifold and ill defined for any useful precise calculation of possible future developments. As in the case of planning by private decision-makers, the choice of the optimum time-span for a governmental control plan is a question of the balance between the sensitivity of present decisions to possible events in the more distant future and the costs of extending the time-span of the plan in a meaningful way. Also, as in the case of planning by private decision-makers, the fact that the time-span covered by the plan is limited carries with it the implication that any governmental control plan should be subject to frequent revision and should be used solely to decide the best use of today's controls, the actual level of tomorrow's controls being left for decision in the light of tomorrow's revised control plan.

(4) THE SOCIAL WELFARE FUNCTION

In the modern developed economy, even when the basic principle of free enterprise is maintained, there are a large number of reasons why the government may feel called upon to intervene directly in the economy. These reasons may be grouped under six headings.

(i) It may be considered desirable to influence the demographic developments in the community, that is to say, to raise or to lower the rate of growth of the population.

(ii) It may be considered desirable to affect the distribution of income and wealth between the present and future generations, that is to say, to raise or to lower the proportion of the national income which is not consumed at once but which is saved and invested for the advantage of the citizens in the future.

(iii) It may be considered desirable to take steps to redistribute income and wealth between the various classes of the citizens of any one generation, that is to say, to increase the welfare of the poor and needy at the expense of the rich and prosperous.

(iv) The free enterprise competitive system will not work in the efficient manner of the perfectly competitive system if there are important indivisibilities in the economy which are bound to lead to the existence of monopolistic or monopsonistic influences in the economy. The government may wish to intervene in order to correct distortions to the efficient pattern of the use of resources caused by monopolistic elements.

(v) Next, there is the huge category of external economies and diseconomies. This includes, at the one extreme, the need for the government itself to provide certain services, such as the police, the benefits from which are entirely social or 'external' as contrasted, with the 'individual' or 'internal' benefits gained from some activity which affects directly only one or two particular citizens. At the other extreme, this category covers those cases where the individual activity has only some incidental external effects (such as the proverbial smoke nuisance of a factory) which the government can hope to control by some partial regulation or tax or subsidy without taking over the whole activity from the private sector of the economy. Since, as we are now told, the external diseconomies of fumes from the petrol engine may so pollute the atmosphere as to put an end to all human life, it would be somewhat unrealistic not to allow for such factors in any catalogue of imperfections of the *laissez faire* system.

(vi) Finally, there are all sorts of frictions in economic markets. In pure theory, in a perfectly competitive economy there would never be any continuous unemployment of labour except when the wage rate was zero. All workers would come into the labour market at the beginning of the day or week and offer their services in competition with each other to a set of competing employers and the wage would very quickly be reduced so long as it was positive and any worker remained without work. In fact, of course, workers set a price for their work (which may well, of course, be influenced more or less sluggishly by past and expected levels of unemployment) and there results from week to week a certain level of employment and a certain level of unemployment. Similarly, many producers of manufactured products set prices for their goods (which also may be influenced over time by the level of demand for them) and there results from week to week a level of productive activity and a level of unused capacity in the businesses concerned. The fact that many producers of goods and suppliers of labour react to a change in demand, not by an immediate change in the price of the goods or the wage of the labour, but by a change in the amount of goods sold or the amount of labour which finds employment can lead to large cumulative swings—an initial change in demand leading to a change in output and employment, leading to a change in real income, leading to a change in the amounts of goods and services demanded and so on in a cumulative vicious circle. But these swings could be offset by governmental measures which affect the level of demand for goods and services and so for labour at any given level of money wage rates and prices.

These six categories of reason for governmental intervention in the economy are closely interrelated. It is impossible to separate into unconnected watertight compartments the use of controls by the government for various purposes such as (i) affecting the distribution of income and property, (ii) coping with externalities and indivisibilities, and (iii) stabilizing total demand. The controls which are employed primarily for the one purpose will in almost all cases have some effect upon the other purposes. Thus changes in tax designed primarily to help to stabilize total demand will almost certainly have some effect upon the distribution of income and property and perhaps also upon the balance between expenditure on road-building and expenditure upon the vehicles to use the roads. Or, to take another example, a change in road-building programmes designed to obtain the best balance in the resources devoted to transport and to other social uses will almost certainly have some effect in stabilizing or destabilizing the total level of demand. Theoretically, therefore, it is necessary to conceive of one single governmental control plan under which all the effects of all its controls are considered simultaneously.

An important implication of this is that the government must be able to evaluate as a whole the social desirability of the various effects of its controls under the six headings (i) to (vi) given above. Thus a change in the rate of income tax or in the level of some governmental expenditures may effect the distribution of income and wealth; it may simultaneously affect the level of employment and thus of the total real national income; it may affect various departmental plans for roads, defence, schools, etc. How does the government decide how much extra employment is worth how much greater inequality in the distribution of income or how much extra education is worth how much reduction in the battle against pollution? The government must have some politically determined mechanism for judging between the social values to be put upon its various social and economic objectives. That is to say, in some sense or another it must be thought of as acting upon a social welfare function which gives due and balanced weight to all its different objectives and as setting its controls with the object of maximizing expected future social welfare. In the next chapter we will consider in much more detail one example of this way of looking at the problem.[2]

[2] Important issues of moral and political philosophy arise in this connection. For example, in a democratic community, what are the legitimate limits to the use which any government should make of its particular social welfare function, i.e. of its own relative evaluation of different social ojbectives? Should it commit present resources in as rigid a manner as possible to those uses which will ensure the satisfaction of its own social values in the distant future, leaving little or no flexibility for the satisfaction of the alternative social values of the opposition party, which may well in turn constitute the government? In other words, to what extent should a government recognize and plan to meet the uncertain future wishes of the electorate itself?

(5) THE TERMINAL CONDITIONS

We have seen in (3) above that the time-span covered by a governmental control plan will necessarily be limited. But this is simply due to the multiplication of uncertainties as one peers into the more and more distant future; it does not mean that the government is indifferent to what will happen to the economy beyond the period of the plan. The government must, therefore, be concerned with an evaluation of the terminal conditions in which on any given control plan it will leave the economy at the end of the plan period on each of the possible environmental paths which it is considering in its plan. These evaluations of terminal conditions make up an essential part of a social welfare function; but in the very nature of things, simply because *ex hypothesi* their implications for periods beyond the time-span of the plan are not explored, these evaluations must be extremely rough and ready rule of thumb affairs. We will consider this problem in greater detail in the example of a social welfare function examined in the next chapter.

(6) THE CHOICE OF CONTROL WEAPONS

In the dynamic model of the economy used for illustrative purposes in Chapter VII and depicted in Figure 29, the government's control weapons were marked by a double asterisk and were nine in number, namely: t_q^{**}, H_q^{**}, t_w^{**}, H_w^{**}, G_1^{**}, G_2^{**}, i_{lg}^{**}, i_{sg}^{**} and i_{sp}^{**}. These represent rates of direct tax on incomes of various classes (the 't's), subsidies to the incomes of various classes (the 'H's), governmental demands for various goods and services (the 'G's), and the various interest rates at which the financial authorities were prepared to deal in various securities (the 'i's).

This is in fact a very restricted list of possible weapons of control. If the government is planning ahead in order to maximize the expected value of some general comprehensive social welfare function, it must take into account the net combined effects of all its policies and acts which will have any economic effect at all:—and this is almost to say simply, all its policies and acts. In principle, the government must be facing the most general question of the following kind: "If our whole collection of policies is so-and-so, what will be the result on all the things in which we are interested? If, however, our whole collection of policies were changed in this and this respect, what would be the net changes in all the things in which we are interested? Would we regard the whole collection of net changes as constituting a net social loss or gain?" In other words, an implication of the conclusion mentioned earlier, that governmental action must be regarded as a whole, is that all possible governmental policies must be regarded as controls for our present purposes.

Of course, in the real world the problem must be broken down in some way into manageable parts and in Chapter XVII we will discuss this aspect of the problem. But, in any case, we can make some preliminary and useful distinctions between various types of governmental policy decisions which have very different implications for the purposes of a dynamic control plan.

(i) There are first of all what we may call REVOLUTIONARY POLICIES. If a political change in the USSR were to result in a change over to a comprehensive system of *laissez faire* competitive free enterprise capitalism or if a political change in the USA were to result in the socialization of all the means of production, distribution and exchange, it would be difficult to say that there had been no change of economic policy or that the change in economic policy was such as would have no significant effects upon social welfare. But the total change of economic structure would be such that any existing econometric model of the economy would become totally irrelevant and any attempt to calculate the resulting effects upon social welfare by the methods considered in this volume would be absurd. We are discussing in this volume changes in economic policies that can take place within the general existing structural framework of the economy.

(ii) This does not, however, mean that our type of analysis can be of no use in the examination of the effects of what may be called POLICIES OF STRUCTURAL ADJUSTMENT. By this we mean governmental policies which introduce a once-for-all structural change in some limited section of the economy. Many examples may be given: legislation which prevents certain restrictive business practices; legislation which reduces the power of labour monopolies to push up money wage rates; the nationalization of an important industry like steel, together with the application of certain new rules for its pricing and output decisions; the introduction of a new tax on capital gains; the substitution of a value-added tax for some other form of indirect taxation on commodities; the replacement of certain social security benefits by a general negative income tax; the introduction of new legislation prohibiting the emission of smoke or other forms of pollution of the environment; and so on and so on.

Measures of this are once and for all and do affect the behavioural relationship in the economy and this means that the econometric model of the economy must be revised. But unlike the revolutionary policies under (i) they are only partial. The general structure of the economy and so of the econometric model can remain unchanged; it is only the structure of, or the value of the parameters in, one or two of the relationships which must be revised. Such revision presents great difficulty. But if it is not too extensive—and the distinction between revolutionary policies and policies of structural adjustment is, of course, only one of degree—it may well be useful to attempt to calculate what the future effects of these once-for-all limited changes in certain parameters of the econometric model will be and to assess on the general principles discussed in this volume whether the net effect is socially desirable.

(iii) There remains the category of what may be called FLEXIBLE CONTROLS. These comprise the measures of policy which the government is prepared to vary at relatively frequent intervals. The nine control variables of Figure 29 listed above all fall into this category, though many more could be added. They include tax rates (as contrasted with tax structures), rates of subsidy, monetary and national debt policies affecting interest rates and supplies of assets of various degrees of liquidity, and government demands for goods and services of all kinds. They may also include a number of quantitative controls such as the limitation of some activity by the issue of licenses permitting that activity; thus, the volume of imports of a given commodity or the amount of building of houses or of factories that may take place in a given region may be controlled by the issue of licenses to import or to build, the number of licenses issued being varied from time to time. Or, to take another example, expenditure on durable consumer goods may be controlled by official regulation of the terms on which hire-purchase finance can be offered for their acquisition.

It is this class of policy decision for which the analysis developed in this volume is most directly relevant. But, once again, the distinction between policies of structural adjustment and flexible controls is only a matter of degree. Consider, for example, a revision of the scale of progression in an income tax. A government raises the rates of tax on high incomes and exempts from tax a range of low incomes previously subject to tax as a more or less permanent change of social policy for the redistribution of income. Do we regard this as a structural adjustment or merely as a change of certain rates of tax which we consider as the particular use of a flexible control? The choice is a matter of personal taste.

But extremes meet and there is a possibility that just because it is so flexible a particular control will consciously be used by a government in a way which has the same sort of effect as a once-for-all structural adjustment. An example of this would occur if the government linked the rate of some particular tax automatically to the level of some other variable, such as the level of unemployment. Suppose that the government wished to adjust total tax-free personal incomes and thus total personal consumption, so as to maintain a stable level of effective demand for goods and so for labour. Suppose that for this purpose it introduced, as a once-for-all institutional change, the rule that a particular personal tax (e.g. an income tax or a compulsory contribution to national insurance) should automatically be lowered (or raised) on a given sliding scale according as the unemployment percentage rose (or fell). This it could do only if that particular tax rate were extremely flexible in the sense that it could be readily and promptly raised or lowered in so far as its administration was concerned. But the net effect of the once-for-all introduction of the automatic sliding scale would be to revise the structural relationship in the economy between the receipt of income and its expenditure.

We will consider this aspect of the use of flexible controls at greater length in Part 5 of this volume. For the present, we concentrate attention on the planning ahead of a pattern for the flexible controls which is calculated to maximize expected social welfare. This is the essence of governmental optimal control planning.

(7) THE METHOD FOR DECIDING UPON THE OPTIMUM USE OF THE CONTROLS

The problem then remains for the government to find some means for discovering what set of sub-plans for its controls along the various future environmental paths will in fact maximize its expectation of social welfare. This problem is formally exactly equivalent to the problem which private decision-makers face when they have to decide what set of sub-plans for the variables which they can control will maximize the expectation of their own private utility. This we have already discussed in Chapter XII and in the Note to that chapter.

A complete control plan consists of a sub-plan for the movement of the controls along each environmental path. There is a vast number of such patterns. Each pattern will produce a given result along each environmental path, and thus a given level of social welfare along each path, and thus—given the government's assessment of the probability of each path—a given level of expected social welfare. The problem is to choose that pattern for the controls which results in the highest level of expected social welfare.

Given the econometric model which represents the technological and behavioural relationships in the economy, given the starting point of the economy, given the description of the different possible environmental developments and an assessment of their probabilities and given some principle for the measurement of the social welfare accruing from each possible development of the economy, it should, theoretically, be possible to calculate mathematically the optimum pattern for the controls. It is not the purpose of this volume—indeed it does not lie within the competence of the author—to discuss the mathematical techniques involved. A sketch of one possible technique has been given in the Note to Chapter XII in the case of planning by private decision-makers; with the substitution of a social welfare function for a private utility function the analysis in that Note can be directly applied to the problem of governmental control planning.

In the text of Chapter XII, we discussed another method. The decision-maker can start with any set of sub-plans for his controls along each environmental path; he then modifies this pattern of controls in certain marginal ways, considers the total effect of such modification, and assesses whether it has resulted in an increase or decrease in total expected utility; he adopts the modification if expected utility has been increased; he then tries a yet further modification; and so on, as long as any substantial gains in expected utility can be obtained. This method can be regarded simply as a method of calculating the optimum pattern for the controls. In this case the marginal modifications are not in fact made but merely imagined; the results are calculated; further modifications are imagined and their results calculated; and so on until some final pattern of controls is reached which can constitute the strategic control plan actually adopted.

On the other hand, this method can also be regarded as a method of actually improving a strategic plan in a step-by-step fashion. Today some plan for the controls is in operation, the actual controls of today being set in accordance with this plan. Tomorrow the plan will be revised for two reasons: (i) because more will be known about the actual environmental development so that the plan would need revision even if the previous plan had been optimal; and (ii) because the previous plan was not optimal and, even if the environmental uncertainties were completely unchanged, some modifications of the plan might be adopted because they would in any case have led to a better outcome. By a process of this kind, a plan may hopefully be gradually improved as time passes.

Let us consider the implications of this method in somewhat greater detail. We will do so in terms of the simple three-day four-environmental path model of Figures 34 and 35. That is to say, let us suppose that the government has a three-day plan for the development of its controls over four environmental paths. For example, it knows what levels of motor-vehicle taxation and road building it will impose today and it has an idea of the levels of road-building and of motor-vehicle taxation which it intends to impose tomorrow if it is at point 12 and the levels which it intends to impose tomorrow if it is at point 34, and similarly for the alternative levels which it plans to impose the day after tomorrow if it is then at points 1, 2, 3 or 4 on the possible environmental paths. It then considers whether a small change of a particular kind in this pattern of planned controls—e.g. a little more to be spent on the roads tomorrow if at point 12—is an improvement or not.

Let us first consider whether this is a sensible sort of question to ask. One can see the point of the procedure if the question is whether a small change in the controls actually to be imposed today would improve things or not, always taking into account the direct and indirect effects of the change in today's controls on possible events tomorrow and the day after tomorrow. But is there any point in asking today whether a small change in the controls planned for tomorrow would improve matters? After all, tomorrow's controls need not be actually finally determined till tomorrow comes. What is the point then of fussing one's head with the question whether a slight rise in the amount planned for road expenditure tomorrow if tomorrow turns out to be fine will improve social welfare or not?

The answer is twofold.

In the first place, there is much to be said for publishing the government's control plan. To obtain the best informed decisions by private citizens today it is necessary that they should have the most accurate information available about future conditions. The potential purchaser of a car today may properly be influenced by the question whether or not a particular road will be built tomorrow. If, therefore, the government's control plan is published, today's events (e.g. the number of cars bought today) may be influenced by a change in the government's plans for its future controls (e.g. the amount of road-building tomorrow). Future plans can thus have an actual effect on today's events and so on social welfare.[3]

But, secondly, there is a much more fundamental point than this. Suppose that a change in the plans for the government's future controls are not made public so that they can have no effect upon today's events in the private sector of the economy. Nevertheless, there may be some point in the government considering whether a small change in its controls planned for the future would increase

---

[3] We are, however, for the time being assuming that the government's control plans are not being published (see p. 226 above). But, at a later stage, we will consider the effects of the publication of the governmental plans (see Chapter XVIII) and at that point we will return to the above argument.

or decrease the social welfare expected over the period of the plan, for the simple reason that an improvement in the pattern of tomorrow's planned controls (given today's controls) will enable the government to consider whether there might not then be a possible improvement in today's controls (given the new and improved level of the controls planned for tomorrow). Thus given the actual level of today's motor-vehicle taxation and road-building programme, the question may be asked whether it would not increase the total of social welfare to be expected over the three-day plan period if there were not some increase in the road expenditure planned for tomorrow if tomorrow is fine (i.e. for point 34 on Figure 34). Suppose the answer is "Yes". Then the question may be raised whether a reduction in today's motor-vehicle taxation would increase the social welfare expected over the planned period. The answer to this question might have been "No" if the old plan for low expenditure on road-building tomorrow had been maintained, since to stimulate the demand for cars today would merely add to tomorrow's congestion. But the answer might be "Yes" if tomorrow's plan for road expenditure had been raised to the improved and higher level. Thus, to improve tomorrow's plan (given today's controls) may be a useful way of finding out whether today's actual controls might not be improved.

This procedure is, of course, merely a gradient method of climbing the hill of social welfare. If a marginal change in today's actual controls or in tomorrow's planned controls is made only if it would increase the total social welfare expected over the period of the plan, then any series of such marginal changes will move one continually up hill until one reaches the summit.[4]

The procedure is subject to two serious limitations.

In the first place, there is the well-known point that one may be climbing the wrong peak, in the sense that nearby on the mountain range there may be a still higher peak. Some structural change might improve the final prospects for social welfare, although this might involve in the first place moving one's plan of controls in a direction which, if the changes were kept to small marginal adjustments, would decrease expected welfare. One must first descend into the valley in order to start on the ascent of the higher peak.

Secondly, the procedure may, of course, be an extremely roundabout way of getting near the top of the peak. Consider, for example, two commodities X and Y which are good substitutes for each other in demand. Consider two tax controls, a tax rate of t_x on the consumption of X and of t_y on the consumption of Y. The best

---

[4] Assuming that, if there is any point of inflexion, one can perturb the system so as to find out whether there is any remaining direction in which one can still climb.

course might be to reduce both taxes to zero. But damage may in fact be done not only by the average height of t_x and t_y (which undesirably diverts demands away from these two goods in general) but also by the difference between t_x and t_y. If t_x is much greater than t_y, then high-cost Y will be being produced which could better be replaced by low-cost X. A rise in t_y will help to remove this particular inefficiency. Thus, with t_x considerably greater than t_y, some rise in t_y might improve things. But when t_y has been raised as near t_x as is necessary to attain the maximum benefit, t_y will still be less than t_x, since a low level of t_y has advantage in not diverting demand away from Y onto goods other than X. It will then, of course, improve matters to reduce t_x since a reduction in t_x will attract demand from high cost Y and also from the other goods. t_x will then be reduced below t_y until the advantage of attracting demand on to X from other goods is offset by the disadvantage of attracting demand from the now relatively low cost Y. Then it will be desirable to reduce t_y. And so on, until t_x and t_y have both been reduced to zero. Clearly it would be a roundabout way to reach this final state by starting, as we did in this example, with a rise in t_y, even though it remains true that every step in the above sequence marked an improvement.

The moral of this is that the government, in considering a marginal change in its control plan, should enlist what help it can from its economic advisers to start on an initial set of exploratory changes which on general economic principles is likely to provide a fairly direct route towards the best attainable position with the existing structure of the economy.

CHAPTER XVI

THE APPLICATION OF THE PRINCIPLES OF CONTROL TO A PARTICULAR SOCIAL WELFARE FUNCTION: AN ILLUSTRATIVE CASE

The purpose of the present chapter is solely to provide an illustration of a possible way of treating a social welfare function, to apply to this social welfare function the step-by-step method of control planning discussed at the end of the last chapter, and to consider some of the implications for governmental organization and action.[1]

We will present a simplified model based upon the three-day four-environmental path model already depicted in Figures 34 and 35. But in the case of the discussion of Figures 34 and 35 in Chapter X we confined our attention to a three-day plan period because we were assuming that the world was known to be coming to an abrupt end at midnight between days 2 and 3, so that there was no problem of evaluating the terminal conditions of the plan. We now assume, however, that the government is confining its attention to a three-day plan period not because 'Kingdom Come' is anticipated at the end of day 2, but simply because it cannot cope with more than four paths of environmental uncertainty. The government will now be interested in the state in which its sub-plans will leave the economy at the end of day 2 at the termination of each of the four environmental paths. We are thus faced with the scheme depicted in Figure 41.

The government is considering its strategic control plan at the beginning of today knowing already whether it is wet or fine. It is faced with four possible environmental paths over the remaining two days of its plan, namely sequences of (1) wet-wet, (2) wet-fine, (3) fine-wet, and (4) fine-fine. There are now eleven relevant states of the economy to be considered. The four terminal points which we

[1] This chapter contains a dose of differential calculus and is thus an exception to the rule hitherto observed in these volumes that such mathematical analysis is confined to footnotes or to notes appended to the various chapters. The present chapter could be treated as a note appended to Chapter XV and the thread of the argument is not lost if the reader omits the present chapter. The matters discussed in it are, however, of such basic importance that it deserves, and is presented as, a chapter in its own right.

will call T_1, T_2, T_3, and T_4 respectively, which refer to the states of the economy which will exist at the end of day 2 (i.e. the beginning of day 3) if the weather has moved on paths 1, 2, 3 or 4 respectively must be added to the seven other points, namely 1234, 12, 34, 1, 2, 3 and 4, which we have already discussed in connection with Figures 34 and 35.

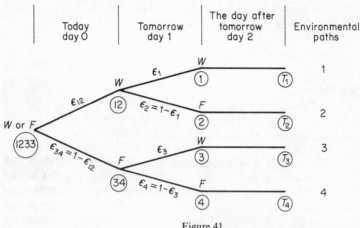

Figure 41

In order to make a rational choice of policies, the governmental authorities must form some estimate of the probabilities of moving along the different environmental paths. This involves estimating (1) ε_{12}, i.e. the probability of moving from point 1234 to point 12 which also implies ε_{34} the probability of moving to point 34, since $\varepsilon_{12} + \varepsilon_{34} = 1$; (2) ε_1, i.e. the probability of moving from point 12 to point 1 which implies $\varepsilon_2 = 1 - \varepsilon_1$; and (3) ε_3, i.e. the probability of moving from point 34 to point 3, which implies also $\varepsilon_4 = 1 - \varepsilon_3$.

If we make the assumption that in some sense or another the community clocks up units of social welfare or utility as it passes through the various points along any one environmental path and that the objective of the government is so to set the levels of its controls as to maximize the total social wefare or utility which it (the government) expects to be clocked up over the period of the plan, we can express our problem formally as the formulation today of a plan for the use of the governmental controls along each environmental path which will maximize:

$$\mathscr{E}(U) = U_{1234} + \varepsilon_{12}U_{12} + \varepsilon_{34}U_{34} + \varepsilon_1\varepsilon_{12}(U_1 + U_{T1})$$
$$+ \varepsilon_2\varepsilon_{12}(U_2 + U_{T2}) + \varepsilon_3\varepsilon_{34}(U_3 + U_{T3}) + \varepsilon_4\varepsilon_{34}(U_4 + U_{T4})$$
$$\dots\dots(16.1)$$

where U_q stands for the amount of Social Welfare which would be clocked up if and when the economy passed through point q and U_{Tq} stands for the social valuation to be placed on the state in which the economy would be left at the end of path q.

The purpose of this chapter is to consider what might be the forms of the social welfare function (i.e. of U_q and U_{Tq}) if one was to try to formulate it and, more realistically, how far the sort of deliberations and actions of actual governments in the choice of policies could in reality be interpreted and even perhaps assisted by working out some of the implications of any such social welfare function. This chapter is thus concerned only with the 'normative' side of planning; and it neglects the whole of the 'positive' side of the problem, namely all the questions connected with the estimation of the actual effect which any given time pattern of the governmental controls will actually have on the course of the economy—i.e. on the total national income, on its distribution between rich and poor, on the level of employment, on the output and consumption of various particular goods and services, and so on, as the economy moves along any one environmental path. It is simply assumed that by means of clever work in its statistical, economic and planning offices, through the construction of an econometric model, the authorities make the best possible estimates of the effect which any given time pattern of their controls along each given environmental time-path will have upon the relevant variables in the economy.

How then might the government handle its policy objectives in such a setting?

Suppose that there are only two products X and Y—the generalization to n products would present no difficulty of principle. Then if one tried in a liberal free enterprise economy to formulate a function U_q—namely the amount of Social Welfare clocked up by the community as one passed through point q—one might express it as:

$$U_q = a\{eN\hat{U}(\hat{C}_{xa}, \hat{C}_{ya}, \hat{L}_a)\}_q + b\{eN\hat{U}(\hat{C}_{xb}, \hat{C}_{yb}, \hat{L}_b)\}_q$$
$$+ \{(1 - e)N\hat{U}(\hat{C}_{xu}, \hat{C}_{yu})\}_q + \{U_s(C_x, C_y, \overline{X}, \overline{Y})\}_q$$
$$+ \{U_g(G_x, G_y)\}_q \dots\dots\dots\dots\dots\dots\dots\dots\dots\dots\dots\dots (16.2)$$

where $\overline{X}$ and $\overline{Y}$ are the total gross outputs of X and Y, C_x and C_y are the total amounts consumed by individuals, G_x and G_y are the amounts bought by the government for public use, N is the total population, e is the proportion of the population in work so that $1 - e$ is the proportion unemployed, a and b (where $a + b = 1$) are two constant fractions which divide the employed population into two groups aeN and beN, such that the least rich person in group *aeN* is better off than (or perhaps rather, at least as well off as) the least poor person in group *beN*, and $\hat{C}$ and $\hat{L}$ represent the amounts of consumption per head and of work done per head in the various groups in society.

The philosophy behind this is as follows. Social Welfare is represented primarily as the sum of the welfare of the individual citizens which depends directly upon the amount of each product consumed and the amount of work done by each individual citizen; but this sum is subject to two qualifications, first, the addition to or subtraction from the citizens' welfare due to the social costs or benefits (i.e. the external economies or diseconomies) associated with various economic activities and, second, the contribution to welfare due to governmental expenditure upon goods for public consumption.

Let us first consider these qualifications. $U_s(C_x, C_y, \overline{X}, \overline{Y})$ expresses the valuation of the external social costs and benefits which may be associated with the private consumption and production of the two commodities. It is only illustrative, since external social costs and benefits might well be associated with other variables, such for example as the number of persons employed in a certain productive activity. Such elements could readily be added. $U_g(G_x, G_y)$ expresses the valuation placed upon the public services fed by the governmental purchases of the two goods.

As for the basic elements, namely the individual citizens' individual utilities from their individual consumptions and leisure, it would be unreasonable to ask any government to assess every individual's welfare separately and to add up the result—to assess the happiness of Mr Smith, of Mr Jones, of Mr Brown, and so on separately and add them all up. The thing clearly must be done in broad classes of persons. In equation 16.2, solely for illustrative purposes, the population is divided into three groups. There are the unemployed, namely $(1 - e) N$, who are unwillingly debarred from working and whose private utility depends solely upon their private consumption, the utility of an unemployed man being thus $\hat{U}(\hat{C}_{xu}, \hat{C}_{yu})$. The employed, namely *eN*, are then divided into two classes, the rich, namely *aeN* and the poor, namely *beN*, where $a + b = 1$. Clearly it would be possible to divide the population up into any number of gradations of wealth and poverty. For example if one divided them up into a hundred 1% classes (i.e. $a_1 + a_2 + \dots + a_{100} = 1$)—where a_1 denoted the 1% richest citizens, a_2 the 1% next richest citizens, and so on—one would obtain an almost continuous description of the distribution of wealth and poverty. The two classes $a + b = 1$ are chosen solely for purposes of simple illustration.

The $\hat{U}$'s of the social welfare function must be valuations made by the government in so far as they involve interpersonal comparisons, but for the rest they are valuations which respect individual choice in the market. Thus, simply to illustrate the principle, let us suppose that all citizens have the same tastes (i.e. the same indifference map) and have only to choose between the consumption of X and Y (i.e. $\hat{C}_x$ and $\hat{C}_y$). Then the individual's indifference map might be as in Figure 42. If the income of a citizen in each of our three classes allowed consumption at points a, b, and u respectively, then the '$\hat{U}$'s in the Social Welfare function would be based on the citizen's indifference map, but with governmental cardinal numbers allotted to the indifference curves $\hat{U}_a$, $\hat{U}_b$, and $\hat{U}_u$.

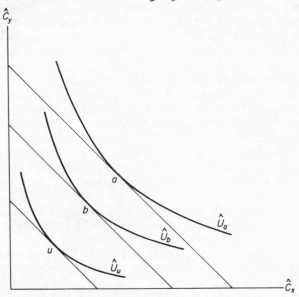

Figure 42

The simple classification of the citizens into the three classes a, b, and u skates over a number of difficulties of which two may be mentioned. First, how does one measure the degree of wealth and poverty in order to order the citizens according to their wealth? Is it by income after tax? Or is it solely by the amount spent on consumption? In either case, does one take into account the amount of work done? Is a man who chooses a relatively low income from earnings and thus a relatively low level of consumption because he greatly prefers leisure, in a real sense 'poorer' than one who, with the same opportunities, chooses to work more and earn more? Is the ownership of property itself, quite apart from the income from property, to be counted as making a man richer for the purposes of our classification? For the purposes of the present chapter it will be simply assumed that these considerations are in fact relatively unimportant.

Second, there are demographic facts of the utmost importance in the real world which the formulation in equation 16.2 entirely ignores. This formulation would be correct if the whole population was comprised of male fully adult workers. But the age and sex composition of the population is, of course, of fundamental importance for the standard of living. The immortal Athene may have sprung fully armed from the head of Zeus, but workers do not spring fully trained from their mothers' wombs, and they grow old and incapable of work. Governmental policies which affect fertility, nuptiality and mortality rates are of immense importance; the first effect of a change in fertility is, of course, to increase the number of dependent children, later to increase the number of workers, and still later to increase the number of the dependent old aged in retirement.[2] These dynamic demographic developments are of fundamental economic importance and are disgracefully neglected by economic theorists interested in economic growth and dynamic developments. We shall ourselves incur the shame of neglecting them in this chapter and assume that governmental policies may affect the number of adult males of working age who comprise the whole population.

To return to our main problem: How might a social welfare function of the kind depicted in equations 16.1 and 16.2 be used to judge whether any given small modification in the pattern of the controls planned over the plan period along each of the environmental paths would or would not be an improvement? It will be seen from equation 16.2 that a small change in the controls will affect Social Welfare through its effect on the sixteen variables e, N, $\hat{C}_{xa}$, $\hat{C}_{ya}$, L_a, $\hat{C}_{xb}$, $\hat{C}_{yb}$, $\hat{L}_b$, $\hat{C}_{xu}$, $\hat{C}_{yu}$, $\hat{C}_x$, $\hat{C}_y$, $\bar{X}$, $\bar{Y}$, G_x and G_y—all of which are direct causes of change in the amount of Social Welfare (U_q) which the community will clock up on its meter of Social Welfare if and when it passes through the point q. The first step is thus the 'positive' task of the government's economists, statisticians and econometricians to inform the government of the way in which the movement of each of these sixteen variables[3] along each of the

---

[2] Cf. Note to Chapter X of *The Growing Economy*.

[3] G_x and G_y are, of course, themselves controls. They may change as a DIRECT part of the change in the planned pattern of controls. The remaining fourteen variables given above may change as an INDIRECT effect of the changed pattern of controls.

environmental paths would be affected by the change in the controls. The second step is the 'normative' step which we wish to discuss in this chapter, namely how these small changes in each of the sixteen variables listed above would at each point q affect the amount of Social Welfare clocked up at that point (namely U_q).

This second step requires the differentiation of the expression for U_q in equation 16.2 in respect of each of the sixteen variables listed above. We will obtain the resulting expression for dU_q after the introduction of a certain number of constraints and new definitions.

Let us first write:

$$\mu_{aq} = \left\{\frac{\partial \hat{U}_a}{\partial \hat{C}_{xa}} \div P_x\right\}_q = \left\{\frac{\partial \hat{U}_a}{\partial \hat{C}_{ya}} \div P_y\right\}_q$$

$$= -\left\{\frac{\partial \hat{U}_a}{\partial \hat{L}_a} \div \overline{W}(1 + \delta_{la})\right\}_q$$

and similarly for μ_{bq} while:

$$\mu_{uq} = \left\{\frac{\partial \hat{U}_u}{\partial \hat{C}_{xu}} \div P_x\right\}_q = \left\{\frac{\partial \hat{U}_u}{\partial \hat{C}_{yu}} \div P_y\right\}_q \quad \dots\dots\dots\dots\dots (16.3)$$

where μ_{aq}, μ_{bq} and μ_{uq} represent the marginal utility of money income to our three classes of citizens—rich, poor and unemployed —P_{xq} and P_{yq} represent the market prices ruling for the two commodities, and $\overline{W}_q$ represents the money wage rate fixed for the employment of a unit of labour at the beginning of day q, and payable at the beginning of day q.[4]

As far as the purchase of the two goods is concerned, equations 16.3 simply assume that all consumers can purchase any amount of any good for final consumption at the same current market price (which must therefore include any rate of tax levied on that good) without the price being affected by the purchases of any individual consumer. But this assumption is not made about the purchase of leisure by the employed citizens in classes a and b. $\overline{W}$ represents the price paid by the employer of labour for a unit of labour. The worker may add less than $\overline{W}$ to his income for an additional unit of work provided by him. This would happen if the supplier of labour were a monopolist. But the direct taxation of earnings provides a much more certain and universal reason for this phenomenon, and the more progressive the system of direct taxation the greater the divergence

[4] We use the notation $\overline{W}$ instead of W for the wage rate to distinguish it from the usage in *The Growing Economy* where it is assumed that the wage rate for work done during day t (W_t) is fixed at the beginning of day t, but payable at the beginning of day $t + 1$. If i_t were the rate of interest ruling for a day's loan made at the beginning of day t, then $\overline{W}_t(1 + i_t) = W_t$.

between the wage paid by the employer and the amount added to his disposable income by the worker. If the marginal rate of tax were 20%, then out of a $\overline{W}$ of \$1 only \$0·8 would be received by the worker as a net addition to his income. The net wage would be $(1 - 0·2)\overline{W}$. This divergence is represented by the terms δ_{la} and δ_{lb} in equations 16.3.

Let us introduce a variable μ_q representing the marginal utility of income to the average citizen at point q. We will discuss later what sort of average of μ_{aq}, μ_{bq} and μ_{uq} is best used for μ_q but for the next stage of our analysis any arbitrary value of μ_q may be chosen. We can then write

$$\{\partial U_s/\partial C_x\}_q = \{\mu P_x \delta_{scx}\}_q \dots\dots\dots\dots\dots\dots\dots (16.4)$$

with similar expressions for $\partial U_s/\partial C_y$, $\partial U_s/\partial \overline{X}$ and $\partial U_s/\partial \overline{Y}$ and

$$\{\partial U_g/\partial G_x\}_q = \{\mu P_x(1 + \delta_{gx})\}_q \dots\dots\dots\dots\dots\dots (16.5)$$

with a similar expression for $\{\partial U_g/\partial G_y\}_q$.

In equations 16.4 the term δ_{scx} measures the divergence between marginal social and marginal private utility in the private consumption of X, since the addition to total social utility of an extra unit of private consumption of X is $\mu P_x + (\partial U_s/\partial C_x)$ (i.e. the sum of private utility and the valuation of any external benefit), so that $1 + \delta_{scx}$ = marginal social utility/marginal private utility. In equation 16.5 the term δ_{gx} represents the proportion by which one should raise the market value of the goods bought by the government for public purposes in order to get the marginal social valuation of the use of these goods for governmental purposes. If $\delta_{gx} > 0$ then— apart from other indirect repercussions—to transfer a unit of X from private to public consumption would add to Social Welfare.

We may also note that the total amount of private consumption of each good is the sum of the consumption by the three classes of citizens so that:

$$C_x = N(ae\hat{C}_{xa} + be\hat{C}_{xb} + [1 - e]\hat{C}_{xu}) \dots\dots\dots\dots (16.6)$$

and similarly for C_y. From these equations we can get an expression for dC_x in terms of dN, de, $d\hat{C}_{xa}$, $d\hat{C}_{xb}$ and $d\hat{C}_{xu}$; and similarly for $d\hat{C}_y$.

Moreover if we write L for the total amount of work done we have:

$$L = eN(a\hat{L}_a + b\hat{L}_b) \dots\dots\dots\dots\dots\dots\dots\dots (16.7)$$

From this expression we can obtain an expression for dL in terms of dN, de, $d\hat{L}_a$ and $d\hat{L}_b$.

We may next consider the technical, production constraints on the economy. We assume production functions of the form:

$$\overline{X}_q = F_{xq}(L_{xq}, X_{xq}, Y_{xq})$$

and

$$\overline{Y}_q = F_{yq}(L_{yq}, X_{yq}, Y_{yq}) \dots \dots \dots \dots \dots \dots \dots \dots \text{(16.8)}$$

where $\overline{X}_q$ and $\overline{Y}_q$ are the gross outputs of goods produced at the end of the day q (including all the stock of capital equipment handed over from day q to the next day and all the consumption goods produced during day q and available for consumption on the next day) while L_{xq}, X_{xq} and Y_{xq} are the amounts of labour and intermediate products and capital goods put at the beginning of day q into the industry producing $\overline{X}$, and similarly for L_{yq}, X_{yq} and Y_{yq}. We also have:

$$C_{xq} = \overline{X}_{\overline{q-1}} - X_{xq} - X_{yq} - G_{xq} \dots \dots \dots \dots \dots \text{(16.9)}$$

and

$$C_{yq} = \overline{Y}_{\overline{q-1}} - Y_{xq} - Y_{yq} - C_{xyq} \dots \dots \dots \dots \dots \text{(16.9)}$$

where $\overline{q-1}$ represents the point on our diagram from which the point q must have proceeded—for example, if point q is point 1 on our diagram then point $\overline{q-1}$ is point 12, and so on. These equations state that the amount of any good available for private consumption on day q is the gross amount produced as a result of the productive operations of day $\overline{q-1}$ less the amounts set aside on day q as inputs into the productive processes of day q and less the amounts consumed by the government for public services on day q.

Let us also write

$$\left. \begin{array}{l} L_q = L_{xq} + L_{yq} \\ X_q = X_{xq} + X_{yq} \\ Y_q = Y_{xq} + Y_{yq} \end{array} \right\} \dots \dots \dots \dots \dots \dots \dots \dots \dots \text{(16.10)}$$

Let us write

$$1 + \delta_{l_x \overline{q-1}} = P_{xq} \left(\partial F_{x\overline{q-1}} / \partial L_{x\overline{q-1}} \right) \div \overline{W}_{\overline{q-1}} (1 + i_{\overline{q-1}}) \dots \text{(16.11)}$$

In this case $\delta_{l_x \overline{q-1}}$ measures the divergence between the value at time q of the wage fixed and paid at time $\overline{q-1}$ for a unit of labour employed at $\overline{q-1}$ and the value of its marginal product (namely $\partial F_{x\overline{q-1}} / \partial L_{x\overline{q-1}}$) to be sold at time q for a price P_{xq}. And similarly for $\delta_{ly\overline{q-1}}$.

Let us also write

$$1 + \delta_{yx\overline{q-1}} = P_{xq}\,(\partial F_{x\overline{q-1}}/\partial Y_{x\overline{q-1}}) \div P_{y\overline{q-1}}(1 + i_{\overline{q-1}}).\ .\ (16.12)$$

In this case $\delta_{yx\overline{q-1}}$ measures the divergence between the cost of a unit input of Y at point $q - 1$ into the X industry reckoned at its value at point q when the additional output of X will be sold (i.e. $P_{y\overline{q-1}}[1 + i_{\overline{q-1}}]$) and the value at point q of that additional product when it is sold (i.e. $P_{xq}\,(\partial F_{x\overline{q-1}}/\partial Y_{x\overline{q-1}})$). And similarly for $\delta_{xx\overline{q-1}}$, $\delta_{xy\overline{q-1}}$ and $\delta_{yy\overline{q-1}}$.

Then differentiating equations 16.8, 16.9 and 16.10, using equations 16.11 and 16.12, and rearranging the terms we get:

$$\{P_x(dC_x + dG_x + dX) + P_y(dC_y + dG_y + dY)\}\,q$$
$$= \{(1 + i)(P_x dX + P_y dY + \overline{W}dL + P_x[\delta_{xx}dX_x + \delta_{xy}dX_y]$$
$$+ P_y[\delta_{yx}dY_x + \delta_{yy}dY_y] + \overline{W}[\delta_{lx}dL_x + \delta_{ly}dL_y])\}_{\overline{q-1}}\ .\ .\ (16.13)$$

If we now differentiate the expression for U_q in equation 16.2 and make use of equations 16.3, 16.4, 16.5, 16.6, 16.7 and 16.13, we obtain the following expression which breaks down the change in Social Welfare clocked up as the economy passes through point q into a number of component parts:

$$dU_q = \qquad\qquad\qquad \text{COMPONENT CONNECTED WITH}$$

$$\mu_q\left\{\frac{dN}{N}\left(\frac{U_p}{\mu} - PC + \overline{W}L\right)\right\}_q \qquad \text{I Optimum Population}$$

$$+ \mu_q\left\{\frac{de}{e}\left(\frac{U_p - N\hat{U}_u}{\mu} - [PC - PN\hat{C}_u] + \overline{W}L\right)\right\}_q \qquad \begin{array}{l}\text{II Full}\\ \text{Employment}\end{array}$$

$$+ \mu_q\{(1 + i)PdI\}_{\overline{q-1}} - \mu_q\{PdI\}_q \qquad \text{III Optimum Savings}$$

$$+ \mu_q\left\{\begin{array}{l}aeN(\alpha - 1)(Pd\hat{C}_a - [1 - \delta_{la}]\overline{W}d\hat{L}_a)\\ + beN(\beta - 1)(Pd\hat{C}_b - [1 - \delta_{lb}]\overline{W}d\hat{L}_b)\\ + (1 - e)\,N(\gamma - 1)\,Pd\hat{C}_u\end{array}\right\}_q \qquad \begin{array}{l}\text{IV}\\ \text{Redistributi}\\ \text{of Income}\end{array}$$

$$+ \mu_q\{eN\overline{W}(a\delta_{la}d\hat{L}_a + b\delta_{lb}d\hat{L}_b)\}_q \qquad \text{V Incentives}$$

$$+ \mu_q\left\{\begin{array}{l}P_x(\delta_{scx}dC_x + \delta_{s\overline{x}}d\overline{X} + \delta_{gx}d\overline{G}_x)\\ P_y(\delta_{scy}dC_y + \delta_{s\overline{y}}d\overline{Y} + \delta_{gy}d\overline{G}_y)\end{array}\right\}_q \qquad \begin{array}{l}\text{VI External}\\ \text{Divergences}\end{array}$$

$$+ \mu_q \left\{ \begin{array}{l} (1 + i)(P_x[\delta_{xx}dX_x + \delta_{xy}dX_y] \\ + P_y[\delta_{yx}dY_x + \delta_{yy}dY_y] \\ + \overline{W}[\delta_{lx}dL_x + \delta_{ly}dL_y]) \end{array} \right\}$$

VII INTERNAL
DIVERGENCES
$\overline{q-1}$ . . . . (16.14)

where $U_p \equiv aeN\hat{U}_a + beN\hat{U}_b + (1 - e)N\hat{U}_w$ thus measuring the total utility obtained from the personal consumptions of private individuals; $PC \equiv P_xC_x + P_yC_y$, thus measuring the total money expenditure on private consumption; $PN\hat{C}_u \equiv N(P_x\hat{C}_{xu} + P_y\hat{C}_{yu})$, thus measuring what the total expenditure on personal consumption would be if everyone lived on the standard of an unemployed man; $Pd\hat{C}_a \equiv P_xd\hat{C}_{xa} + P_yd\hat{C}_{ya}$, thus measuring the increase in the total quantity consumed by an individual in class a valued at the current prices of consumption goods and similarly for $Pd\hat{C}_b$ and $Pd\hat{C}_u$; $PdI \equiv P_x dX + P_y dY + \overline{W}dL$, thus measuring the additional quantity of resources, valued at their current prices, invested at the beginning of the productive process on any day; and $\alpha \equiv \mu_a/\mu$ or the ratio of the marginal utility of money income to an individual in class a to the general average marginal utility of money income and similarly for $\beta = \mu_b/\mu$ and $\gamma = \mu_u/\mu$.

It is to be observed that all the items on the RHS of equation 16.14 are increments of social welfare clocked up at point q measured in money terms at the money prices ruling at point q,[5] which are then multiplied by μ_q, which measures the marginal utility of money income at point q, a measure which we will discuss below.

We will now comment in turn on the various components of equation 16.14.

COMPONENT I This component is positive if

$$\frac{U_p}{N} > \mu \frac{PC - \overline{W}L}{N}$$

Suppose that there were a small representative increase in the population (dN). U_p/N is the average utility per head of the population so that total utility would increase by $(U_p/N) dN$ if (in the absence of any distributive effect which would be included in component IV) the new members of society enjoyed the same standard of living as the existing members and if there were no further change. But there would be a further change in so far as the consumption per head of the new members differed from the additional output

[5] Thus $U_p/\mu N$ measures the 'money value of a man' in the sense of the total utility enjoyed by a representative citizen valued in terms of current dollars.

per head of the new members. Since any distributional effects will be separately shown under component IV we can assume that consumption per head of the new members is equal to the existing average (PC/N); and since any divergence between the wage earning capacity of the new members and that of existing population will be shown in a change of the employment ratio e in component II and any divergence between the wage paid and the additional product of labour will be shown in component VII, we can assume that the additional product per head of the new members is equal to the existing wage per head of the existing population (namely $\overline{W}L/N$). $(\overline{W}L/N - PC/N)\,dN$ thus measures the total excess (or, if negative, the deficiency) of the additional output produced by a small number of new members (dN) over the total amount which they would absorb at the current level of consumption per head of population, and $\mu(\overline{W}L/N - PC/N)\,dN$ thus measures the addition (subtraction) to total utility which would be brought about by using this excess product to increase the average consumption of the population (by making up this deficiency by reducing the average consumption of the population) at the current marginal utility of income (μ). $(U_p/N)\,dN - \mu\left[(PC - \overline{W}L/N\right]\,dN$ thus represents the net total addition to utility.[6]

COMPONENT II There are two alternative commonsensical ways of thinking about the Full Employment component.

(i) Given a small increase in employment out of a given population, namely Nde, Social Welfare will be increased to the extent that

$$\frac{1}{\mu}\left\{\frac{U_p - N\hat{U}_u}{eN} - \mu\left(\frac{PC - PN\hat{C}_u - \overline{W}L}{eN}\right)\right\} > 0.$$

$U_p - N\hat{U}_u$ is the total excess of the private utility of the total population over what it would be if all the members were at the unemployed's standards. Since the unemployed are in any case at the unemployed's standards, this is the same as the excess of the total private utility of the employed population over what it would have been if they had been at the unemployed standards, so that $(U_p - N\hat{U}_u)/eN$ is the increase in utility for a man moving from the unemployed to the employed sector of the economy. But by a

---

[6] This formula is the same as that given on page 91 of my *Trade and Welfare* except that I was there assuming full employment (i.e. $L = N$) so that I spoke of $\overline{W}L/N$ in terms of $\overline{W}$ or 'the marginal product of a workers'. To allow for an unchanged unemployment percentage, I should have spoken in terms of $\overline{W}L/N$ or 'the marginal product of a representative citizen'.

similar reasoning it can be seen that $(PC - PN\hat{C}_u)/eN$ is the increase in consumption for a man so moving. If this excess consumption had to come at the margin from others' consumption, it would impose a loss on others equal to $\mu (PC - PN\hat{C})/eN$. But, in so far as the employed man's wage is equal to the value of his marginal product (and in so far as this is not so, the divergence is accounted in component VII), there is an addition to the social value of output of $\mu\overline{W}(L/eN)$, where L/eN is the amount of work done per employed man. The net gain from the transfer of one man from the unemployed to the employed sector is therefore

$$\frac{U_p - N\hat{U}_u - \mu(PC - PN\hat{C}_u - \overline{W}L)}{eN}$$

(ii) Another way of looking at the matter is to say that $\overline{W}(L/eN)$ is the contribution to additional output due to having one more man in employment (apart from any divergences between marginal products and rewards which appear in component VII) and that $\mu\overline{W}(L/eN)$ is, therefore, the 'efficiency' contribution of fuller employment. The remaining term, $\{U_p - N\hat{U}_u - \mu(PC - PN\hat{C}_u)\}/eN$, is a change in Social Welfare due to the alteration of the 'distribution' of income as a result of paying more to the newly employed man and so much less than would otherwise be the case to other members of the population. We will return to this interpretation when we consider component IV.

COMPONENT III $\{PdI\}_q \equiv \{P_x dX + P_y dY + \overline{W}dL\}_q$ is the value at current prices of the increment of productive resources on which capital funds are laid out at the beginning of day q to produce goods for sale at the beginning of the next day; that is to say it is the value of the increment of real resources invested in the productive process at the beginning of day q. An inspection of component III indicates that this element, which appears with a negative sign at point q, will reappear with a positive sign at all points to which the economy could move on the day after q. Suppose point q is point 12 on Figure 41; then it is clear that $\{PdI\}_{12}$ will reappear with a positive sign at points 1 and 2. An inspection of equation 16.1 together with component III of equation 16.14 then shows that the net contribution of $\{PdI\}_{12}$ to expected Social Welfare is $\varepsilon_{12}\{PdI\}_{12}\{(1 + i_{12})(\varepsilon_1\mu_1 + \varepsilon_2\mu_2) - \mu_{12}\}$ which is positive if $i_{12} > \{\mu_{12} - (\varepsilon_1\mu_1 + \varepsilon_2\mu_2)\}/(\varepsilon_1\mu_1 + \varepsilon_2\mu_2)$ i.e. if the rate of interest is greater than the expected rate of decline of the marginal utility of income. This is the familiar formula for expressing the condition on which an increment of savings can add more to expected future utility through increased future consumption than it subtracts from present utility through decreased present consumption.[7]

Two comments on this expression may be useful. First, there may be divergences between the rate of interest and the expected value on the subsequent day of the net marginal product of the additional real resources invested at the beginning of day q. The formula without modification would be true only if there were no such divergences; but these divergences are accounted for in the δ terms in component VII of equation 16.14.

Second, the i used in the formula is the money, not the real, rate of interest. But this does not present us with any difficulty. Suppose that all prices are rising by a proportion p between one day and the next. Then the marginal utility of income will be falling for two reasons, first because a unit of money will buy less consumption goods and second because a unit of consumption goods will 'buy' less 'utility'. The decline in the marginal utility of real consumption is thus $\{\mu_{12} - (\varepsilon_1\mu_1 + \varepsilon_2\mu_2)\}/(\varepsilon_1\mu_1 + \varepsilon_2\mu_2) - p$. But the real rate of interest is now $i - p$. The balance between the money rate of interest and the rate of decline in the marginal utility of money remains unchanged.

COMPONENT IV The algebra by which equation 16.14 is reached would be correct for any arbitrary value of μ_q which we might have cared to choose at equations 16.4 and 16.5. In fact, in a second-best problem of the kind with which we are at present concerned, any division of the effects of a policy change between their 'efficiency' effects and their 'distributional' effects is arbitrary. The change may make some people better off by a large amount and others worse off by a smaller amount; and that is that. Any attempt to say how much of this change is an 'efficiency' change and how much a 'distributional' change is arbitrary.[8] Yet it may be useful for a policy-maker to make some arbitrary distinction of this kind. But how might one proceed to make a useful distinction of this kind?

The basic need is to compare the marginal utility of income to different groups both within a given generation (i.e. on any one day)

[7] If $\varepsilon_1 = 1$ so that $\varepsilon_2 = 0$ the condition would become $i_{12} > [(\mu_{12} - \mu_1)/\mu_1]$ or $i_t > [(\mu_t - \mu_{t+1})/\mu_{t+1}]$. For any individual the elasticity of substitution σ between consumption at t and consumption at $t + 1$ can be expressed as (the proportionate increase in consumption) ÷ (the proportionate fall in the marginal utility of consumption.) If money prices were constant, $(\mu_t - \mu_{t+1})/\mu_{t+1}$ would measure the proportionate fall in the marginal utility of consumption and i_t would measure the real rate of interest. If $\hat{c}$ were the proportionate increase in an individual's consumption, then the expression becomes $i > \hat{c}/\sigma$, which is the form used on page 205 of *The Growing Economy*.

[8] When I wrote Part I of *Trade and Welfare*, I was not, I think, clear about the arbitrariness of this distinction. What follows should be read in this respect as an addendum to that volume.

and as between generations (i.e. as between one day and another). For this we need a bench mark measure. We might, for example, take the additional utility obtained from \$1 more to spend on consumption by an unemployed man at point 1234 on Figure 41 as our measuring rod, i.e. $\mu_{u,\,1234} = 1$. At point q the basic measures would then be μ_{aq}, μ_{bq} and μ_{uq}. These measures depend upon value judgements made by the policy-makers and they imply, for example, that the policy-makers would be equally satisfied by a policy change which gave \$1 more to a man with the standard of living of an unemployed man at point 1234 faced with the cost of living of point 1234 and by a policy change which gave \$ $1/\mu_{aq}$ to a rich man with the standard of living of a rich man at point q and with the cost of living ruling at point q.

But the formulation of these distributional weights is not sufficient to say whether a given change has had any, and if so what, distributional effect. In order to make any statement of this kind, it is necessary to formulate an arbitrary definition of what sort of distribution of any given improvement between the various classes is said to be such as to leave the distribution of welfare unchanged. This is an arbitrary definition, though it has no doubt the overtones of a value judgment. Suppose \$1 more was available for expenditure on consumption at point q at the prices current at point q. The policy-makers must define a distribution of this \$1 among the various groups in society (namely ae_qN_q, be_qN_q and $\left[1 - e_q\right] N_q$) which is such as to leave distribution unchanged. Let λ_{aq}, λ_{bq} and λ_{uq} (where $\lambda_a + \lambda_b + \lambda_u = 1$) be the fractions of the \$1 which, according to the chosen definition, must go to the three groups if the distribution of welfare is to be unchanged. Then μ_q is defined as $\lambda_{aq}\mu_{aq} + \lambda_{bq}\mu_{bq} + \lambda_{uq}\mu_{uq}$ and it measures the increase in private utility which would be gained by society having \$1 more to spend on consumption, if that \$1 were distributed so as to have what has been defined as no distributional effect.[9]

[9] There are many different possible definitions of the absence of distributional effect. (i) If it involves giving an equal amount of additional income to every citizen, then $\lambda_a = ae$. (ii) If it involves dividing the \$1 in the ratio of citizens existing consumption levels, then $\lambda_a = [PC]_a / \{ [PC]_a + [PC]_b + [PC]_c \}$ (iii) If it involves dividing the \$1 in the ratio of citizens' existing total utilities, then

$$\lambda_a = ae\hat{U}_a / \{ae\hat{U}_a + be\hat{U}_b + [1 - e] \hat{U}_u\}$$

(iv) If it involves dividing the \$1 so as to raise every individual's utility by the same proportion, then

$$\lambda_a = \frac{ae\hat{U}_a/\mu_a}{ae\hat{U}_a/\mu_a + be\hat{U}_b/\mu_b + (1 - e) \hat{U}_u/\mu_u}$$

(v) If it involves dividing the \$1 so as to give each individual the same absolute increase in utility, then

$$\lambda_a = \frac{ae/\mu_a}{ae/\mu_a + be/\mu_b + (1 - e)/\mu_u}.$$

If a proportion λ_a of any increase in total expenditure on consumption $[PdC]$ did in fact go to group a, then $\lambda_a[PdC]/aeN$ would be the increase in consumption of an individual in group a. It can then be seen from equation 16.14 that component IV of that equation would be zero if the distribution of $[PdC]$ among the three groups were in the proportions λ_a, λ_b and λ_u. Since $\alpha = \mu_a/\mu$, $\beta = \mu_b/\mu$ and $\gamma = \mu_u/\mu$, the total component would become:

$$[PdC]\{(\mu_a - \mu)\lambda_a + (\mu_b - \mu)\lambda_b + (\mu_u - \mu)\lambda_u\}$$

which is equal to zero since

$$\lambda_a + \lambda_b + \lambda_u = 1 \text{ and } \mu = \lambda_a\mu_a + \lambda_b\mu_b + \lambda_u\mu_u.$$

We may now revert to the distributional element in the Full Employment component which was mentioned in connection with component II above namely $\{U_p - N\hat{U}_u - \mu(PC - PN\hat{C}_u)\}/eN$. If we substitute the values for U_p, PC and $PN\hat{C}_n$ given after equation 16·14 above, we can see that this distributional component will be positive if:

$$\mu < (a\hat{U}_a + b\hat{U}_b - \hat{U}_u)/P(a\hat{C}_a + b\hat{C}_b - \hat{C}_u).$$

In order to simplify the exposition of the commonsense which lies behind this formula, let us suppose that all the employed are similar in their standards (i.e. $a = 1$ and $b = 0$) so that we have solely a distinction employed (a) and unemployed (u). Then our condition becomes $\mu < \hat{U}_a - \hat{U}_u)/P(\hat{C}_a - \hat{C}_u)$. We may write the RHS of this expression as $\Delta(\hat{U})/\Delta(P\hat{C})$ to represent the ratio of the increase in utility to the increase in expenditure resulting from an unemployed man finding employment. Now a citizen who moves from unemployment to employment will have a high marginal utility of income when he is unemployed (μ_u) and a low marginal utility of income when he is employed (μ_a). We may assume, therefore, that $\mu_u > \Delta(\hat{U})/\Delta(P\hat{C}) > \mu_a$.

If the employed and the unemployed had the same utility function with a diminishing marginal utility of money income and if the only difference in their situations were that the employed had more income to spend on the consumption of products than the unemployed, then we could argue as follows. $\Delta(\hat{U})/\Delta(P\hat{C})$ would be the average utility of the increment of consumption of products and this would lie somewhere between the high marginal utility of the first additional units of consumption (μ_u) and the low marginal utility of the last additional units of consumption (μ_a). But this argument overlooks the fact that there is a further distinction between the situations of the employed and the unemployed in that the former can choose how much work and how much leisure to enjoy, whereas the latter are constrained without choice to do no work. Nevertheless, we may reasonably make the assumption that $\Delta(\hat{U})/\Delta(P\hat{C})$ lies somewhere between μ_u and μ_a.

But μ is a weighted average of μ_u and μ_a, namely $(1 - \lambda_u)\mu_a + \lambda_u\mu_u$. If λ_u is sufficiently small, then μ will be $< \Delta(\hat{U})/\Delta(P\hat{C})$. Let us take a numerical example. Suppose $\Delta(\hat{U})/\Delta(P\hat{C}) = 0\cdot5\ \mu_a + 0\cdot5\ \mu_u$.[10] Then with $\mu_u > \mu_a$, the condition $\mu = (1 - \lambda_u)\ \mu_a + \lambda_u\mu_u < \Delta(\hat{U})/\Delta(P\hat{C}) = 0\cdot5\ \mu_a + 0\cdot5\ \mu_u$ is satisfied if $\lambda_u < 0\cdot5$.

The commonsense of this is clear. When one man shifts from the unemployed to the employed class, his standard of living is increased. Apart from what he produces (and this is already taken account of in the 'efficiency' element of the Full Employment component), this increase in his consumption must be taken from the community in general. Now his marginal utility was μ_u in his previous position; but he has had a structural change in his position and his marginal utility is now μ_a. Giving him an extra income is (with our assumption that $\Delta(\hat{U})/\Delta(P\hat{C}) = 0\cdot5\ \mu_a + 0\cdot5\ \mu_u$) equivalent to giving $0\cdot5$ to an employed man with marginal utility, μ_a and $0\cdot5$ to an unemployed man with marginal utility, μ_u. The loss of utility to the community in general assumes a proportion λ_u to have been raised from the existing unemployed. If $\lambda_u < 0\cdot5$ (as will almost certainly be the case) the result is, as it were, a net redistribution from the 'rich' employed to the 'poor' unemployed.

COMPONENT V. This component needs little comment. If as a result, for example, of direct taxation the net wage received by the worker is less than the wage paid by the employer, then an incentive which induces an increased effort has a positive efficiency effect.

COMPONENT VI The δ here may be positive measuring the external social benefits, or negative measuring the external social costs, of increases in the private or governmental consumption or in the production of the various goods.

COMPONENT VII The δ here measures divergences within the productive system between the price paid to a factor by an employer and the price paid by the purchaser of the product for the marginal product of that factor. The most obvious causes of such divergences are monopolistic or monopsonistic factors and rates of indirect taxation. Subsidization of a product could make such a divergence negative in sign. It will be observed that these divergences are in respect of the productive operations carried out during day $\overline{q - 1}$ but they must be evaluated with the marginal utility of income of day q which is when the product will be available for use.

[10] This would be the case if all citizens had the same utility function dependent only on the amount of products consumed with the marginal utility of income a linear function of the amount spent on consumption. But this neglects the qualification noted in the previous paragraph.

So far we have said nothing about the terminal conditions of the government's control plan, that is to say about the elements U_{T1}, U_{T2}, U_{T3} and U_{T4} in equation 16.1. This is in fact a particularly difficult matter in the sort of control planning which we are discussing. At first sight, a normal procedure would seem to be to say that the government must place some social valuation, however arbitrary, upon the total goods which will be carried over from the last day of the plan to the beginning of the next day and to leave the matter there. In this case we could write the terminal utility elements of equation 16.1 as:

$$U_{Tq} = U_{Tq}(\overline{X}_q, \overline{Y}_q) \dots \dots \dots \dots \dots (16.15)$$

where the point q represents point 1, 2, 3 or 4 in our diagram, since $\overline{X}_q$ and $\overline{Y}_q$ represent the total gross outputs which will be produced during day q and left over till the beginning of the next day which is outside the plan period. If we differentiate this expression, using equations 16.8, 16.11 and 16.12, and write

$$\partial U_{Tq}/\partial \overline{X}_q = \mu_{Tq}P_{\bar{x}Tq}(1 + \delta_{\bar{x}Tq})$$

and similarly for $\partial U_{Tq}/\partial \overline{Y}_q$, we get:

$$\begin{aligned} dU_{Tq} = \ & \mu_{Tq}\{(1 + i)PdI\}_q \\ & + \mu_{Tq}\{(1 + i)(P_x[\delta_{xx}dX_x + \delta_{xy}dX_g] \\ & + P_y[\delta_{yx}dY_x + \delta_{yy}dY_y] \\ & + \overline{W}[\delta_{lx}dL_x + \delta_{ly}dL_y])\}_q \\ & + \mu_{Tq}\{P_{xTq}\delta_{\bar{x}Tq}d\overline{X} + P_{yTq}\delta_{\bar{y}Tq}d\overline{Y}\}_q \dots \dots \dots (16.16) \end{aligned}$$

where μ_{Tq} represents the policy-makers' attribution of a marginal utility of income at the beginning of the first day after the end of the plan, where P_{xTq} and P_{yTq} represent the econometricians' estimates of the market prices then ruling, and where $\delta_{\bar{x}Tq}$ and $\delta_{\bar{y}Tq}$ (which, as we shall see, must cover a multitude of sins) represent any divergences between the marginal social utilities to be attributed to $\overline{X}_q$ and $\overline{Y}_q$ and the marginal utilities of their prices, $\mu_{Tq}P_{xTq}$ and $\mu_{Tq}P_{yTq}$.

From equation 16.1 it can be seen that, for the end points of the possible environmental paths during the period of the plan, we need to evaluate not simply dU_q (as is done in equation 16.14) but $d(U_q + U_{Tq})$, which means adding the terms in equation 16.16 to those in equation 16.14. Equation 16.14 is then modified in the following three ways.

First, the 'optimum savings' component has added to it the term $\mu_{Tq}\{(1 + i)PdI\}_q$, which means that the element $\{PdI\}_q$ is now multiplied by $\{\mu_{Tq}(1 + i_q) - \mu_q\}$. On the basis of the argument given above in discussing component III this means that the optimum savings criterion can be carried on until the termination of the plan.

Second, the 'internal divergences' component has added to it a term expressing the internal divergences of the last day of the plan period and thus enabling the internal divergences criteria also to be carried on until the termination of the plan.

Thirdly, there is the addition of the new and last item in equation 16.16, namely any divergences between the social values of the additional goods carried over from the end of the plan and their market values.

This last item is, of course, vague and arbitrary in the extreme, as it is not known whether these goods will be used for consumption, for governmental purposes, or for investment for future production nor, if they are used for consumption, whether they will go to the rich or the poor, nor in what conditions they will be consumed privately or by the government or invested. The period is *ex hypothesi* unplanned and uninvestigated.

But the trouble, in fact, goes much deeper than that. Suppose that it were known that the small change in controls the effect of which we are examining would have no effect on the amount of goods carried over from the end of the plan period so that $d\overline{X}_q = d\overline{Y}_q = 0$. It would still, alas, not be true that $d(U_q + U_{Tq})$, as reckoned from equations 16.14 and 16.16, would account for the whole of the story. The change in the controls might have caused a rise in population $(dN_q > 0)$ which would continue to live into the post-plan period and thus affect future welfare.

An attempt might perhaps be made to include N_q as well as $\overline{X}_q$ and $\overline{Y}_q$ in equation 16.15 and then in one way or another to evaluate $\partial U_{Tq}/\partial N_q$ in terms of its probable future implications. But even that is not the end of the story. Even if $d\overline{X}_q = d\overline{Y}_q = dN_q = 0$ so that the small change in controls which is under study would have no direct effect upon the material or demographic resources of the post-plan period, nevertheless, it might affect Social Welfare after the close of the plan period. A change in a control at one time may have a delayed as well as an immediate effect. Thus a change in income tax on day t (even if the old rate of tax were restored on day $t + 1$) may affect people's expenditures on day $t + 1$ since the purchases of one day may be affected by the tax-free disposable income of a previous day. In other words, changes in controls during the plan period may affect not only the initial material and demographic resources with which the post-plan period is endowed, but also behaviour during the post-plan period. In a hunch-like manner, policy-makers will no doubt try to take such possibilities into account but there is presumably no precise way of quantifying them.

Does the type of analysis developed here in fact have any practical significance? Does it point at all to ways in which governments in the sort of mixed economies of which we have been speaking might consider the implications of their policy objectives?

The analysis in this chapter has relevance only to marginal decisions, i.e. only to the question whether small changes in control policies would make things better or worse. But subject to this very important limitation it does perhaps help in three ways.

First, the analysis suggests that it is legitimate to consider the effects of a given small change in a control plan separately under the different component heads of equation 16.14 and to add up the results to obtain the net effect on Social Welfare. This could be of importance. A great deal of the analysis of the causal effects of different policy changes and of the consequential policy-making is bound to remain rather rough and ready. Some policy changes will have very significant effects on some of the components of Social Welfare while their effects on other components are probably relatively small and in any case almost impossible to estimate. The analysis in this chapter suggests that it may not be totally illegitimate to treat the effects of such controls in a partial manner and to add up these partial, but important, results of the various controls on the components which they are most likely to affect significantly. The possibility of treating the different effects of the various controls separately and then adding up the results on Social Welfare enormously simplifies the problem of decentralizing planning operations among the different departments and agencies of government. We will return to this problem in the following chapter.

Second, the procedures discussed in this chapter may help to draw a line between the 'positive' and the 'normative' elements in policy-making. The policy-makers must put to their administrators, statisticians, economists and econometricians all questions concerning the positive relationships in the economy, asking them to explain how the relevant and directly quantifiable variables (population, inputs, outputs, prices, amounts of work done, etc.) would be affected by any given control plan along the different environmental paths. The estimation of a number of the divergences due to taxation, monopolistic conditions, etc., between the values of effort and rewards and of inputs and their marginal products (see components V and VII of equation 16.14) is also a 'positive' matter to be left to the technical experts concerned. But it is for the policy-makers themselves to form value judgments on many of the social benefits and costs associated with various activities (see component VI of equation 16.14), on all the factors which involve interpersonal comparisons of utility, and, in particular, on the distributional weights (the 'μ's) to be ascribed in different conditions to marginal changes in the incomes of various groups. As a series of small changes in control plans are considered (moving always from a lower to a higher total social welfare, as suggested on pages 242–5), so, of course, the policy-makers must be prepared to revise these distributional weights. If, for example, a series of small policy changes is adopted which has the effect of raising progressively the income per head of one group and reducing that of another, so the policy-makers at each stage may want to reduce the μ attached to the former, and to raise the μ attached to the latter group.

Third, the method of considering only small marginal changes in the controls enables a large number of the components in the Social Welfare function to be judged solely in terms of marginal, and not total, interpersonal comparisons, i.e. in terms of μ and not of $\hat{U}$ (see components III, IV, V, VI and VII of equation 16.14). Questions of the kind: "How many dollars would you have to give to a man in situation I in order to bring about the same increase in social welfare as giving one dollar to a man in situation II?" would, one may suspect, be much more meaningful to a policy-maker than questions of the kind: "How much would total welfare be increased by moving a man from situation II to situation I?"

Unfortunately, as we have already seen in discussing components I and II of equation 16.14, the latter type of question cannot always be avoided even in the case of small marginal changes in the controls. One more citizen in the population (component I) is a small marginal change in the population, but it makes a structural change for the individual who comes out of the nowhere into here. Similarly, one more citizen in employment is a small marginal change in the total labour force but marks a structural change in the standard of living of the man himself. One cannot avoid measuring the total difference between the 'money value of the happiness of a representative citizen' ($U_p/\mu N$) and the 'money value of the happiness of an unemployed man' ($\hat{U}_u/\mu$), if one is adding up the contribution to Social Welfare in dollars.

There is one further case of great importance which necessitates comparisons of total rather than of marginal utilities and which has so far been neglected in this chapter. A change in a control may affect the probability with which a government expects one of the environmental paths. Thus some governmental expenditure on research and development may increase the probability with which a particular technological breakthrough is expected. In terms of the simple example depicted in Figure 41, suppose that a given change would increase the probability of tomorrow being wet by $d\varepsilon_{12}$. Then, remembering that $\varepsilon_{34} = 1 - \varepsilon_{12}$, the effect on $\mathscr{E}(U)$ in equation 16.1 would be:

$$d\varepsilon_{12}\{U_{12} - U_{34} + \varepsilon_1(U_1 + U_{T1}) + \varepsilon_2(U_2 + U_{T2})$$
$$- \varepsilon_3(U_3 + U_{T3}) - \varepsilon_4(U_4 + U_{T4})\}.$$

A glance at equations 16.2 and 16.15 is sufficient to remind one that this would involve, in an extreme form, the comparison of the total utilities of citizens on one environmental path with their total utilities if they could be shifted on to another environmental path. The difference between one environmental path and another may well involve structural, rather than merely marginal, changes for the individuals concerned.

There is one further major omission in the analysis of the present chapter. Nothing has been said about residual uncertainty. The whole analysis has been conducted on the assumption that, for the period covered by the plan, the government can consider the possibilities of the development of the economy along every possible environmental path. We have already argued that this will be impossible and that the government, just like any other decision-maker, will be able to consider in a carefully calculated manner only a very limited representative number out of all the multitudinous possible environmental paths.

We shall return to this matter in Part 5 of this volume; but it may be useful to stress at this point one significant implication of this omission. It will be observed that while Full Employment (component II of equation 16.14) figures among the objectives of economic policy, price stability as such does not appear at all as a *desideratum* in equation 16.14. This is as it should be because presumably no one cares about the stability of money prices itself. Price inflation may, of course, have undesirable effects on the distribution of income or, by making it very unprofitable to hold money as a liquid asset, may impede the efficient working of the economy.

In principle, these effects should show themselves through the behavioural relationships in the econometric model. Thus if some change in controls increases total demand and if this causes a price inflation and if this price inflation causes a redistribution of income from fixed income to variable income classes or if, through its effects on the willingness to remain liquid and to hold money, it causes a reduction in real output, then in principle those who have constructed the econometric model should have made allowance for these indirect adverse effects upon the level and the distribution of real income. In this case, the evaluation of the adverse social effects of price inflation will have been properly included in the other components of equation 16.14 and there will be no separate weight to be attached to price inflation or price stability itself.

But, as we shall argue in Part 5, the whole question of liquidity is concerned with residual uncertainty which has been assumed away in this chapter. For this very reason it is true that the formulation of the measurement of Social Welfare in equation 16.14 does not in fact allow for any adverse effects of price inflation upon economic efficiency. We shall attempt to repair this omission in Part 5 of this volume.

CHAPTER XVII

THE DECENTRALIZATION OF GOVERNMENTAL CONTROL PLANNING

We have argued (Chapter XV, p. 237) that a governmental control plan must be treated as a single entity, since there must be some mechanism for making a single balanced judgement of the social value of any change in a control, when all the different effects of that control are taken into account. Yet modern government is such a vast affair that there must necessarily be some decentralization of operations among a large number of different governmental agencies and departments. No single department could run the police, education, old age pensioners, road-building and defence to mention a few of the fields in which governmental policies must be determined. Can decentralization be made compatible with the formulation of a single coherent governmental control plan?

We have already discussed at some length in connection with the formation of an indicative plan (Chapter XIII, pp. 214–7) one aspect of the decentralization of planning. The purpose of indicative planning as we described it was to remove market uncertainties by a comparison of the individual plans of the multitude of individual decision-makers so that these plans could be made consistent with each other. Since the economy is a single equilibrium system, this theoretically implies a single indicative plan in which every individual's decisions for every future period is related to every other individual's decisions. But, as we argued, the economy is so complicated that to proceed directly in this way to a single plan would involve so complicated a system of interrelationships that it could not be handled. In fact, different groups of individuals whose decisions reacted most closely on each other (e.g. the producers in a particular industry or in a particular region) might well get together to formulate certain decentralized, partial indicative plans, taking for their purposes as exogenous given data the results suggested by other partial decentralized plans. The outputs of one partial plan would then be used as the inputs of another partial plan and vice versa; and these revisions of the decentralized partial plans might continue until these partial plans were consistent with each other. Such harmonizations of the various decentralized, partial plans, might,

271

so we argued, be greatly assisted by the formation of a much simplified overall framework plan, based upon the aggregation of economic variables into a small number of large classes.

We have already argued (Chapter XIV) that, in the absence of an indicative plan, a governmental control plan can be formulated only if some governmental econometric model of the working of the economy is constructed in order to know what will be the effect upon the economy of a given pattern of governmental controls. The construction of such an econometric model presents exactly the same problems of decentralization as those discussed in Chapter XIII in connection with the formation of an indicative plan. A single econometric model which accounted for every possible variable in the economy could not possibly be handled. A number of decentralized, partial models, might be constructed by the different departments and agencies of government. The outputs of one such model (to take a very simple example, an estimate by the Ministry of Agriculture of the total wages which would be paid to agricultural wage earners if certain conditions, including the level of governmental subsidies to agriculture, were given) could be used as the inputs of another model (for example, an estimate by the Treasury of the demand for consumption goods by all wage earners). These partial models could be revised until they were consistent with each other, the whole process of revision being helped by a highly simplified but comprehensive framework model of the broad aggregates in the economy. This whole process has been described (pp. 205–6) as a possible procedure between the different sections of a single central statistical office. Clearly it could operate in a very similar manner between all the various departments and agencies of government with some central statistical office ultimately responsible only for the aggregated, framework model.

But the construction in this decentralized manner of a set of consistent econometric models of how different sectors of the economy would behave in given conditions, including given levels of the relevant governmental controls, is not the end of the problem of decentralization of governmental control planning. In indicative planning the planners are not themselves planning the use of any controls. Each private decision-maker has his own controls (e.g. the price which a particular producer will decide to charge for his product); the indicative planners are concerned only with the problem of enabling the private decision-makers to choose a set of consistent plans for their controls. The use of the controls is itself totally decentralized. But this is not the case with governmental control planning where, typically, there is one control to be determined centrally (e.g. the rate of income tax) which itself has a large number of decentralized or departmental effects (e.g. on the distribution of income, on the general level of employment, and so on). As we have already explained, governmental control planning shares with indicative planning the problem of determining by a decentralized procedure what, given the behaviour of all the various groups of private individual decision-makers, will be the effects of a given level of governmental controls. But in addition there arises the question whether in the selection of the optimum level of the controls themselves any decentralized procedures are possible. This is the essential problem of decentralisation in governmental control planning.

We start, then, by imagining a modern governmental machine divided up into a number of departments and agencies each dealing with a different set of administrative problems—defence, law and order, education, health, social security, transport, and so on. In connection with each of these departments, there will be certain social objectives, which can be enumerated under certain broad headings such as those shown in equation 16.14 in the previous chapter—the influencing of the demographic development, the stabilization of the total effective demand for goods and services and for labour, the influencing of the total proportion of income saved, the redistribution of income and wealth and the provision in the most efficient manner but with due regard to their social or external effects of various goods and services (ranging from purely 'private' goods like clothes, through 'semi-public' services like transport which may be 'privately' produced and consumed but which at the same time have widespread 'public' external effects, to purely 'public' goods like law and order). At the same time, we must envisage a limited number of governmental controls which can be set to influence these various objectives.

The problem is that each control can be set at only one level at any one point of time, but may affect a large number of social objectives. Some controls will affect in important ways a large number of these objectives. Thus a change in income tax will affect in an important way the distribution of income, the amount of savings, the total demand for goods and services and incentives to work and effort. Some controls—for example, regulations about smoke abatement—may affect almost exclusively only one limited social objective, although, even in a case such as this, there are likely to be some repercussions in other directions as well. Thus a smoke abatement regulation in a particular region might affect the output of a particular commodity which itself carried with it certain important social benefits and costs.

But even if the social effects of a particular control were completely concentrated and thus affected only the social objectives which were the concern of one single governmental department or agency, it would not be true that the use of that control could be simply delegated to that department without any further concern of the central authority. It would still be a matter of central concern to evaluate the social objective which was served by the control in question. Thus a smoke abatement regulation may raise the cost of production of a certain product by a certain amount. The question then arises whether the social benefit due to the absence of this degree of smoke nuisance is worth this degree of cost. The evaluation of the social benefits or cost of an activity affected by a particular control is clearly a matter of concern to the central policy-makers, and is not a matter to be left entirely to the free determination of those in charge of the particular department concerned with the administrative arrangements for the control.

Thus in any duet between the central governmental authority and the various subsidiary governmental departments and agencies, there are two themes to be developed: (1) the manifold effects of a single control on the different concerns of the different departments have to be considered as a whole; and (2) centrally agreed social evaluations must be put upon these various effects (which involves central determination of the values to be given to the 'μ's and to many of the 'δ's in equation 16.14). Both of these themes call for decentralized procedures. Just as in the construction of an econometric model of the economy the individual department can help to construct that part of the model with which it is most directly concerned, so each individual department can help the central authority to assess the effect of a change in the centrally determined controls on those particular social objectives with which its activities are most directly related. Moreover, in evaluating these effects on the various social objectives each individual department can help the central authority by drawing its attention to the detailed implications of the changes with which it is most intimately concerned.

Let us take as an example a proposal to raise the level of state pensions paid to the old. Such a proposal could come originally either from the central governmental authority or else from the department—e.g. a department of social welfare—directly concerned with old age pensioners. Let us suppose that the proposal comes to the central government authority from the department of social welfare. It would at that stage need to be backed by information from the department about (i) the effect of the change on the income levels of various categories of old persons—the married and the unmarried, those with and those without various amounts of property, those earning and those not earning some wages, and so on, and (ii) the needs and special circumstances of these categories of persons in order to evaluate the importance to be attached to the improvements in their incomes.

The central authority before reaching a decision would need to know the effect of the increased pensions in other sectors of the economy upon other social objectives. One such obvious effect would be in increasing the total level of consumers' purchases of goods and services. Whether or not this in itself is to be reckoned as an advantage or as a disadvantage of the proposal would depend upon the answer to the question whether, from the point of view of full employment and the avoidance of inflation, total effective demand was already likely to be too low or too high. Such a question would have to be referred to the department concerned with general stabilization policy—e.g. the ministry of finance.

The ministry of finance might report that the change in old age pensions would through its inflationary pressure have such and such adverse effects upon money prices and so (i) upon the standards of those with fixed money incomes and (ii) upon the foreign demand for the country's exports and so the country's balance of payments. Such disadvantageous effects would have to be evaluated and weighed against the advantages of higher pensions for the old.

The ministry of finance might be asked by the central authority to propose, or it might itself take the initiative in proposing, reductions in other government expenditures or increases in certain governmental taxes or levies in order to mitigate the disadvantageous inflationary effects of the rise in old age pensions. Suppose that for this purpose it proposed a rise in certain commodity taxes. Then it would become necessary to determine and evaluate the effects of these taxes on social welfare (i) by decreasing the demand for goods on which there might for one reason or another be marginal social divergencies between cost and benefit (the 'δ's of equation 16.14) or (ii) by altering the standard of living of various classes of the community through the effect upon the prices at which the taxed goods were available. This, in its turn, would require consultation between the central governmental authority and the departments most directly concerned with these various effects of the proposed commodity taxation.

And so on in cycle of proposal and counter proposal and of discussion and criticism between the various departments and the central authority, leading to the decision to adopt a more or less complicated pattern of adjustment of controls, comprising perhaps the combined changes in a large number of controls, the net effect of which was considered to be definitely beneficial. The analysis in the preceding chapter suggests that if the basic Social Welfare function is of the kind described in that chapter and if attention is confined to the effects of relatively small changes in the controls, then it is a legitimate procedure to consider the effects on each social objective of each change in each control separately, to evaluate each such change separately and to add up the resulting effects upon social welfare in order to see whether the total net value of all the combined changes represents a plus or minus quantity in terms of Social Welfare.

In the application of any such decentralized procedures, there is, however, one very serious complication which must not be overlooked. We have argued at length in the earlier chapters of this Part that any change in the controls needs to be planned in terms of its effects over a period of future time, that these effects will depend upon future unpredictable environmental developments and that the present social value of the effects of any alteration in the controls must, therefore, be reckoned in terms of the net expected value of the effects, taking into account the central authority's assessment of the probabilities of the different environmental paths. This means that, in considering with any departments the effects of any change in a control and in evaluating those effects, the central authority and the department concerned must in principle consider those effects and evaluate them along each possible environmental path —or, at least, along each of the representative environmental paths which the central government has chosen to take into account in the calculations of its control plans. The final assessment of the probabilities to be attached to each environmental path, in order to make the final assessment of the net expected outcome of any change in the controls, must in the end be the responsibility of the central government authority. But here again, consultation with the departments concerned may be of great assistance, since one department of government may be in a much better position than another —and indeed in a much better position than the central government itself—to assess the probability of a particular environmental development. Thus the probabilities of different technological advances in, say, transport may be much more sensibly assessed by those working in a ministry of transport than by officials in other parts of the governmental machine. Thus the process of consultation between the central governmental authority and the particular departments about the various aspects of a single change in a control has in reality three themes: (i) the detailed effects of the change on various assumptions about future environmental developments; (ii) the social evaluations to be put upon these various detailed effects; and (iii) the probabilities of the various environmental developments.

CHAPTER XVIII

AN INDICATIVE CONTROL PLAN

We have already argued (Chapter XIV) that if there is to be any formal indicative planning which is at all comprehensive and adequate, then there must be some governmental control planning and that the resulting plans cannot be regarded as strict state secrets but must in large measure be revealed to the public. A modern government is such an important user and supplier of goods and services that it is pointless to assess future balances between total supplies and demands without estimating governmental supplies and demands; governmental controls (such as rates of taxation) are so pervasive and important in their effects that it is pointless to forecast how the private section of the economy will behave in the future without consideration of the way in which governmental controls are expected to move in the future.

To publish its control plans means that the government must reveal its secret hopes and fears. It is, of course, possible for it to reveal such secrets and in this way to marry the ideas of an indicative plan and of a control plan. We may call the offspring of this marriage an indicative control plan. Let us consider what the child would look like and whether it would be a healthy creature.

In order to bring out the basic problems involved let us caricature the formulation of an indicative control plan in the same way in which we previously caricatured the formulation of an indicative plan (see Chapter IX above). The necessary modifications for a practical procedure are similar to those discussed in Chapter XIII in the case of an indicative plan. The government once more summons to a meeting in the Albert Hall all the citizens in the country. Each citizen is then presented with lists of every price for every good and service, and also lists of every tax rate, of every rate of subsidy, of every rate of interest and of every other governmental control for every day on every environmental path in the future. Each citizen then writes down how much of everything he or she would plan to buy or to sell at every future date on every environmental path if these prices and controls were operative. There is then a prolonged coffee break. It is necessary, as before, for the bureaucrats to add up the demands and supplies of each good or

277

service for each future day on each environmental path including any future governmental demands and supplies in order to estimate the planned excesses of demand or supply. But now it is not sufficient for the planners simply to adjust upwards or downwards the future price of any good for which there is an excess demand or supply and to return to the meeting with a new price list for a second round of estimations. The planners can now attempt to remove an excess demand either by raising the price or by raising a tax or by reducing a public expenditure. In other words, at each round of indicative estimation the planners must present a future schedule of control levels as well as a future schedule of prices; and they must decide which type of adjustment they will suggest to the assembled citizens in the light of an answer to the question which type of adjustment will help most to attain the ultimate economic and social goals of the government. And this, of course, involves all the problems involved in governmental optimal control planning which we have discussed in earlier chapters of this Part of the present volume.

The arguments in favour of this process of indicative control planning are obvious. Indeed, the whole purpose of Parts 3 and 4 has been to show how control planning may be useful for a good choice by the government of today's controls and how indicative planning may help to improve today's actions in the private sector by removing market uncertainties due to the absence of forward markets. Since one cannot have a meaningful indicative plan without taking into account the future level of taxes and other controls, the case for an indicative control plan is apparent.

But there are important snags which we may discuss under three heads.

(1) First, as we have already pointed out in the earlier discussion of a purely indicative plan, the formal organization of such a plan by a governmental authority will lead to the danger that private producers in order to avoid losses due to the revelation of trade secrets may either supply misleading and biased information to the planners or may be encouraged to form collusive monopolistic groups in which trade secrets can be shared, but which may have other obvious dangers to the public interest. When one allows for the fact that an indicative control plan will involve and affect the government's control strategy these dangers are much increased. In an indicative control plan the rate of tax or subsidy which will be imposed on a given activity may well depend upon the assessment by the governmental authorities, from information gathered in conversations with the private entrepreneurs concerned, of its effect on the relevant activity. Clearly there may be a strong incentive for the private entrepreneurs concerned to present a united front in

persuading the authorities concerned that a low tax or a high subsidy is required to obtain a socially desirable result. The processes of an indicative control plan may greatly encourage such collusive action.

(2) The second set of problems arises from the possible political effects of the revelation of the probable future level of the controls by the authorities concerned. This might cause adverse inflexibilities of policy. The revelation of future budgetary plans could readily be interpreted as having implied certain moral commitments by the government to certain policies, whereas, as we have already argued, the purpose of the forecasts of future controls should be only to make it easier to choose the best level for today's controls. As the environment changes, so control plans must be flexibly revised; and the publication of control plans might endanger this flexibility. This danger of political inflexibility will be the smaller, the greater the number of representative environmental time-paths covered by the plan. For when there are more than one such time-path, all commitments become conditional in form from the very outset; and a number of alternative paths for the future controls will be stated in the plan itself.

(3) Finally, there are serious speculative problems. These are particularly marked in the case of controls whose levels cannot be, or by convention are not, changed except at rather infrequent intervals and then by appreciable steps. This is the basic reason for budget secrecy. With an annual budget coming up for decision in, say, six months' time, a minister of finance does not announce that as at present advised he thinks that the tax on the purchase of new cars will have to be raised by 50% in six months' time when the budget is finally settled. Or, rather, he does not do so unless for economic control reasons he wishes to cause a six months' buying spree. But this would be just the sort of statement which might have to be made if there were a completely open marriage between a control plan and an indicative plan. If this course were really adopted, it would be necessary to build into the behavioural relationships of the econometric model some very important speculative parameters. Thus the demand for cars would have to be made dependent upon the future course of the tax on the purchase of new cars as predicted in the control plan itself. It is not difficult to see how greatly this would complicate the problem of control. The speculative rather than the currently operative effect of controls might become of paramount importance.

This speculative problem is also reduced in so far as a number of environmental time-paths are covered by the governmental control plan, since in this case the planned future changes in tax rates remain conditional and, therefore, uncertain. This speculative problem would be further greatly reduced if changes in tax rates and in other governmental controls could all be carried out by small amounts at any point of time rather than by infrequent jerks at predetermined points of time. If, for example, the rate of tax on the purchase of new cars could be adjusted by small amounts at any moment upwards or downwards as changing conditions required and if, in consequence, future planned paths for the controls showed gradual upward or downward movements, the incentive for concentrated speculative bursts of purchasing and other activities would be removed. The problem remains an acute one, where, for administrative or other reasons, changes in controls must be concentrated at certain relatively infrequent points of time.

If the above difficulties in a complete marriage between indicative and control plans are considered decisive, then one is left with two possibilities. It may be wise to go to the other extreme, to keep the control plans as strict state secrets, and, on the lines already mentioned, to allow indicative planning to remain an iterative unorganized and informal conversation between academic research institutes, financial journalists, business concerns, etc.—all guessing what the future rates of tax may be. On the other hand, it may be possible to compromise and for purposes of indicative planning to reveal from the government's control plan the complete plan in the case of those controls with little speculative implication (e.g. the planned levels of governmental expenditure on goods and services), but in other cases only some general indications of probable directions of the controls without specific and detailed information in the case of those particular controls where speculative effects would be important.

PART 5

RESIDUAL UNCERTAINTY AND ECONOMIC STABILIZATION

Let us cease to consider what,
perhaps, may never happen, and what,
when it shall happen, will laugh at
human speculation.

There are a thousand familiar
disputes which reason can never
decide; questions that elude
investigation and make logick
ridiculous; cases where something
must be done, and where little can be
said.

Many things difficult to design prove
easy to performance.

SAMUEL JOHNSON : *Rasselas*

CHAPTER XIX

RESIDUAL UNCERTAINTY AND PUBLIC POLICY: PROPORTIONAL, INTEGRAL AND DERIVATIVE CONTROL

In Parts 3 and 4 of this volume we have considered the problems which arise in forecasting and in governmental control of an economy in conditions of environmental uncertainty. But the analysis which we developed there would be adequate only on the very unrealistic assumption that there was no residual uncertainty, as defined earlier, that is to say, on the assumption that precise, calculated plans had been prepared as to the action which could be taken along every possible environmental path. But this, as we have already argued, is an impossible requirement. In fact, economic agents must be prepared to cope with unexpected situations to meet which no previous precisely calculated plan of action has been prepared. In this final part of this volume we shall consider the problems which arise as a result of the need to cope with such residual uncertainty.

We will start by considering in this chapter one very important implication of this state of affairs for governmental action. An unexpected primary increase or decrease in the demand for goods and services in general can in the ways already discussed through many channels of positive feedback in the economy cause a large secondary inflation or deflation of demand. For example, there is an unexpected increase in the fashionable age for marriage; fewer new families are formed; there is an unexpected fall in the demand for new houses and for furniture and other durable consumption goods. The producers of these goods have smaller incomes and spend less on other goods and services for their own consumption; and, since the prospects of their industries are worsened, they also spend less on the installation of new capital equipment designed to produce houses, furniture and other durable consumption goods in the future. The reduction of expenditures on consumption and on capital development by the producers of houses, furniture and other durable consumption goods, reduces the incomes and worsens the prospects of other producers who, in their turn, reduce their outlays on consumption goods and on new capital equipment.

Moreover, since most producers and most workers are price-setters in the sense that each day they go into the market offering their products or their labour at a predetermined money price or wage rate, the impact effect of a general reduction in money demand will be a fall in the quantity of goods sold and in the number of workers employed rather than in the money prices charged for the goods and for the labour. A vicious cumulative circle of reduction in real output, real employment and real income may develop.

In the opposite circumstances, an unexpected primary increase in the general demand for goods and services might give rise to a vicious cumulative circle of inflationary pressures. We will discuss at a later stage why it may be desirable to check cumulative inflations of demand as well as cumulative deflations.

If arrangements for forecasting, planning and control on the lines discussed in Parts 3 and 4 were able to cover all environmental paths, then these problems of cumulative deflations and inflations would never arise. The government would have had plans ready for reductions of taxation, for increases in governmental expenditures, for making the investment of funds in other lines of activity more easy and for other suitable policies which would have led to increases in other forms of demand occurring as quickly as the fall in the demand for houses, furniture and other durable consumption goods occurred. Private producers and workers would have had their programmes ready for shifting, in the light of the pre-arranged governmental policies, to other lines—including perhaps a planned shift to leisure by the all-round reduction of working hours.

One very important result of the existence of what we have called 'residual uncertainty' is, therefore, the need for the government to be ready to react quickly to unexpected incipient declines or rises in the total demand for goods and services so as to nip in the bud the possible vicious cumulative effects of such unexpected disturbances. There must in fact be a governmental 'stabilization programme', which is a question of quick response to the unexpected to supplement the type of governmental control plan discussed in Part 4, which is a pre-arranged plan for the avoidance of fluctuations in demand in the case of those environmental developments for which full plans have been made in advance.

At first sight, this problem of quick governmental response in order to stabilize total demand may seem a relatively simple matter. There are a number of governmental policies which can affect the level of demand—in particular, monetary policies which make it easier or more difficult for private producers and consumers to raise funds of money for expenditure, tax measures which leave private producers and consumers with more or less money of their own to spend, and measures to increase or decrease governmental expenditure itself on goods and services. We shall discuss these measures at greater length in later chapters of this part. But given that it can by one means or another affect total demand, can one not merely say that the government should take measures to raise demand when demand is deficient and to reduce demand when demand is excessive, and leave it at that?

Unfortunately, there are some extremely important general considerations of the timing and form of governmental stabilization policies which arise from the nature of the dynamic interconnections in a modern economy which we discussed in Part 1 and in particular in Chapters IV and V of this volume. We will illustrate these problems of stabilization control by means of the example of the very simple accelerator-multiplier model considered in Chapter V. From equations 5.21 to 5.24, we have:

$$D'(t) = I_c^*(t) + v\{D'(t-1) - D'(t-2)\} + cD'(t-1) \ldots (19.1)$$

That is to say, we are considering an economy in which total demand in period t is made up of three elements: first, an exogenous element, namely $I_c^*(t)$; second, an accelerator demand, i.e. demand for new capital goods which depends simply upon the rate at which the demand for goods and services has gone up in the immediate past, namely $v\{D'(t-1) - D'(t-2)\}$; and third, a multiplier demand, i.e. a demand which depends upon the immediate past level of income, which in turn depends upon the immediate past level of demand, namely $cD'(t-1)$. Let us assume for our present illustrative purposes (i) that the system starts with $I_c^* = 1,250$ and with D' at its equilibrium level of 5,000; (ii) that I_c^* then rises unexpectedly on day 1 once and for all to a new level of 1,300; (iii) that $v = 0.5$; and (iv) that $c = 0.75$. Then the movement of the economy through time will be as shown by the curve marked (iii) on Figure 21. The total level of demand, will rise with diminishing fluctuations to a new equilibrium level of 5,200.[1] This uncontrolled time-path of D' is reproduced as curve (i) on Figures 43 and 44.

Let us suppose that the government wishes to stabilize total demand at its previous level of 5,000. We are assuming that we are dealing with a case in which the initial disturbance (the rise of I_c^* from 1,250 to 1,300) is unexpected and that we are concerned solely with the possibility of governmental reactions to undesired and un-expected movements of D' from the target level of 5,000.

The first possibility is for the government to introduce an element of PROPORTIONAL control. Suppose that, through its monetary or

[1] See pp. 66–73 above for a full discussion of these assumptions and of the resulting time-path for D'.

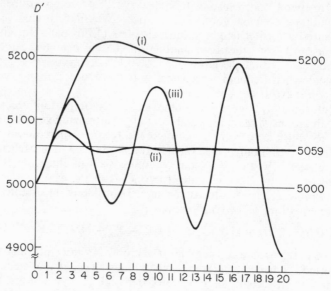

Figure 43

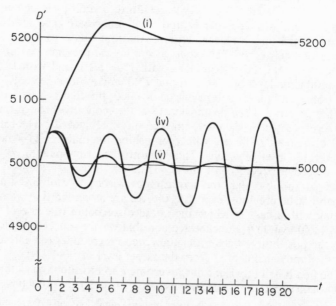

Figure 44

fiscal policy, it is able to arrange that total demand on any day t—namely $D'(t)$—is raised (or lowered) by a proportion—for example 60%—of the amount by which total demand on the previous day—namely $D'(t - 1)$—fell below (or exceeded) the target level of 5,000. Then we should have to add a fourth element of demand in equation 19.1, namely $0.6\{5,000 - D'(t - 1)\}$. Equation 19.1 would now become:

$$D'(t) = I_c^*(t) + 0.5\{D'(t - 1) - D'(t - 2)\} + 0.75\{D'(t - 1)\}$$
$$+ 0.6\{5,000 - D'(t - 1)\} \dots\dots\dots\dots\dots\dots\dots\dots\dots(19.2)$$

Given that I_c^* rises once and for all from 1,250 to 1,300 on day 1, and that D' had been at its constant equilibrium level of 5,000 for at least two days immediately preceding day 0 we can work out the future course of D' on the principles illustrated in Table IV, including now the fourth element of governmental proportional control in the level of D' on any day t. The resulting time-path for D' is shown by the curve marked (ii) on Figure 43.

The result of the governmental proportional control has been to reduce the excess demand and to bring D', with some fluctuations, to a new equilibrium level of 5,059.[2] This is less than the uncontrolled level of 5,200 but it is still in excess of the target level of 5,000. The reason for this is clear. A proportional control will operate only if there is some divergence between the actual (5,059) and the target (5,000) level of D'. If D' were brought down to the target level, then there would be no excess demand; 60% of zero is zero, so that there would be no governmental disinflation of demand; and with I_c^* permanently at the excess figure of 1,300, the actual level of D' could not remain at the target level of 5,000.

Before we go on to consider how this defect of proportional control might be remedied, we will point out another serious danger. Suppose that because of administrative, political and possibly also bureaucratic difficulties in the collection of statistical information about what is happening to D' and in operating the governmental control measures, there is a longer delay than we have allowed so far in the effective impact on the economy of the governmental control measures. Suppose by way of illustration that there is a two-day instead of merely a one-day delay between the excess or deficiency of total demand which it is desired to correct and the effective operation of the element of governmental proportional control. That is to say, instead of adding $0.6\{5,000 - D'(t - 1)\}$ to

---

[2] The new equilibrium level of D' can be seen to be approximately 5,059. If we assume that $D'(t) = D'(t - 1) = D'(t - 2)$, i.e. that D' is at a constant equilibrium level, then equation 19.2 becomes $(1 - 0.75 + 0.6) D'(t) = I_c^*(t) + 0.6 \times 5,000$. With $I_c^*(t) = 1,300$, this gives $D'(t) = 5,059$ (approximately).

equation 19.1 as was done in equation 19.2, we would have to add $0.6\{5,000 - D'(t - 2)\}$ and obtain:

$$D'(t) = I_c^*(t) + 0.5\{D'(t - 1) - D'(t - 2)\} + 0.75\,D'(t - 1)$$
$$+ 0.6\{5,000 - D'(t - 2)\} \quad\ldots\ldots\ldots (19.3)$$

The resulting time-path for D' is now shown by curve (iii) instead of by curve (ii) in Figure 43.

There has been a dramatic deterioration in the situation. The level of D' once more fluctuates round the new level of 5,059, but the fluctuations have now become explosive and the whole system has become highly unstable. What in fact has happened is that, because of the undue delay, a corrective governmental deflation of demand often does not come into operation until the peak of the inflation which it was intended to check is already past, so that the governmentally induced deflation is excessive and serves to reinforce a deflationary movement instead. Conversely, a corrective governmental inflationary policy may come when the deflation which it was intended to correct has already passed its peak, and the economy is already on an upward path which the governmental measure merely reinforces. Ill-timed governmental control measures can do more harm than good.

But let us suppose that the government can operate promptly enough as in the case of curve (ii) of Figure 43 and let us return to the problem raised by the fact, which we discussed above, that a proportional control cannot in the nature of things wholly offset some permanent inflationary or deflationary disturbance. What can be done?

What is clearly needed is some system whereby the government, as it were, learns by experience and gradually intensifies its deflationary (or inflationary) control as experience shows that its present control is inadequate to bring the level of demand permanently down to (or up to) the target level. This principle is recognized by the introduction of an element of INTEGRAL CONTROL. Suppose that the government keeps a record of the excess (or deficiency) of actual demand as compared with the target demand experienced in every period since the initiation of its control policy, and that it sums up the total of these excesses (or deficiencies) of demand over the whole period. If there is a permanent excess of demand (as in the case of the 5,059 level of curve (ii) in Figure 43), this total of excess demand will get larger and larger as time passes. If the government introduces an element of integral control, whereby there is some governmental deflation (or inflation) of demand which is related to the past sum of total excesses (or deficiencies) of the actual demand, then demand can be brought back permanently to its desired equilibrium level. In the case of curve (ii) of Figure 43, as time passed an excess of 59 would be added each period to the sum (the integral) of all past excesses of demand and this would gradually add a corresponding permanent element to the government deflationary policy. If and when as a result of this the total level of demand reached the target level of 5,000, it could now remain there permanently; for the element of integral control depends upon the sum of all past excess demands which would remain unchanged, so that the element of integral control could remain permanently unchanged at the level necessary to preserve total demand at its target level. And this target level of total demand is the only one which can be permanently maintained; for at any other level of demand there would be some current discrepancy between the actual and the target levels of demand, so that the total sum of discrepancies would be changing with the result that the level of the integral control, and so the level of the total demand itself, would be changing.

Suppose then that the government adds to the proportional control of equation 19.2 an element of integral control equal to the total sum of past deficiencies of total demand below its target level. Such an element of integral control at time t would be equal to:

$$\{[5,000 - D'(t - 1)] + [5,000 - D'(t - 2)]$$
$$+ [5,000 - D'(t - 3)] + \ldots + [5,000 - D'(1)]\}$$

If we add this element to the factors making up current demand— $D'(t)$—in equation 19.2, we obtain the equation:

$$D'(t) = I_c^*(t) + 0\cdot5\{D'(t - 1) - D'(t - 2)\} + 0\cdot75\,D'(t - 1)$$
$$+ 0\cdot6\,\{5,000 - D'(t - 1)\} + \{[5,000 - D'(t - 1)]$$
$$+ [5,000 - D'(t - 2)] + \ldots + [5,000 - D'(1)]\} \ldots (19.4)$$

From this we can calculate the time-path for D' from time 0 onwards on the assumption that D' was constant at its equilibrium level of 5,000 up to time $t = 0$ and that I_c^* rose once and for all from 1,250 to 1,300 at time $t = 1$. The resulting time-path for D' is that shown by curve (iv) in Figure 44.

It will be seen that the level of D' does now fluctuate round the target level of 5,000, but that unfortunately these fluctuations which were damped and disappearing in the case of curves (i)—which fluctuated round the excess level of 5,200—and curve (ii)—which fluctuated round the excess level of 5059—have now become explosive. The introduction of integral control has brought the equilibrium level down to the target level, but unfortunately it has made the whole system unstable. The reason for this result can be understood intuitively. Since, in an integral control mechanism, the excess demand for past periods (e.g. that of two days ago) will be playing its part as well as the immediately past excess demand (e.g. that of one day ago), it has some of the features of a delayed proportional control. This, as we saw in comparing curve (iii) with curve (ii), can make the system unstable because it may mean that a deflationary control is being exercised when the level of demand has already passed its peak and needs a less deflationary, or indeed some inflationary, control to stabilize it.

Can one preserve the integral control which does have the advantage of bringing the equilibrium value of D' into line with its target value, and yet do something to offset its possible destabilizing effect? As can be seen from curves (iii) and (iv), instability implies that D' will be either rising or falling particularly rapidly as it passes its equilibrium level and either overshoots or undershoots it. Instability may accordingly be offset by introducing an element of DERIVATIVE CONTROL whereby the government reduces expenditure when total expenditure is rising rapidly and increases expenditure when expenditure is falling rapidly.[3] For this purpose, let us subtract from total expenditure at time t—namely $D'(t)$—in equation 19.4 an element of governmental derivative control equal to $0.25\{D'(t-1) - D'(t-2)\}$. Equation 19.4 now becomes:

$$D'(t) = I_c^*(t) + \{0.5 - 0.25\} \{D'(t-1) - D'(t-2)\} + 0.75\,D'(t-1)$$
$$+ 0.6\{5,000 - D'(t-1)\} + \{[5,000 - D'(t-1)]$$
$$+ [5,000 - D'(t-2)\} + \dots + [5,000 - D'(1)]\} \dots (19.5)$$

If once more we assume that D' is constant at its equilibrium level of 5,000 up to time $t = 0$ and that $I_c^*(t)$ rises once and for all from 1,250 to 1,300 at time $t = 1$, we can, from equation 19.5, once more calculate the time-path of D', which is shown in curve (v) of Figure 44. It will be seen that while the system still fluctuates, these fluctuations are now quite rapidly damped. The system is both stable and total demand moves to its target level of 5,000.

The preceding paragraphs are, of course, nothing more than a very simple numerical example of an exceedingly oversimplified economic system. Even so, it is very difficult to reach any general conclusions about the nature of a good stabilizing policy. The precise nature of that policy—namely, how powerful should be the elements of

---

[3] This is the exact opposite of the influence of the type of speculative expenditure or of the accelerator expenditure discussed on pages 61–72, which represent an additional element of expenditure which is high when total expenditure is rising rapidly and low when total expenditure is falling rapidly, and which, as we have seen, exercise very destabilizing influences.

proportional, integral and derivative control[4] and how important is the avoidance of delays in their application—depends quite basically upon the nature of the dynamic forces and the delays at work in the system which it is desired to stabilize. There are, however, perhaps two features which our analysis suggests to be desirable in a control policy. In the first place, the government should arrange to be able to react as promptly as possible and with controls whose effects are as immediate as possible, when it is confronted with an unexpected and undesired rise or fall in total demand. Secondly, the amount of its deflationary (or inflationary) control should depend not only upon (i) the level of the most recent excess (or deficiencies) of actual over desired total demand (PROPORTIONAL CONTROL) but also should be the greater (ii) the longer and more persistent that excess (or deficiency) has been (INTEGRAL CONTROL) and (iii) the more quickly that excess (or deficiency) is growing or the less quickly it is falling (DERIVATIVE CONTROL).

For this sort of purpose the government needs flexible and quickly acting controls over the total demands for goods and services. In the following chapters we will examine the question how far such controls can be exercised through monetary policy or through fiscal policy. We will start with an examination of monetary policy. But in order to be in a position to do so we must first examine (as is done in Chapters XX and XXI) the nature of money and the reasons why people use and hold money.

Note to Chapter XIX

A MATHEMATICAL NOTE ON THE ILLUSTRATIVE MODEL USED IN CHAPTER XIX

(i) With $v = 0.5$ and $c = 0.75$, equation 19.1 can be rewritten as:
$$D'(t) - 1.25 D'(t - 1) + 0.5 D'(t - 2) = I_c^*(t) \ldots\ldots\ldots (19.6)$$

By writing $D'(t) = D'(t - 1) = D'(t - 2)$ and confining our attention to periods after $t = 0$ when $I_c^*(t)$ is assumed to be constant at 1,300, we obtain $\bar{D}' = 5,200$, which is the stationary equilibrium value of D' after period 0. The characteristic equation derived from 19.6 is of the form:
$$d'^2 + ad' + b = 0 \ldots\ldots\ldots\ldots\ldots\ldots\ldots\ldots\ldots\ldots\ldots\ldots\ldots (19.7)$$

where $a = -1.25$ and $b = 0.5$. Since $a^2 - 4b = (1.25)^2 - 2 < 0$, the system is oscillatory; and then since $b = 0.5 < 1$, the oscillations are damped.

---

[4] In the example given we gave the proportional control a weight of 0.6, the integral control a weight of 1.0, and the derivative control a weight of 0.25. Other weights would have led to very different results.

(ii) Equation 19.2 can be rewritten as:

$$D'(t) - 0.65 D'(t-1) + 0.5 D'(t-2) = I_c^*(t) + 3,000 \ldots (19.8)$$

With D' constant at $\bar{D}'$ and confining our attention to periods after $t = 0$ when I_c^* is assumed to be constant at 1,300, this gives a stationary equilibrium value of $\bar{D}' = 5,059$. The characteristic equation from 19.8 is:

$$d'^2 - 0.65 d' + 0.5 = 0$$

and with $(0.65)^2 - 4 \times 0.5 < 0$, the system is oscillatory; but then with $0.5 < 1$ the oscillations are damped.

(iii) Equation 19.3 can be rewritten as:

$$D'(t) - 1.25 D'(t-1) + 1.1 D'(t-2) = I_c^*(t) + 3,000 \ldots (19.9)$$

Once more the stationary equilibrium value of D' after the once-for-all rise of I_c^* to 1,300 is $\bar{D}' = 5,059$; but the characteristic equation is now:

$$d'^2 - 1.25 d' + 1.1 = 0.$$

With $(1.25)^2 - 4 \times 1.1 < 0$ the system is oscillatory; but then with $1.1 > 1$, the oscillations are explosive.

(iv) If equation 19.4 is rewritten to refer to the level of total demand at time $t - 1$ instead of its level at time t, we have

$$D'(t-1) = I_c^*(t-1) + 0.5 \{D'(t-2) - D'(t-3)\} + 0.75 D'(t-2)$$
$$+ 0.6 \{5,000 - D'(t-2)\} + \{[5,000 - D'(t-2)]$$
$$+ [5,000 - D'(t-3) + \ldots + [5,000 - D'(1)]\} \ldots\ldots (19.10)$$

If we subtract 19.10 from 19.4 and rearrange terms we obtain:

$$D'(t) - 0.65 D'(t-1) + 1.15 D'(t-2) - 0.5 D'(t-3)$$
$$= 5,000 + I_c^*(t) - I_c^*(t-1) \ldots\ldots\ldots\ldots\ldots\ldots (19.11)$$

If we write D' at a constant value $\bar{D}'$, then with $I_c^*(t) = I_c^*(t-1)$ we obtain $\bar{D}' = 5,000$. The introduction of integral control has made the equilibrium level of D' coincide with its target level. The corresponding characteristic equation is

$$d'^3 - 0.65 d'^2 + 1.15 d' - 0.5 = 0 \ldots\ldots\ldots\ldots\ldots (19.12)$$

By trial and error[5] we can find $d' = 0.47$ as the approximate value of a real root of the characteristic equation. Since this root is real

---

[5] With $d' = 0.4$ the LHS of 19.12 is -0.08 and with $d' = 0.5$ it is $+0.0375$. By linear interpolation, $d' = 0.47$ is the approximate value of d' which makes the LHS of 19.12 equal to zero.

and <1, it represents a non-oscillatory damped element in the system. Dividing the LHS of 19.12 through by $d' - 0.47$ gives (approximately):

$$d'^2 - 0.18 d' + 1.0654$$

Since $(0.18)^2 - 4 \times 1.0654 < 0$ and since $1.0654 > 1$, this part of the system gives an explosive oscillatory movement.

(v) If equation 19.5 is now rewritten to refer to $D'(t - 1)$ instead of to $D'(t)$ and if the resulting equation is then subtracted from equation 19.5 (that is to say, if we use a procedure exactly similar to that by which equation 19.11 was derived from equation 19.4), we obtain from equation 19.5:

$$D'(t) - 0.4\,D'(t - 1) + 0.65\,D'(t - 2) - 0.25\,D'(t - 3)$$
$$= 5,000 + I_c^*(t) - I_c^*(t - 1) \quad \ldots\ldots\ldots\ldots\ldots\ldots\ldots (19.13)$$

with its characteristic equation

$$d'^3 - 0.4\,d'^2 + 0.65\,d' - 0.25 = 0 \quad \ldots\ldots\ldots\ldots\ldots (19.14)$$

By trial and error[6] we obtain an approximate value of 0.38 for a real root of 19.14. This root being real and less than unity gives a non-oscillatory damped element in the value of D'. Dividing the LHS of 19.14 through by $d' - 0.38$ gives (approximately):

$$d'^2 + 0.02 d' + 0.6494$$

Since $(0.02)^2 - 4 \times 0.6494$ is < 0, and since $0.6494 < 1$, this gives a damped oscillatory movement.

---

[6] With $d' = 0.3$ the LHS of 19.14 is -0.065 and with $d' = 0.4$ the LHS of 19.14 is $+0.01$. Linear interpolation gives $d' = 0.38$ (approximately).

CHAPTER XX

MONEY AND OTHER ASSETS AS A SAFEGUARD AGAINST RESIDUAL UNCERTAINTY

In the previous chapter we considered one of the important implications for governmental policy arising from the fact that, as we pointed out in Chapter XIII, the number of possible future environmental paths is always so great that decision-makers cannot possibly consider what their future actions would be along each conceivable environmental path. There will remain much residual uncertainty; one object in the formulation of any present plan must be simply to put the planner into a flexible position so as to be able to react quickly and appropriately to unexpected, unforeseen events to meet which no carefully premeditated course of action has been prepared in advance.

In the private sector of the economy, this means essentially holding wealth in the form of assets which are more flexible in their uses than would otherwise be the case. Of course, it may be decided to hold assets in a flexible form to meet carefully calculated and premeditated risks. Thus, to take the example discussed in Chapter XI, a producer of umbrellas and sunshades having carefully calculated the effects of wet weather and of fine weather upon his business and having carefully assessed the probabilities of its being wet or fine may decide to install a flexible plant that can be used in the future to produce either umbrellas if wet or sunshades if fine, even though a more rigidly specialized plant, if devoted to the exclusive production of one of these products, would result in a lower cost of production.

Flexibility to meet residual uncertainty involves something more far-reaching than this. In so far as one does not know at all what the eventuality will be for which one will want to use one's wealth in the future, then one will want to hold one's wealth in forms which will help to cope with any eventuality which may turn up. In a free market economy, for any one individual this quality of helping to cope with unexpected eventualities is possessed in some degree by all assets. If one owns one asset (asset E) and then some quite unexpected event occurs which makes one need some quite other kind of good or service (*F*), one can sell asset *E* and use the proceeds to acquire some amount of *F*.[1]

We may say that an asset provides 'safety' in so far as it gives one a generalized power of being exchanged in the future into any specific good or service which may unexpectedly turn out to be needed. But not all assets are equally useful for this purpose. A sunshade is useful for protecting one from the sun in a fine summer. But if the summer quite unexpectedly turns out to be wet, then—even if there is a perfect market for sunshades and umbrellas—one would not expect to get a very good price for one's redundant sunshade in order to help one to purchase an umbrella in a rainy seller's market for umbrellas. Some assets are in fact safer than others. We must consider what are the qualities needed in an asset to make it a safe asset.[2]

For a market price exchange economy to work efficiently there must be (i) a unit of account and (ii) a means of payment. If an owner of asset *E* wanted to exchange it into good *F*, in the absence of some common unit of account and of some common means of payment, he would have to look for someone who owned *F* and wanted to own *E* in order to arrange an appropriate barter. But it might, of course, be the case that no one who owned *F* wanted *E*, but that someone who owned *F* wanted *A* while someone else who owned *A* wanted *E*. In this case the owner of *E* would have to bring all parties together to form a triangular barter deal—exchanging *E* for *A*, *A* for *F*, and *F* for *E*. It is because (i) there is a generally accepted unit of account (the prices of *A*, *E* and *F* can each separately be quoted in terms of dollars) and (ii) there is some recognized means of payment (for example, a dollar note), that the owner of *E* can sell his asset *E* in the market and buy *F* in the market without discovering all the individual parties and fixing all the individual bargains which ultimately make this exchange possible for him.

The asset which acts as the unit of account and as the means of payment we call 'money'. Let us speak of it as asset *M*. The degree of safety provided by asset *E* depends upon the ability of the owner

---

[1] As a useful mnemonic in what follows, *E* can stand for ordinary shares or Equities, *F* for Final goods (i.e. what one ultimately wishes to purchase), and *M* for Money.

[2] What we have called the quality of 'safety' in an asset might perhaps be better called its degree of 'market flexibility'. To possess assets which can readily and at little cost be exchanged into any other good or service which may be unexpectedly needed is not merely a safeguard against an unexpected calamity; it may also be a safeguard against missing an unexpected golden opportunity of doing well if one could quickly shift one's assets into some specific goods which are unexpectedly desirable. We have chosen to call the quality 'safety' rather than 'market flexibility' solely in order to keep as far as possible to terminology in current use.

of asset E, if some unexpected need turns up, to exchange asset E for good or service A, B, C or D as the case may be according to the nature of the unexpected need. But an exchange of E into A, B, C or D involves two steps: first, an exchange of E into M, and second, an exchange of M into A, B, C or D. The degree of safety provided by asset E thus depends essentially upon two elements: (i) the conditions affecting the knowledge of the owner of E about how much M he will be able to get for his E at any given future date; and (ii) the conditions affecting the knowledge of the owner of E about how much of A, B, C or D he will be able to acquire at any given future date with a given amount of M. Now the owner of E cannot possibly know the money price which he must pay for A, the money price which he must pay for B, and so on for each alternative good or service individually at any given future date. For, *ex hypothesi*, we are dealing with unexpected, unpremeditated events. The relative supply–demand conditions for A, B, C and D cannot be clearly foreseen and the relative prices of A, B, C and D are, therefore, unknown. But their relative prices are not the only possible unknowns. As we shall argue later, financial and other policies on the part of the government will affect the general ABSOLUTE level of money prices within which the RELATIVE prices of A, B, C and D are reflected. If the owner of E does not know whether the general level of money prices will go up or go down in the future nor at what rate they will be inflated or deflated, he clearly knows less about the extent to which a given amount of M at a given future date is likely to safeguard him against unspecified eventualities than he would know if he was certain about what some specified money price index (i.e. the money cost of a specified bundle of goods and services A, B, C and D) would be at that date. Let us from this point on use F to denote this bundle of goods and services (e.g. a ton of steel + a dozen eggs + nine shirts + the work of one man for a week) and $P_f(t)$ to denote its money cost (i.e. the buying price of the bundle F) at any future date t.

The actual composition of the bundle F is essentially arbitrary for the simple reason that its use is to help to deal with the residual uncertainty which is essentially vague and unthought-out in one's mind. Every economic agent can in fact at the back of his mind have his own bundle F according to his own intuitive assessment of the sort of things in which he may be interested if the unexpected happens. There are thus sub-systems of residual uncertainty. Thus, consider a business concern which is going to use some sort of equipment to produce electricity, but does not know whether it will be powered by water, coal, oil, or nuclear energy, because there are a number of uncalculated possibilities as to future technical progress and the future costs of various inputs. It may wish to keep assets which are safe in terms of a bundle F made up of engineering products of many forms.

But while different people can think in terms of different F-bundles, when one comes on to monetary policy one objective of which may be to stabilize or to control the general level of prices, only one general F-bundle can be chosen by the financial authorities. However the main purpose of thinking in terms of a bundle F and of future movements in its money price P_f is to cope with the possibility of a general monetary inflation or deflation of all prices. In so far as this is the case, all price indices which cover a large number of dissimilar goods and services are likely to move in much the same way. And in so far as there may be a marked probability that the prices of one particular group of goods will move in an exceptional way, knowledge of how a general index of prices chosen by the monetary authorities will move in the future will improve the ability of those interested in special groups of goods to guess how their prices will move. For example, those who are specially interested in the price of engineering products may have some reason to guess that their prices will fall by 0.5% per annum relatively to the price index used in connection with monetary policy. If they know how this latter index will move, they will be greatly helped in guessing how the prices of their own special F-bundle will move.

Consider then an economic agent who holds now at time 0 an asset E and is interested in a particular F-bundle. At some future time t he will in fact be able to sell a unit of E at a price $P_e(t)$. The amount of F which he will then be able to acquire for this unit of E will be $P_e(t)/P_f(t)$. If this ratio could be known for certain for every future date, then we might say that E was a perfectly safe asset. An owner of E would know exactly how much of the bundle F he could acquire by selling his E at every future point of time, no matter what unexpected eventuality occurred.

Safety is, of course, not the only quality which is desirable in an asset which is to be held to meet the hazards of residual uncertainty. Consider two assets E_1 and E_2. Let us write P^* for the selling prices and P for the buying prices of assets. Then the ratios between the selling prices of E_1 and E_2 and the buying price of F at future time t would be $P_{e1}^*(t)/P_f(t)$ and $P_{e2}^*(t)/P_f(t)$ respectively; and suppose that both these ratios are known for certain so that both E_1 and E_2 are perfectly safe assets. Then a dollar invested in E_1 now (time 0) will command for certain $P_{e1}^*(t)/\{P_{e1}(0)\,P_f(t)\}$ units of F at time t, while a dollar invested now in E_2 will command $P_{e2}^*(t)/\{P_{e2}(0)\,P_f(t)\}$ units of F at time t. Thus if $P_{e1}^*(t)/P_{e1}(0) > P_{e2}^*(t)/P_{e2}(0)$, E_1 is the preferable safe asset, since its yield in terms of future command over F is greater.

The amount of F obtainable at time t from a dollar invested in E at time 0 is

$$\frac{P_e^*(0)}{P_e(0)} \frac{P_e^*(t)}{P_e^*(0)} \frac{1}{P_f(t)}$$

This investment will be the safer, the more certainly $P_e^*(t)/P_f(t)$ is foreseen; and it will have a higher yield, (i) the lower is the margin between the buying and the selling price of E, (ii) the higher the rate of appreciation of E's selling price, and (iii) the lower the future price of F.

In order to make a fair comparison between various assets $P_e^*(t)$ must be the value which asset E will command if sold in the market, inclusive not only of any appreciation in the market selling price of E but also inclusive of the accumulation at compound interest of any interest or dividend paid on asset E between time 0 and time t. Yield includes interest plus capital gain.

For E to be a perfectly safe asset a necessary condition is that there should be a perfect market for E. E may need to be sold suddenly and unexpectedly to meet some unforeseen eventuality; for the ratio $P_e^*(t)/P_f(t)$ to be known for certain, the selling price of E must not be affected by the speed with which E is to be realized. If there is not a perfect market for E, then to obtain a good price for E may need time to find a purchaser and to negotiate a good price with the purchaser. Or a quick sale on reasonably favourable terms may require heavy expenditure on advertisement. The extent to which the price at which E can be sold in the market at any one time is independent of the amount of time, trouble, and money which has been spent upon negotiating the sale may be called its 'marketability'. For an asset to provide a high degree of safety it must have a high degree of marketability.

But that is, of course, not enough. For $P_e^*(t)/P_f(t)$ to be known in advance, it is not sufficient merely to know that the price $P_e^*(t)$ will not depend upon any selling effort on the owner's part. The additional requirement for E to be a safe asset is that the selling price of E should be correlated at time t with the price of F in the following sense. Consider two environmental states at time t, in the first of which $P_f(t)$ would be 10% higher than in the second. Then E is a safe asset if the selling price of E would also be 10% higher in the first environmental state than in the second. This does not necessarily mean that the movements of $P_e^*(t)$ and $P_f(t)$ are correlated over time, only that they are correlated over the different environmental states at each point of time. If some events would cause the general price index P_f to be 10% higher at time t than it would otherwise be, then E is a safe asset in terms of its purchasing power over F if these same events would cause the selling price of E also to be 10% higher than would otherwise be the case.

A sufficient, though not necessary, condition for the ratio $P_e^*(t)/P_f(t)$ to be known in advance is that future movements in the price $P_e^*(t)$ should be known and that future movements in the price $P_f(t)$ should also be known. Let us consider each of these in turn.

Asset E might be perfectly marketable as defined above; and yet there might be great uncertainty as to what its future market price—P_e^*—would in fact be at time t. Clearly some types of asset will be subject to much more uncertainty than others as to the general demand/supply forces which will affect their market price conditions in the future. We will return to these differences later; here we will merely note them. This means that confidence about the price at which the owner of asset E will be able to realize it for money at time t will depend not only upon its marketability but also upon the extent to which general supply/demand conditions will not greatly affect the market price of asset E. The degree to which the money price of any asset is unaffected by fluctuations in general market conditions we will call the 'price reliability' of the asset.

The extent to which uncertainty surrounds future movements in the general index of money prices—P_f—will depend in large part upon governmental financial policies and we shall return to this subject at some length. At this stage we will merely point out that if future movements in the general index of money prices are not known in advance, then money itself is not a perfectly safe asset, since it will not be known for certain how much command over F will be provided at each future date by holding a certain sum of money. But if the future of $P_f(t)$ is known for certain, then money itself is *par excellence* the safe asset.

This last statement is subject to one qualification. If interest is paid on money, then the selling price at time t (namely $P_m(t)$) of \$1 of money put aside now at time 0 is not \$ 1, since $P_m(t)$ must equal the \$ 1 plus compound interest earned on the \$ 1 from time 0 to time t. If fluctuations in the rate of interest are possible but unknown, then $P_m(t)$ will be unknown so that the yield of the \$1 in terms of F (namely $P_m(t)/P_f(t)$) will itself be unknown. This qualification is probably only of secondary importance: but it draws our attention to the fact that the yield on money in terms of F will depend (i) upon the future course of the general level of prices, being highly negative (or positive) in so far as the rate of inflation (or deflation) of P_f between time 0 and time t is high and (ii) upon the rate of interest—if any—paid on the holding of money balances. The rate of real yield per annum will be $i_m - p_f$, where i_m is the rate of interest paid on money balances and p_f is the rate of inflation of the general price index.

The degree to which future movements in a general price index such as P_f are known for certain we may call the degree of reliability of the purchasing power of money. In passing it should be noted that RELIABILITY of the purchasing power of money is not the same thing as STABILITY of its purchasing power. If the general price index were known to be going to rise at 2% per annum, there would be perfect reliability in the purchasing power of money, though the yield on money in terms of real goods would be 2% per annum less than it would otherwise have been if the price level had been stable, as well as reliable.

In a world in which there is uncertainty about the future general level of prices $P_f(t)$ money is no longer a perfectly safe asset, and it is almost certain that no other perfectly safe asset can be found. Indeed, the only asset whose price would be perfectly correlated with the price of F (in the sense explained above) would be F itself. But F may contain a number of perishable goods or services which simply cannot be held as a store of value or, in less extreme cases, could only be stored at great cost. We may, if we like, say that F is a perfectly safe asset but that the yield of F in terms of F is extremely low, because the cost of holding F is very high so that as time went on these costs would eat away the whole stock of F itself.

In fact, in order to cope with residual uncertainty it will always be a question of choosing to hold a mixed collection of different assets which together will give the best possible combination of safety and probable yield. There is one reason why this collection of assets will nearly always include the holding of some money, even in conditions in which the expected yield on money is very low and very uncertain, that is to say, even in conditions in which the general level of prices is expected on balance to go up rapidly but with considerable possibilities of unforeseeable fluctuation in the rate of inflation. The reason is as follows.

Money is the only asset for which the cost of transaction is zero. To sell \$1 for \$1 costs nothing; to buy \$1 with \$1 costs nothing; one simply does nothing in both cases. Moreover, since money is the medium of exchange, one will continually be receiving money and spending money. But receipts and expenditures will not exactly coincide. To invest in asset E all money immediately upon its receipt and to sell asset E as soon as money was needed for expenditure would involve some transactions cost both in the purchase and the sale of E, even if it were only the psychological cost of taking the necessary thought and trouble. But these transactions costs are the same whether E is held for a short or for a long period. Suppose these costs to be $1 for $100 invested in E. Then if E is held for one year, this cost represents 1% per annum on the investment; but if E is held for one week only, it represents 1% per week or 67% per annum (allowing for the weekly compounding of interest); and if E is held for only one day, it represents 1% per day or no less than 3,600% per annum (allowing for the daily compounding of interest).

Thus transactions costs are a small deterrent to the purchase of an asset which is to be held for a period, but are a strong—indeed, in the limit, a prohibitive—deterrent to investment in an asset which is expected to be needed for turning back into money in a very short time. People will want to hold assets which will give a safe command over F at various dates in the future, including the immediate future. For this reason, some receipts of money will not be immediately invested in other assets even though the yield on money is very low; transactions costs would make the yield on other assets, if they are to be realized almost at once, even lower.

If all assets were perfectly marketable and had no transactions costs associated with them, there would still be a problem of deciding how much of one's wealth to hold in the form of money and how much in the form of other assets in order to achieve the best balance between safety and probable yield, taking into account (i) the possible movements in the prices of the other available assets; (ii) the possible movements in the price index of goods and services in general; and (iii) the extent to which the money prices of the other assets were likely to be correlated with the money price index of goods and services in general. In the Note to this chapter we construct a very simple model to illustrate this problem.

Note to Chapter XX

SAFETY AND YIELD IN THE CHOICE OF ASSETS

In discussing portfolio selection, investment in money is often treated as a perfectly safe investment with a zero, or a very low but certain, yield and investment in other assets, such as ordinary shares, as a risky investment with a variable yield, the expected value of which is relatively high. But in an age of inflation this is a doubtful procedure. It all depends upon what one wants to do with one's wealth at the end of the period over which one is looking ahead. Let us suppose that one will express its value then in terms of a unit called 'final goods' (F), and let us suppose that one can invest one's present money capital (K) without further cost either in money (M) or in ordinary shares or equities (E), M and E being distinct from F. If the money price of final goods (f) is going to change in a given way whether upwards or downwards quite independently of the behaviour of the money price of shares (e), then M is the safe asset. It is true that if the given change in f is upward, one will do worse than if it is downward. But if one knows the future change in f, then investment in M gives a riskless, though perhaps a low, yield in terms of F.

But suppose that the future movements in f are not known. Then investment in M is risky in terms of its real yield of F, because one does not know how much F a given amount of M will command in the future. If future movements of f and e were unknown, but if it were known that f and e would move in exactly the same way,[3] then investment in E would be the riskless investment. The future purchasing power of E over F would be certain. In fact, if it were unknown whether there was going to be a general inflation or deflation of money prices, but it were known that the money prices of shares and of final goods would be affected in the same way, then shares are a safe investment and money is a risky investment.

Reality lies, probably, somewhere between these two extremes. Share prices are more volatile than the general level of prices of final goods and services. Share prices may rise greatly or fall substantially in the near future; the cost of living is much more likely to rise by a relatively moderate amount. But the rise in the cost of living may well be greater in conditions in which share prices rise rapidly, and conversely if conditions turn out to be generally deflationary. Neither M nor E alone gives a riskless return in terms of F. The purpose of this Note is to consider the choice between M and E by an investor who wants to have a future ability to purchase F.

Let us consider an investor who has today a given amount of money capital (K) which he can hold in money (M) or which he can invest in shares (E) and let us choose units of E so that today's price of E is unity. Then after today's investment decision has been taken :

$$K = M + E \dots\dots\dots\dots\dots\dots\dots\dots\dots\dots\dots\dots\dots\dots (20.1)$$

where K is given. Suppose our investor to be interested only in the amount of F which he will be able to purchase tomorrow, and choose units of F so that today's money price of F is also unity. Our investor, having no money illusion, is not basically concerned with tomorrow's money price of money (m), of shares (e), or of final goods (f).[4] What does interest him is tomorrow's value in terms of

---

[3] The necessary condition is in fact somewhat weaker than this. It is sufficient that the future movement of the ratio f/e should be known.

[4] Tomorrow's money price of money (m) is not necessarily unity. If a certain interest (i) can be earned on a unit of money invested in a money loan for one day, then $m = 1 + i$. Similarly, tomorrow's money price of a share (e) measures tomorrow's value of the share inclusive of any dividend or other return paid on that share.

F of a unit of money acquired today (let us call this $\bar{m}$) and tomorrow's value in terms of F of a unit of shares acquired today (let us call this $\bar{e}$).[5]

Let us suppose that our investor considers two possible developments of tomorrow's economic environment. In environment 1 he expects the relevant real prices to be $\bar{m}_1$ and $\bar{e}_1$ and in environment 2 he expects the relevant real prices to be $\bar{m}_2$ and $\bar{e}_2$. Then he expects to be able to purchase $F_1 = M\bar{m}_1 + E\bar{e}_1$ or $F_2 = M\bar{m}_2 + E\bar{e}_2$ units of F in each of the two environments. Using equation 20.1 and writing $\alpha = E/K$ for the proportion of his capital which he invests in shares, we obtain:

$$F_1 = K\{(1 - \alpha)\bar{m}_1 + \alpha\bar{e}_1\}$$
$$F_2 = K\{(1 - \alpha)\bar{m}_2 + \alpha\bar{e}_2\} \quad\dots\dots\dots\dots\dots\dots\dots\dots\dots (20.2)$$

so that:

$$F_1/F_2 = \{(1 - \alpha)\bar{m}_1 + \alpha\bar{e}_1\}/\{(1 - \alpha)\bar{m}_2 + \alpha\bar{e}_2\} \quad\dots\dots (20.3)$$

Let us suppose that our investor has a utility function for wealth in terms of final goods of the form:

$$U(F) = B - \{\sigma/(1 - \sigma)\}\, AF^{-(1-\sigma)/\sigma} \dots\dots\dots\dots\dots\dots (20.4)$$

where A, B and σ are constants with the implications given on pages 217–9 of *The Growing Economy*. In particular, σ will then measure the numerical value of a constant elasticity of substitution between F_1 and F_2. From 20.4 we can derive:

$$\mu \equiv dU/dF = AF^{-1/\sigma} \dots\dots\dots\dots\dots\dots\dots\dots\dots\dots (20.5)$$

so that

$$\mu_1/\mu_2 = (F_1/F_2)^{-1/\sigma} \text{ or } F_1/F_2 = (\mu_1/\mu_2)^{-\sigma} \dots\dots\dots\dots (20.6)$$

Our investor expects environment 1 with probability ε_1 and environment 2 with probability $\varepsilon_2 = 1 - \varepsilon_1$. He wishes to choose a value of α so as to maximize his expected utility,

$$\mathscr{E}(U) = \varepsilon_1 U(F_1) + \varepsilon_2 U(F_2) \dots\dots\dots\dots\dots\dots\dots\dots (20.7)$$

If we differentiate 20.7 in respect to α, using 20.2 and 20.5, we obtain:

$$d\mathscr{E}(U)/d\alpha = K\{\varepsilon_1\mu_1(\bar{e}_1 - \bar{m}_1) + \varepsilon_2\mu_2(\bar{e}_2 - \bar{m}_2)\} \quad\dots\dots\dots (20.8)$$

---

[5] If the money price of F moves from 1 to f between today and tomorrow and if the money prices of M and E move from 1 to m and e respectively, then $\bar{m} = m/f = (1 + i)/f$ and $\bar{e} = e/f$.

Since ε_1, ε_2 and K are constants > 0, the expression in 20.8 will be $\gtrless 0$ as both $(\bar{e}_1 - \bar{m}_1)$ and $(\bar{e}_2 - \bar{m}_2)$ are simultaneously $\gtrless 0$, provided that μ_1 and μ_2 have not both fallen to zero, i.e. provided that the investor's prospects have not become so rosy by being able to bet on a certainty that the marginal utility of F in both environments has fallen to zero. In other words, if in both environments the real value of shares is expected to rise more (or to fall less) than the real value of money, then our investor would wish to borrow in addition to his own capital ($\alpha > 1$) sufficient money to invest in shares to satiate all his needs in both environments. Conversely, if in both environments the real value of shares is expected to rise less (or to fall more) than the real value of money, he will want today to borrow shares (to be repaid tomorrow in shares) ($\alpha < 0$) on a sufficient scale to be able to acquire an amount of money which will satiate all his needs in both environments tomorrow.[6]

The possibility examined in the last paragraph is in fact totally unrealistic. Even in a generally inflationary atmosphere there is always some possibility, however small, that shares between today and tomorrow will do worse than money. We have assumed that our investor knows for certain ($\varepsilon_1 + \varepsilon_2 = 1$) that there are only two possible environmental outcomes with $\bar{e}_1$ and $\bar{m}_1$ in the one case and $\bar{e}_2$ and $\bar{m}_2$ in the other case. In fact, he will always be faced with a very large number of possible outcomes, in some of which shares will do less well than money, even though the expectational weights —the 'ε's—to be attached to these outcomes are small. Indeed, the number of possible environmental outcomes is so great that no investor today could possibly make a precise calculation covering all possible outcomes; at best he can make a representative calculation covering a few typical cases; but to be properly representative these cases must include some with $(\bar{e} - \bar{m}) > 0$ and some with $(\bar{e} - \bar{m}) < 0$.

The illustration with only two precisely defined environmental outcomes as expressed in 20.8 must be taken to cover both the possibility that shares will do better than money and the possibility that money will do better than shares. Accordingly, we will consider only the case where $(\bar{e}_1 - \bar{m}_1)$ and $(\bar{e}_2 - \bar{m}_2)$ have opposite signs. Suppose $(\bar{e}_1 - \bar{m}_1) > 0$ and $(\bar{e}_2 - \bar{m}_2) < 0$, i.e. that in environment 1 the real value of shares will rise relatively to the real value of money, and conversely in environment 2. Then, for $\mathscr{E}(U)$ to be a maximum, α must be chosen so that the expression in 20.8 is zero, i.e.:

$$\mu_1/\mu_2 = \varepsilon_2(\bar{m}_2 - \bar{e}_2)/(\varepsilon_1(\bar{e}_1 - \bar{m}_1)) \dots \dots (20.9)$$

---

[6] Of course, institutional factors may limit the amounts of money or of shares which he can in fact borrow.

This expression has a straightforward economic meaning. From 20.2 we have $dF_1 = K(\bar{e}_1 - \bar{m}_1)\,d\alpha$ and $dF_2 = -K(\bar{m}_2 - \bar{e}_2)\,d\alpha$ so that:

$$\gamma \equiv -\,dF_2/dF_1 = (\bar{m}_2 - \bar{e}_2)/(\bar{e}_1 - \bar{m}_1) \dots\dots\dots\dots (20.10)$$

where γ measures the marginal rate at which F_2 can be exchanged for F_1 by varying α. Equation (20.9) can then be expressed as

$$\varepsilon_1\mu_1/\varepsilon_2\mu_2 = (\bar{m}_2 - \bar{e}_2)/(\bar{e}_1 - \bar{m}_1) = \gamma \dots\dots\dots\dots (20.11)$$

which states that, in order to maximize expected utility, α must be so chosen that F_1 and F_2 are such that the marginal rate of exchange between them is equal to the ratio between their marginal utilities, weighted by the degree of confidence with which each outcome is expected.

From 20.6 and 20.9 we obtain

$$F_1/F_2 = \{\varepsilon_2(\bar{m}_2 - \bar{e}_2)/(\varepsilon_1(\bar{e}_1 - \bar{m}_1)\}^{-\sigma} \dots\dots\dots\dots (20.12)$$

and from 20.3 and 20.12 we obtain:

$$\frac{(1 - \alpha)\bar{m}_1 + \alpha\bar{e}_1}{(1 - \alpha)\bar{m}_2 + \alpha\bar{e}_2} = \left\{\frac{\varepsilon_2\,\bar{m}_2 - \bar{e}_2}{\varepsilon_1\,\bar{e}_1 - \bar{m}_1}\right\}^{-\sigma} \dots\dots\dots\dots (20.13)$$

and solving 20.13 for α we have:

$$\alpha = \frac{\bar{m}_2\{\varepsilon_1(\bar{e}_1 - \bar{m}_1)\}^{\sigma} - \bar{m}_1\{\varepsilon_2(\bar{m}_2 - \bar{e}_2)\}^{\sigma}}{(\bar{m}_2 - \bar{e}_2)\{\varepsilon_1(\bar{e}_1 - \bar{m}_1)\}^{\sigma} + (\bar{e}_1 - \bar{m}_1)\{\varepsilon_2(\bar{m}_2 - \bar{e}_2)\}^{\sigma}}$$

$$\dots\dots\dots\dots (20.14)$$

which expresses in terms of the given parameters ε_1, ε_2, $\bar{m}_1$, $\bar{m}_2$, $\bar{e}_1$, $\bar{e}_2$ and σ the value which α must take in order to maximize expected utility when $(\bar{e}_1 - \bar{m}_1)$ and $(\bar{e}_2 - \bar{m}_2)$ take opposite signs.

Of course, if institutional arrangements were such as to prevent any borrowing of money or of shares, equation 20.14 would be subject to the constraint $0 \leqslant \alpha \leqslant 1$. In the absence of this constraint, our investor may borrow money or shares; but with the utility function specified in 20.4 he will have no incentive to borrow more money or more shares than he can repay. Suppose, for example, that he expects with a very high probability that shares will do very well relatively to money and only with a very low probability that money might do a little better than shares ($\varepsilon_1[\bar{e}_1 - \bar{m}_1]$ very large relatively to $\varepsilon_2[\bar{m}_2 - \bar{e}_2]$). We shall have $\alpha > 1$. But the investor must be prepared in the improbable event of shares doing badly to repay his money debt without having to reduce his command over final goods (F_2) below zero. From 20.2 we can see that $F_2 \geqslant 0$

implies:

$$\alpha \leqslant \overline{m}_2/(\overline{m}_2 - \overline{e}_2) \dots\dots\dots\dots\dots\dots\dots\dots\dots (20.15)$$

Conversely if he borrows shares ($\alpha < 0$), he must be prepared in the event of money doing badly to be able to repay his shares without reducing F_1 below zero. From 20.2 this implies:

$$\alpha \geqslant - \overline{m}_1/(\overline{e}_1 - \overline{m}_1) \dots\dots\dots\dots\dots\dots\dots\dots (20.16)$$

But from 20.14 we can see that α is a weighted average of $\overline{m}_2/(\overline{m}_2 - \overline{e}_2)$ and $-\overline{m}_1/(\overline{e}_1 - \overline{m}_1)$, the weights being $(\overline{m}_2 - \overline{e}_2) \{\varepsilon_1(\overline{e}_1 - \overline{m}_1)\}^\sigma$ and $(\overline{e}_1 - \overline{m}_1) \{\varepsilon_2(\overline{m}_2 - \overline{e}_2)\}^\sigma$. It follows, therefore, directly from 20.14 that $\overline{m}_2/(\overline{m}_2 - \overline{e}_2) > \alpha > -\overline{m}_1/(\overline{e}_1 - \overline{m}_1)$, so that, if our investor maximizes in conformity with 20.14, he will in any case satisfy the conditions 20.15 and 20.16, or in other words he will never be tempted to borrow what he cannot repay. With the utility function given in 20.4 the possibility, however remote, of F_1 or F_2 being reduced to zero is too horrific for him to contemplate.

The expression for α given in 20.14 is in terms of the future values of M and E measured in real values in terms of $F(\overline{m}$ and $\overline{e})$. By substituting m/f for $\overline{m}$ and e/f for $\overline{e}$ in 20.14 we obtain:

$$\alpha = \frac{m_2 f_1 \{\varepsilon_1 f_2(e_1 - m_1)\}^\sigma - m_1 f_2 \{\varepsilon_2 f_1(m_2 - e_2)\}^\sigma}{(m_2 - e_2) f_1 \{\varepsilon_1 f_2(e_1 - m_1)\}^\sigma + (e_1 - m_1) f_2 \{\varepsilon_2 f_1(m_2 - e_2)\}^\sigma}$$

$$\dots\dots\dots\dots (20.17)$$

which gives the expression for α in terms of the three money prices m, e and f instead of the two real prices $\overline{m}$ and $\overline{e}$.[7]

Let us consider a number of special cases in terms of 20.17 with the object of illustrating the effect of expected movements in the money prices of final goods (f_1 and f_2) on the choice between M and E in an investor's portfolio. In all these cases we will assume that no interest is payable on M so that the value of \$1 worth of M is \$1 tomorrow whatever may happen; or in other words $m_1 = m_2 = 1$.

CASE I

If $\sigma = 0$ then from 20.17:

$$\alpha = (f_1 - f_2)/\{(1 - e_2)f_1 + (e_1 - 1)f_2\} \dots\dots\dots (20.18)$$

where $1 - e_2$ is the proportional fall in the money price of E if environmental 2 materializes and $e_1 - 1$ is the proportional rise in the money price of E if environment 1 materializes. This case with $\sigma = 0$ is the case where the investor considers only safety quite regardless of yield. He will not contemplate a possible reduction in

[7] See footnote 5.

F_2, however slight and however improbable, for any increase in F_1, however great and however probable. The formula in 20.18 could in fact be derived by putting $F_1 = F_2$ in 20.3.

It follows from 20.18 that if $f_1/f_2 = 1$ then $\alpha = 0$. This is the case in which the money price of final goods will be the same in environments 1 and 2 so that money is the perfectly safe asset. But if $f_1/f_2 = e_1/e_2$, then from 20.18, $\alpha = 1$. This is the case where the real purchasing power of E will be the same in both environments $(\bar{e}_1 = e_1/f_1 = e_2/f_2 = \bar{e}_2)$ so that E is the riskless asset. An intermediate case is where $1 < f_1/f_2 < e_1/e_2$, which would occur if the money prices of final goods were affected in the same direction as, but to a smaller degree than, the money prices of shares by environmental events. In this case $0 < \alpha < 1$,[8] so that only a mixture of E and M will give a riskless result.

The fact that in our example, our investor can achieve complete certainty in terms of final goods is due to the fact that in our example there are only two environmental outcomes while there are two assets (E and M) which fare very differently in the two environments. If there were three environmental outcomes and only two assets which fared very differently in the three environments, it would no longer be possible for our investor to choose a combination of E and M which would give the same outcome in terms of F in all three environments.[9]

CASE II

If $f_1/f_2 = \varepsilon_1(e_1 - 1)/\varepsilon_2(1 - e_2)$, then from 20.17, regardless of the value of σ, we obtain the same expression for α as that given in 20.18 which in this case can be expressed as:

$$\alpha = \{\varepsilon_1(e_1 - 1) - \varepsilon_2(1 - e_2)\}/(e_1 - 1)(1 - e_2) \quad \dots \dots (20.19)$$

when $f_1/f_2 = \varepsilon_1(e_1 - 1)/\varepsilon_2(1 - e_2)$. The meaning of this is clear. From 20·9 we know that to maximize, $\mathscr{E}(U)$, F_1 and F_2 must be so adjusted that $\mu_1/\mu_2 = \varepsilon_2(\bar{m}_2 - \bar{e}_2)/\varepsilon_1(\bar{e}_1 - \bar{m}_1) = \varepsilon_2 f_1(1 - e_2)/\varepsilon_1 f_2(e_1 - 1)$,

---

[8] From 20.18, $\alpha = (f_1 - f_2)/\{(f_1 - f_2) + (e_1 f_2 - e_2 f_1)\}$. Since in this case both $(e_1 f_2 - e_2 f_1)$ and $(f_1 - f_2)$ are > 0, we have $0 < \alpha < 1$.

[9] If there are m possible environments and n different assets, if $\bar{p}_{ij}$ represents tomorrow's price in terms of F of the jth asset in the ith environment, and if α_j represents the proportion of the investor's capital (K) invested today in asset j then the investor can obtain the same outcome (F) in all environments only if the '$\bar{p}$'s are such that a solution for the $n + 1$ unknowns $\alpha_1, \alpha_2, \dots, \alpha_m$ and F can be obtained from the following $m + 1$ equations:

$$K(\bar{p}_{11}\alpha_1 + \dots + \bar{p}_{ij}\alpha_j + \dots + \bar{p}_{1n}\alpha_n) - F = 0$$

$$K(\bar{p}_{i1}\alpha_1 + \dots + \bar{p}_{ij}\alpha_j + \dots + \bar{p}_{in}\alpha_n) - F = 0$$

$$K(\bar{p}_{m1}\alpha_1 + \dots + \bar{p}_{mj}\alpha_j + \dots + p_{mn}\alpha_n) - F = 0$$

$$\alpha_1 + \dots + \quad \alpha_j + \dots + \quad \alpha_n \quad = 1$$

which in this special case we are assuming to be equal to unity. But with diminishing marginal utility μ_1 will equal μ_2 only when F_1 equals F_2. But this means that α must be so chosen as to give the same certain yield in terms of F, whatever the environment. In other words the expression given in 20.18 for Case I is relevant; and this, with the special value assumed for f_1/f_2, gives the formula in 20.19.

CASE III

If $\sigma = 1$, we have from 20.17 the result:

$$\alpha = \{\varepsilon_1(e_1 - 1) - \varepsilon_2(1 - e_2)\}/(e_1 - 1)(1 - e_2) \quad \ldots \ldots \quad (20.20)$$

which is the same as the expression for α given in 20.19, but in this case the equation is valid regardless of the value of f_1/f_2.

The economic interpretation of the irrelevance of f_1/f_2 to the optimum value of α is clear. From 20.10 we have

$$\gamma = \varepsilon_2 f_1(1 - e_2)/\varepsilon_1 f_2(e_1 - 1)$$

so that $\partial\gamma/\gamma = \partial(f_1/f_2)/(f_1/f_2)$; or, in other words, a 1% rise in f_1/f_2 would itself cause a 1% rise in the rate at which F_2 could be exchanged for F_1.

From 20.3 we have

$$F_1/F_2 = f_2\{(1 - \alpha)m_1 + \alpha e_1\}/f_1\{(1 - \alpha)m_2 + \alpha e_2\}$$

so that $\partial(F_2/F_1)/(F_2/F_1) = \partial(f_1/f_2)/(f_1/f_2)$; or, in other words, at any given value of α the ratio of total F_2 to total F_1, would rise by 1% if f_1/f_2 rose by 1%.

From 20.6 with $\sigma = 1$ we have $d(\mu_1/\mu_2)/(\mu_1/\mu_2) = d(F_2/F_1)/(F_2/F_1)$; or, in other words, with a 1% rise in the ratio of F_2 to F_1 there would be a 1% fall in the ratio of the marginal utility of F_2 to that of F_1.

It follows that a 1% rise in f_1/f_2 will, with α unchanged, cause a 1% fall in the marginal utility of F_2 relatively to the marginal utility of F_1. But this same rise in f_1/f_2 will have made it possible by varying α to obtain 1% more F_2 for each unit of F_1 given up. The fall in the marginal utility of F_2 will be exactly balanced by the fall in its cost; there will be no motive in fact to alter α because of a change in f_1/f_2, if α is already at its optimum level.

CASE IV

Suppose $\sigma \to \infty$; then from 20.17:

$$\alpha \to -1/(e_1 - 1) \text{ if } f_1/f_2 > \varepsilon_1(e_1 - 1)/\varepsilon_2(1 - e_2)$$

and

$$\alpha \to 1/(1 - e_2) \text{ if } f_1/f_2 < \varepsilon_1(e_1 - 1)/\varepsilon_2(1 - e_2). \quad \ldots \ldots \quad (20.21)$$

With $m_1 = m_2 = 1$ and with $\bar{m} = m/f$ and $\bar{e} = e/f$, we have $\bar{m}_1/(\bar{e}_1 - \bar{m}_1) = 1/(e_1 - 1)$ and $\bar{m}_2/(\bar{m}_2 - \bar{e}_2) = 1/(1 - e_2)$. In other words, the two limits for α given in 20.21 are the same as the two limits given in 20.15 and 20.16.

The economic interpretation is clear. $\sigma = \infty$ means that the investor pays no regard to risk but only to expected yield. The loss of one unit of F_1 weighted by its expectation is worthwhile if it will obtain more than one unit of F_2 weighted by its expectation, regardless of how low F_1 and how high F_2 already are, provided only that neither F_1 nor F_2 fall below zero.

From 20.2 and 20.10 we see that $\gamma = f_1(1 - e_2)/f_2(e_1 - 1)$ measures the extra amount of F_2 which can be obtained by giving up one unit of F_1 by decreasing α. It follows that α should be decreased (down to the limit which reduces F_1 to zero) if $\varepsilon_2(1 - e_2)f_1/\varepsilon_1(e_1 - 1)f_2 > 1$ and should be increased (up to the limit which reduces F_2 to zero) if $\varepsilon_2(1 - e_2)f_1/\varepsilon_1(e_1 - 1)f_2 < 1$.

CHAPTER XXI

FINANCIAL INTERMEDIARIES AND THE QUALITIES OF ASSETS

In the last chapter, when we were considering the possibilities for private economic decision-makers of holding various kinds of asset as a safeguard against residual uncertainty, we discussed the problem very generally in terms of the choice between (i) money and (ii) other assets, merely noting in passing that other assets in fact varied very much in their relevant characteristics. We must now consider the various qualities of different assets in more detail.

The ultimate beneficiaries from assets are individual citizens; the basic real things which enable assets to be beneficial to people are the real capital goods of the community—land and other natural resources, houses, factory buildings, plant, equipment, durable consumption goods, stocks of raw materials, of half-finished goods, and of finished goods, and so on. If individual citizens owned directly real capital goods of this kind and nothing else, the problem would be simply to consider what types of real property were most versatile and flexible in their uses. We have already made reference to this aspect of the matter, stressing the fact that in conditions of residual uncertainty there will be a motive to install capital equipment which is less rigidly specialized and less long-lasting than would otherwise be the case.

But there are in society many corporate institutions which act as intermediaries between the assets from which the individuals ultimately but indirectly benefit (i.e. the assets owned by the corporate intermediary) and the assets from which the individuals directly benefit, that is to say, which they actually own themselves (i.e. the 'liabilities' of the corporate institution to the individuals to whom it is 'indebted'). In a modern society we may note five types of such intermediary.

(1) There are productive companies which own land, plant machinery, stocks of raw materials, etc., and use these to produce other goods and services. These companies may have raised the funds[1] necessary to acquire and hold these real assets by the issue

---

[1] In what follows we shall use 'bills' to represent all short-term borrowings and 'bonds' to represent all long-term borrowings.

of bills, by the issue of bonds, or by the issue of equities or ordinary shares which give to their owners not a direct ownership of the company's machines, etc., but a right to participate in any profits which it may make. Individuals can own bills, bonds, and equities which are issued by the company which in turn owns the real property.

(2) There are central governments and other public authorities who may own real property (e.g. government offices, the plant and equipment of, for example, the Post Office, and so on) and this property may have been acquried by borrowing from the public in the form of the issue of governmental debt, whether of short-term bills or of long-term bonds.

Because of their possession of a compulsory taxing power, governmental authorities differ in one very important way from all other intermediaries. If a government has financed its purchases of real property in the past from taxation and not by borrowing, it may own real property in excess of the governmental debt issued to, and held by, the private sector of the economy. On the other hand, it may have borrowed in the past to finance current as well as capital expenditure; in this case the debt issued by the government may at any one time greatly exceed the value of the real property owned by it, the debt nevertheless maintaining its value because of the government's power to use taxation to meet interest and repayment obligations on the debt.

(3) There are a whole range of financial institutions which we will divide into (i) banks and (ii) other financial institutions. Let us first consider these other financial institutions. They can be of the most varied kind but we will illustrate the sort of arrangements which occur by considering insurance companies and building societies. An insurance company owns assets which may take the form of real property but are still more likely to take the form of the financial liabilities of other intermediaries (e.g. bills and bonds issued by the government or bills, bonds, or equities issued by productive companies). Individuals in turn in addition to owning insurance shares or equities giving them a right to participate in any profits made by the insurance company also own insurance policies which are the obligations of the insurance company to pay out funds in certain contingencies (e.g. on the death of the insured or on the destruction of his house by fire). A building society is a body which holds as its main assets mortgages on houses which are obligations of the house owners to pay given sums to the building society or to surrender the houses to the building society; against this other individuals own shares or deposits with the building society which represent an indebtedness on the part of the society to repay at

short notice the capital sum of money lent by the individual depositors to the society.

(4) The banks constitute, as we shall see, a very special form of financial intermediary because their main liabilities consist of deposits of money, the ownership of which can be readily transferred by cheque from one depositor to another; this form of transfer of the ownership of a short-term debt of the bank has in fact become the main means of payment, replacing the actual handing over of cash (i.e. notes and coin) from a buyer to a seller. This provides the individual owner of the deposit with a very special form of asset, and against this the banks hold various assets; they will hold a small amount of real assets (their own buildings and equipment), but in the main they will hold the short-term and long-term debts (bills and bonds) of other individuals and institutions, both governmental and private.

(5) We must, however, distinguish between the ordinary banks (described in the previous paragraph) and the central bank. In most modern free enterprise economies, there are a number of competing ordinary banks (we will call them commercial banks). When a payment is made by cheque by a depositor in one commercial bank to a depositor in another commercial bank, the former bank must have some means of transferring funds (i.e. of some part of its own assets) to the recipient commercial bank. This mechanism is provided by means of a central bank. Each commercial bank holds among its assets a deposit of money with the central bank (i.e. an obligation on the part of the central bank to pay cash to the commercial bank on demand). Commercial bank A pays commercial bank B by transferring part of A's deposit with the central bank to the ownership of B.

But what in the end is money itself? Consider an insurance policy, which is an obligation on the part of insurance company A to pay $1000 to citizen B's heir, namely C, when B dies. B dies. A pays C by drawing a cheque on A's deposit with commercial bank D. But C wishes to add to his deposit with commercial bank E. D pays E by transferring part of D's deposit with the central bank F to E. But D's (and now E's) deposit with F is a right of D (and now of E) to demand a payment of $1000 from F. But what is this right? We can consider this best by supposing that C wanted not to add to his deposit with E but to obtain 'real money'. What would he have obtained and how would he have obtained it?

Here we reach the ultimate modern financial make-belief. Legal tender money is that thing, denominated in the unit of account (e.g. in terms of dollars) the payment of which is held in law to satisfy the obligation to pay any debt expressed in the unit of account (in our example, the $1,000 owed by the insurance company to C.) And this legal tender money is nowadays, in a modern free enterprise economy, often defined as the notes issued by the central bank. Now the notes issued by the central bank do not differ in any meaningful economic way from the deposit liabilities of the central bank.[2] We will assume that the only form of legal tender money are the notes issued by the central bank.[3]

The central bank often, in addition, acts as the government's banker, with whom the government holds its deposits of money to finance its day-to-day payments. The central bank will, therefore, have as its liabilities (i) all notes or legal tender money held throughout the economy; (ii) its deposit liabilities to the commercial banks; and (iii) its deposit liability to the government. Against this, it will hold assets which normally take the form of short-term and long-term debt of the government.

In what follows, we shall assume that the central bank holds only governmental bills and bonds. This assumption needs consideration in view of the fact that the central bank must play the role of 'lender in the last resort'. Suppose that, for some reason or another, individual owners of deposits with the commercial banks and other financial institutions wish simultaneously on a large scale to change their deposits into legal tender money, i.e. notes. Each bank and other financial institution will normally have only a fraction of its deposit liabilities covered with its holdings of notes or of deposits with another bank or financial institution. In so far as any one of the banks or financial institutions tries to cash its deposits with another such institution, it merely passes the problem on to that other member of the group. In the end, as a group, they can obtain notes to encash their deposit liabilities to individual depositors only by (i) using up their own holdings of notes; (ii) cashing their own deposits with the central bank in which case the central bank will simply substitute its notes issued for its deposit liabilities to the commercial banks; or (iii) directly or indirectly selling some other form of asset to the central bank in return for a new issue of notes. Being lender in the last resort means essentially that the central bank must be prepared to employ (iii) if the resources under (i) and (ii) are insufficient.

[2] In the United Kingdom notes issued by the Bank of England are legal tender. But what is a Bank of England note? If one examines a Bank of England £1 note one sees written on it: "I promise to pay the bearer on demand the sum of One Pound" signed by the Chief Cashier of the Bank of England, who, if asked to redeem this obligation, could legally satisfy it by handing a £1 note to the owner of the £1 note in exchange for his £1 note.

[3] Coin has in fact become a very small part of the circulation of cash in a modern free enterprise economy.

But there are many ways in which (iii) can be performed. Broadly speaking, the commercial banks can (i) borrow from the central bank, i.e. sell to the central bank for newly issued notes some bills issued by the commercial banks; (ii) recall commercial bank loans to other financial institutions (e.g. the discount houses) who then sell bills (e.g. government bills) to the central bank for newly issued notes; or (iii) sell bills (e.g. government bills at present held by the commercial banks) to the central bank for newly issued notes. Method (i) would involve the central bank holding assets other than government debt. We assume that either method (ii) or method (iii) is used, only because the exposition will be simpler if we can treat the central bank merely as an agent dealing in government debt. The basic analysis is not affected.

To return to our main theme, the effect of financial intermediation is to place some financial institution between the individual owner of property and the ultimate real property plus net government debt which is to be held by the private sector of the economy. But this link between ultimate individual property owners on the one hand and ultimate real property on the other may not in every case be provided directly. Intermediary A may have as part of its liabilities, not a liability to an ultimate individual, but a liability to another intermediary, and may hold as part of its assets, not real property or government debt, but the liabilities of another intermediary. The whole resulting possible structure of assets and liabilities is illustrated in Table VII.

In that table we assume that there are only seven forms of asset: (1) A or real property; (2) N or legal tender money, i.e. the notes issued by the central bank; (3) D or the deposit liabilities of various financial institutions, i.e. obligations to produce on demand a given amount of N; (4) S or bills which represent all other forms of short-term debt; (5) L or bonds which represent long-term debt; (6) E or equities which represent the rights to participate in the profits of an enterprise, such as are provided by the ordinary shares issued by a company; and (7) I or insurance policies, which are taken to represent obligations to pay certain sums in the case of specified contingencies. We assume, also, that holders of assets can be divided into the various categories discussed above: namely, individuals (denoted by a subscript i), productive companies (subscript p), other financial institutions (subscript o), commercial banks (subscript c), the central bank (subscript b), and the government (subscript g). Issuers of assets include the above holders of assets plus an additional 'issuer' which we have called the 'real world', which must be regarded as 'issuing' land, buildings, machinery, stocks, etc., to be held by the various asset holders. A

Table VII

	Individuals		Productive Companies			Other Financial Institutions					Commercial Banks		Central Bank			Government		Real World
Assets Held by	$_iS$	$_iL$	$_pS$	$_pL$	$_pE$	$_oD$	$_oS$	$_oL$	$_oE$	$_oI$	$_cD$	$_cE$	$_bN$	$_bD$	$_bE$	$_gS$	$_gL$	A
Individuals N_i													$_bN_i$					
D_i						$_oD_i$					$_cD_i$		0					
S_i	$_iS_i$		$_pS_i$				$_oS_i$									$_gS_i$		
L_i		$_iL_i$		$_pL_i$				$_oL_i$									$_gL_i$	
E_i					$_pE_i$				$_oE_i$			$_cE_i$			0			
I_i										$_oI_i$								
A_i																		A_i
Productive Companies N_p													$_bN_p$					
D_p						$_oD_p$					D_p		0					
S_p	0		$_pS_p$				$_oS_p$									$_gS_p$		
L_p		0		$_pL_p$				$_oL_p$									$_gL_p$	
E_p					$_pE_p$				$_oE_p$			E_p			0			
I_p										$_oI_p$								
A_p																		A_p
Other Financial Institutions N_o													$_bN_o$					
D_o						$_oD_o$					D_o		0					
S_o	$_iS_o$		$_pS_o$				$_oS_o$									$_gS_o$		
L_o		$_iL_o$		$_pL_o$				$_oL_o$									$_gL_o$	
E_o					$_pE_o$				$_oE_o$			$_cE_o$			0			
A_o																		A_o
Commercial Banks N_c						0					0		$_bN_c$					
D_c	$_iS_c$		$_pS_c$											$_bD_c$				
S_c							$_oS_c$									$_gS_c$		
L_c		0		$_pL_c$				$_oL_c$									$_gL_c$	
E_c					$_pE_c$				$_oE_c$			0			0			
A_c																		A_c
Central Bank S_b	0		0			0										$_gS_b$		
L_b		0		0				0									$_gL_b$	
Government N_g						0					0		$_bN_g$					
D_g														$_bD_g$				
E_g					0							$_cE_g$			$_bE_g$			
A_g																		A_g

subscript before an asset denotes the issuer of that asset, and a subscript after an asset denotes the holder of that asset. Thus $_pE_i$ represents the equities issued by productive companies and held by individuals. $_pE$ represents the total of equities issued by productive companies, no matter who holds them; and E_i represents the total of equities owned by individuals, no matter who issued them.[4]

Thus, looking down any one column in the table, one can see the distribution among different holders of the total of one particular kind of asset issued by one particular issuer. And looking along any one row of the table, one can see the distribution by issuers of any one particular kind of asset held by any one particular sort of holder.[5] All the blank cells in the matrix in the table refer to elements that cannot logically exist. A deposit issued by issuer A can only be held as a deposit (and not as an equity or an insurance policy) by holder B. It is therefore, only the intersection of a deposit column with a deposit row that can have meaning; all other intersections of deposit column are blank. The cells which contain a zero are cells which could logically be filled but which we assume by law or institutional custom always to be empty. Thus, looking down the first two columns, it will be seen that individuals are assumed never to borrow from the central bank or from productive companies and to borrow only on short-term (bills) from the commercial banks. Or looking along the two rows referring to the central bank, we see that that institution is assumed to hold no bills or bonds issued by individuals, productive companies, or other financial institutions, but only governmental debt. And looking down the three central bank columns, one sees that while its notes are held by all types of asset holders, its deposits are owned only by commercial banks and the government, while the whole of its equity is assumed to be owned by the government.

Moreover, certain other elements which could logically exist do not exist in the table because we have assumed that, for similar legal or customary institutional reasons, some forms of assets are never issued at all by certain issuers or never held at all by certain holders. Thus, while individuals are assumed to hold all seven types of asset (see the first seven rows of the table), they are assumed only to issue bills and bonds, i.e. to borrow on short or long-term from various institutions (see the first two columns of the table); by assumption

[4] In Table VII, the various assets—*A, N, D, S, L, E* and *I*—are all measured in money values. The money value of the *E* issued by any one issuer represents the net worth of that issuer (i.e. the difference between the value of the assets which it holds and the value of the other assets which it has issued). It follows that if, for example, the money price of some real capital good goes up, so that this element of *A* goes up, the *E* issued by the holders of this element of *A* will go up by an equal amount.

[5] It is to be noted that the real world only issues assets. It does not itself hold any.

they do not, for example, issue insurance policies; thus, $_iI_p$ (insurance policies issued by individuals to productive companies)—a logical possibility—is not shown in the table simply because no column for $_iI$ exists in the table so that the cell for $_iI_p$ is not displayed.

The reader must be left, by considering what possible columns and rows are omitted and by examining the cells marked with a zero in the intersections of those columns and rows which are displayed, to work out for himself the details of the institutional assumptions illustrated in the table. He can construct any number of similar tables for himself with simpler or more elaborate sub-divisions of classes of assets and of asset issuers and asset holders and with different assumptions about the legal or institutional structure of the type of assets issued by, and held by, each type of issuer and holder. Table VII is put forward merely as an illustration of what the present author considers to be the most salient relationships in a modern free enterprise capital market.

In any case, it should be apparent that the interlacings on a modern capital market can be very complicated. We shall use Table VII from time to time in what follows to illustrate the relevance of some of these interlacings. But before we do that it is useful to show what happens when we net out all the intermediary issuers and holders. Every element in Table VII is both an asset issued by some agent (named at the top of the table) and an asset held by some agent (named at the left-hand side of the table); thus the total of assets issued is equal to the total of assets held. Let T stand for the total value of assets issued or held by a particular issuer or holder, the particular issuer being denoted as before by a subscript before T and the particular holder by a subscript after T. Then we have:

$$\text{Total Assets Issued} = {}_iT + {}_pT + {}_oT + {}_cT + {}_bT + {}_gT + A$$
$$= \text{Total Assets Held} = T_i + T_p + T_o + T_c + T_b + T_g$$

But we suppose that in the case of productive companies, other financial institutions, commercial banks, and the central bank, assets issued must equal assets held; the balance sheet must balance if, in the case of all private institutions, we define the equity as covering the whole of the excess of the value of assets held over the value of liabilities. But if $_pT = T_p, {}_oT = T_o, {}_cT = T_c$ and $_bT = T_b$, we obtain from the above relationship $(T_i - {}_iT) = A + ({}_gT - T_g)$ or the net excess of individual assets over liabilities is equal to the value of the community's real property plus what we may call the governmental deadweight debt or the excess of its debt over the value of any assets which it may hold. With the description of assets held and issued implied in Table VII we obtain

$$N_i + D_i + (S_i - {}_iS) + (L_i - {}_iL) + E_i + I_i + A_i$$
$$= A + ({}_gS + {}_gL - N_g - D_g - E_g - A_g)$$

or the notes, deposits, net bills, net bonds, equities, insurance policies and real property owned by individuals is equal to the total real property in the community plus the governmental deadweight debt, i.e. its short-term and long-term debt net of any money, deposits, equities, or real property which the government may itself own.

Financial intermediation cannot, of course, in itself, alter the nature of the real resources of the community—the land, buildings, machinery, stocks of raw materials, etc.,—which are to be held. But it can greatly affect the nature of the assets held by the individual citizens. By forming a corporate group which holds property in common, individuals can change the nature of the rights which they own.

Consider the equities of a productive company. The actual physical plant and equipment owned by a productive company makes up one single complex whole as a going concern. One cannot have one individual owning this brick on the factory wall and another owning that brick, each deciding whether this is the best use which is being made of his particular brick.[6] One man could own the whole business. But even if an individual were rich enough to do so, he might well prefer to spread his risk by owning instead a part share in many businesses instead of the whole of one business. The issue of ordinary shares (equities) by a joint stock company enables individuals to own rights to part shares in the profit-making capacity of a company, while the company itself owns the actual indivisible physical resources.

Moreover, a company may finance its investment in physical equipment not merely by increasing the equity issue[7] but by borrowing through the issue of bills or bonds to be purchased by other individuals. Those who acquire the company's bills and bonds acquire a right to certain money payments of interest and repayment of capital. They, unlike the owners of the equities, do not share in

---

[6] We now approach the problem of indivisibilities, assumed away by assumption 7 on page 27 of *The Stationary Economy*, but which we hope to discuss fully in a subsequent volume.

[7] In so far as a company finances new investment out of its own profits which it refrains from distributing to the ordinary shareholders, it increases the value of the profit earning capacity of the company and so the value of the existing shares. This we treat as an additional 'issue' of equities by the company to the existing shareholders.

the chance of a high income if the company does well and (apart from the ultimate risk of the company going bankrupt and defaulting on its obligation) they do not face the risk of a low income if it does badly. The more bills and bonds the company issues, the greater the risks born by the owners of the equity. Thus suppose the company faces an equal chance of earning \$150,000 and \$50,000 on real capital costing \$1,000,000. If there are no bills and bonds outstanding, the equity owners will receive an equal chance of earning \$150,000 or \$50,000 on \$1,000,000, i.e. of earning 15% or 5% on their money.

But suppose now that half or \$500,000 of the real capital of the company has been financed by the issue of bonds on which interest of \$50,000 must be paid. The equity owners will have subscribed only the remaining \$500,000 of the capital of the company; but on this they now have an equal chance of \$150,000 − \$50,000 = \$100,000 and of \$50,000 − \$50,000 = \$0, i.e. an equal chance of 20% and 0%. Thus, by financing more of its capital requirements through the issue of fixed debt, the company can concentrate the risk bearing onto a smaller group of equity owners. Thus financial intermediation through joint stock companies enables the risk element in the real situation to be concentrated on those property owners who are most willing to undertake risks.

If we turn to 'other financial institutions' such as insurance companies and building societies the change in the nature of the assets owned by individuals through the corporate pooling of assets is even more apparent. If there is a 1 in 1,000 chance that any one house will be burnt down in the course of the year, this real risk is not changed by fire insurance. But the risk which the individual householder faces is, of course, completely transformed. By taking out an insurance policy issued by an insurance company he owns an asset which gives him a right to the value of his house if it is destroyed by fire. The insurance company in turn owns assets (e.g. bills and bonds issued by the government) which it can realize in money value at any time which is necessary to meet its contingent liabilities to householders. The insurance company by pooling the fire risks has converted the unconditional liability of the government (the government bills and bonds) into a large number of contingent liabilities to the individual householders. The risk of fire has not been affected; the burden of bearing the risk has been reduced by spreading it over a large body of householders.[8]

Building societies and ordinary commercial banks perform a different function through the pooling of individual resources. A

---

[8] Cf. the discussion of the problem in *The Growing Economy*, Chapter XXII.

building society lends money to persons to invest in houses; the building society raises the money for this purpose by borrowing money which is put on deposit with it by a large number of individual savers; these savers with deposits with the building society have the right to withdraw their deposits at short notice, though the loans made by the building society to the house owners cannot be recalled at short notice. The individual borrower (the individual house owner) wants a fairly long-term loan which he must repay with a fixed annual payment over a period of years; the individual lender (the individual depositor) wants to lend out his savings in a form in which he can get them back at short notice if any unexpected need should turn up. Just as the insurance company operates on the principle that, while any one particular house may be burnt down, not all will be burnt down at once, so the building society works on the principle that, while any one depositor may want to withdraw his deposit at any moment, not all depositors will want to do so at the same time. It is, therefore, sufficient for the building society to hold only a relatively small proportion of its own assets in a readily realizable form, even though all its deposit liabilities are readily realizable by its depositors. The financial intermediary in this case has turned long-term loans (to the individual householder) into short-term loans (by the individual depositor) through the pooling principle that not all short-term loans will be recalled at once.

Commercial banks perform this same function. They lend for longer periods, or invest in longer-term bonds, funds which have been deposited with them on conditions which allow the withdrawal of the funds on sight or at very short notice. A particular commercial bank (bank A) may lose funds either because a depositor with bank A asks bank A for cash or else because the depositor wishes to transfer by cheque his deposit to someone else who wishes to deposit the money with bank B, in which case bank A must transfer some of its own deposits with the central bank from its own ownership to that of bank B. But bank A keeps only a small proportion of its total deposit liabilities covered by cash and by its own deposit with the central bank because it knows that, while all its depositors have the right to cash their deposits or to transfer them to another bank, in fact they will not all want to do so at the same time. Moreover, it also knows that while some of its depositors will be withdrawing cash, others will be paying cash in, and that some depositors with banks B, C, D, etc., will be making transfers to people who bank with bank A at the same time that some who bank with bank A will be making transfers to people who bank with banks B, C, D, etc. The pooling principle again allows the banks to borrow short and lend long.

M

In a competitive economy, one must imagine various kinds of financial intermediary being set up, making use of the pooling principle in a number of different ways in order to alter the nature of the assets held by the ultimate individual asset holders. If the form of asset which they issue is more acceptable to the ultimate asset holder than the form of asset which the financial intermediary itself holds, there is scope for a profitable operation by the financial intermediary; for example, it can borrow short-term at a lower rate of interest than the long-term rate at which it lends, the margin being the price which the individual lender pays for the transfer of a long-term into a short-term tying up of his savings.

The result in a modern developed economy is a very large assortment of different kinds of assets which differ very much in their qualities and characteristics.

First, there are differences of probable yields. The financial intermediary often makes its living, as we have seen, by issuing assets with a relatively low yield and holding assets with a relatively high yield, giving in return some other quality in the assets which it issues such as certainty in place of risk, quick instead of slow realizability, and so on.

Secondly, different assets will vary in the transactions costs involved in transferring them from one ownership to another. A financial intermediary may hold assets with high transfer costs and issue assets with low transfer costs.

Thirdly, different assets will carry with them different degrees of risk that the issuer will default on his obligations.

Fourthly, different assets vary very greatly in the certainty attached to their monetary yields and the money value at which they can be realized.

We have already seen that the degree of risk attached to equities or participations in the right to profits depends not only upon whether the business itself is a risky one or not, but also upon the degree to which the business has been financed by the issue of bills and bonds.

There are also all sorts of contingency debts, that is to say, of assets which give the right to a definite sum of money, but only if some specified contingency is realized. Insurance policies are the most obvious form of this.[9]

In the case of ordinary debts (bills and bonds), the certainty of the value of the capital sum of the debt will vary greatly with the length of time before the debt is repayable. In the case of an

---

[9] But they are not the only possible form. Debts may include a price index clause by which the amount of money to be paid is a precisely defined sum which depends, however, upon the level of the money prices of goods and services in general when the debt comes to be paid.

irredeemable debt, e.g. a promise to pay $1 a year in perpetuity, the capital value of the debt will vary inversely with the rate of interest. Thus if the long-term rate of interest is 1 % per annum this debt will be worth $100, but if the rate of interest rises to 2 % per annum it will be worth only $50. Short-term debts—e.g. a bill which represents simply an obligation to pay $100 in, say, a year's time—will be liable to vary very much less with the rate of interest; if the rate of interest is 1 % per annum, it will now be worth approximately $99 and if the rate rises to 2 % per annum it will still be worth approximately $98.[10] Thus the capital value of a bill is a much more certain quantity than the capital value of a bond.

Fifthly, there remains one other very special characteristic of an asset, namely the degree to which it is in fact acceptable in lieu of actual legal tender money in the settlement of debt. This quality is possessed *par excellence* by the deposit liabilities of the commercial banks, the transfer of which by cheque from one owner to another is the most important means in fact for settling debts in the modern developed free enterprise economy. In fact, we may regard such bank deposits as being perfect substitutes for legal tender money. We shall use the term 'money', denoted by M, for notes plus the deposit of the commercial banks ($M = {}_bN + {}_cD$) i.e. for the sum of all instruments which are in fact used for the settlement of debts as if they were legal tender money.

But many assets which are not in fact actual substitutes for money, since they are not in fact generally acceptable in lieu of legal tender money for the settlement of debts, may nevertheless be almost as good as money because they can be readily exchanged at a certain value into money at little or no notice and with little or no cost. If an asset (such as a government bill) has little transactions cost, a low risk of default and a certain immediate money value, it may be held instead of money by a holder who feels that he may need money in the future; he can readily and quickly change it into money at a more or less certain value. Assets may be said to be 'liquid' in so far as they possess this characteristic of easy, costless, certain exchangeability into money; the more liquid are his other assets, the less actual money (notes and deposits) will any economic agent need to hold.

---

[10] The investor earns the capital appreciation from $98 to $100 on a capital investment of $98; and ($100 − $98)/$98 = $2/$98 = approximately 2 %.

CHAPTER XXII

MONETARY POLICY

At any one time in a modern developed free enterprise economy there will be a market for money and for various forms of capital asset of the kind depicted in Table VII. There will be various kinds of real and of financial assets issued and offered to the market by the real world (e.g. land, plant, equipment, etc.), by productive enterprises, by the government, by banks, and by other financial intermediaries. There will be various potential holders of these assets, namely individual citizens, productive enterprises, the government, banks and other financial intermediaries coming on to the market to invest their wealth in, and to hold, these various assets. The prices of these various assets relatively to each other—a set of relationships which can be expressed by the money price of each asset, if we take the asset 'money' as our numeraire—will move from day to day as the conditions of supply or of demand for the various assets change.

An adequate discussion of the facts which influence the demand and supply conditions for various assets on the capital market would require a long volume devoted exclusively to that subject and it is not the intention of the present author to embark on that work. Here it is possible to give merely one or two illustrations of some of the most important general factors at work, which will tend to change the demand for, relatively to the supply of, an asset.

(1) The current money price offered for any asset will be the higher, the higher is the future money yield expected to be earned on it. In some cases the future money yield is fixed and known for certain, as in the case of a government bond for which there is a quite negligible risk of default. But, in other cases, the money yield is not fixed or known for certain. Thus if anything happens in the economy to make it seem more probable than before that company A will do well and company B do badly in the future, the price of the equities of A will rise and of B will fall.

(2) There may be speculative influences of the kind described in Chapter V (pp. 61–6) affecting the demand for any one asset or group of assets. Future capital gains are as attractive as future income yields; and if the price of an asset is expected to rise in the future—

325

perhaps simply because it has been rising in the immediate past— then the present demand for it may be high. Indeed any one purchaser of the asset may think that in terms of probable future income yield it is basically overvalued, but if he believes that others are going to purchase the asset and drive its price up in spite of its relatively low future income yield, then he too will wish to purchase the asset now. Thus A may buy an asset X because he thinks B, C, D and E are going to purchase it, although he considers its price to be already high having regard to its future yield of income. At the same time B may be buying because he thinks that A, C, D and E are going to buy, although he (B) considers X to be basically overvalued. And thus, everyone may be speculating on everyone else's speculation. It is for this sort of reason that a capital market in fixed assets can show very marked fluctuations, fluctuations which are much more marked than the fluctuations which are occurring in those other underlying sections of the economy (for example, the labour market or the market for perishable consumer goods) where similar speculative epidemics cannot operate.

(3) Where the future income yield of the asset is fixed and known for certain but will in whole or part be received in the relatively distant future, the present price which people will pay for the asset will be greatly influenced by their expectations of the future course of interest rates. If the future course of short-term interest rates were known for certain, then the current price of an asset today (time 0) which would give certain money yields of B_1, B_2 and B_3 on days 1, 2, and 3 with zero yields thereafter would be given by the formula

$$P = \frac{B_1}{1 + i_0} + \frac{B_2}{(1 + i_0)(1 + i_1)} + \frac{B_3}{(1 + i_0)(1 + i_1)(1 + i_2)}$$

where i_0, i_1 and i_2 are the short-term rates of interest which will rule during days 0, 1, and 2 respectively. Clearly the present value of a bill (i.e. a promise to pay B_1 in a day's time and nothing thereafter) will depend solely on today's rate of interest (i_0), whereas the price of a longer-term bond (i.e. a promise to pay B_1 in a day's time, B_2 in two day's time, and so on) will also be affected by the future short term interest rates (i_1, i_2, etc.). An expectation that future interest rates will fall will, therefore, raise the price of bonds relatively to bills.[1]

(4) If all economic agents are risk averters, then, given the average expected future yield on an asset, an increase in the element of risk (e.g. a simultaneous increase in the possibility that the yield may be

[1] Or, in other words, it will reduce the long-term rate of interest relatively to the short-term interest rate. See the discussion of these relationships in *The Growing Economy*, pp. 313–8.

very much above or very much below the expected average yield) will reduce the demand for the asset. Thus events which make the future profitability of company A seem more risky and that of company B less risky are likely to cause a fall in the money price of A's equities and a rise in the money price of B's equities. There may, however, be changes—due, for example, to political events or to the appearance of very far-reaching possible technological changes—which increase risk simultaneously over a very wide range of economic activities. Such a change might cause a widespread shift from other assets into money or near substitutes for money (i.e. an increased demand for liquid assets, as defined on page 323), thus causing a fall in the money prices of a large range of real assets and of other non-liquid assets. This would be the case if the future course of the level of money prices for final goods and services in general were not itself made more uncertain by the events in question; economic decision-makers would be shifting from a wide range of real durable assets (each of whose future money value had become less certain) into money (whose future purchasing power in terms of final goods and services in general had not become less certain). But if the change were one which greatly increased the uncertainty as to what future monetary and fiscal policy would be and as to whether a general inflation or deflation were to be expected, the result might be exactly the opposite, namely a desire to shift from money and near substitutes for money into a wide range of real assets, thus causing an immediate inflation of their money prices.

(5) Finally, there may be policy changes on the part of governmental issuers and holders of assets which are designed expressly to alter the relative net supply of various assets to the private sector of the economy and thus to influence their prices. Our primary concern in this chapter is to consider the effects of such policy changes, given the current forces of the factors enumerated under items (1) to (4) above.

There are two kinds of financial intermediaries, namely the governmental and the banking authorities, who by altering the composition and scale of the assets which they issue and hold (as illustrated in Table VII) may take positive policy steps to affect prices on the capital market. In the rest of this chapter, we shall discuss what these steps might be, what their immediate effects on the capital market are likely to be and how these changes on the capital market may affect the demand for goods and services in the rest of the economy.

As far as the government is concerned, we will leave to the next chapter on fiscal policy any changes in governmental expenditures on real goods and services or any changes in rates of taxation which may alter the movement over time of the total of debt (bills and bonds) issued by the government. We consider in this chapter only a change in the composition of the national debt. Let us suppose, by way of illustration, that the government decides to unfund some part of the national debt, that is to say it borrows more money on short-term (issues more bills) and uses the proceeds to buy up part of its long-term debt (issues less bonds). There are now more bills and less bonds in the market; some individual citizens or financial institutions must be persuaded to shift from bonds to bills; this can only be done by lowering the price of bills relatively to that of bonds, so that the short-term rate of interest will go up and the long-term rate will go down.[2]

Let us suppose then that the immediate effect of the unfunding of part of the national debt is to cause a rise in the short-term, and a fall in the long-term rate of interest, or, in other words, a fall in bill prices and a rise in bond prices until certain holders of government bonds are prepared to hold government bills instead on a sufficient scale. There are now likely to be further repercussions on asset prices in so far as there are other substitutes for either (i) government bills and/or (ii) government bonds.

(i) Bills are liquid assets, which for many holders are near-substitutes for money. We assume for the present that no interest is payable on money (i.e. on notes issued by the central bank or on the deposit liabilities of the commercial banks). In this case, holders of money may wish to shift from money into bills on which a higher rate of interest can be earned. This will tend to keep up the money price of bills until people are willing to hold the existing amount of money together with the increased supply of bills as the appropriate form of being more liquid than before. But the more the money price of bills is maintained in this way, the greater, of course, must be the rise in the price of bonds in order to give people the necessary incentive to hold more bills and less bonds.

(ii) Government bonds are less liquid than bills because uncertainty as to what may happen to future interest rates introduces uncertainty as to what may happen to the money price of bonds. Bonds may to some holders be in competition to some degree with some other forms of assets whose future money value is uncertain, such as equities issued by some productive concerns. In so far as this is the case the rise in the price of bonds and the fall in the

---

[2] This is equivalent to a reduction in the actual 'forward' interest rates; and those economic agents will shift from bonds to bills who, as a result, are prepared to bet that the future 'spot' rates of interest will in fact be higher than the new 'forward' rates of interest. See *The Growing Economy*, p. 317.

average yield expected from bonds may cause some holders of bonds to wish to sell bonds and purchase equities. In so far as this is the case, the money price of equities will be driven up.

Thus, if we greatly simplify things by imagining only four types of asset in a linear progression of substitutability for each other from the most liquid to the most illiquid and risky, namely money → bills → bonds → equities, we can say that a rise in the amount of bills and a fall in the amount of bonds brought about by governmental debt management policy will (1) raise the money price of equities and will do so the more (i) the greater the substitutability between money and bills, (ii) the less the substitutability between bills and bonds, and (iii) the greater the substitutability between bonds and equities; (2) raise the short-term bill rate of interest; (3) lower the long-term bond rate of interest; and (4) cause asset holders to be in general more liquid than before since the total of liquid assets (money and bills) will have risen and the total of illiquid assets (bonds and equities) will have fallen.[3]

We have seen how the government, regarded as a financial intermediary, can alter the composition of assets on the capital market by funding or unfunding part of the national debt. Action by the central bank is of a similar kind except that the central bank can alter the composition of assets available to the other sectors of the economy on the capital market not merely by altering the supply of bills relatively to bonds, but also by altering the supply of money (i.e. of notes and deposits) relatively to bills and bonds. Thus the central bank can (i) sell some of the government bills which it holds and purchase bonds instead or vice versa; (ii) sell some of the government bills which it holds and cancel the money (i.e. the notes or its deposit liabilities to the commercial banks) with which the bills are bought from it or vice versa; or (iii) sell some of the government bonds which it holds and cancel the money with which the bonds are bought, or vice versa.

In so far as these transactions are simply between the central bank and the government, there will be no effect upon the supply/demand situation in the capital market for the private sectors of the economy. Thus if under (i) above when the central bank holds (i.e. purchases) less bills and more bonds, the government simply issues (i.e. sells) less bills and more bonds, there will be no change at

---

[3] The government will, of course, have become so much the less liquid since its liquid liabilities will be greater and its illiquid liabilities the smaller. But we are assuming that the government can just grin and bear it without any further consequential change in its actions, whereas we shall, later in this chapter, consider the effects of the greater liquidity in the private sector upon the decisions of economic agents in the private sector.

all in the market conditions for any assets. We assume that the government and the central bank are not at loggerheads, that they are operating a single financial policy and that we need, therefore, interest ourselves only in the combined effect of governmental debt policy and central bank monetary policy. For this purpose we need to examine a consolidated balance sheet of the government and the central bank. This is obtained by writing down as the combined assets issued by the government and the central bank all the items in the columns of Table VII marked $_bN$, $_bD$, $_bE$, $_gS$ and $_gL$ as assets issued, by writing down all the items in the rows of the Table marked S_b, L_b, N_g, D_g, E_g and A_g as assets held, and by cancelling all the items which appear in both lists (i.e. which are a liability of the government to the central bank or of the central bank to the government.) The result is shown in Table VIII.

Table VIII

Consolidated Balance Sheet of the Government and Central Bank

Assets Issued	Assets Held
1. Money, i.e. Notes and Deposits, held by Individuals, Productive Companies, Commercial Banks, and Other Financial Intermediaries $(_bN_i + _bN_p + _bN_c + _bN_o + _bD_c)$	4. Real Assets held by government (A_g)
2. Government Bills held by Individuals, Productive Companies, Commercial Banks, and Other Financial Intermediaries $(_gS_i + _gS_p + _gS_c + _gS_o)$	5. Balance equal to + Net National Debt or − Net National Asset
3. Government Bonds held by Individuals, Productive Companies, Commercial Banks, and Other Financial Intermediaries $(_gL_i + _gL_p + _gL_c + _gL_o)$	

We can consider the impact effect of national debt and monetary policy on the capital market by considering changes in the composition of the assets issued by the financial authorities (i.e. by the government and the central bank combined) as listed on the left hand side of Table VIII.

As far as a shift as between bills and bonds is concerned (items 2 and 3 of Table VIII) we need add nothing to what has already been said before. It makes no difference on the capital market whether the supply of bills is reduced and that of bonds increased by (i) the government unfunding part of the national debt or (ii) the central bank selling bonds from, and buying bills into, the portfolio of assets which it holds.

The new possibility which arises when we add monetary policy to national debt policy is that the central bank may (e.g. by indulging in an open market policy) cause more (less) money and less (more) government bills and bonds to be issued to the private sector of the economy; that is to say, it may cause the items under (1) to be increased (or decreased) with a corresponding decrease (or increase) in the items under (2) or (3) of Table VIII. Suppose, for example, that the central bank purchases some bills and some bonds in the market with newly issued notes. Then government bills and bonds available to the private sectors of the economy under items (2) and (3) go down. At the same time the amount of notes held by those who have sold these bills and bonds to the central bank goes up under item (1). If, as is probable, those who have sold the bills and bonds do not wish to hold notes, they will pay these notes into the commercial banks with which they bank and the commercial banks will probably deposit these notes with the central bank. The net result then will be (i) that the private sector of the economy holds less bills and bonds; (ii) that these same persons hold more deposits with a commercial bank; (iii) that this increase in the deposit liabilities of the commercial banks is offset by their increased deposits with the central bank; and (iv) the central bank holds more bills and bonds against which it owes more deposits to the commercial banks.[4]

In order to induce the private sectors of the economy to hold more money and less bills and bonds the money price of bills and bonds will have to rise; that is to say, the purchase of bills and bonds by the central bank with newly issued money will raise the money price of bills and bonds or, in other words, will lead to a fall in the short-term rate of interest and in the long-term rate of interest. There will then be further repercussions. If, for the time being, we confine our attention once more to the simple progression of the four assets; money → bills → bonds → equities, we must consider the following interconnections.

---

[4] It is assumed in the above account that the central bank's purchase of bills or bonds is not directly from the commercial banks. If it were we would have simply the result (i) that the commercial banks' holding of bills or bonds goes down but its deposits with the central bank go up and (ii) that the central bank's holding of bills or bonds goes up against which its deposit liabilities to the commercial banks goes up.

The story given in the text implies in terms of Table VII (i) a fall in $_gS_i$, $_gS_p$ or $_gS_o$ and in $_gL_i$, $_gL_p$ or $_gL_o$; (ii) an equal rise in $_cD_i$, $_cD_p$ or $_cD_o$ as the case may be; (iii) an equal rise in $_bD_c$; and (iv) an equal rise in $_gS_b$ or $_gL_b$. Changes (i) and (iii) will appear in the consolidated balance sheet shown in Table VIII.

(1) If we continue to assume that no interest is paid on money, then the fall in interest payable on bills will increase the attractiveness of money relatively to bills as a form for the holding of liquid assets. If a small fall in the interest on bills causes a large shift from bills to money, then the fall in the short-term rate of interest will be small; a given reduction in the supply of bills will easily be absorbed by a willing shift into the alternative holding of money.

(2) To what extent the short-term rate of interest falls relatively to the long-term rate of interest will depend essentially upon the extent to which the central bank has bought bills or bonds in its expansionary open market operation. The more it has concentrated on the purchase of bills rather than bonds, the more the short-term rate will have fallen relatively to the long-term rate.

(3) But the final result will depend upon the extent to which bills and bonds are substitutes for each other in the capital market. The extent to which this is so will depend upon the extent to which investors as a whole allow changes in the current short-term rate of interest to affect their expectations about the future course of interest rates. If, to take an extreme example, everyone always expected future rates of interest to be at whatever level the current short-term rate of interest might be, then there would never be any difference between the short-term and the long-term rates of interest.[5] The more people are influenced by the current level of the short-term interest rate in forming their expectations of the future course of interest rates, the greater will be the extent to which people shift from bills to bonds (or vice versa) when the bill rate falls (or rises) relatively to the rate of interest on bonds.

(4) Once again, we must allow for the possibility of substitutability between bonds and equities when the yield on bonds falls, as has been explained earlier.

When we take into account these possible substitutabilities, the upshot of the central bank's open market purchase of bills and bonds is as follows.

(A) The money price of equities will be raised by the shift from bonds to equities resulting from the higher price of bonds. This rise in equity prices will be the greater, (i) the greater is the substitutability between bonds and equities; (ii) the less is the substitutability between bills and money, since this will tend to keep up the price of bills which will tend to keep up the price of bonds; and (iii) the greater is the substitutability between bills and bonds if the central bank has operated mainly by purchasing bills, since this will tend to drive up the price of bonds in sympathy with the price of bills; but (iv) the less is the substitutability between bonds and bills if the

[5] See *The Growing Economy*, pp. 313–8.

central bank has operated mainly by purchasing bonds, since in this case a large shift of holders from bonds to bills would tend to keep down the price of bonds and thus keep down the price of equities.

(B) The short-term rate of interest on bills will fall.

(C) The long-term rate of interest on bonds will fall.

(D) Asset holders will in general be in a more liquid position since the amount of money has increased while the amounts of bills and bonds have declined, and money is the most liquid asset of all.

The effects both of the management of the national debt and of monetary policy which we have so far examined in this chapter leave out of account certain very far-reaching effects—what we may call pyramiding effects—which result from the existence of the commercial banks and of other financial intermediaries.

Consider first the effect on the commercial banks of some unfunding of the national debt which, as we have seen, is represented by an increase in the supply of bills and a reduction in the supply of bonds to the private sectors of the economy. The yield on bills will rise and the yield on bonds will fall. This will cause private holders to shift from bonds to bills, and thus to become more liquid. The commercial banks will be no exception to this general rule. With a lower yield on bonds and a higher yield on bills, they too may shift from holding bonds to holding bills and they too will thus become more liquid.

When the commercial banks become more liquid, that is to say when the ratio of their liquid assets (their holdings of notes, deposits with the central bank, and government bills) to their own deposit liabilities to their customers rises, they will be in a position to expand their own operations. For, as we have seen, their operations depend upon the possibility of meeting a proportion, but not on the whole, of their liabilities from their liquid assets at any one point of time.

The commercial banks may thus well become more liquid when the government unfunds some part of the national debt. *A fortiori* will this be the case when the central bank operates by purchasing bills and bonds with new money. If these bills and bonds are purchased directly from the commercial banks, then these banks are obviously more liquid since they themselves then hold more money and less bills and bonds among their assets. If these bills and bonds are purchased from other private holders, then, as we have seen already, the effect on the commercial banks is likely to be that their deposit liabilities to their customers and the central bank's deposit liability to them go up by the same amounts. This will make them more liquid than before.

Thus if at the outset the commercial banks' deposit liabilities were 1,000 and their liquid assets were 20% of their deposit liabilities and if their deposit liabilities and their liquid assets (i.e. their deposits with the central banks) both go up by the same absolute amount, say 100, then the ratio of their liquid assets to their deposit liabilities rises from 200/1,000 = 20% to 300/1,100 = 27·27%.

When the commercial banks become more liquid and wish to expand their operations in consequence, they will take steps to expand their non-liquid assets by purchasing more bonds and by lending more to their private customers.[6] Each bank can finance such operations by crediting the person from whom the bonds are purchased or to whom the bank loan is extended with an extra deposit with the bank in question. Of course, if bank A purchases a bond from individual B who banks with bank C, then B will draw down his deposit with A to pay it into bank C; and in this case A would have to transfer to C some of its deposit with the central bank. But if all the commercial banks keep in step, these interbank transfers will cancel out; as bank A purchases a bond from B who banks with bank C, bank C in turn will be purchasing a bond from D who banks with bank A.

To return to our previous numerical example. Suppose that the commercial banks keep 20% of their deposit liabilities covered with liquid assets and suppose that, initially, their deposit liabilities are 1,000 and their liquid assets 200. Suppose then, that as a result of the central bank's purchases of bills and bonds, the deposit liabilities and the liquid assets of the banks both go up by 100 to 1,100 and 300 respectively. Then the process of expansion by the commercial banks will go on until their deposit liabilities have risen to 1,500. Then, the ratio of their liquid assets to deposit liabilities will have fallen to 300/1,500 or to the original figure of 20%.

But this is by no means the end of the pyramiding effect. Some of the original holders of bills and bonds which were originally sold to the central bank or of the original holders of bonds sold to the commercial banks may wish to hold some of the money received from the sale of these bills and bonds on deposit with other financial institutions rather than on deposit with the commercial banks. In other words, some of the additional 500 deposits mentioned in the example given in the last paragraph may now be paid by the holders

---

[6] We have so far in this chapter spoken as if the only short-term assets in the market were liquid government bills. This is, of course, far from the case. Short-term advances by a bank to a customer (i.e. the bills issued by the private sector) are not so liquid since they cannot be so readily changed back into money at a moment's notice by the bank.

to another financial intermediary (e.g. a building society) to be held as a deposit with that institution.

The building society may well keep its reserves in the form of deposits with a commercial bank, since it can cash these deposits at any time it wishes to do so. If this is the case, then the transfer by citizen A of a deposit with bank B to a building society C which banks with bank B will have no effect upon banks B's balance sheet. It will simply owe the deposit liability to C instead of to A. But the building society will now be in a more liquid position. Its deposit liabilities and its liquid reserves will have gone up by the same absolute amounts; its ratio of liquid reserves to deposit liabilities will have risen; and it will wish to expand its illiquid assets, e.g. to lend more on mortgages to persons who wish to purchase houses.

The net result of these pyramiding effects is to intensify all the effects of the central banks' open market purchases of bills and bonds. Interest rates will be further reduced as the commercial banks and other financial institutions go out into the market to purchase with their deposits various forms of asset. More funds will be available on easier terms to lend to private individuals and to productive companies; and these private individuals and productive companies will become still more liquid as they hold more deposits with banks and other financial institutions and less illiquid assets.

It is the effect on these private individuals and productive companies which will determine the extent to which the expansionary national debt and monetary policies lead to an actual increase in expenditures on goods and services. There are at least five influences which may bring this about.

(1) In the first place, the fall in interest rates and, in particular, in the long-term rate of interest may increase the willingness of producers, whether individuals or productive companies, to borrow money in order to purchase new capital equipment of one kind or another. On pages 307–13 of *The Growing Economy* we have explained how the present value of a machine depends upon the discounted value of its future yields; the lower is the rate of interest, the higher will be this discounted value and the more willing will any producer be to purchase the machine at the current price at which it is on offer to him.

(2) Similarly, individual citizens may be more willing to purchase durable consumption goods when the rate of interest at which the funds for its hire-purchase can be obtained are reduced.

(3) Quite apart from any reduction in the actual rate of interest charged, potential borrowers from banks and other financial institutions, who would otherwise have been refused a loan, may now find that they can obtain such funds, now that the banks and

other financial institutions are looking for new outlets for their funds.

(4) The rise in the price of equities may induce companies to issue new ordinary shares in order to carry out a project of capital development which would not otherwise have been undertaken. A numerical example may serve to make the principle clear. Suppose that, at present, the company can expect to earn a total profit per annum of $100,000 and that by purchasing a given piece of capital equipment at a cost of $600,000 it could expect to raise its profit per annum by $50,000, i.e. by 50% from $100,000 to $150,000. If its outstanding ordinary shares are worth $1.000,000 in the market, then it will have to increase its total number of ordinary shares issued by 60% in order to raise the funds needed for the new project. Its profits would go up by 50%, but these profits would have to be spread over 60% more shares. Each existing shareholder would be worse off. But suppose now that the existing shares went up in price so that they were worth $1,500,000 instead of $1,000,000. The the number of new shares needed to be issued in order to raise the capital sum of $600,000 would now be only 40% of the existing number. Profits would go up by 50% and these would have to be spread over only 40% more shares. The existing owners of the company would benefit by the expansion.

(5) The fact that private individuals and productive companies were now more liquid than before might encourage them to take more risks and thus to embark on enterprises involving investment of some of their own liquid funds in real capital equipment of one kind or another.

One outstanding feature of this whole process is the probable existence of considerable time-lags and of uncertainty in the amount of the ultimate effects of monetary policy upon actual expenditures by private individuals and productive companies on real goods and services. This is due in the first place to the pyramiding effects which we have discussed above. When the central bank by purchasing bills and bonds in the market makes the commercial banks more liquid, there will be delays while the commercial banks decide how to react to this and delays as they in turn actually expand and invest in less liquid assets. This in due course may make other financial intermediaries such as building societies more liquid; and there will be further delays while these institutions decide how to react and while they in turn actually build up their less liquid assets. Moreover, as individuals and private companies become more liquid as they receive funds from the central bank, the commercial banks and other financial institutions, they may in many cases at first use these funds, not to purchase more goods and services, but simply to repay outstanding debts. Thus company A may use new liquid funds to repay its trade debts to company B, which in turn uses these funds to repay trade debts to company C. In the process all these companies will become more liquid, and in the end this may well cause them to launch out on new expenditure in ways in which they would not otherwise have done. But the process will be a slack one and the timing and the extent of the final effect upon the demand for goods and services will be difficult to estimate.

Similar delays and uncertainties can occur if the central bank is adopting a restrictive monetary policy in order to restrain private expenditure on goods and services. A sale of bills and bonds by the central bank will make the rest of the economy less liquid. But there will be delays while the commercial banks react to their less liquid position by calling in loans previously made to their customers or by selling bonds; this, after a time, will make other financial instititutions less liquid and there will be delays while they adjust their position; and the first reaction of some individuals and private companies to the fact that less funds are available to them from banks and other financial institutions may be in part to pay their debts to each other less rapidly, while they in turn seek time before they cut down their own expenditures on goods and services.

Some part of this general slackness in monetary control can be removed if the central bank has more direct control over the actions of the commercial banks and possibly also of other financial institutions. It need then no longer induce the commercial banks to restrict their loans by making these commercial banks less liquid and waiting for them to react; it could directly instruct the commercial banks to reduce their loans by a stated amount. The most extreme form of such control would be the complete nationalization of the commercial banks and the amalgamation of all the banking institutions in one single bank, whose policy would be directly determined at the centre. The resulting consolidated balance sheet of the government plus central bank plus commercial banks is shown in Table IX.[7]

It is clear from this table how very much greater is the direct monetary control over the economy. The financial authorities can now not only purchase government bills or bonds direct from (or

---

[7] The table is obtained by writing down as combined assets issued all the items in the columns of Table VII marked $_cD$, $_cE$, $_bN$, $_bD$, $_bE$, $_gS$ and $_gL$ and by writing down as combined assets held all the items in the rows of Table VII marked N_c, D_c, S_c, L_c, E_c, A_c, S_b, L_b, N_g, D_g, E_g and A_g and cancelling out those items which appear in both lists. We assume now that $_cE_p = {}_cE_o = 0$ i.e. that all the equity in the banking system belongs to the government.

Table IX

Consolidated Balance Sheet of the Government and All Banks

Assets Issued	Assets Held
1. Money Held by Individuals, Productive Companies and Other Financial Institutions $(_bN_i + _bN_p + _bN_o + _cD_i + _cD_p + _cD_o)$	4. Real Assets held by the Government and by the Banks $(A_g + A_c)$
2. Government Bills held by Individuals, Productive Companies, and Other Financial Institutions $(_gS_i + _gS_p + _gS_o)$	5. Short-term loans by the Banks to Individuals, Productive Companies, and other Financial Institutions $(_iS_c + _pS_c + _oS_c)$
3. Government Bonds held by Individuals, Productive Companies, and other Financial Institutions $(_gL_i + _gL_p + _gL_o)$	6. Long-term loans by the Banks to Individuals, Private Companies and Other Financial Institutions. $(_iL_c + _pL_c + _oL_c)$
	7. The Banks' ownership of the Equities of Private Companies and Other Financial Institutions $(_pE_c + _oE_c)$
	8. Balance equal to $+$ Net National Debt or $-$ Net National Asset.

sell them direct to) private individuals, productive companies or other financial institutions; they can also issue new money by direct loans to individuals, productive companies, and other financial institution or by investment in the equities of productive companies and other financial institutions; and they can call in money and cancel it by directly recalling loans from, or realizing previous investments in, these other private sectors of the economy. Monetary control can be tauter and more direct in its effect, although there will still remain many delays and slacknesses due to the uncontrolled immediate reactions of individuals, productive companies and other financial institutions to changes in their general liquidity.

Table IX allows us to consider one further element in monetary control. We have assumed up to this point that no interest is paid upon holdings of money. In so far as notes are concerned, it may be difficult to envisage the payment of interest. Let us for the time being confine our attention to deposit money. There is no difficulty in conceiving the payment of interest on balances of money held on deposit with the commercial banks. So far in discussing the choice between assets (for example, the substitutability between money, bills, bonds and equities, discussed earlier), we have assumed that investors will be comparing a zero rate of interest on money with the short-term rate on bills and with the long-term yields and prospects of capital gains on bonds and equities. We can still envisage the combined financial authority (of government, central bank and commercial banks) as buying or selling bills or bonds with money. But it can now decide what rate of interest should be offered on the money with which it is offering to purchase the bills or bonds (or on the money which any purchasers of bills or bonds from it must pay for their purchases). This introduces another dimension into monetary policy.

Let us for the moment—solely for simplicity in explaining the basic point—assume that we can talk about THE rate of interest because the financial authorities are so adjusting the relative supplies of bills and bonds in the market that the short-term rate of interest on bills is the same as the long-term rate on bonds. Let us then compare the two following situations.

(1) In situation 1 the financial authorities offer to buy or sell bills and bonds in unlimited amounts at prices which represent a rate of interest of 10%, and they also pay a rate of interest of 10% on the deposit money which they offer in exchange for the bills and bonds.

(2) In situation 2 the financial authorities offer to buy or sell bills and bonds in unlimited amounts at prices which represent a rate of interest of only 8% on them but in this case they pay no interest on the deposit money which is exchanged for the bills and bonds.

In situation 1, private asset holders are likely to hold much more money and less bills and bonds than in situation 2. Money has not only the advantage of being the most liquid asset but in situation 1 it earns no less in interest than bills and bonds. In situation 1 investors will choose to be much more liquid than in situation 2. But in situation 2 the general level of interest rates will be lower, the price of bonds will be higher and, in consequence, the price of equities will be high.

Now it is possible that there will be the same incentive to spend on goods and services in situation 1 and in situation 2. In situation 1, interest rates will be relatively high and equity prices will be relatively low (factors which will discourage investment under items

(1), (2) and (4) on pages 335–6 above), but liquidity will be higher (a factor which will encourage investment under item (5) on page 336 above). In other words, the monetary authorities can encourage (discourage) expenditure on goods and services either by reducing (increasing) the cost of borrowing and thus encouraging (discouraging) people to think of embarking on projects with a given average expected yield or by increasing (reducing) liquidity and this encouraging (discouraging) readiness to face the risks involved in any given enterprise.

At first sight, it may appear as if, except in so far as the actual book-keeping involved in banking carries a real cost with it, the policy of the monetary authorities should be to create all the liquidity which private investors want, since, apart from the costs of book-keeping, it costs the community nothing for the banks to hold the bills and bonds while private individuals and productive companies hold deposits in their place. But this view overlooks a basic feature of a monetary economy.

Many financial intermediaries issue assets which are much more liquid than the assets which they hold. This is outstandingly true of the commercial banks which hold as large part of their assets more or less illiquid loans or bonds, but whose deposit liabilities are used as perfect money substitutes. It may be true of a government which finances the purchase of physical assets such as school buildings in part with the issue of reliable short-term bills. It is true of a building society; the deposits which it issues can be much more readily changed into money than can the house mortgages which it holds. But while liquidity can be deficient, it is also possible from the social point of view for the economy to be in an excessively liquid position.

An individual can obtain flexibility in his assets in either of two ways. He can invest in a flexible form of real assets (that is to say, in a flexible, all-purpose, relatively short-lived machine instead of a long-lived, rigid, one-purpose machine), or he can hold a liquid asset issued by a financial intermediary. He obtains flexibility in both cases; but the position from the point of view of society as a whole is totally different. The flexible machine gives society as well as the individual real flexibility; flexibility through financial intermediaries gives flexibility to the individual but not to society.

In principle, the conclusion to be drawn from this is straightforward. Flexibility through liquidity is appropriate where the unexpected turn of events may affect only a few individuals at a time so that the need for flexibility can be pooled, just as the need for insurance against a fire risk can be pooled. But where the unexpected turn of events may affect the whole, or a very large part of the community at once, real social flexibility through the flexibility of real assets is needed. But the more easily individuals can obtain flexibility through the liquidity provided by financial intermediaries, the less incentive they will have to seek flexibility through the installation of flexible, short-lived, multi-purpose instruments of production. The difficult (and to the present author unsolved) problem of social choice is how, in the light of these considerations, to ensure that the correct degree of flexibility is provided through monetary liquidity.

This choice has very far reaching consequences from the point of view of the control of the economy by monetary policy. Suppose that the monetary authorities are controlling the total demand for goods and services at the socially desirable level, but that they are doing this through the provision of great liquidity rather than through a reduction in the cost of raising capital funds. Each separate private asset holder will feel confident that he can realize his assets if he wants to obtain money for expenditure on some quite unexpected need. If one individual feels such a need, well and good; he can spend freely to satisfy it without by his own action having any very profound disturbing effect upon the total economy. But suppose now that some quite unexpected event takes place which makes everyone, or at least a very large proportion of the population, want simultaneously to increase greatly their purchases of goods and services. It may be an important unexpected invention which opens up simultaneously opportunities for the profitable investment of new plant and machinery in a large range of activities; it may be a rumour of war or other trouble which makes everyone want to hoard goods simultaneously; it might conceivably be a widespread and infectious change of taste and habit on the part of consumers. The safer and the more liquid are the assets held by final holders (even though the real capital equipment of the community may be very specialized and rigid), the greater will be the sudden, simultaneous and unexpected attempt to increase the purchase of goods and services.

The problem can be seen best by considering the deposits of the commercial banks. Everyone will simultaneously be trying to spend his deposits on acquiring more real goods. But there will be no more real goods in the community to be bought. The surge of money expenditure can cause only price rises, depletion of stocks held by producers and traders, or unsatisfied orders.

This phenomenon of a simultaneous desire on the part of holders of deposits to change their deposits into goods must not be confused with a possible 'run on the banks' when depositors simultaneously attempt to turn their deposits into notes. A general rush from deposits into goods could cause real difficulties to the economy as described above, but it need cause no difficulties to the banks as such. The individual banks have no incentive to limit liquidity on this account. The fact that everyone is paying his deposit away by cheque more frequently and more quickly merely means that the banks will be kept busier transferring deposits from one account to another.

But if all depositors desired simultaneously to cash their deposits merely in order to hold notes instead, this need not cause any direct upset in the markets for real goods and services. If, however, the commercial banks were separate from the central bank and kept only a small proportion of their total deposits covered with notes or with deposits with the central bank, then such a run on the banks could cause serious banking difficulties unless the central bank acted on a sufficient scale, by one of the means discussed on pages 314–5, as lender in the last resort—issuing all the notes necessary to pay off the deposits which were being withdrawn. This would, however, be basically a book-keeping rearrangement with no direct real effect— an arrangement which would be most simply effected by drawing no distinction between the issue of notes and the supply of deposits in a consolidated banking system of the kind illustrated in Table IX.

The two types of phenomena may, however, well be combined in the following way. If people wished suddenly and unexpectedly to increase their money expenditures they might well try to turn various liquid assets (such as deposits with building societies) into money. If holders of deposits with building societies all attempted to cash these deposits in order to pay them directly or indirectly into ordinary transferable deposit accounts with the commercial banks, the building societies who themselves keep only a small proportion of their deposit liabilities covered by cash or other very liquid assets would experience a run on their reserves. They would be forced to repudiate on their obligations to their depositors unless by some means or another they were enabled to borrow directly or indirectly from the banking system.

In so far as they were enabled to do so, the total amount of money in the form of ordinary transferable bank deposits would go up by the amount of deposits transferred from the building societies to the member banks.[8] In order to prevent a bankruptcy of the building societies, their deposits would have been turned into transferable

---

[8] In Table VII, $_oD_i$ would go down and $_cD_i$ would go up by the amount of deposits which individuals transferred from the building societies to the member banks. If the building societies borrowed this amount from the commercial banks, $_oS_c$ or $_oL_c$ would go up by this same amount. Everyone's books would still balance.

money which would enable the inflation of the demand for goods and services to be *pro tanto* reinforced.[9]

The phenomenon of a general unexpected shift from money and other liquid assets into goods and services has been expounded in an exaggerated and dramatic form in order to illustrate its nature. It need not, of course, be as dramatic. The point is, however, a simple one. The more liquid and safe are the ultimate assets which are provided by the financial intermediaries, the better will this be in so far as it will enable an individual's special unexpected needs to be met. This is not only a good thing in itself, but it will also have the effect of making people more willing to take risks and to launch out on enterprising new undertakings which may in the end prove to be of great social benefit. But, at the same time, it will make the economic system less stable and more difficult to control in so far as some unexpected general economic development may occur which causes all individuals to wish to increase their expenditures simultaneously.

In our discussion of the possibility of paying interest on deposits, we have so far made no reference to the fact that it is very difficult to devise an administratively workable scheme whereby interest could be made payable on notes and coin. Thus, although people could be induced to hold deposits by paying interest on them, it would not be possible in this way to induce people to hold notes. If interest rates on other assets (including deposits) were very high, people might be induced to economize very much in the holding of notes. Notes are not perfect substitutes for deposits. It is not normally possible to pay one's bus fare by means of a cheque drawn against one's bank deposit. Thus situations could arise in which people were very liquid 'depositwise', but very illiquid 'notewise'. This could be a source of some inconvenience and inefficiency, since people might be caught in unexpected situations with quite inadequate holdings of notes.

Although this is not probably more than a minor matter in a modern developed economy in which the vast majority of all important transactions are carried out by cheque and not by cash, yet it is worth investigating the situation further because of the light which it can throw on more general relationships between money and liquidity. We have seen already[10] that, in order to exercise a given restraint on borrowing for new expenditure, the rate of interest in terms of money must be *pro tanto* higher, the more rapid is the

[9] A further possibility is that when people wish to spend their money more quickly they may want to hold a larger ratio of notes to deposits. In this case, the desire to spend deposits more quickly would be combined with a desire to cash their deposits into notes.

[10] Cf. *The Growing Economy*, pp. 38–9.

expected rate of rise of money prices, since the yield on a machine is equal to its income yield plus the capital gain expected on it. If the general level of prices is expected to go up by 10% per annum, then the money yields on bills and bonds must be 14% per annum in order to give a real yield of 4% per annum. If the general level of prices is expected to fall by 2% per annum, then a money yield on bills and bonds of only 2% per annum is sufficient to give a real yield of 4% per annum. If, therefore, the monetary authorities could manipulate at will the expected future rate of inflation or deflation of the general level of money prices, then it could induce the desired degree of liquidity in notes as well as in deposits.

Suppose, simply by way of illustration, that to get the desired degree of general liquidity it was desired by the authorities to have the rate of interest on notes and deposits one point below the rate on bills and bonds, and suppose that at the same time, in the interests of controlling total demand, it was desired to have the real rate of interest on bills and bonds at 5% per annum. Then if the monetary authorities could manipulate an expected rate of decline of money prices of 4% per annum, they could achieve their object with a zero rate of interest on notes and deposits and a 1% rate of interest on bills and bonds. The margin between the rate of interest on notes and deposits on the one hand and on bills and bonds on the other would be $1 - 0 = 1\%$ per annum, while the real rate of interest on bills and bonds would be $1 + 4 = 5\%$ per annum.

In other words, an inducement to remain liquid by holding money can be provided by either or both of two means: (i) by paying interest on money (an arrangement which may be administratively simple for deposit money, but impracticable for notes and coin) and (ii) by a general deflationary movement of money prices which gives rise to the expectation that if money is held it will appreciate in real purchasing power. The second of these points can be made in a more realistic way by saying that the expectation of a rapid inflation of prices will cause people to choose to be very illiquid (in order to avoid holding money which is quickly falling in real purchasing power) in so far as a high offsetting money rate of interest cannot be paid on money. Excessive illiquidity brought about by the fear of inflation can be socially very undesirable if it induces private decision-makers to choose policies which, by making them very illiquid, make them very vulnerable to unexpected misfortunes or make it impossible for them to seize fleeting golden opportunities.

We may summarize the conclusions of this long chapter in the following way.

(1) Monetary and national debt policies, by altering the mix of liquid and illiquid assets and by affecting interest rates, can exert

an influence on the total level of money expenditure on goods and services.

(2) There are, however, almost certainly considerable delays and considerable margins of uncertainty in the degree of effect upon total money demand.

(3) Monetary and national debt policies can operate in two conceptually separate ways: (i) by making finance cheaper and easier for projects of capital development or (ii) by putting people into more liquid position for the taking of risks.

(4) Liquidity in the form of holding deposits can be induced by offering interest on deposits, but liquidity in the form of holding notes can be induced only by avoiding expectations of rapid price inflations.

(5) Liquidity can be overdone as well as underdone from a social point of view.

The proper mix of policies for the control of the total expenditure on goods and services can, however, be finally considered only when we have brought into the mix not only the degree of liquidity and the cost of capital finance through monetary policy, but also the fiscal measures which are the subject of discussion in the next chapter.

CHAPTER XXIII

FISCAL POLICY

In the previous chapter we have considered the various ways in which the financial authorities can vary the structure of the different kinds of assets available to be held by the private sector of the economy. There are, broadly speaking, two ways in which the financial authorities can apply their powers to affect this structure of assets.[1] In the first place, the financial authorities might determine the amount of the various kinds of assets which were to be made available to the private sector of the economy, i.e. determine and control the totals of the assets shown under each of the three items on the left hand side of Table VIII.[2] If this were done, then the forces of supply and demand on the capital market would determine the relative prices of the various assets, which might change as the asset holders in the private sector changed their attitudes to liquidity, their expectations and so on. Alternatively, the financial authorities could set prices at which they were willing to buy and sell assets of various kinds, being ready to exchange one asset for another at the given price.

To take an example: with the first type of policy, the financial authorities would decide how many government bills and how many government bonds to put on the market; if people's expectations about future interest rates changed so that they increased their desire for long-term bonds relatively to short-term bills, the price of bonds would go up (the long-term rate of interest would fall) and the price of bills would fall (the short-term rate of interest would rise). With the second type of policy, the financial authorities would determine the price of bills and of bonds (i.e. determine the short-term and the long-term rates of interest) and would buy (or sell) bills or bonds in the market as soon as the price of bills or bonds fell (or rose) above the policy-determined level.

With the first type of arrangement, monetary policy would be implemented by choosing and changing the quantities of assets

---

[1] Cf. pages 125–7 of Chapter VII.

[2] Or of Table IX, if the commercial banks are also to be regarded as part of the policy-making financial authorities.

provided; if the financial authorities wished to increase liquidity they would issue more money and with it buy up and remove from the private sector's ownership some bills and bonds. With the second type of arrangement, monetary policy would be implemented by choosing and changing the rates of interest; if the financial authorities wished to increase liquidity they would raise the money prices at which they offered to buy bills and bonds from the private sector.

Both types of arrangement would thus enable an effective monetary policy to be applied. But in order to understand the impact effects of other policy changes, and in particular of the fiscal policy changes which we shall examine in this chapter, it is necessary to decide which type of monetary policy is assumed to be in operation. In this chapter we shall assume that monetary policy is of the second type and also that the financial authorities have in their direct control the commercial banks as well as the central bank and the management of the national debt. That is to say, we shall be dealing with the state of affairs depicted in Table IX and we shall assume that, at any one time, there is a fixed rate of interest on deposit money, a fixed price of government bills (determining the corresponding short-term rate of interest), a fixed price of government bonds (determining the corresponding long-term rate of interest), and fixed rates of interest at which the banks will lend to the private sectors of the economy for loans of various durations and various grades of risk.[3] The composition of the consolidated balance sheet in Table IX is then determined by the amounts of the various assets which the private sector will determine to hold (or, in the case of borrowing from the bank, to issue) on these given terms.

Against this background of monetary policy, we can turn to a consideration of fiscal policies as means for stabilizing the total level of demand for goods and services in conditions of residual uncertainty. By fiscal policies are meant changes in governmental taxes or expenditures designed for the purpose of influencing the demand for goods or services.

Normally, a fiscal policy designed to stimulate demand will involve an increased budget deficit or a decreased budget surplus, and thus an increase in the rate at which the deadweight national debt is rising or a decrease in the rate at which it is falling. For a reduction in taxation by leaving more tax-free purchasing power in the private sector will give some incentive for increased private expenditure of one kind or another on goods and services, while an

---

[3] This last assumption is not altogether a straightforward one; but we assume broadly that the terms of bank lending of various kinds are predetermined and that on those terms all borrowers judged to fall within any given category are accommodated.

increase in governmental expenditure on goods and services will itself be a direct stimulation of the total demand for goods and services. And, conversely, fiscal policies designed to restrict total demand will normally involve increased tax revenue and/or decreased governmental expenditures and so a decrease in the budget deficit and in the rate of growth of the national debt (or an increase in the budget surplus and in the rate of decrease of the national debt).

But this is not necessarily the case. With the monetary policy which we are assuming, a combination of two or more changes in fiscal arrangements may well leave the balance between government revenue and expenditure unchanged and yet lead to a net effect upon the total demand for goods and services. The following are two possible examples of this phenomenon.

First, suppose that the government raised the rates of death duties levied on properties passing from benefactor to beneficiary on the death of the benefactor and at the same time lowered the rates of taxation on current incomes so that the total of tax revenue was unchanged. Suppose further that the death duties were paid simply by the sale of government bills and bonds out of the estates passing at death without any further immediate effects. Suppose, however, that a large part of the increased income tax was paid through the reduction of personal expenditures on consumption goods. With the monetary policy which we are assuming the sale of government bills and bonds to raise the duties payable on the estates passing at death would have no effects upon rates of interest or upon funds available in any part of the capital market; they would be taken up by the monetary authorities at the predetermined prices and there would thus be no further repercussions upon the demands for goods and services from this source. Those who were paying less income tax would, however, increase their demands for goods and services. As a result there would be no change in the government's budget balance between total revenue and expenditure, but the total demand for goods and services in the economy as a whole would be stimulated.

Or, to take another example, suppose that the government increases its own expenditures on goods and services by a given amount, but that at the same time it raises the rate of income tax so as to obtain an additional tax revenue exactly equal to the increase of government expenditure. Once more the existing budget surplus or deficit will be unaffected. But suppose that those who have to pay income tax meet their increased tax liabilities only in part by cutting down their expenditures on goods and services, and for the rest that they raise the funds by cutting down their savings and purchasing less governmental bills and bonds. Once more, with the monetary policy which we are assuming, their reduced demand for bills and bonds can have no effect upon interest rates in the capital market; the monetary authorities will make good any immediate deficiency of demand for bills and bonds at their predetermined prices. But the taxpayers' reduction in their demands for goods and services will be so much less than the government's increased demand for goods and services. There will once more be no change in the budget surplus or deficit, combined with an increase in the total demand for goods and services.[4]

If, however, a fiscal policy stimulus to the total demand for goods and services is given either solely by a reduction in taxation (leaving a higher purchasing power to the taxpayers) or solely by an increase in governmental expenditures, the result will, of course, be an increased budget deficit or a reduced budget surplus. And, conversely, a restrictive fiscal policy which depends either solely on higher taxes or solely on reduced governmental expenditures will result in a reduced budget deficit or an increased budget surplus. From the point of view of long-term structural planning, i.e. the sort of planning which we discussed in Part 4 and in particular in Chapter XVI, it will be very important to draw the distinction between fiscal policies for the control of total demand which do, and those which do not, involve a change in the balance between total governmental revenue and expenditure. To take one example, compare situation 1 in which personal demand is stimulated by a given reduction in the income tax leading to a given increase in the budget deficit with situation 2 in which there is the same stimulus to private demand brought about by the same reduction in income tax, but in which this is accompanied by an increase in the revenue from death

---

[4] The final net increase in the total demand for goods and services, taking into account the multiplier effects of the initial net excess of the government's increased expenditures over taxpayers' reduced consumption, will of course be greater than this initial net excess of government increased expenditures over taxpayers' reduced consumption. On certain plausible assumptions, the final total increase in demand for goods and services will be equal to the initial increase in government expenditures. The final increase in the demand for goods and services and so in incomes (ΔD) will be equal to the increased government expenditure (ΔG) plus any net increase in personal consumption (ΔC), so that $\Delta D = \Delta G + \Delta C$. But there will be two influences on consumption. Suppose that a proportion c of net disposable income is always spent. Then if there were no increase in tax rates, there would be an increment of personal consumption equal to $c\Delta D$. But with an increase of tax revenue equal to the government expenditure (ΔG) we would have a consequential reduction of consumption equal to $c\Delta G$, since a proportion c of the fall in net disposable income due to the increased tax payments ΔG would be met by reduced consumption. Thus $\Delta C = c(\Delta D - \Delta G)$. Thus we have $\Delta D = \Delta G + \Delta C = \Delta G + c(\Delta D - \Delta G)$, so that $\Delta D = \Delta G$.

duties, the immediate effect of which on personal consumption is negligible, but which causes there to be no change in the budget balance between total tax revenue and total governmental expenditure. The immediate effect on total demand is the same, but in situation 1 the national debt will grow more rapidly than in situation 2. As time passes, in situation 1 people will individually be more wealthy than in situation 2.[5] As time passes, therefore, people who are otherwise in basically the same economic position will hold more property in situation 1 than in situation 2; they will have inherited more because of the lower level of death duties; and they will probably, therefore, have a smaller incentive to save. The growth of deadweight national debt will in time affect the proportion of income saved[6] and thus the choice between the fiscal policies of situation 1 and situation 2 will be relevant for the achievement of the optimum level of savings (component III of equation 16.14) in any longer-term plan.

But we are at the moment concerned not with these longer-term implications, but with the short-run problem of achieving a quick and rapid effect through fiscal changes on the total level of demand. We must look upon fiscal policy decisions as having these two aspects. From time to time, perhaps once a year at the time of the formulation of an annual governmental budget, the whole structure of government taxes and expenditures must be adjusted to achieve the longer-term objectives discussed in Chapter XVI. These objectives will include, of course, the maintenance of total demand so as to achieve the full employment of resources (component II of equation 16.14) but they will be considered only in the light of one or two representative environmental paths. More frequently than once a year, it must be possible to adjust taxes or expenditures not so much in such a way as to implement a revised, fully calculated long-term plan—that must wait for the next annual budget—but in such a way as to have the most rapid and effective influence in interrupting any threatened cumulative spiral of deflation or inflation of the total demand for goods and services, resulting from some unexpected and unpremeditated change in the economic environment. For such a temporary purpose, the net effect upon the budget surplus or deficit and so upon the size of the national debt can be neglected, since corrections can be made at the next annual revision

---

[5] The total net wealth of individuals is equal to the total real capital of the community plus the deadweight national debt. The deadweight national debt will grow more quickly in situation 1 than in situation 2.

[6] See *The Growing Economy*, pp. 501–7.

of the longer-term fiscal plan; the immediate issue is a quick effect upon total demand. For the remainder of this chapter we shall, therefore, be considering fiscal changes solely from this point of view.

Any change in fiscal policy which causes a larger budget deficit, e.g. a cut in the rate of income tax, will cause the government to have to borrow more than would otherwise be the case. It will have to issue more debt of one kind or another to finance the increased budget deficit. It should be remembered, however, that with the monetary policy which we are assuming the form in which this debt will be held by the private sector will be left to the choice of the private sector at the given prices of the various assets (i.e. at the various rates of interest) predetermined by the monetary authorities. To take an example, suppose that the government issues more bonds to finance the increased deficit but that at the given rates of interest offered by the monetary authorities on deposits, bills and bonds, the private sector wishes to hold its increased wealth in the liquid form of deposit money. Then the sale of bonds by the government will tend to depress their price; in order to maintain the price of bonds (i.e. to prevent a rise in the long-term rate of interest), the banks will purchase bonds with new deposit money. The private sector will hold increased deposits with the banks who, in their turn, will hold increased bonds. And, conversely, if the government adopts a restrictive fiscal policy which leads to a budget surplus and the redemption of debt, the form of assets (deposits, bills, bonds, etc.) which the private sector of the economy chooses to give up will be at the choice of the private sector, given our monetary assumption that the banking system will without limit exchange one type of asset for another at given predetermined prices.

Let us then turn to a consideration of the forms of fiscal policy change which will have the most rapid and effective impact upon the demand for goods and services.

At first sight, it might appear that the most obvious direct fiscal influence upon the total demand for goods and services would be exercised through changes in the government's own demands for goods and services. This influence is, of course, direct and effective, but for the great bulk of most governmental expenditures on goods and services it is impossible to arrange that the effect should be rapid and prompt without incurring great waste and inefficiency. Most governmental expenditures on goods and services—defence, police, education, health, roads, and so on—are in respect of public services requiring careful forward planning; the plans can and should, of course, be altered gradually to take into account new needs and developments, including the longer-term considerations of the basic balance between the total national resources and the total demands on these resources for other purposes.[7] Plans to build a new road take much time to prepare before any money can usefully be spent on the actual construction of the new road; and suddenly and unexpectedly to stop the construction of a half-built road clearly involves waste of a kind which is to be avoided if possible.

There is, however, one particular kind of direct governmental expenditure on goods which may have an important short-run stabilizing or destabilizing effect upon the total demand for goods and services. In order to reduce market uncertainties for a particular group of producers, the government may introduce marketing schemes for the products of these producers which stabilize the price or, alternatively, guarantee a minimum price below which the market selling price for the product will not be permitted to fall. Schemes of this kind may take the form of the government holding a buffer stock of the product in question, buying up surplus supplies in the market when the market price falls below some predetermined minimum level and selling from the buffer stock when there is a deficiency of supply in the market so that the market price rises above some predetermined maximum level. Alternatively, a scheme can be operated whereby, when the price of the product falls below a minimum guaranteed level, the government does not buy up the surplus stock and store but simply subsidizes the revenue of the producers by paying a subsidy on their product equal to the deficiency of the current market price below the guaranteed minimum; and with such a scheme the government could levy a tax on the sale of the product equal to any excess of the ruling market price over a predetermined maximum price.

Both types of scheme, in so far as they merely stabilize the market, will involve the government borrowing funds to purchase supplies for the buffer stock or to subsidize selling prices in times of deficient demand—a debt which can be repaid by the proceeds from the sales of the commodity from the buffer stock or from the imposition of the tax on selling prices in times of excess demand.

Schemes of this kind can be applied only to products of a very standardized kind with clearly distinguished grades and qualities for which predetermined minimum and maximum prices can be precisely defined. A buffer stock scheme can be applied only to a durable product involving moderate costs of storage, but stabilizing subsidy-cum-tax arrangements can be applied to any standardized product, even if it is a perishable commodity.

Schemes of this kind can, without doubt, operate to interrupt the positive feedback effect of reduced incomes leading to reduced

[7] This is implied in component II of equation 16.14.

N

demand leading to reduced incomes, and can thus mitigate the vicious spirals of deflation and inflation. Thus if there is some unexpected change in the economic situation which initiates an increase (or decrease) in total demand, the incomes of the producers of the products covered by buffer stock or stabilizing tax-cum-subsidy arrangements will not be subject to the full market increase (or decrease) which they would otherwise have experienced. As far as their contribution to total demand is of any importance, there will be a stabilizing element introduced into the economy, which can be very rapid, prompt and effective in its operation. As far as a buffer stock is concerned, the action is extremely prompt. The buffer stock authority automatically buys (or sells) as soon as the market demand falls below (or rises above) the critical level. As far as subsidy and tax arrangements are concerned, it may not be administratively possible to pay the subsidy (or raise the tax) so promptly. The subsidy may have to be paid (or the tax levied) retrospectively, after the commodity has been sold in the market. But if the producer knows that his income will in fact be supplemented by the subsidy (or curtailed by the tax) in due course, he is likely to adjust his own expenditures in advance to what his income will be after allowing for the fully anticipated retrospective fiscal adjustment to which he knows he is ultimately liable. The effect may thus be almost as prompt as in the case of a buffer stock.

In a number of countries, a large part of agricultural output has been covered by schemes of this kind and there is no doubt that they have thus provided an important contributory safeguard against serious cumulative deflations of demand.

But such schemes bring with them their own serious politico-economic problems. In so far as farmers' pressure groups can cause the guaranteed prices to be pushed up further than would be needed purely for stabilization purposes, a buffer stock scheme will be burdened with ever growing stocks and an automatic subsidy-cum-tax scheme will work with a perpetual deficit, always paying out subsidies and never receiving taxes. Moreover, schemes of this kind, while they will certainly act to mitigate fluctuations in demand originating in other sectors of the economy, can at the same time be originators of fluctuations in total demand if the trouble arises from the conditions of supply in the production of the commodities covered by the schemes themselves.

Consider, for example, a scheme covering the marketing of wheat, Suppose that there is an exceptionally good harvest. With a buffer stock scheme which prevented any fall in the market price, the consumers of wheat would continue to purchase the same amount as before at the same price as before. But the government would borrow additional funds (which, with our assumptions about monetary policy, would have no further immediate repercussions in the capital market) in order to purchase the whole of the additional output at the old price and the whole of this government purchase would represent an increase in the incomes of wheat farmers which might induce them to increase their expenditures and thus initiate some increase in demand. In these conditions, the exceptionally good harvest would undoubtedly lead to some initial destabilizing inflation of total demand.

But one must compare this result with what would happen in the absence of any marketing scheme for wheat. This depends upon the price elasticity of demand for wheat. If this elasticity of demand were unity, then the consumers would spend the same amount as before on wheat, the increased amount purchased being exactly offset by the fall in its price. Since, in this case, the producers would have the same money income as before and the consumers would be spending out of their incomes the same amount on wheat as before, there would be no reason to expect any noticeable repercussions upon total expenditures. If the demand for wheat had an elasticity much below (above) unity, then the expenditure on wheat would fall (rise) and while the wheat producers would have smaller (larger) incomes to spend, the consumers would have just so much more (less) of their money incomes left over after their purchases of wheat. If the producers adjusted their further purchases in the same way and at the same speed to a change in their incomes as the consumers did their purchases to a change in the incomes left over after their purchases of wheat, then once again there would be no general destabilizing initial impact from the good wheat harvest. There would only be a shift of purchasing power over other goods and services as between the producers and consumers.

This does not, however, mean that a good wheat harvest in the absence of a wheat marketing scheme could not have any general destabilizing effect. We may note three possibilities. First, the change in the producers' incomes and purchasing power will be concentrated on a relatively small group, whereas the equal offsetting change in the consumers' purchasing power over other goods and services will be spread over the whole population. The effect on total expenditure of a large change in purchasing power per head concentrated on a small number of heads may be very different from that of a small change in purchasing power per head spread over a large number of heads. If farmers' incomes per head fell drastically, they might have to make a drastic cut in their consumption expenditures, while the corresponding small rise in the standards of living of all other citizens might be absorbed mainly in increased savings. Secondly, it is possible that farmers (e.g. because they are generally richer or poorer than, or differ in their social habits from, other members of the community) behave differently from the rest of the community in the speed and nature of their reactions, e.g. spending a higher and saving a lower proportion of any change in their incomes. Third, it is possible that people in general cut down their consumption more quickly when their incomes fall unexpectedly than they raise their consumption when their incomes rise unexpectedly. In this case, if the elasticity of demand for wheat was different from unity, whether greater or less than unity, an unexpectedly good or bad harvest, since it would cause some incomes to fall and some to rise, would have some immediate deflationary effect on total demand and vice versa if people reacted less quickly to a fall than to a rise in their incomes.

If there is an automatic subsidy and tax scheme which prevents a good harvest from causing any net reduction in the price received by the producer, the impact effect of a particularly good harvest on the producer will be exactly the same as it would have been with a buffer stock scheme. In both cases, he sells the increased quantity at an unchanged price and has that much more income to spend. But as far as the consumer is concerned the impact effect is different, since the increased quantity is allowed to have its uncontrolled market effect upon the price of wheat. If the consumers' demand is very elastic, consumers will spend more on wheat at the low price under the subsidy tax scheme than they would under the buffer stock scheme; this will mean that the government has to find less funds to finance the increased incomes of the farmers. But in so far as some at least of this increment of consumers' expenditure on wheat comes from income that would otherwise have been spent on other goods so that it involves a decrement of expenditure on other goods, the tax and subsidy scheme will be rather less inflationary than the buffer stock scheme; and vice versa if the consumers' elasticity of demand for wheat is less than unity.

We may conclude that buffer stock or automatic subsidy-tax schemes which stabilize the price offered to the producers of certain standardised products can exert an important stabilizing influence in the economy in so far as unexpected fluctuations in demand are liable to originate in other sectors of the economy, but that they could become destabilizing factors if unexpected fluctuations are more likely to originate within the productive operations in the stabilized sector rather than in demand originating in the other sectors.

There is one other form of government expenditure which might be capable of prompt administrative adjustment so as to provide an effective stabilizing device, namely transfer payments or payments by the government of direct supplements to the incomes and so to the purchasing power of the individual citizens. Such governmental expenditures do not represent direct demands by the government itself for goods and services and they are comparable in their effects to changes in individuals' disposable incomes brought about by increases or decreases in the governmental taxation of incomes. We will, therefore, consider variations in governmental transfer payments as part of our discussion of attempts to stabilize total demand through variations in the taxation of income.

There are two kinds of variation in governmental taxes which may be considered as effective means for the prompt control of private expenditures: first, changes in the indirect taxes imposed on the purchase of certain goods and services; and, second, changes in the direct taxation of incomes. The merits and demerits of these two types of tax control are very different. We will discuss each in turn.

Administratively, it is quite possible to put up or down fairly frequently and at relatively short notice the rate of tax levied on the consumption of various goods and services. If a large range of such goods and services are subject to such taxation, this instrument of control could be not only prompt, but also effective in its use, since it would be quantitatively important. There are certain disadvantages in the use of this instrument if it is confined to variations in the rate of tax on only one good or a very limited group of goods. If the short-run price elasticities of demand and supply for that good or group of goods were very high it is possible that a rise in the rate of tax per unit consumed would actually cause an increase, and not a decrease in the total expenditure on goods and services. The increase in the tax raises the price to the consumer and reduces the price to the producer; this causes a great deal less to be bought and sold; this could cause a reduction in the total revenue from the tax since the reduction in the amount bought and sold if very great might outweigh the rise in the tax per unit bought; if consumers spent on other untaxed goods the whole of the sum which they saved from spending less on the more highly taxed goods, then total incomes would be increased; the producers of the untaxed goods would receive a boost to their incomes equal to the whole reduction of the consumers' expenditures on the more highly taxed goods; but this reduction in receipts from the sale of the taxed goods is partly absorbed by a reduction in tax payments to the government and only for the remainder represents a reduction of the incomes of the producers of the more highly taxed goods.[8]

Even if the elasticities of supply and demand for the product are not so great that the tax revenue is actually reduced, there are disadvantages in concentrating the tax charged too heavily on one commodity or group of commodities. For unless the elasticities of demand and supply are very small, there is likely to be a reduction in the total activity in the taxed sector relatively to the activity in the untaxed sector; the concentration of the deflation of incomes and spending, needed to offset a general inflationary tendency, will then be concentrated on one particular sector or set of sectors. A vicious spiral of inflation may be broken at the expense of engineering a particularly severe local pocket of deflation in order to counterbalance the widespread effects of whatever particular inflationary cause (occurring probably in some quite different sector) has started the trouble.

To offset general inflationary (or deflationary) repercussions, it is useful to be able to raise (or lower) indirect taxation over a very wide range of goods and services both because this will not concentrate the offsetting tendency fortuitously on some particular sector of the economy and also because the wider the range of taxation involved the greater the quantitative effect that can be achieved from any given moderate percentage rise or fall in the rates of taxation.

Variations in the rates of indirect taxation on goods and services as a means of stabilizing total demand carry certain speculative implications which must be borne in mind. Suppose, for example, there is some unexpected inflationary development in the economy and it is desired to offset this temporarily by means of a rise in the rates of indirect taxation. For the policy to be most effective it is

---

[8] Let $D(p) = S(p - t)$ represent the equilibrium between the demand and supply of the taxed good, where p is the selling price including tax and t is a specific rate of duty on the good. By differentiation we obtain $dp/dt = e_s/\{e_s - (1 - \theta)e_d\}$ where $e_s = \{dS/S\}/\{d(p - t)/(p - t)\}$ equals the elasticity of supply, $e_d = \{dD/D\}/\{dp/p\}$ equals the elasticity of demand and $\theta = t/p$ equals the proportion of the selling price paid in tax. We have also $R = Dt$ as a measure of the revenue so that $dR/dt = D + t\, dD/dt = D(1 + \theta e_d\, dp/dt)$ so that using the above expression for dp/dt, we have $dR/dt = D\{e_s + e_d[\theta(1 + e_s) - 1]\}/\{e_s - (1 - \theta)e_d\}$. Since $-e_d$, the numerical value of the elasticity of demand, is always > 0 and since $0 < \theta < 1$, it follows that dR/dt is $\lessgtr 0$ as $-e_d\{\theta - (1 - \theta)/e_s\} \lessgtr 1$. It follows that if $e_s < (1 - \theta)/\theta$, dR/dt will always be > 0 however large e_d may be. If, for example, one-tenth of the selling price were taken in tax, the revenue would necessarily rise as a result of a rise in the rate of tax if the elasticity of supply were less than 9; if the elasticity of demand were not great enough, it might rise even if the elasticity of supply were greater than 9. If the elasticity of supply were infinite, then the condition for $dR/dt < 0$ is $-e_d > 1/\theta$, so that with the tax equal to one-tenth of the consumer's purchase price the elasticity of demand would have to be greater than 10 for the revenue to be reduced by a rise in the rate of tax.

necessary that the rise in the rates of tax should be (i) unexpected and (ii), when imposed, expected to be only temporary.

If the rise in the rates of tax are anticipated, then consumers may well speed up their purchases in order to buy before the higher tax rates are in operation—this being particularly true, of course, in the case of durable consumption goods. This could represent a very destabilizing influence, since consumers might thus be encouraged to speed up their purchases whenever an inflation of total demand started, in anticipation of the imposition of higher tax rates to control the inflation; and vice versa when a deflation of demand started. The moral is that if this weapon is going to be used the government must be prepared to raise (or lower) the rates of tax very promptly upon the inception of an unexpected inflation (or deflation) of total demand. Moreover, the government must be prepared to change the rates frequently. When an unexpected inflation or deflation of total demand starts, the government must not wait and see, while the inflationary or deflationary forces gather strength, and only change the rate of tax when the need for the change is fully apparent to it—and thus to every individual citizen as well. It must be ready to make the change promptly and to reverse its action promptly if it turns out that it has overestimated the inflationary or deflationary danger.

Suppose that, at the same time, it is known that in due course (for example, at the time of the next annual budget) the whole apparatus of government controls will be reviewed and revised in the way discussed in Chapter XVI above, so that the stabilization of the economy in the light of the new unexpected inflationary or deflationary events will be implemented by the whole range of governmental controls. Thus the changes in the particular rates of indirect taxation designed to have a prompt impact upon total demand will be thought to be only temporary. If a rise in an indirect tax is unforeseen (so that it cannot have been anticipated by additional purchases) and if it is then expected to be temporary (so that there will be the maximum incentive to postpone purchases so long as the higher rates of tax are in operation), this fiscal instrument will have the optimum effect in restricting purchases during an unexpected temporary threat of an inflation of total demand; and, *mutatis mutandis*, it will have the optimum effect in stimulating purchases during an unexpected temporary threat of a deflation of total demand.

The other tax changes which may be used to effect a prompt influence over total demand are changes in the direct taxation of incomes which leave consumers with a larger tax-free spendable income when the rates are lowered, and vice versa when the rates of

tax are raised. It is of importance to note that the speculative considerations regarding changes in direct taxes are the exact reverse
of the speculative changes regarding the use of indirect taxes. While
the anticipation that the money prices of goods may be raised in the
future through a rise in the rates of indirect taxation is likely to
cause an immediate speculative increase in purchases, the anticipation that one's net spendable money income is likely to be reduced
in the future by a rise in the rate of income tax is likely to cause one
to be more economical immediately in one's consumption. And
the more permanent the reduction in net spendable incomes is
expected to be, the greater will be its immediate effect in curtailing
consumption; if a fall (or rise) in net spendable income is expected
to be only temporary, then most of it may be met by a temporary
fall (or a rise) in savings—which with our monetary assumption will
have no effect on the capital markets—rather than by a temporary
change in the standard of living.

The implication of this for fiscal policy is clear. If the government
wishes to effect a prompt and marked, but temporary, influence
over total demand through changes in rates of direct taxation, it
need not be so concerned with the administrative problem of
bringing into actual operation very quick, unexpected changes of
tax. To announce that it is going shortly to raise rates of tax on
income will itself help to curtail present expenditures; citizens'
speculations on the government's intentions to use this weapon
will in themselves be a helpful stabilizing factor. On the other hand,
if the weapon is going to be used only as a temporary device for
affecting the demands of consumers, the changes in tax rates may
have to be on rather a large scale, since much of the variations in
net spendable incomes may be offset by variations in the amounts
saved.

It remains to consider whether it is administratively practicable to
devise suitable fiscal measures to bring about frequent and reasonably prompt variations in the net spendable incomes of individual
citizens. One practicable means would be to vary the amounts of
money paid out by the government in direct transfer payments to
individuals. In most modern developed economies such transfer
payments are made in one form or another: family allowances
payable according to the number of children in the family, old age
pensioners and various other social security benefits. It is possible
also to envisage negative income tax schemes which are primarily
devised to bring about a more equal distribution of income and
which involve payments of income subsidies to those whose incomes
are low as well as the levy of income taxes on those whose incomes
are high. One such scheme would involve the payment of a fixed

tax-free social dividend to every individual, regardless of his or her other income, combined with the progressive taxation of all other income.

Provided that any transfer payments to individuals of this kind were made at frequent intervals, either weekly or monthly—as they usually are—there would be no insuperable administrative difficulty in reducing the payments in times of unexpected inflationary pressures and increasing them in times of unexpected deflationary pressures. Moreover, in most developed economies, there are schemes which involve the raising of special levies, contributions, or taxes from workers and their employers for the finance of social security benefits, such as unemployment benefits, sickness benefits, and old age pensions. These contributions are sometimes in the form of a given absolute amount of money for each person employed and sometimes in the form of a given percentage of the wage paid to each person employed. In either case, provided once again that the levies were made at frequent intervals, e.g. weekly or monthly—as they usually are—there would again be no insuperable administrative difficulty in making prompt arrangements for larger levies to be raised in times of unexpected inflation and for prompt reductions in the levies in times of unexpected deflation.

Schemes of this kind would bring about very widespread and prompt changes in net spendable incomes and from that point of view would make admirable control instruments. They would, however, in many cases be open to serious objection from the point of view of their distributive effects. In so far as they involved changes in fixed lump sum transfer payments or levies—e.g. in the size of the same family allowance paid to each child, of the same old age pension paid to each elderly citizen, of the same social dividend paid to every citizen, or of the same national insurance contribution paid by each worker—they would throw the same absolute variation in spendable income on every citizen, whether rich or poor. This constitutes a grave disadvantage of such schemes. Suppose that it is desired to reduce spendable incomes to cope with an unexpected inflationary situation. The same absolute reduction for each citizen, if it were on a sufficient scale to cope with the inflationary situation, might involve a cut in spendable incomes for the poorest citizens which was intolerable from the point of view of their standard of living. In this case, either the control would have to be used on an inadequate scale or else grave social injustice would have to be inflicted.

For this reason it would be desirable to find a fiscal measure which would reduce spendable incomes in proportion to, or better still on some progressive scale in relation to, each individual's existing spendable incomes. The rich would face a larger absolute reduction than the poor (the poorest facing, perhaps, no reduction at all) when it was desired to curtail consumtion. Variations in the rate of contributions or taxes which are levied as a proportion of wage payments (for example, national insurance contributions or payroll taxes levied as a stated proportion of the wage paid) would be much less open to objections of this kind. In the first place, they would not affect transfer payments to those who were not in work (such as family allowances, old age pensions, unemployment benefit, sickness benefit) and in the second place, the highly paid worker would experience a bigger absolute adjustment of his spendable income than would the low paid worker.

In most highly developed economies, there is a system of income taxation which levies tax on a very wide range of citizens (even though no income tax is levied on the poorest) and in which the tax is levied at the source. In such cases, it might be possible to arrange for supplements or decrements of the tax deductible and payable to the government to be paid from time to time. For example, it might be ruled that any tax deductible and payable to the government in, say, the second quarter of a given year should be 1% greater than it would have been with the existing regular tax schedules.[9] Such a system could bring about a prompt increase or decrease in the spendable incomes of all those liable to income tax. The fact that the adjustment to the spendable income would be in proportion to the tax liability which would in turn be related progressively to the income of the tax payer would imply some rough and ready element of progression in the control instrument.

[9] With any such scheme, there would have to be adjustments of tax liabilities at the end of each year. Thus suppose that for a given tax year there had been supplements of 1%, 3%, 2% and 0% for the four quarters of the year. This would mean that for the year as a whole $(1 + 3 + 2 + 0) \div 4 = 1.5\%$ more tax should be paid than would otherwise have been payable according to the regular tax schedules operative for the year. In the case of incomes subject to wide seasonal variations or payable only annually at some one point of time, fairness would necessitate some such smoothing adjustment; for example, an annual income received and taxable solely in the fourth quarter of the year would, in the above example, be liable to a zero tax supplement unless there were some such retrospective smoothing process.

CHAPTER XXIV

PRICE STABILITY VERSUS FULL EMPLOYMENT—CONCLUSION

The monetary and fiscal policies which we have been examining in the preceding chapters of this part are designed solely as temporary measures to cut short the possible cumulative inflationary or deflationary effects of unanticipated fluctuations in the total demand for goods and services; we have argued that they must be applied promptly and on a scale which depends not only upon the current level of inflation or deflation, but also upon the degree to which an inflationary or deflationary situation has persisted in the past and the speed with which it is increasing or decreasing in intensity. It remains only to consider what measure of the degree of inflationary or deflationary pressure of demand should be used for this purpose.

There are two principal candidates for this role: (1) the extent to which there is an abnormal tension or an abnormal slackness in the use of the real productive resources of the economy; and (2) the extent to which inflationary or deflationary pressures of demand are causing market prices to rise or to fall. The degree of tension or slackness in the demands made on the real productive resources of the community can be measured by such things as the extent to which there is spare, unused productive capacity in the various industries, the extent to which there is unemployment of labour in various sectors of the economy and the extent to which order books are empty or are full of the names of a long list of customers impatiently waiting for supplies. Perhaps the most convenient and generally used single index of the overall state of pressure on the real resources in the community is the percentage of the labour force which is unemployed.

At any one time, there is bound to be some unemployment of labour in any dynamic economy. As some economic activities contract and others expand, there is bound to be some interval between the reduction in employment of resources in the contracting, and the increase of employment in the expanding, sectors. Such unemployment may simply take the 'frictional' form of a short interval while a worker moves from one job to a similar job in the same district, or, it can take the much more serious form of the 'structural' unemployment which exists during the prolonged transfer of activity from one type of occupation in one district to another type of occupation in another district. Levels of frictional and structural unemployment may, of course, vary over time as the economy develops in ways which make the movement of labour between occupations more or less necessary or more or less difficult. Such movements are, however, unlikely to develop suddenly and short-run fluctuations in the percentage of total workers unemployed is much more likely to be an index of short-run fluctuations in the total level of demand for all goods and services rather than an index of increasing or decreasing problems of mobility between occupations.

When figures of unfilled vacancies are available, it may be possible to distinguish between the two types of variation in the unemployment percentage. If unemployment and unfilled vacancies rise together, it is probable that the trouble is due to the increased need for mobility, since more employers are looking in vain for workers at the same time that more workers are looking in vain for jobs. When unemployment rises and unfilled vacancies simultaneously fall, then there would appear to be a general decline in the demand for labour. It may, therefore, be better to judge the general pressure of demand upon real resources not merely by the unemployment percentage but also by the ratio of unemployment to unfilled vacancies.

Another snag arises in using the general unemployment percentage as index of the pressure of demand on real resources. When demand falls off, the impact on the producer of the goods and the employer of the labour may well be not to dismiss workers, but to arrange for short-time working or for a less intensive use in some form or another of his existing work force. This will be particularly likely if his work force consists of a team of skilled workers well experienced in his own methods of production; he will not wish to reduce his work force until he is sure that the redundancy of labour is more than a mere passing phenomenon. Thus the growth of unemployment may lag behind the reduction in demand. Similarly, when there is an increase in demand, producers may arrange for more overtime or the more intensive use of their existing labour force, while they consider whether the increase in demand is at all likely to last and while they take steps to build up their labour force. For these reasons, variations in the unemployment percentage may only follow with some time-lag the variations in the level of effective demand to which they are due. If, as we have argued, it is important that stabilizing changes of monetary and fiscal policy should be taken very promptly in response to changes in the total level of demand for goods and services, it is important to avoid this delay. For this purpose, it is important if one uses the unemployment percentage as a general index of unused real resources to attempt to anticipate changes in the unemployment percentage in so far as it is possible to obtain sufficiently quickly any supplementary information about the actual outputs of various industries.

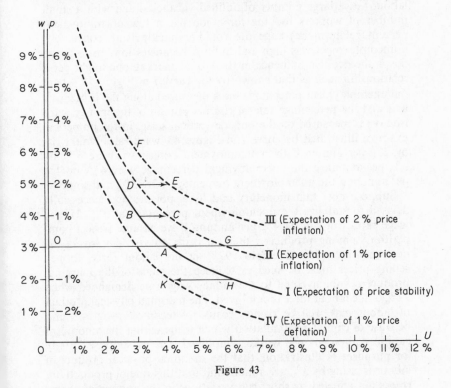

Figure 43

Suppose that, subject to these modifications and qualifications, it were decided to use the unemployment percentage as the general index of excesses or deficiencies in the level of the total demand for goods and services, what level of the unemployment percentage —1%, 3%, 5%—would one take as the 'target' level for the general stabilization through short-term monetary and fiscal policies? It is at this point that one must consider also the alternative criterion— namely price stability—for the guidance of short-run financial stabilization measures. For the criterion of the degree of pressure on the use of real resources and the criterion of the degree of in- flationary increases or deflationary falls in money prices are not independent of each other.

In the sort of labour market which we described earlier in this volume (see Chapter I) one of the factors, though not the only factor, which would determine the rate of increase or decrease in money wage rates would be the degree of tension or of slackness in the labour market. With employers trying to obtain a lot more labour (i.e. a large number of unfilled vacancies) and with a small number of workers looking for a job (i.e. a low unemployment percentage) the money wage rate would be quickly rising; conversely, if unemployment was high and unfilled vacancies low. In so far as this is the decisive influence in the labour market, one might get a relationship such as that shown by the curve I in Figure 45, where the unemployment percentage (u) is measured along the horizontal axis and the percentage rate of rise per annum of the money wage rate (w) is measured on the outside vertical scale. In the numerical example illustrated by curve I in Figure 45, wage rates would rise by 2% per annum if the unemployment percentage were 6%, by 3% per annum if the unemployment percentage were 4%, by 4% per annum if the unemployment percentage were 3%, and so on.

Suppose now that monetary and fiscal policies are successfully devised to stabilize the unemployment percentage at 3%. Money wage rates will rise by 4% per annum. If we assume perfect competition[1] among producers, then, in order to give employers the necessary incentive to employ 97% of the labour force, money selling prices must be such as to keep the value of the marginal product of labour equal to the money wage rate demanded when 97% of the labour force is employed. The marginal physical product of labour may well be rising because of technical progress[2] and because of capital accumulation which is increasing the amount of capital equipment per worker employed. Let us suppose, purely for purposes of illustration, that the marginal physical product of labour is rising by 3% per annum and that this rate of productivity rise is not affected by short-run variations in the volume of unemployment. Then, with money rates rising by 4% per annum, but the marginal physical product of labour rising by only 3% per annum, monetary and fiscal policies must be such as to permit or,

---

[1] The argument in the text is expounded in terms of perfect competition between producers. But this is not a necessary assumption for the main conclusions to stand. These conclusions are valid so long as conditions are such that prices must rise as quickly as labour costs. This would be so if prices were in fact set by producers with a given constant mark-up on labour costs or if producers maximized profits with wage costs making up the whole of short-run variable costs and with a constant elasticity of the demand curve facing each producer.

[2] Provided that technical progress is not of such a labour-saving variety as to cause a reduction in the physical marginal product of labour.

if necessary, induce the total level of money demand so to expand as to cover a rise in the money prices of products of 1% per annum. With a 3% rise in physical productivity and a 1% rise in prices, the money value of the marginal physical product will rise by 4% in line with the rise in the money wage rate. The rate of rise of money prices of products which will be necessary to maintain a given volume of employment is thus shown on the inside vertical scale of Figure 45. With marginal physical productivities always rising by 3% per annum, the necessary percentage rate of annual rise of product prices will always be three points below that of money wage rates.

We have so far considered the point marked *B* on curve *I* on Figure 45. The financial authorities are so controlling total money demand as to maintain a 3% unemployment index; as a result, money wage rates are rising by 4% per annum; and to fill the gap between the 4% rise in money wage rates and an assumed 3% rise in productivity, the money prices at which the products of labour can be sold will have to be permitted or induced to rise by 1% per annum.

But even in the sort of labour market described earlier, the degree of tension or slackness in the labour market may not be the only factor affecting the rate of change of the money wage rate. Let us suppose workers to be concerned with the real purchasing power of their wages and producers to be concerned with real costs, i.e. with the relationship between money costs and money selling prices. Suppose further that the money prices of all products have been going up by 1% per annum and are expected by everyone to continue to go up by 1% per annum. In these circumstances, a 1% per annum rise in money wage rates would be confidently expected to, mean no change in the real wage of the worker and no change in the real cost of a unit of labour to the employer. One might expect in these conditions that each worker would be demanding and each employer would be willing to offer, an annual percentage rate of increase of money wage rates which would be one point higher than it would have been if no increase in product prices was expected but if the circumstances had otherwise been the same. In other words with the confident expectation by everyone concerned that product prices would go up by 1% per annum, the curve *I* in Figure 45 (which depicted the state of affairs when no rise in product prices was expected) would rise to the position of curve *II*, i.e. one percentage point above curve *I* along the whole of its range.

If financial policies are such as to maintain the unemployment percentage at 3%, then we should move to the point *D*. Money wage rates would go up by 5% per annum (1% per annum to allow for the anticipated rise of the cost of living by 1% per annum plus 4% per annum because of the tension in the labour market). With wage rates rising by 5% per annum and productivity rising by only 3% per annum, the financial authorities would have to allow for a rate of expansion of total money demand which would cause selling prices to rise by 2% per annum in order to give employers the necessary incentive to maintain employment.

It is important to note that if we are at the point B on curve I and if people then get used to the rise of product prices of 1% per annum so that the curve rises to the position of curve II, the inflation will not be stopped by a more restrictive financial policy which raises the unemployment percentage to 4%. Such a restrictive policy would have been sufficient to prevent the inflation from starting. If, that is to say, we had been at point A with no anticipation of an upward movement of prices, we should have stayed put at point A; the degree of tension in the labour market would have caused wage rates to rise by 3% per annum and this would have been exactly offset by the rise in productivity of 3% per annum. But if we are at point C with the anticipation of a 1% per annum inflation of product prices, we will stay put at point C; wages will rise by 4% per annum (3% due to the degree of tension in the labour market and 1% to offset the rising cost of living); as a result, product prices will have to rise by 1% per annum to close the gap between the 4% rise in money wage rates and the 3% rise in productivity; as a result the expectation of a 1% rise in product prices will be justified.

If it were desired to move from point C to point A (i.e. to reach the point at which product prices could be permanently stabilized), it would be necessary to change the expectation of a 1% per annum rise in product prices to the expectation of price stability. This could be achieved by adopting a more restrictive financial policy which raised the unemployment percentage to 6%, thus moving from point C to point G on curve II. At point G product prices will be stable since the money wages will be rising by 3% per annum (2% due to the degree of tension in the labour market and 1% due to the expectation of price inflation) and this will just offset the 3% per annum rise in productivity. At point G price expectations will, therefore, be disappointed; and as people come to expect price stability because prices are stable at point G, it will be possible to adopt a less restrictive financial policy, to lower the unemployment percentage to 4%, and to move from point G to point A. The 4% unemployment percentage (i.e. the unemployment level at which the solid curve I cuts the 3% per annum productivity line) is the level at which whatever level of price inflation or deflation is expected will in fact be realized. It is the level at which inflation or deflation will continue at a constant percentage rate equal to whatever rate is generally anticipated.[3]

At any other unemployment percentage the inflation or deflation of product prices would become explosive. Suppose, for example, that one was on curve *I* at point *B*; product prices would have to be allowed to rise by 1% per annum to maintain the demand for labour; as people got used to, and came fully to anticipate the 1% price inflation, the curve would rise to curve *II*; we should be at point *D* and prices would rise by 2% per annum; as people came to anticipate a 2% price inflation, the curve would rise to curve *III* and we would be at point *F* with a 3% price inflation; and so on without limit.

In so far then as the labour market is affected by (i) the shortage or abundance of the supply of labour relatively to the demand and (ii) the anticipation of price inflation or deflation, and in the absence of other relevant changes, there will be only one level of the unemployment percentage which can be permanently maintained without the danger of an infinite inflationary or deflationary explosion. There are two very good reasons why explosive inflations or deflations of this kind should be avoided.

First, there is the danger of an ultimate complete breakdown of the monetary system as the actual and anticipated rate of price inflation reaches infinity. The most obvious point is that if there are certain liquid assets like notes on which money interest cannot be paid, but which play a vital, even if humble, role in the monetary system, then an infinite rate at which these assets lose their real value will make it impossible to maintain their use as an effective medium of exchange.[4]

Second, there is an important adverse effect on the economy which becomes operative long before the inflation finally explodes. The

[3] It was argued on pages 343–4 that one could not easily arrange to pay interest on notes, but that an $x\%$ per annum rate of deflation of product prices gives the same real return on money as an $x\%$ money rate of interest with stable money prices. If in order to encourage the holding of liquid assets in the form of notes, it is desired to provide a real return on notes of $x\%$ per annum, one method would be to engineer a perpetual, fully anticipated rate of deflation of money prices by $x\%$ per annum. In terms of Figure 45, if one wanted to engineer a 1% per annum price deflation, starting at point *A*, one could raise the unemployment percentage to 6% and move to point *H*. This would enable a 1% per annum deflation of prices to take place; when this had persisted long enough for the expectation of this degree of deflation to be generally adopted, one could lower the unemployment percentage one more and move to point *K*.

[4] At the height of the runaway inflation in Germany after World War I, workers on being paid their wages in cash would literally run to the shops to purchase goods in order to avoid the loss of value between the moment of receipt and expenditure of the currency.

situation is basically one in which anticipations are disappointed. For example, at each of the points B, D and F on Figure 45, people are anticipating a rate of rise of product prices which is 1% per annum lower than the rate of rise which actually takes place. This means that real expectations will be disappointed; the worker who expects to be 5% better off in real terms next year will in fact be only 4% better off; the producer who is making his plans on the basis of a real rate of interest of 7% will find that the real rate turns out to be 6%.[5] We have argued at length (see Chapter XXIII of *The Growing Economy*) that in order that the use of resources should be used in the best possible way it is important that economic decision-makers should make their plans on the basis of correct anticipations of future market developments. This is impossible in an explosive inflationary or deflationary situation.

It is not maintained that the mechanism described by Figure 45 (i.e. the interplay of the degree of scarcity or abundance in the labour market and of the degree to which price inflation is expected) is the only possible cause of an explosive inflationary or deflationary situation. The essence of this explosive inflationary situation is that workers' money wage rates are being pushed up at a rate higher than that which the rise in productivity will stand; the community as a whole is trying to get a quart out of a pint pot.

There are other mechanisms which may lead to an explosive inflationary situation because the community as a whole is trying to obtain shares of the total available for distribution which together are excessive and inconsistent. One example is an attempt by group A to obtain, say, 10% more than group B, while group B is simultaneously trying to obtain 10% more than A. Suppose A and B both start with a wage rate of $10. A pushes A's wage rate up to $11 in order to be 10% ahead of B. B then pushes B's wage rate up to $12.1 in order to be 10% above A. A then pushes A's wage rate up to $13.31 in order to be 10% above B. And so on without limit. Wage leap-frogging of this kind in order to maintain inconsistent wage differentials could equally well lead to an infinite price explosion if the financial authorities, in order to maintain employment at some predetermined level, allowed, or if necessary took positive measures to induce, an expansion of total money demand such as to allow the prices offered by consumers to rise as rapidly as the

[5] For example, he can borrow money at a money rate of interest of 8% and expects a rate of price inflation of 1%, so that in real terms he must pay 7% on any money which he borrows. If prices in fact rise by 2%, he will, in fact, have to pay only 6% in real terms.

[6] See the Note at the end of this chapter for a mathematical expression of such explosive situations.

wage costs.[6] If it was decided to prevent any such explosive inflationary situation by means of the control of total money demand, the financial authorities would have to restrict demand so as to maintain so high a level of unemployment that the great excess of labour supply in the market exerted a sufficiently deflationary pressure to offset these other inflationary influences.

Given all these and other relevant conditions in the labour market, there will be one level of the unemployment percentage (in the numerical example of Figure 45, a 4% level) which must be maintained in order to prevent the development over time of an infinitely rapid price inflation or deflation. This means that, subject to the possible need to deviate temporarily from this percentage in order to influence the expectation of price inflation or deflation, the financial policies for short-run stabilization purposes must take this unemployment percentage as their target. Monetary and fiscal policies must be more expansive (i) in so far as the actual unemployment percentage is above this figure; (ii) in so far as the unemployment percentage has been for a long time persistently above this figure; and (iii) in so far as the unemployment percentage is rising, with converse rules for monetary and fiscal restrictive policies.

But the question immediately arises whether this rule for short-run stabilization is consistent with the principles of long-term control planning discussed in Chapter XVI above; clearly there is an important inconsistency unless the rules suggested in Chapter XVI (which for short we will call 'the structural planning rules') are modified. The Full Employment element in the criteria for the structural planning rules (component II in equation 16.14) would instruct the planners in the periodic revision of the structural plans (for example, at the time of each annual budget) to regard every increase in employment and output as so much social gain; there is no element in the other parts of the criteria for the structural planning rules (i.e. no other component in equation 16.14) which would set off as a cost against the increased employment and output the danger of this leading to an explosive inflation of money prices. This is no mere accident or oversight in formulation of the structural plan. The simple point is that the holding of money, the whole question of monetary liquidity and the dangers of explosive monetary movements are, as we have argued in this present part of this volume, matters connected with residual uncertainty; and the structural planning of Part 4 takes no account of such residual uncertainty.

Some interconnection is, however, obviously necessary. It would be absurd that the revision of structural plans (e.g. the annual budget) should always arrange for an excessive inflationary development of total demand and that it should be left to the more frequent stabilization adjustments of fiscal and monetary policies continually to offset these excess demands. The fiscal weapons chosen for short-run stabilization purposes will, as we have seen, be chosen principally for their merits in making possible prompt, unplanned changes in the level of total demand; they are not necessarily the ideal instruments for the long-run planned control of total demand.

One way in which this inconsistency could be removed would be to add an additional constraint to the rules for long-run structural planning, namely that the controls should be planned so as to maximize expected Social Welfare in the manner discussed in Chapter XVI—subject, however, to the constraint that no plan should be acceptable which reduced the unemployment percentage at any future environmental point below some stated critical level. This level would be the lowest level of unemployment at which it was thought that the danger of an explosive inflation could be avoided.[7]

In the very simple case analysed in Figure 45, this critical level of the employment percentage would be 4%. The vital question which remains to be examined is: "What measures if any can be taken to lower this critical level?" From Figure 45, it can be seen that the critical level of the unemployment percentage would be reduced (i) by a rise in the productivity line and (ii) by a shift of the basic curve I to the left.[8]

As far as productivity is concerned, this is a result of such factors as technical progress and of the accumulation of new capital equipment. Increased productivity is desirable basically because it enables an increased output per head to be realized and enjoyed and only incidentally as a means of reducing the risks of monetary inflation. The main considerations in the choice of policies to promote research and development of new ideas and to determine

[7] It is not intended in this volume to discuss the technical problems involved in planning to maximize Social Welfare subject to such a constraint. In the procedure outlined on pages 241–5, it would be necessary to stop the upward or downward adjustment of any control at any environmental point as soon as it either (i) began to cause a decline rather than an increase in expected Social Welfare, as defined and analysed in Chapter XVI, or (ii) it caused the unemployment percentage at any environmental point to fall below the stated critical level.

[8] The two movements are not necessarily independent. Thus a faster rate of technical progress will raise the height of the productivity line in Figure 45 from, say, 3% to 3·5% per annum. But faster technical progress may mean that some occupations and industries are expanding and others are contracting more rapidly than would otherwise be the case. The result may be that the inevitable level of frictional and structural unemployment is greater than would otherwise be the case. A rise in the productivity line may be combined with a shift to the right of the basic curve I. The critical unemployment percentage might actually be increased.

the level of savings and investment in new capital equipment will be the effect on the welfare components of equation 16.14. There may, however, be some additional advantage to be gained in making it easier to avoid explosive inflationary developments.

But the main emphasis in the search for measures specifically designed to reduce the critical level of the unemployment percentage must undoubtedly be placed on the possibility of institutional changes in the labour market which will reduce the rate at which money wage rates rise at any given level of unemployment.

The critical level of the unemployment percentage would be reduced if it were possible to increase the degree of mobility of the labour force and thus to reduce the level of frictional and structural unemployment. Suppose that it was proposed to reduce the unemployment percentage from 5% to 3% and that this involved reducing the number of unemployed from 500,000 to 300,000. Consider two alternative methods of achieving this objective. The 500,000 unemployed workers will be attached to certain industries, occupations and regions. If it were possible for the unemployed workers to move readily to the unfilled vacancies, unemployment could be reduced without any very substantial change in the upward pressure on wage rates in the economy as a whole. For while the bargaining power of labour would be somewhat increased in those parts of the economy from which the labour was moving, it would be somewhat decreased in those parts of the economy into which labour was moving. Contrast this with a policy of reducing the level of unemployment from 500,000 to 300,000 by a general expansion of the money demand for goods and services without any mobility of labour. The demand for labour would have to be raised in all industries, occupations and regions (both in those in which there was a redundancy and also in those in which there was already a shortage of labour) until the market for labour had been expanded by the required 200,000 in the industries, occupations and regions to which the labour was already attached. There would be a great increase in the upward pressure on wage rates throughout the economy. Thus the critical level of the unemployment percentage will be the lower, the more mobile is the labour force. This consideration gives greatly added support to the case for governmental policies designed to aid the retraining, removal and rehousing of unemployed workers and their families.

Moreover, there are a number of restrictive practices in the labour market which reduce the mobility of the labour force. Demarcation rules which unnecessarily prevent one body of workers from shifting from one job to another, apprenticeship rules which prevent the easy entry of new labour into highly paid or expanding trades and insistence upon national bargaining which makes it difficult to adapt conditions of work to the needs of particular producers—these are important examples. The more effectively such practices can be restrained, the lower will be the critical unemployment percentage at which an explosive inflationary threat occurs.

The phenomena mentioned in the preceding paragraph are all instances of monopolistic practices. Trade unions are in fact monopolistic bodies which, by combining the individuals concerned into a single bargaining unit, prevent unimpeded competition among the individual workers concerned from undermining a level of wage rates or some other conditions of work which the monopolistic trade union has established in its bargain with the employers. It may, therefore, be asked whether the most effective method of reducing the level of the ciritical unemployment percentage would not be to remove the monopolistic powers of the trade unions.

There can in fact be little doubt that, if there were perfectly competitive conditions in the labour market, the critical unemployment percentage would be greatly lowered. But the restoration of competitive conditions in the labour market would depend upon the restoration of competitive conditions among the employers of labour as well as among the workers. Since one employer (for example, a single industrial company) may employ many thousands of workers, and since in any one region or industry there may be only a very few employers but a very large number of workers, perfectly competitive conditions in the labour market cannot be restored. Monopolistic trade unions are an inevitable and proper institution in such market conditions.

But because monopolistic institutions must necessarily exist, it does not follow that they should not be subject to some measures of government control. The real question is not whether trade union bargaining should exist, but to what measures of social control it should be subjected. All this raises issues connected with conditions of monopoly which, it is hoped, will be the subject of a later volume in this series but which have been considered as little as possible in the present volume. However, it is difficult to leave the present topic totally unconsidered at this point and the remaining paragraphs of this chapter are devoted to a few superficial observations on the matter.

One possible set of institutional arrangements which might serve to control excessive wage inflations without impeding the legitimate trade union function in wage bargaining might be on the following lines.

(1) The government would establish some body whose job it would be to establish from time to time the proper norms by which the

merits of changes in wage rates should be judged. Such a general norm would be set at an annual percentage rate of rise in hourly wage earnings equal to the expected general rate of rise in the marginal physical productivity of labour in the economy as a whole (the 3% per annum of Figure 45). But the principle would be recognized that where there was a threat of a serious shortage of labour the rate of rise might appropriately be greater, both to attract labour into that market and also to restrain the demand for labour in that market and, conversely, that where a serious surplus of labour threatened, the rate of rise of hourly wage earnings might properly be less than the general norm.

(2) All bodies of workers and employers would be completely free to agree to any wage bargain which was mutually satisfactory to both parties.

(3) However, a system of appropriate industrial tribunals would instituted, so that when a dispute arose about a wage bargain either side could appeal to the appropriate tribunal. The tribunal would rule whether the claim by the trade unions was outside the norms as established under (1) or whether the employers were refusing to admit a claim within the norms established under (1). Such rulings would have to be accepted and would be enforced by the imposition of important financial penalties on the employer or the trade union which disregarded them.

An institutional arrangement of this kind would allow complete freedom to the workers and employers to make any bargains they wished. There would be no legal restrictions at all on the trade unions claiming, and the employers granting, any level of wage increase in any particular instance (for example where the employers were short of labour and desired to attract labour from other employments) where it was to their mutual benefit. There would, however, be a serious curb on the unjustifiable use of monopoly bargaining power by a trade union to push up a wage rate or by an employer or an employers' association to hold a wage rate down.

Two final comments may be in order.

In the first place, while the general norm for the general rate of rise of money wage rates would be determined by the general rate of rise of productivity throughout the economy (the 3% line of Figure 45), it is important to realize that this must not be done by arrangements to tie wage rates in particular industries and occupations to changes in productivity in those same industries and occupations. Suppose that there were only two products, agricultural output and industrial output. Suppose further that technical progress is such that in the course of the year productivity does not rise in manufactures, but rises by 5% in agriculture. If wage rates remained unchanged, the cost and price of agricultural products might fall by the full 5%. If the general level of product prices is to be stabilized, this would involve monetary and fiscal policies which stimulated total demand until the general level of prices had been raised back to its old level. This might mean the price of manufactures had to be raised 2·5% above the initial level while the price of agricultural products was pulled half way back to its initial level, so that it fell by only 2·5% instead of 5%. The competition for labour between the two industries might then lead to a bidding up of the wage rate by 2·5% in both industries. In this case the industrial workers would enjoy a rise of wage rates by 2·5% even though their productivity had not increased, and the agricultural workers would enjoy a rise of wage rates by only 2·5% even though their productivity had risen by 5%.

Indeed, the outcome for some time might well have to be even more favourable to the industrial workers whose productivity had not increased. Suppose that when people's real incomes rise (as they would when productivity in agriculture rose) consumers want to buy little more agricultural products but many more industrial products. Then labour will become redundant in agriculture where output per head has gone up but the demand for the product has scarcely risen, and labour will be scarce in industry where output per head has not risen but the demand for the product has increased. There will be a tendency for prices to fall still further in agriculture where there is now a glut of produce and to rise further in industry where there is a shortage of produce. This should be allowed to lead to a rise in industrial wages relatively to agricultural wages so long as it is necessary to attract workers from agriculture to industry. The rise in productivity is in agriculture but the consequential rise in wages should be in industry.

When, against a background of a general stabilization of the total demand for goods and services, there are a series of increases of productivity at varying rates in different industries and occupations, redundancy of labour may appear in some industries, occupations and regions, and shortages of labour in other industries, occupations and regions; there will be no obvious simple connection between the rate of increase of productivity in any one industry, occupation or region, and the redundancy or shortage of labour in that industry, occupation or region. Wage rates must rise in those parts of the economy in which these developments tend to cause a shortage of labour relatively to wage rates in those parts of the economy in which these developments tend to cause a redundancy of labour. Any attempt to preserve pre-existing differentials by raising wage rates in the latter group of industries to catch up those in the former group can only lead to a general upward pressure on wage costs which will adversely affect the critical unemployment percentage.

This leads to the second and final observation on this matter. If wage fixing arrangements are such as to keep a non-inflationary balance of bargaining power and thus to allow supply and demand to be adjusted to each other in the various labour markets, then wage rates cannot be used as a major weapon to determine the distribution of income either between wage earners and property owners or as between one group of wage earners and another. The distribution of income and wealth must be controlled in the main by other measures: the taxation of high incomes and property; the subsidization of low incomes; the payment of family allowances, old age pensions and similar transfer payments; the development of educational opportunities and of similar social services. But a full discussion of the principles for the redistribution of income and wealth must be postponed for another occasion.

In conclusion, we may point out that governmental control of a dynamic economy in which there is a large free enterprise sector requires three types of planning.

(1) First, it requires governmental encouragement of a formal or informal system of INDICATIVE PLANNING of the kind discussed in Part 3, designed to enable all decision-makers (both those in the private sector and also the government itself) to make better forecasts of future market conditions.

(2) Second, it requires a frequently revised governmental STRUCTURAL PLAN of the kind discussed in Part 4, designed to enable the government to set its own controls at any point of time in such a way as to obtain the best present and future use of the community's resources along a limited number of carefully considered representative environmental paths.

(3) Third, it requires a short-run STABILIZATION PROGRAMME. Since the structural control plan under (2) will leave much residual uncertainty and since unexpected events may lead to cumulative inflations or deflations, the government must be able and ready, probably mainly through fiscal measures, promptly to restrain or to stimulate the total level of demand.

The main link between the structural control plan of (2) and the stabilization programme of (3) will be the lowest level at which it is safe to attempt to maintain the unemployment percentage without running the risk of an explosive inflation. This critical unemployment percentage can itself be reduced if satisfactory means can be found for exercising a social control over the monopolistic bodies which determine wage rates and other conditions of work in the labour market.

Note to Chapter XXIV

THE GENERATION OF EXPLOSIVE INFLATIONS AND DEFLATIONS

I

Suppose that the proportional growth rate of the money wage rate (w) at any point of time is equal to the sum of two terms: first, the proportional growth rate in the real wage rate at which those fixing the wage bargain aim ($\overline{w}$); and, second, the expected proportional growth rate in the cost of living, i.e. in the price of the products of labour (p_e). Suppose further that the proportional growth rate in the real wage rate at which the wage-fixers aim is a function of the degree of tension in the labour market, measured by the unemployment percentage (U), so that $\overline{w} = \overline{w}(U)$. Then:

$$w = \overline{w}(U) + p_e \quad\ldots\ldots\ldots\ldots\ldots\ldots\ldots\ldots (24.1)$$

Suppose that the expected rate of rise in the price of products is a lagged function of the actual rate of rise in the price of products, such that:

$$p_e = \{\lambda/(D + \lambda)\} p \quad\ldots\ldots\ldots\ldots\ldots\ldots\ldots (24.2)$$

Suppose, finally, that the conditions of production and marketing of final products is such that, in order to maintain a given level of employment, the financial authorities must arrange for demand to rise in such a way that the proportional growth rate of the selling prices of final products (p) is equal to the proportional growth rate of money wage rates (w) less a constant proportional growth rate of productivity (r), so that:

$$p = w - r \quad\ldots\ldots\ldots\ldots\ldots\ldots\ldots\ldots\ldots (24.3)$$

If one eliminates w and p_e from 24.1, 24.2 and 24.3, one obtains:

$$p = \overline{w}(U) - r + \{\lambda/(D + \lambda)\}p$$

so that:

$$dp/dt = \lambda\{\overline{w}(U) - r\} \quad\ldots\ldots\ldots\ldots\ldots\ldots (24.4)$$

The solution of 24.4 for any given constant value of U gives:

$$p(t) = \lambda\{\overline{w}(U) - r\} t + p(0)$$

and substituting for $p(0)$ from 24.1 and 24.3, one obtains:

$$p(t) = \lambda\{\overline{w}(U) - r\} t + \overline{w}(U) - r + p_e(0) \quad\ldots\ldots (24.5)$$

From this one may conclude (i) that if U is so chosen as to make $\overline{w}(U) = r$, then the rate of price inflation, $p(t)$, remains constant at whatever was the initially expected rate of inflation, $p_e(0)$; (ii) that if U is chosen so as to make $\overline{w}(U) > r$, then, although prices will initially fall if the expected rate of deflation, $- p_e(0)$, is greater than the bargained rate of rise of real wage rates, $\overline{w}(U) - r$, yet ultimately inflation will set in, since, with $\lambda\{\overline{w}(U) - r\} > 0$, at some value of t $\lambda\{\overline{w}(U) - r\}t$ will become $> - \{\overline{w}(U) - r + p_e(0)\}$; and (iii) with $\overline{w}(U) - r > 0$, the rate of inflation will become explosive since as $t \to \infty$ so $\lambda\{\overline{w}(U) - r\}t$ will $\to \infty$. Conversely, an explosive deflation will set in if U is so chosen as to make $\overline{w}(U) < r$.

II

Suppose that there are two groups of wage earners, A and B, with money wage rates W_a and W_b. Suppose that group A aims at keeping W_a equal to θ times W_b and with this in view W_a is set as a lagged function of W_b such that:

$$dW_a/dt = \lambda\,(\theta W_b - W_a) \text{ or } W_a = \{\lambda/(D + \lambda)\}\,\theta W_b \quad \ldots \ldots .(24.6)$$

and similarly:

$$W_b = \{\lambda/(D + \lambda)\}\,\theta W_a \quad \ldots \ldots \ldots \ldots \ldots (24.7)$$

Eliminating W_b between 24·6 and 24·7, we get:

$$W_a = \{\lambda^2/(D + \lambda)^2\}\,\theta^2 W_a$$

so that:

$$d^2 W_a/dt^2 + 2\lambda\,dW_a/dt - \lambda^2(\theta^2 - 1)W_a = 0 \quad \ldots \ldots .(24.8)$$

The roots of 24.8 are $\lambda(\theta - 1)$ and $- \lambda(\theta + 1)$, so that:

$$W_a(t) = Fe^{\lambda(\theta - 1)t} + Ge^{-\lambda(\theta + 1)t} \ldots \ldots \ldots \ldots .(24.9)$$

where F and G are constants depending on the initial conditions. From 24.9 we can see that:

$$W(0) = F + G \quad \ldots \ldots \ldots \ldots \ldots \ldots (24.10)$$

and

$$dW_a(0)/dt = \lambda(\theta - 1)F - \lambda(\theta + 1)G$$

or from 24.6:

$$\lambda\{\theta W_b(0) - W_a(0)\} = \lambda(\theta - 1)F - \lambda(\theta + 1)G \quad \ldots \ldots .(24.11)$$

Solving for F and G from 24.10 and 24.11 and substituting the resulting values of F and G in 24·9, we obtain:

$$W_a(t) = \tfrac{1}{2}\{W_a(0) + W_b(0)\}\,e^{\lambda(\theta - 1)t}$$
$$+ \tfrac{1}{2}\{W_a(0) - W_b(0)\}\,e^{-\lambda(\theta + 1)t} \ldots \ldots \ldots \ldots (24.12)$$

Since $W_a(0) + W_b(0) > 0$ and $\theta > 1$, the first component on the RHS of 24.12 will $\to +\infty$ as $t \to \infty$ and since $-\lambda(\theta + 1) < 0$, the second component will $\to 0$ as $t \to \infty$. W_a will, therefore, rise without limit, ultimately at a proportional growth rate equal to $\lambda(\theta - 1)$. With the symmetrical relationship between W_b and W_a assumed in our example, the same conclusion is true also of W_b.

INDEX